# THE *Promise* OF EUROCOMMUNISM

**LAWRENCE HILL & COMPANY**
*Westport, Connecticut*

## By the Same Author

WE CAN BE FRIENDS: THE ORIGINS OF THE COLD WAR
THE WOUNDED EARTH: AN ECOLOGICAL SURVEY
CUBA VS. THE CIA
*With Robert Light*
DOLLARS AND SENSE OF DISARMAMENT
*With Victor Perlo*
THE OPEN MARXISM OF ANTONIO GRAMSCI
THE GAPS IN THE WARREN REPORT
THE THREAT OF AMERICAN NEO-FASCISM: A PRUDENTIAL INQUIRY
THE SURVIVOR, A NOVEL

# THE *Promise* OF EUROCOMMUNISM

## *by Carl Marzani*

INTRODUCTION BY JOHN M. CAMMETT

**LAWRENCE HILL & COMPANY**

*Westport, Connecticut*

Library of Congress Cataloging in Publication Data

Marzani, Carl.
The promise of Eurocommunism.

  Bibliography: p.
  Includes index.
  1. Communism—Europe.  I. Title.
HX238.5.M395     335.43′094     80-80526
ISBN 0-88208-110-1
ISBN 0-88208-111-X (pbk.)

*Copyright © 1980 by Carl Marzani*

*Introduction copyright © by John M. Cammett*

*ISBN: cloth edition 0-88208-110-1*
*ISBN: paperback edition 0-88208-072-5*
*Library of Congress Catalogue Card Number: 80-80526*

*Lawrence Hill and Company, Publishers, Inc.*
**2 3 4 5 6 7 8 9 10**

to
my departed comrade Betty Brazil
and to the living ones,
Anita, Attilio, Paula, Salvatore;
and to our brethren,
Michele Cardinal Pellegrino and
Luigi Bettazzi, Bishop of Ivrea.
*Camminando insieme per nutrir speranze*

# Contents

# Introduction

## by JOHN M. CAMMETT

On June 3, 1976, Enrico Berlinguer, general secretary of the Italian Communist party, publicly used the term "Eurocommunism" to describe some common positions of the major Communist parties of Western Europe. The occasion was a mass meeting on the outskirts of Paris presided over by Berlinguer and his French counterpart, Georges Marchais.

A few weeks later, in his address to the Berlin Conference of European Communist parties, Berlinguer again referred to the "new type of elaboration and searching that some people have referred to as 'Eurocommunism.' "* At the same conference, Santiago Carrillo, general secretary of the Spanish Communist party, also referred to "Eurocommunism," a term "recently employed in circles far removed from our own."† Carrillo further declared that "the term is not exact. A Eurocommunism does not exist. Still, it is clear that the Communist parties of developed capitalist countries, or those at an advanced level of development, must confront . . . specific problems which will lead us toward paths and forms of socialism that will not be the same as those of other countries."

To many Americans, Berlinguer's and Carrillo's use of the term occasions no surprise since they are generally identified with it. But the fact is that the expression "Eurocommunism" was coined about a

---

* "For New Roads towards Socialism in Italy and Europe," *The Italian Communists*, no. 2–3 (April-July 1976), p. 60.

† See Bernardo Valli, *Gli eurocomunisti*, p. 255.

year earlier by avowed enemies of Communist parties of any kind.* Some have identified the Catholic philosopher Augusto Del Noce (see page 108 of this book) as the originator of the term; others name Arrigo Levi, editor of the liberal Torinese daily *La Stampa*. But the most likely claim to this honor goes to the Italo-Croat Frane Barbieri, a writer for the Milanese anti-Communist daily *Il Giornale nuovo*, founded in 1974. Recently, Barbieri himself has claimed that he chose that expression because it emphasized the *geographic* location of the phenomenon and not its *ideological* character, which he believed was not fundamentally different from communism *tout court*.

After Berlin—more precisely, in the early months of 1978—the mass Communist parties of Western Europe occasionally began to employ the term "Eurocommunism" without the quotation marks. Thus we have the anomaly of Communists adopting for their own use a term which was originally anti-Communist. Why so?

First, because a progressive and more autonomous Europe seemed more and more crucial to the world struggle for détente and positive social change. Within that framework, certain Communist parties, as Western Europeans, could make an important contribution. Second, and perhaps more important, because the term, however inexact, could be used to convey the essence of the *problematique* of the large Western Communist parties: a mass struggle for a democratic socialism within the conditions of advanced capitalism. The "Euro" context provided a good framework for presenting the main elements of current Western Communist strategy. In New York in October 1979, Giovanni Berlinguer (Enrico's brother) suggested these were: (1) the struggle for an ever broader system of alliances of the working class—not just with the peasants but also with the middle classes and the intellectuals, as well as with those groups (the feminist movement, youth, students, unemployed, etc.) increasingly threatened by "marginalization" under late capitalism; (2) the fundamental importance of democracy in every stage in the struggle for socialism; (3) the full autonomy and independence of each Communist party; and (4) an internal party organization characterized by ever freer and more open discussion, though within the framework of democratic centralism. Berlinguer was speaking of the Italian Communists, but those general propositions are fully applicable to the Spanish and French parties as well.

Shortly after the major Communist parties of Western Europe had elected to fight on the terrain of Eurocommunism, publications on that question became much more frequent, as is demonstrated by the bibliography of this work. At the risk of being far too schematic, I

---

* For more information on the origins of the term, see the fine article by Philip Elliot and Philip Schlesinger, "On the Stratification of Political Knowledge. . . ." pp. 57–59.

would summarize the debate of 1976–79 in the following way. The conservative journals and those of the Establishment usually took a position equivalent to "*plus ça change, plus c'est la même chose,*" or that of the rhetorical question, "Has the leopard changed its spots?" For them, Eurocommunism was the same enemy, but presented in a new and more dangerous form. Especially typical of this attitude were the articles published by *Commentary* and—in somewhat more sophisticated fashion—those in *Encounter*. But there was an important variant of the conservative response which can be found in such authoritative publications as *Foreign Affairs* and *Foreign Policy* (the former even published three solicited articles by the Eurocommunists Jean Kanapa, Sergio Segre, and Giorgio Napolitano). The informing slogan of this group might be "The enemy of my enemy is my friend." These enlightened conservatives thought of Eurocommunism as potentially useful for its many criticisms of "real" socialism in Eastern Europe and the Soviet Union and, in the case of Italy, for the contribution which the PCI might make to avoid political and economic chaos in that country.

Eurocommunism and its implications also figured prominently in a number of American leftist publications. Many, if not most, have been very suspicious of the phenomenon. Major concerns of this literature were a supposed return of the "Euros" to the "social democracy" of the Second International and a purported "sell-out" of the working class. Examples of this are the editorial opinions of *Monthly Review* and several articles published in *Radical America*. I am reminded of Régis Debray's observation that for certain people "everything that actually exists must be guilty of compromising with reality." On the other hand, several publications, perhaps sharing Gilbert Seldes's belief that "nothing is inevitable—not even revolution," have provided us with a number of critically sympathetic articles on Eurocommunism. Outstanding in this respect are the *Socialist Review* (till 1978, *Socialist Revolution*), *Marxist Perspectives,* and the Chicago weekly *In These Times.*

The literature on Eurocommunism is by now, even in English, rather extensive. Whether pro or con, whether inspired by narrow political reasons or by plain desire to know the facts, it does give careful readers a more or less accurate picture of the present stances of the Italian, French, and Spanish Communist parties. However, most of this work is seriously lacking in two respects. First, it fails to convey any sense of the daily activities and concrete life of members of those parties. Here Carl Marzani's book makes a precious contribution, and to this I shall return shortly. Second, few or no historical data (with rare exceptions) are given to explain or "legitimize" the idea of Eurocommunism. In this area too, Marzani is greatly illuminating. But much of the literature reads as though this approach to socialism arose like a phoenix out of the crisis of world capitalism of 1973. Now, it is unquestionably true that that crisis made it possible for the Communist parties in question to move rapidly from marginal positions to positions of central importance in their respective countries. This also is why it is wrong to speak of an "integration" of those parties into the capitalist system or of a process of "social-democratization," as many leftist critics have said. The crisis of the 1970s gave those parties with their *significant otherness*—their leading presence in still unassimilated working classes (and their growing importance in other social groups)—an authority which could no longer be ignored.

Part of the reason, it is true, for the relative success of these parties is based on certain historical peculiarities within their respective countries. The Italian party, the "epicenter" of Eurocommunism, prospers in a country which is both modern and backward—first world and third world at once. Curiously, this has encouraged a greater autonomy of the working class, which has so far stubbornly resisted the kind of pulverization and integration that has occurred elsewhere. The French Communist party has continued to profit from the still vital class-consciousness of its great revolutionary tradition and from the inability of its bourgeoisie, in its prosperous complacency, to establish a national "hegemony." Finally, the long delayed demise of the Franco regime enabled the Spanish party, the most outspoken in its Eurocommunism, to become the heir for many Spaniards to the old Republican tradition.

But the main reason for the stubborn persistence of these parties as major political forces is that each in its own way has created a "usable past," thus providing a sense of *continuity* clearly lacking in most of the other Communist parties of the West. Naturally, this does not imply that "Eurocommunism" is only or even mainly a product of the distant past. Far from it! The martyrs of Italian, French, and Spanish communism of the 1930s would scarcely recognize their parties if they were permitted to revisit them. Yet it seems undeniable that by the thirties all these "Latin" parties had arrived at one common decision: a resolve to move, somehow or other, beyond the condition of "vanguard parties"—with their attendant "purity" of doctrine and historical determinism—toward the creation of *mass national parties*. The threat or actual experience of fascism was the catalytic agent in this important change, and the Popular Front governments of France and Spain were its first historical embodiments.

The theoretical and practical weaknesses of Frontism are by now notorious. In fact, the Comintern, initially suspicious of the whole idea, limited the PCF to mere support of the Blum government of 1936, rather than actual participation. Nobody at that time, so far as I know, even attempted to theorize a connection between the Popular Front and the "transition to socialism." Yet the decision of revolutionary Communist parties to behave "politically," to participate concretely in the political life of bourgeois states, was a major turning point. Once that happened, everything identified with the Eurocommunism of the 1970s became a possibility.

True enough, the defeat of the Spanish Republic and the Nazi-Soviet Pact temporarily ended the Popular Front, but it was revived and strengthened during the wartime resistance movement. By 1947, it appeared that the PCF, as a member of the postwar government, was about to accept Frontism in a theoretical and not merely practical way. In a remarkable interview in the London *Times* of November 1947, Maurice Thorez declared that "we are and we remain a government party, a party conscious of its responsibilities before the country. . . . We continue to think, to say, that 'the most happy perspective for France is the prolonged maintenance in office of a democratic government of large national unity.' "* Even more significant was Thorez's connection of democracy with socialism: "The progress of democracy throughout the world, despite the rare exceptions which confirm the rule, permits the envisioning of different roads for the march to socialism than that followed by the Russian Communists."†

But six months later, the French Communists were thrown out of the government, the Cold War began, and the whole process was not resumed until after 1956. Even then, it must be said, the French Communists were very slow to reaffirm in a new way these elements of their heritage.

The Italian Communist party, though eventually of crucial importance to Eurocommunism, began its career most inauspiciously. Founded in 1921, when the activities of the fascist *squadristi* were already well underway, the PCI was semiclandestine from the beginning. By the end of 1926, it was completely illegal and remained so until the fall of Mussolini in July 1943. Paradoxically (or should I say dialectically?), it was precisely the fact that the PCI began as a party of losers which forced it into a creative re-examination of the reasons for its near obliteration. The key to all of Antonio Gramsci's work is derived from his considerations on the defeat of the Italian labor and

---

\* Tiersky, *French Communism*, p. 161.
† Ellenstein, *Le P.C.*, p. 15.

socialist movements. Especially significant for the future were his views on Marxist strategies in countries with triumphant and "hegemonic" bourgeoisies, and his conclusions on the importance of the struggle against determinism and for the establishment of "hegemony" on the cultural front.

Similarly, the key to all of Palmiro Togliatti's work is derived from his efforts to establish conditions, both inside and outside the party, so that another such defeat would not occur. In their work and thought, both of these men had a profound impact on what would later be known as Eurocommunism. Carl Marzani is well aware of all this, and that is why his pages in this book on Gramsci and Togliatti are so valuable.

Carl Marzani is an unusual man and therefore has had an unusual life, one peculiarly suited to writing a book on Eurocommunism for American readers.* He was born in Rome, on the eve of World War I, to an antifascist family which was compelled to emigrate to the United States in 1924. After attending public schools in Pennsylvania, Carl went to Williams College, from which he graduated in 1935. Despite his frequent expressions of "premature antifascism" (remember the indulgent attitude of many Americans toward Mussolini before 1936), the college awarded Marzani a fellowship to study at Oxford University. While en route, he heard that Mussolini was supporting Franco, and therefore went to Spain to fight against both. He spent some time there with an anarchist brigade on the Aragon front and finally did arrive at Oxford. Spain, as Carl has said, "was a cram course in isms"; hence, the experience turned him sharply leftward. At Oxford, he met and married a young American Communist and both joined the British Communist party.

In 1938, Marzani received his degree from Oxford. After a brief and bitter period in Prague (it was the time of the Munich capitulation), the Marzanis returned to New York. A day after the signing of the Nazi-Soviet Pact, Carl joined the CPUSA. The Pact troubled but did not dismay him, for he believed that French and British policies throughout the thirties had left the USSR with no alternatives. Two years later, after intensive organizational work in New York's Lower East side, Marzani left the party, "with some bitterness but no regrets."

Meanwhile, Carl taught economics at New York University. But after Pearl Harbor, on March 4, 1942, he joined the Office of Strategic Services. The OSS was the well-known predecessor of the CIA, but it

---

* Those curious to know more about Carl Marzani will find their interest well rewarded by reading Barton Bernstein's 1971 introduction to the reprinting of Marzani's 1952 book, *We Can Be Friends*, and the interview with a certain "Eric Lanzetti" in Vivian Gornick's *Romance of American Communism*.

played a very different and much more positive role in world history. Its director, General William Donovan, hired Marzani in the full knowledge that he had been a member of the Communist party. According to Carl, Donovan suggested that he not admit to past membership in the CPUSA, for the general despised the reactionary J. Edgar Hoover and distrusted the FBI.

While in the OSS, Marzani served in Washington, London, Paris, and Rome, and worked directly for General George C. Marshall and his deputy, General Joseph T. McNarney, as well as for Under-secretary of War Robert P. Patterson. At war's end he was transferred to the State Department Intelligence Office, and a year later, after Churchill's Fulton speech, resigned in protest against Truman's Cold War policies.

While on terminal leave, Marzani was commissioned to do a film for the progressive CIO union, the United Electrical, Radio and Machine Workers of America (UE). The film documented the connections between General Electric and Westinghouse and Axis firms and Washington's role in beginning the Cold War. Naturally, it infuriated the corporations, the FBI, and the State Department. The result was Marzani's indictment under the newly devised loyalty oath program on numerous charges of defrauding the government. The fraud? Collecting his salary (half the time as a GI) while concealing past Communist membership. The jury found him guilty, and the judge sentenced him to three years. Subsequently, the U.S. Supreme Court split 4–4 on the constitutionality of his case and thereby "legitimized" his sentence.

The relative severity of the sentence was bad enough. Even more absurd was the fact that he actually spent thirty-two months (seven of them in isolation) in four penitentiaries! Characteristically, he did not waste his time. In this period, he wrote two books. One was the first book-length history of the origins of the Cold War. It was published in 1952 and called *We Can Be Friends*. Because it charged the Truman administration with major responsibility for the Cold War, the book was almost completely ignored. Twenty years later, however, it was reprinted with a fine introduction by a leading historian, Professor Barton J. Bernstein. While Bernstein did not ignore the inevitable shortcomings and partialities of the book, he concluded,

This path-breaking volume . . . must command our respect . . . because it focused upon so many of the right issues, because it sought to alert Americans to serious dangers, because it challenged the Cold War consensus, because it offered an important, often astute, interpretation of recent history, and because it held out the hope of peace. . . . Carl Marzani taught a lesson that many Americans were not prepared to learn until Vietnam.

Marzani's other book of this period was a novel of politics in the early years of the Cold War. Finally published in 1958, it was titled *The Survivor* (New York: Cameron Associates). Though selected with no reference to himself, that title is perfect as a description of Carl Marzani. Beginning with imprisonment, he has had far more than his share of misfortunes. Yet his energy, enthusiasm for life, and faith in the possibility of a better world have never faltered. Some might call his attitude excessively optimistic, but I and many others find it inspiring and essential to the creation of that better world which he envisions and most of us want.

After prison, he edited the *UE Steward* for four years (until the purge of 1954). Thereafter he became a partner in a small left-wing publishing company. After a fire destroyed his firm, he earned a living for some years as a contractor and builder remodeling brownstones. During all this, he continued to write articles, pamphlets, and books on a variety of subjects, including Cuba, bomb shelters, Vietnam, disarmament, and ecology. Especially significant for this book was his annotated translation of significant passages from the *Prison Notebooks* of Antonio Gramsci.* This was the first translation of Gramsci made by an American.

Carl Marzani's Roman birth, almost instinctive antifascism (and peculiarly *Catholic* atheism), his participation in the Spanish Civil War, his sojourns in France and Czechoslovakia, his university degree earned over several years in England, and his earlier experiences of the Communist parties in Great Britain and the United States make him a kind of walking *homo eurocommunista!* He began thinking about this book in the mid-seventies after the stunning victories of the Italian Communist party in the divorce referendum of 1974 and the regional elections of 1975, the early successes of the Common Program of the Communist and Socialist parties in France, and the imminent demise of the Franco regime and re-emergence of the Communist party in Spain. But only in 1977 was it possible for him to return to Europe to carry out the field work for this book.

The trip began in England at the Labour party's Seventy-seventh Conference in Brighton where, for the first time in its history, the Labour party had invited three Communist parties—the French, Italian, and Spanish—to send official observers. Then he went to Paris, Madrid, Belgrade, and Bucharest. In the capitals of Yugoslavia and Romania, he found that many of the fundamental ideas of Eurocommunism were well understood and deeply appreciated. Finally, Marzani arrived in Italy, where he talked to literally hundreds of men and women of every conceivable background.

---

* *The Open Marxism of Antonio Gramsci* (New York: Cameron Associates, 1957).

The result of all this, the book before us, is divided into three parts. The first ("The Foundations of Eurocommunism") discusses the genesis and growth of the major ideas of Eurocommunism as experienced in widely separated parts of Europe. I say, "as experienced," because these ideas are not abstractly cataloged, as they usually are, but presented within the context of specific political struggles. Examples of this are his account of the Berlin Conference of European Communist parties of July 1976 and the chapter on "The Vatican and Eurocommunism." The latter, bound to be "controversial," is a unique and arresting contribution to our knowledge of the way in which the Church from John XXIII to John Paul II has reacted to the challenge of Communism and the "social gospel." This part concludes with a historical discussion, emphasizing the ideas of Gramsci and the earlier Togliatti, on the "long march" of the PCI toward a "new party" and a new society.

Part II differs from the first partly because it is confined to Italy and the Italian Communist party as a case study of the oldest and most developed form of Eurocommunism. Besides, it emphasizes, not political theory as such (though that, too, is constantly present), but the concrete political, social, and economic problems of the country and the struggle of the PCI to overcome them. Here Marzani has recorded most vividly, sometimes unforgettably, how the party has penetrated every aspect of Italian life, whether it be the life of workers in factories or in agriculture, the struggle for the enhancement of local government, for women's liberation and industrial and governmental reform, or against corruption and terrorism.

In the concluding section ("The Perspectives of Eurocommunism"), Marzani takes on the Trotskyist Ernest Mandel, one of the ablest critics of Eurocommunism. He argues that Mandel, perhaps precisely because of the brilliance and completeness of his theoretical arguments, is blind to the concrete possibilities of a mass "national-popular" movement like that of the Italian party. Needless to say, only the judgment of history can decide who is the more correct.

Marzani is, as ever, an optimist and very sympathetic to the Italian Communists, but I do not think he minimizes the enormous obstacles which the party has yet to overcome. His book will convince many that the Italian Communists have undertaken one of the nobler political and social tasks of our time—but its ultimate success is far from guaranteed.

JOHN JAY COLLEGE OF CRIMINAL JUSTICE (C.U.N.Y.)
NEW YORK, JUNE 15, 1980

# Preface

EUROCOMMUNISM is an effort to adapt socialism to advanced capitalist societies, integrating each Communist party into the mores and traditions of its country. While such countries have much in common, they also have substantial differences in their history and levels of development. Consequently, Eurocommunism as a political movement is as varied as the countries in which it exists. Its common denominator is a mood: a mood of liberty and democracy attuned to the humanism of the early Marx; of pride in the species; of self-reliance and confidence in the future. It is an optimistic mood with which Americans can still identify.

The parties concerned—notably the Spanish, the Italian, and the French—do not share a coherent and closed philosophy; as of 1980, no new orthodoxy has in fact developed, and Eurocommunist parties differ a great deal. For example, the Spanish party is more strident toward the Soviet Union than is the Italian, which, in its turn, is more critical than the French. The French and the Portuguese parties supported Soviet intervention in Afghanistan; the Spanish and the Italian rejected it. Further, although all accept democratic pluralistic governments, the Italian and the Spanish are opting for coalitions with capitalist parties, the French and the Portuguese look for alliances only on the left.

As the most recent variant of socialism, Eurocommunism is a response to conditions in the postwar world. In that world, two elements were predominant. The first element was the existence of thermonuclear weapons in the hands of the United States and the

Soviet Union. This fact rendered obsolete armed class struggle in the advanced countries: confrontations between the superpowers can be contained in areas not crucial to one or both—Cuba, Angola, Vietnam—but a civil war in France or Italy would be explosive. Hence, for the Eurocommunists, a *peaceful* transition to socialism in Europe became a categorical imperative—indisputable, ineluctable, inexorable.

The second element in postwar Europe that contributed to the birth of Eurocommunism was the decided shift to the left with a concomitant rise in Communist membership. This was a natural result of the defeat of fascism and of the consequent prestige of the Soviet Union. Paradoxically, however, while Soviet prestige helped Communist growth, the very growth of the parties made them ripe for self-determination: They began to resist Soviet tutelage.

Moreover, if the transition to socialism in Western Europe had to be peaceful, the nature and role of Communist parties as conceived by Lenin and enshrined by Stalin had to be modified. Under tsarist conditions, the insurrectionary politics of Lenin required a mobile striking force, a party of professional revolutionaries welded together by an unwavering ideology and a strict discipline. Of necessity, such a party would be a party of cadres, their numbers less important than their dedication. As Lenin put it, "better fewer but better."

In contrast, a peaceful transition required the conscious support of tens of millions of people, and this could be achieved only by a large mass party of the working class permeating every crevice of society. Of necessity, the members of such a party would be less disciplined, less doctrinaire, and more in tune with the daily experiences of the general population. In mobilizing the population, such a party would have to make alliances with other parties and groups, give up any attempt to manipulate them, and function in an open, democratic manner. Palmiro Togliatti, the Italian Communist leader, was the first to understand these requirements, and the Italian Communist party was the first mass party of a new type, committed to pluralistic government, civil liberties, and democratic procedures.

One by one the Communist parties of Western Europe began to distance themselves from the Soviet Union and to criticize its flaws. Unplanned and unperceived, a process was set in motion which steadily eroded Soviet hegemony in the Communist world. In that process, and under the pressure of events, aspects of Marxist-Leninist theories began to be questioned; received notions began to be modified. Eurocommunism emerged, not as a complete and coherent doctrine, but rather as a current within Marxism, clarifying many ambiguous tenets of Marxism, updating others, and in so doing, shaping certain concepts which are forming the foundations of Eurocommunism. The erosion of Soviet hegemony was a necessary precondition of the birth of Eurocommunism.

## ACKNOWLEDGMENTS

Among those who helped make this book a reality are:

Paul Sweezey and Harry Magdoff of *Monthly Review,* who published my reply to their attack on Eurocommunism in the July 1977 issue of *MR*

Vivian Gornick, who suggested the possibility of a book on the subject, and Erwin Glikes, who suggested the title.

The German Marshall Fund of the United States, which provided a travel grant to the Second International Conference on U.S. History in June of 1979.

Others who generously gave of their time and expertise are: Lord Thomas Balogh, Antonio Bronda (*L'Unità* correspondent), Dick Clemens, Stanley Harrison, Stuart Holland, Ian Mikardo, Edward Mortimer, Eric Shaw, Donald Sassoon and Jack Woddis of England.

Christine Buci-Glucksmann, Michelle Fogel, Monique and Pierre Leveque, Marie-Claude Lluillies, Yvette Jarrico, Augusto Pancaldi (*L'Unità* correspondent) and Gerard Streif of France.

Manuel Azcarate, Gabriel Albiac and Vidal Villa of Spain.

Peko Dapčevič, Andrej Grahor, Ivo Vejvoda, Simeon Pobolilc, Vera Beakovic, and Marja and Joža Vilfan of Yugoslavia.

Corneliu Bogdan, Ion Botar, Dorin Ruzzu and Mirka Malitsa of Romania.

E. E. Mallia and Sammut Michele of Malta.

Giuseppe Boffa, Gianfranco Corsini, my nephews Enrico Girardi and Paolo Marzani, Professor Nico Perrone and Corrado "Tappabuco" Zucchi, Ferdinando Adornato, Professor Adriano Bausola, Sante Bugnoli, Anna Maria Catalan, Umberto Cerroni, Claudio Cristofani, Graziella Civilletti, Bishop Benito Cocchi, John Crane, Crusca D'Etrusca, Rocco Di Blasi, Professor Ambrogio Donini, Franco Ferri, Alberto Garrochio, Luciano Lambertini, Romano Ledda, Silvio Lega, Professor Giuseppe Lazzati, Giangiacomo Magoni, Adalberto Minucci, Maria Teresa Noto, Mario Rodriguez, Vincenzo Rotolo, Gaetano Saterale, Sergio Segre and Professor Maria Rosaria Stabili of Italy.

Professor Ronald Duncan, Rena Gordon, Professor Yereth Knowles, Amelia Ocasio, Pedro Santana Ronda and Carl Wheeler of Puerto Rico.

Doctor Percy Brazil, Joe Curry, Max Gordon, Josie Ingrisani, John Lewis, Ricki Marzani Spector, Grazia Gugliotta and the staff of the Italian Information Service and Library of the United States.

Special thanks to my publisher, Lawrence Hill, who stinted neither time nor effort nor money and to Professor John Cammett for his thoughtful introduction, for his editorial guidance and for his work on every page as well as the notes and bibliography. My thanks also to my wife, Charlotte Pomerantz Marzani, who critically read and helped to shape each succeeding draft; to Donald J. Davidson for careful and tireless editing; and to Professor Eugene D. Genovese, who criticized the manuscript with professional severity.

The contribution of many others, not included here, is acknowledged in the text of the book or the critical notes.

# PART ONE

# Foundations
# of Eurocommunism

# CHAPTER 1

# The End of
# Soviet Hegemony

THE DISTINGUISHING CHARACTERISTIC of Eurocommunism as compared to other forms of Communism—Soviet, Chinese, Cuban, etc.—is its stress on democratic procedures, including those which have developed under capitalism. For Leninists and Maoists, capitalist "democracy" is a way of deceiving workers about who controls society; the American Bill of Rights, constantly breached for blacks and other minorities, is considered a mask for economic oppression. For Eurocommunists this view is accepted as true but one-sided; the Bill of Rights was a major step forward in self-government. Similar constitutional provisions, fully implemented and accompanied by economic democracy, become a necessary component of socialist democracy.

The only example in history of a complete democracy, one that controlled *both* politics *and* economics, was the Paris Commune of 1871. Marx extolled it as a prototype, however imperfect, of a future socialist society. Since then, in no society have citizens had a direct say in both government and production. The United States, for example, has made considerable progress in political democracy and very little in economic democracy, whereas in Yugoslavia the situation is reversed. China and the Soviet Union have tended to authoritarianism in both spheres.

For a complex of historical reasons, the Soviet Union has exercised a dominant influence on all Communist parties, instilling into them Soviet concepts of socialist democracy. Within Western mores, these concepts were neither socialist nor democratic. If to Eurocommunists socialism meant *both* political and economic democracy, then a challenge to Soviet authority was inevitable.

The erosion of Soviet hegemony spans three decades. In this process, four events punctuate the road to Soviet capitulation: June 1948, the expulsion of Yugoslavia from the Cominform; February 1956, Khrushchev's secret report to the Twentieth Congress; February 1964, open rupture between China and USSR; July 1976, the Berlin Conference of the Pan-European Communist parties. Each event, of course, had its history.

The Soviet-Yugoslav conflict was slow in developing: neither Joseph Stalin nor Josip Broz Tito sought the rupture, and when it came each felt surprise and betrayal. Of the two, Stalin had greater reason for chagrin: Tito, a minor Comintern figure, had been hand-picked in 1937 to become general secretary of a quarrelsome Yugoslav party.[1] As general secretary he gathered a new Central Committee of young people, most of them in their twenties, who called the forty-five-year-old Tito *stari* ("the old man"). Under his leadership, the party network throughout the country was strengthened, and so, when Yugoslavia was invaded by Adolf Hitler in April 1941, the party was able to move quickly and effectively.

The invasion of Yugoslavia was not in Hitler's plans, then geared to the invasion of Russia. But when Hitler forced the right-wing government of Prince Paul of Yugoslavia to adhere to the Axis powers (March 25, 1941), the people rebelled. There were huge riots in Belgrade, and the army went over to the side of the rioters. A group of officers effected a coup d'état, and a new government was formed. Hitler was furious; planes, troops, and tanks destined for the assault on Russia were diverted to the south; Yugoslavia was invaded, her army destroyed, and her government exiled. Although the entire operation lasted only ten days (April 6–16), it delayed, in Winston Churchill's judgment, the invasion of Russia by five weeks. If the attack on the USSR had begun on May 15 rather than June 22, Moscow might have fallen, and the course of the war could have been profoundly altered.[2]

The Yugoslavs have always considered their revolt of 1941 a concrete act of assistance to the Soviet Union. Further assistance came as Tito organized the partisans to fight the Germans. Starting with a few people, the partisans comprised more than a hundred thousand fighters by the end of 1943, holding down five hundred thousand German and puppet troops. The cost to Yugoslavia was enormous: 1,685,000 dead out of a population of 16 million—one in ten persons, the same casualty rate as the Soviet Union's. The Comintern cabled: "You are doing a great thing, which our Soviet land will never forget."[3]

When the war ended, Tito was not the minor Comintern functionary he had been in 1935. He was prime minister of Yugoslavia, marshal of an army of a quarter million battle-hardened fighters, and head of a seasoned Communist party of young men and women. Proud of his people and his country, he considered himself to be the independent leader of an independent nation. Stalin began to be irritated. He still regarded Tito as a second-rank Comintern functionary from a small nation having negligible power. The Soviet Union counted its marshals by the score, its soldiers by the millions, and its casualties by the tens of millions. Tito boasted of beating the Germans, but a Soviet army corps had helped take Belgrade. Without the Soviet's advance on a three thousand mile front, outflanking the Germans in Yugoslavia and forcing them to retreat, Tito would never have won.

Furthermore, Tito's nationalistic and intransigeant stance on foreign affairs was a nuisance to the Soviet Union. Despite strong hints from Stalin that Tito should consult with the USSR before taking any action, he acted on his own: he confronted the Allied armies over Trieste; he shot down American planes that intruded over Yugoslav territory; he assisted the Greek guerrillas, thus contravening Stalin's understanding with Churchill.[4]

Equally important was Tito's independence in economic and political matters. He refused to set up Soviet-Yugoslav joint-stock companies, a tested Soviet method of controlling the planning of its satellites. He also refused to accept Soviet military and police advisers, while maintaining his wartime connections with the British. Moreover, he was making treaties with his socialist neighbors without consulting the Russians, and in his state visits to those countries he was received with tumultous acclaim by the people. Tito had become a legendary hero in the Communist world, and his independence might be contagious; it was time to trim his wings.

Stalin instructed his secret services to build up a spy network in Yugoslavia, to approach disgruntled army officers and to infiltrate government and party organs. A Central Committee member was successfully blackmailed into becoming an informer. Simultaneously, as a cover, Stalin waived the joint-stock companies, offered Yugoslavia credits amounting to $135 million, and heaped honors on the Yugoslavs. At the funeral of Soviet President Mikhail Kalinin, in May 1946, the Yugoslavs were asked to provide the honor guard at the catafalque, and Tito was chosen to stand with Stalin and the Politbureau on the balcony of Lenin's tomb, the only foreign guest to do so.

One other instrument was devised by Stalin to control Yugoslavia and the other satellites—the Cominform. Ostensibly an information service, it united the parties in power in Eastern Europe and the Italian and the French parties. Its headquarters were to be in Belgrade, a periodical would be published there, and its editor would be a Russian philosopher, a certain Yudin, who turned out to be an

NKVD agent. The Yugoslavs were soon to institute surveillance over Yudin, spying on the spy.

As the Yugoslavs caught on to the Soviet covert activities, they remonstrated sharply. In early 1948 an angry exchange of letters between Belgrade and Moscow developed into bitter recriminations. The issue was clearly one of national independence: Would Tito and his co-workers subordinate themselves to Stalin? Tito stood firm. Finally, in June 1948, the Cominform expelled him. A tremendous campaign of vilification was whipped up: Tito was a British agent, the Yugoslavs had sold out to capitalism, and so on. At the same time, an economic boycott was instituted by the USSR and its satellites.

Yugoslavia's trade had been largely within the socialist bloc; a serious disruption of its economy seemed inevitable. Stalin was confident that Tito was finished: "I will shake my little finger," he told Khrushchev, "and there will be no more Tito. He will fall."[5] But Stalin was proved wrong.

In a burst of fierce national pride, the Communist party of Yugoslavia, the army, and the people rallied around Tito and the government. The British stepped in with economic aid, which was given without political strings. In a rare display of diplomatic wisdom, the United States followed suit, accepting Tito's communism for the sake of his apostasy. Titoism survived, an irreparable crack in the Stalinist monolith. Stalin moved to contain the damage: in 1949, in a series of trials, independent Communist leaders in various countries were framed, tried, condemned, and executed. Nationalist stirrings in Eastern Europe were eliminated—more precisely, driven underground.

Stalin could not hold back the tide: the damage to Soviet authority was permanent. Tito's surviving of his excommunication initiated the erosion of Soviet hegemony. The challenge of Titoism was crucial to the development of Eurocommunism, not only because it undermined Stalinism, but also because it had internal consequences in Yugoslavia. To rally his people and to gain further aid from the West, Tito had to liberalize his regime; he had to restrain the secret police, diminish the persecution of dissidents, allow freedom of travel, and open up the country to the periodicals, books, and ideas of the West. Ideologically, Tito, Edvard Kardelj, Mosa Pijade, Milovan Djilas, and others challenged Stalin's reduction of Marxism to a sterile catechism. Internationally, Tito concentrated on developing the influence of the emerging nations, what later came to be called the third world. Working with Nehru, he began to weld together a coalition of nonaligned nations whose interest, like that of Yugoslavia and other European nations, lay in a diminution of the Cold War.

Most important, perhaps, was Tito's ability to make a Communist regime acceptable to the West. Outgoing in manner but self-possessed, vivid in speech, lucid in thought, Tito bore lightly the legend of a doughty warrior. His role as David to the Soviet's Goliath captivated the West, which, in its admiration (mingled with self-interest), glossed over the one-party nature of the Yugoslav government and its avowedly Communist orientation.

After the death of Stalin, the Soviet government moved to improve relations with Tito. In May 1955, Nikita Khrushchev, Nikolai Bulganin, and Anastas Mikoyan visited Yugoslavia to make amends. Upon their arrival at the Belgrade airport, Khrushchev delivered a speech of abject apology, blaming Lavrenti Beria (the executed chief of the secret police) for the past treatment of Yugoslavia. Impassive and aloof, Tito made no reply, merely waving the Russian leaders to the waiting cars. After two days of negotiations, a joint declaration signed by Tito and Bulganin as heads of state (there was no mention of Communist parties) stated that "questions of internal organization, of different social systems and of different forms of socialist development . . . [should be] solely the concern of individual countries."[6]

The heretic had triumphed. For two decades Stalinism had rested on the twin pillars of dictatorship and infallibility. Now the dictator was dead and the Kremlin was admitting error. Soviet hegemony was at an end . . . on paper. In truth, another twenty-five years would pass before the Soviet government accepted the inevitable, but an era had ended.

In the genesis of Eurocommunism, Khrushchev was as important as Tito. In February 1956, in a secret report to the Twentieth Congress of the Communist Party of the Soviet Union (CPSU), Khrushchev revealed the dark side of Stalin's regime, and his terrorization and megalomania were explicitly documented. Even top Soviet officials, aware of Stalin's ruthlessness, were astounded at the extent to which the Communist party itself had been decimated.[7]

The anger and disillusionment following Khrushchev's revelations were enormous. The Italian party, for example, lost two hundred fifty thousand members in a few months—20 percent of its total membership. The foreign delegates at the Twentieth Congress who had been uneasy in the past over the divisive fight against Tito and the executions of many party leaders—Rudolf Slansky in Czechoslovakia, Laszlo Rajk in Hungary, Traicho Kostov in Bulgaria—felt disoriented, betrayed, and defiled. Among these delegates the need for independent thinking now arose imperiously, a feeling well expressed in the diary of an Italian delegate, Vittorio Vidali.

Vidali, born in 1900, joined the Socialist party in 1917 and the Communist party in 1921. Imprisoned and tortured under the fascist regime, he escaped to the United States, whence he was deported in

1927. He fought in the Spanish Civil War as Carlos Contreras, organizer and commander of the legendary Fifth Regiment, which was the model for the rebuilding of the Republican Army. After World War II Vidali had become a member of the Central Committee of the Italian Communist party (*Partito Communista Italiano*, PCI), a Communist senator, and a delegate to the Twentieth Congress. Though he resented Khrushchev's attacks on Stalin as one-sided denigration, he could not deny the evidence of Stalin's crimes. On the way back from Moscow, after the congress, he wrote in his diary: "Rajk? Slansky? Kostov? Gomulka? And so many others? Here and now we see passing out of history the concept of a leading nation, a model party, and guiding individuals. It is as well that all this should end. At least this much will be of use: we shall begin to think with our own heads, to say what we really believe, to learn to say no."[8]

"To think with our own heads" is a foundation stone of Eurocommunism. But Soviet leaders were not prepared to face the consequences of the Twentieth Congress, and fought a bitter, and sometimes bloody, rearguard action to preserve Soviet hegemony. They threatened Poland; they sent tanks into Hungary.

Khrushchev became alarmed by the centrifugal forces released by Tito's successful heresy and his own secret report at the Twentieth Congress. He called a world conference of Communist parties in 1957 where he proposed a new international Communist organization. Most parties demurred. Palmiro Togliatti, leader of the Italian party, expressed the general sentiments: "There is no immediate need to create new international organs. . . . What is needed is a high degree of autonomy so that the individual parties can determine their strategies and forms of collaboration with other political forces in each country. . . ."[9]

Khrushchev walked out on the speech. The Russians were distinctly cool toward the Italians, but many delegates, including the Poles, supported Togliatti in private. Mao Tse-tung, it was noted, went out of his way to be cordial to the Italians. Despite his surface acquiescence in Soviet leadership, Mao had no intention of accepting any organization that might infringe even remotely on Chinese autonomy.[10]

The 1957 conference was the first of a series designed to reestablish Soviet hegemony. Paradoxically, each conference further undermined Soviet authority because the Sino-Soviet conflict came to dominate each.

The causes of the Sino-Soviet split are many, but a major issue, as in the conflict with Tito, was the Soviet claim to a degree of authority in the Communist world that was incompatible with Chinese national independence. At the Twentieth Congress, in 1956, Mao had been angered by the secret report: he felt he should have been consulted in such an important matter, and he disagreed with the tone of the report, believing that Stalin's contributions had been minimized. He proceeded to show a critical, though friendly, stance toward Soviet policies. In 1957 he supported the Polish Wladislaw Gomulka against Khrushchev (he thought Gomulka a good Communist), but backed Soviet intervention in Hungary (he thought Imre Nagy a renegade Communist), though with a subtle rebuke: Khrushchev should have intervened sooner. On the whole, however, Mao was supportive of the Soviet Union, and at the 1957 conference he declared that "the socialist camp must have a head, and this head is the USSR." Presumably, this obeisance was an exchange for substantial Soviet aid that had been granted to China a month before.[11]

In 1958 the conflict sharpened. Mao was planning to take Taiwan and demanded an open commitment of Soviet aid. Khrushchev refused, fearing a nuclear confrontation with the United States. In August 1959 China fought India over a border dispute, and Khrushchev stayed neutral—a betrayal from the Chinese point of view. A month later, Khrushchev went to the United States to negotiate with Eisenhower on détente, and this, too, was seen as a betrayal. Khrushchev then went to Peking and spoke plainly: Chinese foreign policy was "fraught with negative consequences not only for Sino-Indian relations, but for the entire international situation." He further outraged his hosts by warning them publicly against "testing by force the stability of the capitalist system."[12]

In April 1960 the Chinese retaliated with a massive campaign against the policies—and the authority—of the Soviet Communist party. According to the Chinese, Moscow's desire for détente showed an exaggerated fear of nuclear destruction on the one hand and, on the other, illusions about coexistence with imperialism. Soviet policy was undermining Communist revolutionary strategies, braking liberation movements all over the world, and, objectively, strengthening imperialism. Soon after the Chinese campaign began, the U-2 incident reinforced Mao's position, since it exposed the United States as an aggressor which was lulling the Soviet Union with talk of peace. China gloatingly taunted Khrushchev as a gullible peasant. A month later, at a meeting in Peking of the World Federation of Trade Unions, the Chinese Communist party (CCP) attacked Soviet policies in intemperate and hostile language.

Khrushchev moved for a showdown. He called for a November conference of Communist parties to iron out differences with the Chinese. Mao agreed. This was early in June. In late June, at the Romanian party congress in Bucharest, the CPSU circulated a letter attacking the CCP, and orchestrated its speeches to reinforce the letter. The Russians accused the Chinese of fomenting war, of Trotskyism, and of national chauvinism in their conflict with India. In the following months, Soviet journals pronounced that the policy of "peaceful coexistence" was binding on *all* Communist parties, an implicit assertion of Moscow's authority over the socialist bloc.

The Soviet attack was not limited to words. In July 1960 Moscow unilaterally recalled all Soviet advisers from China. Within a month hundreds of engineers and technical experts had left, taking with them thousands of blueprints, manuals, and technical papers. It was a brutal, heavy-handed action, clearly coercive in intent.[13] As a consequence, scores of plants would remain unfinished, an appalling waste of labor and materials. To the frugal Chinese, painfully husbanding their scarce resources, this was treachery on a grand scale.

Presumably, Khrushchev thought that the Chinese would capitulate. Alternatively, they would refuse to attend the November conference where the Soviet Union could manipulate a Chinese excommunication. If that was his strategy, he miscalculated: the Chinese did not capitulate, and they did attend the conference in November 1960. Further, they counterattacked the Soviet Union and fought it to a standstill. Neither side having gained the necessary support, an ambiguous document was concocted. On the key issue of national independence the Soviet Union lost. There was no condemnation of "factional" (i.e., Chinese) activities; there was no acceptance of Soviet authority on foreign policy. The Chinese were satisfied, calling the conference "an event of great historical significance," because it "changed the previous highly abnormal situation in which not even the slightest criticism of the errors of the CPSU leadership was tolerated."[14]

By this time the erosion of Soviet hegemony, so basic to the development of Eurocommunism, was well advanced, and the Italians were joining the Chinese and the Yugoslavs in open defiance. As we have seen, at the 1957 conference Togliatti had torpedoed the Soviet proposal for a new organization. At the same time he had questioned Khrushchev's analysis of Stalin's crimes. Writing in the magazine *Nuovi argomenti,* Togliatti said that to put all the blame on Stalin (Khrushchev's "cult of personality" argument) was too simple; there had been "a certain degeneration" in the Soviet party and the Soviet bureaucracy.[15]

There was another dimension to the Sino-Soviet conflict beyond the political one of national independence, and that was the ideological dimension. Mao put an end to the papal authority which Stalin had established within Marxism. Mao's writings had been revisionist vis-à-vis Lenin's theories, but Stalin had prudently overlooked this and treated Mao as an equal. After Stalin's death Mao considered himself the leading Marxist theoretician and looked on Khrushchev's pretentions as ludicrous. In the ensuing Sino-Soviet polemics, it became clear that there was no Marxist "pope." Such being the case, any Eurocommunist party had as much theoretical clout as its opponents. Ironically, Mao and Khrushchev were closer to each other ideologically—more Leninist—than either of them was to Tito or Togliatti. Yet Mao was furthering Eurocommunism by destroying Soviet ideological hegemony.

It was apparent to Togliatti, and to other Communist leaders, that the Sino-Soviet dispute weakened the Communist camp, benefited the imperialist side, and had to be mediated. Tito and Togliatti were well fitted to be mediators: they sided with Khrushchev on the dangers of thermonuclear war and the need for caution in foreign affairs; they sided with Mao on the issue of national independence and the stagnation of Marxist studies in the Soviet Union.

The mediation failed (although it enhanced the stature of Togliatti and Tito), and the Sino-Soviet split broke into the open in 1964. It was exacerbated by a clash of personalities. Khrushchev's lack of culture and his extroverted vulgarity grated on the sensibilities of Mao, who, steeped in an ancient culture, was introspective and something of a poet. To Khrushchev, Mao appeared as a great visionary, a Moses who could lead his people in a time of revolution, but too impractical to administer a socialist society. In foreign affairs, he saw Mao as a stubborn—and dangerous—neophyte.

The clash of character reflected the clash of cultures. The Chinese found the Russians to be as hard, as elitist, and as barbarian, as the other "big noses" of the white world—the Americans, the Germans, the British. The Russians, on their side, had their grievances. The Chinese were aloof and untrained. They showed little gratitude for the Soviet aid, which was made at a considerable sacrifice. They didn't treat the Russians with the respect due elder brothers in communism; the Russians after all were the first to make a revolution, the first to build a socialist industrial state. They had stopped Hitler, and they had taken Manchuria from the Japanese, thus contributing to the Maoist victory.

The irritations and clashes over such matters might have been mediated; the deep conflict over foreign policy could not. The Soviet Union wished to pursue détente to minimize the dangers of thermonuclear war; the Chinese thought this a dangerous policy of appeasement. Mao argued that the Communist bloc was stronger than the imperialist bloc and that détente would simply give the United States a breathing space in which to turn the tables. At the 1957 conference, in a major speech, Mao had said: "The east wind is prevailing over the west wind." He cited ten reasons for this judgment, including the victory of the Chinese Revolution, the dismantling of the colonial empires, and the Soviet superiority in placing two sputniks into space while the United States couldn't launch a potato. The United States was a paper tiger and Communists shouldn't fear a thermonuclear war. If such a war were to occur, capitalism would perish, whereas even if China were to lose half her population, the surviving 300 million Chinese would create a new civilization.[16]

To the Soviet leaders Mao's position was lunacy. They knew that their superiority in sputniks was an exception to their general inferiority in technology and armaments. Moreover, neither Russia nor Europe could look with equanimity to a war that would destroy their lands even though 300 million Chinese would survive. If Chinese adventurism plunged the world into a thermonuclear war, it would be the Soviet Union that would bear the brunt of the destruction; hence Chinese foreign policy had to be subordinate to Soviet policy. To the Chinese, this was an intolerable interference in their national independence. The stalemate was clear-cut. But the more China insisted on going her own way, the more she strengthened the resolve of other parties to be equally independent.

By the spring of 1964 the schism had become irreparable, and the Chinese took the offensive in every part of the world. In several countries small factions of old Communist parties had shifted their allegiance to Peking and had been recognized by Peking as the only "true" and "revolutionary" parties in those countries. If Leon Trotsky had set out to create a Fourth International, Mao now was intent on creating a Fifth.* Togliatti was conscious that if this development continued, there would be no road back. In August he went to Moscow to make a supreme effort at mediation. Togliatti disagreed with the Maoist line: aghast at Mao's 1957 speech, he was said to have muttered, "He's crazy!"[17] But he also disagreed with Khrushchev's heavy-handed way of dealing with China and felt confident enough of his international prestige to argue with him. When he got to Moscow, he was greeted by Leonid I. Brezhnev; Khrushchev had gone to tour the great agricultural experiment on the virgin lands of the East. It was suggested that Togliatti go to Yalta to await the leader's return.

At Yalta Togliatti drafted a long memorandum to be presented to Khrushchev as a basis for discussion. He finished this *memoriale* on August 12, and the next day he was struck down by a massive cerebral hemorrhage. He died on August 21, 1964. A copy of the *memoriale* had been sent to Rome, and despite Soviet objections it was published in full.† Its conclusion was unequivocal:

We know that nationalist sentiments remain a constant of the socialist and working-class movement long after the conquest of

---

* By 1980, Chinese alignment with the United States in many parts of the world had effectively stultified the Maoist groupings.

† *Memoriale* has a double meaning: "memorandum" and "testament." In the circumstances, both meanings are valid.

power. Economic progress does not extinguish these sentiments; it feeds them. In the socialist camp. . . we must guard against a coerced outward uniformity; we must believe that unity is achieved and maintained on the basis of diversity and the fullest autonomy of the individual countries.[18]

Togliatti's testament is, though not intended as such, a major document of Eurocommunism, at once a point of arrival and of departure. The erosion of Soviet hegemony, begun by the Yugoslavs, accelerated by the secret report, and completed by the Chinese, was a necessary precondition of Eurocommunism. But it was not a sufficient condition. To establish Eurocommunism, the Soviet Union had to be reconciled to it. This required another twelve years and two more international conferences.

The third international conference of Communist parties was scheduled for the end of 1968. However, in August of 1968 the Soviet army marched into Czechoslovakia. The invasion brought a sharp and immediate condemnation from many Communist parties—the Italian, the French, and the Spanish in the van—placing the Soviet Union in a precariously isolated position.

The conference took place in Moscow in 1969. China, Yugoslavia, Vietnam, North Korea, Albania, and the Netherlands refused to attend. Of those attending, only sixty signed the final declaration without objections or reservations—twenty-one fewer than had signed the declaration of the second world conference of 1960. For the first time a satellite, Romania, expressed major reservations. The Italians refused to sign because the Soviet Union would not accept a statement approving alternate "models" of socialism. The Italian Communist party emerged as the leader of the opposition to the Brezhnev doctrine; its general secretary, Enrico Berlinguer, presented the clearest exposition of the line that was soon to be called Eurocommunism.[19]

The Italian, Spanish, and French parties moved closer to common positions. In 1971 they jointly criticized the trial of a group of Jews in Leningrad who wanted to leave the USSR; in 1973 they criticized the Soviet Union for not publishing the works of Alexander Solzhenitsyn; in 1975 they protested the internment of the mathematician Leonid Plyusch in a psychiatric hospital. Moscow fought back, attacking the Spanish party in particular, both because it was the most critical of the Soviet Union and because it was the weakest of the three. Moscow also pushed for another world conference of Communist parties—the fourth since 1957.

The three Eurocommunist parties (the term was coming into use at this time) countered with a proposal for a pan-European conference where they would have more weight. At first Moscow refused, but as the polemics sharpened and the Soviet Union began to get the worst of the various arguments,* the Soviet leaders gave in. A consultative conference was called in Warsaw in October 1974.

There followed two years of inner wrangling and public maneuverings which culminated in the Berlin Conference in July 1976. In the process, Eurocommunism came of age: two meetings were hosted by the Italian Communist party: one with the Spanish party at Livorno, in July 1975, and one with the French party at Rome, in November 1975. In the declarations of Livorno and Rome, the three parties provided the clearest statement of Eurocommunism, a term which was finally accepted in the Rome declaration.[20]

The Berlin Conference marked the official end of Soviet hegemony, and it was accepted as such by the Soviet Union. The inner history of the two years of negotiations, hitherto unavailable, was given to me by one of the participants at a meeting in Bucharest.†[21]

*In October 1977 I sat kitty-corner at a table with Stefan Voicu, editor of* Era socialista, *the theoretical journal of the Romanian Communist party. Voicu was a short, wiry man in his sixties, with a small, grizzled mustache. We spoke French, and Voicu opened the conversation by telling me how much he had enjoyed the weekly column, datelined New York, I had written for* Romania libera *in 1958–60. I told him the $12.50 paid for each column had helped me to survive in the rough aftermath of McCarthyism. We then proceeded to business.*

*"Malitsa told me," I began, "that you were on the Romanian delegation and that Romania played a leading role in the negotiations."*

*Voicu shook his head impatiently. "I would go further," he said, "Romania played a decisive role, decisive." He leaned back, clasped his arms across his chest, and quirked his head to one side. "I should like to speak freely, yes? But there were many people involved and so much was said that I fear I might use inappropriate phrases. So—no names and no direct quotes on each party's position. Agreed?"*

*"Agreed."*

*He was happy to tell me about the conference, he said, because someone should set the record straight and give Romania its due. True, the Spanish party had been the one to suggest an all-European conference, and the Italian and Polish parties had pressured the Soviet Union to accept it; but once preparations began, it was the*

---

* The Eurocommunist parties were following the Chinese party's new practice of publishing letters to and from the CPSU.

† The meeting had been set up by Professor M. Malitsa, whom I had known at United Nations headquarters in 1950.

*Romanian delegation that had stood up to the Russians on issue after issue. The Yugoslavs, too, had been militant and outspoken, whereas the Italians had been reticent. Yet the Italians had got more credit for the outcome.*

*Despite the passage of a year, Voicu viewed this as an injustice, and it still rankled. The Italians, as he put it delicately, had been more expert at public relations. I didn't say anything, but I could imagine the Italians being more open with reporters—passing on interesting tidbits in a style that governing Communist parties might find too free.*

*I pointed out to Voicu that this interview might help "set the record straight." The point had not escaped him.*

*The Berlin Conference, as it came to be called, began with a preparatory meeting at Warsaw, in October 1974. It opened two years of wrangling among the parties, with the Soviet leaders trying to re-establish their old hegemony and further their goals—the expulsion of the Chinese and restoration of the unity of all parties under the leadership of the USSR.*

*To achieve its purpose, the Soviet delegation brought to Warsaw a lengthy document. Immediately, there were arguments about terminology. To an outsider, many of the phrases sound as metaphysical as the ancient scholastic argument over how many angels can dance on the head of a pin (What is the difference between "proletarian internationalism" and "proletarian solidarity"?), but, in fact, these code phrases express consequential policies. Hence the tenacity of the struggle over words.*

*With so many parties, and so many policies, there was a constant shift of alliances and combinations that took weeks to disentangle. Right off, the Soviet document was found unacceptable by many delegates, and after heated arguments the Romanian delegation suggested another meeting in two months, at which time each delegation would present a position paper. The meeting was set for December 1974 in Bucharest.*

*The position papers turned out to be uneven in quality, partial in coverage, and sharply divergent. Lacking a consensus, the Soviet Union managed to get its paper accepted, although it had the weaknesses of the earlier document—the isolation of China, the Brezhnev doctrine, etc.—as well as a self-serving analysis of postwar history. This last was dropped immediately when the Yugoslavs acidly commented that if the past was under discussion, they had a great deal to say: events had taken place for which neither the Yugoslavs nor the imperialists were responsible.*

*The Soviets proposed that the conference take place at Berlin in May 1975, the thirtieth anniversary of the victory over fascism. An early date would pressure the opposing delegations to accept the*

*Soviet paper. President Nicolae Ceausescu of Romania instructed his delegation to accept the date but not the paper: it would be impossible to thrash out the conflicts in the time available, so the date was meaningless.*

*The Soviet Union suggested that the East German delegation (friendly to the USSR) write a draft combining the various position papers, to be reviewed by a committee of eight parties, including a couple of Eurocommunist parties. Voicu would not name the eight parties, but the Italian and the Romanian were among them. The German draft proved to be hardly more than a rewrite of the Soviet paper and, to the surprise of the CPSU, the committee rejected it. The Eurocommunist position was much stronger than expected. The Soviet Union fought back. In the interests of a "more balanced representation," it demanded the committee be enlarged to sixteen nations—two of the additions being Portugal and Denmark. The mavericks, relying on their momentum, went along.*

*By now the line-up was clear: the pro-Soviet parties versus the Eurocommunist bloc strengthened by the two Eastern European parties, Yugoslav and Romanian. Several other parties, hitherto on the fence, were displaying increasing independence. The CPSU found itself on the defensive, but confident of its power, it remained adamant on two points: a reaffirmation of "proletarian internationalism" and a condemnation of "anti-Sovietism." These were acknowledged code phrases for Moscow's primacy on foreign policy and her immunity from criticism. The Italians decisively rejected "proletarian internationalism" and counterproposed "proletarian solidarity"; the Romanians and the Yugoslavs resisted "anti-Sovietism" and proposed "anticommunism."*

*In August 1975 the Helsinki agreements and many of its provisions were accepted for the draft resolution; but the fundamental issues of Soviet authority and immunity from criticism could not be resolved. The Soviet Union began to blackmail the other parties by saying that there would be no conference and that the non-Communist world would see the disunity of the Communist world. It was an effective threat and delegations began to waver, but at this point, in April 1976, the Romanian delegation spoke up. It would never agree to something it did not believe in, and if the price was scuttling the conference, so be it. The Yugoslav, Italian, Spanish, and British delegations supported Romania, and the meeting broke up, presumably for good.*

*In fact, said Voicu, it was the Russians who, in the face of the Chinese challenge, could least afford a display of European disunity. In a matter of days, they sent a delegation to Bucharest for bilateral talks to break the stalemate. Fierce arguments took place. "It is not easy," said Voicu, "for a small nation to confront a great power.*

*Besides, we were a party long accustomed to a certain reverence, so to speak." He smiled grimly. "No, it wasn't easy. But we held."*

*Finally, the Russians capitulated. The Berlin Conference would take place on the basis of a new understanding among the pan-European parties. As a consolation prize the Romanian president, Ceausescu, had handwritten into the final draft a sentence to the effect that all the parties concerned resented and rejected anticommunism and all slander of the Soviet people. "This," said Voicu, "seemed to please the Russians no end, although it was not what they originally proposed—it was a different phrase, in a different context, with a different meaning."*

*Voicu had talked uninterruptedly for almost an hour. It was becoming clear, as he relived the arguments and struggles of those years, that he felt that he had participated in a decisive event—a historic turning point. He was proud of his party and of his own role.*

*He had prepared for me a package containing the proceedings of the Berlin Conference, some of the major speeches, press releases, and related materials. "Read the speeches," he said. "They give a better sense of what happened in Berlin than the resolutions do. And remember this: the Eastern European countries have a single party system that has become structured into our societies. It will not change for a long time. You, in America, may not think it democratic. Perhaps it isn't, in your terms. But don't forget that it was the Romanians and the Yugoslavs, the governments often slandered as totalitarian, which held the door open for Eurocommunism—for a future united, democratic left and a peaceful transition to socialism."*

*An old-fashioned, grandiloquent speech—yet neither rhetorical nor pompous. And quite possibly true.*

The extent of the Soviet capitulation is reflected in the document issued at the end of the conference.[22] While the emphasis is on questions of peace and coexistence, on which agreement had been relatively easy, four major tenets of Marxist orthodoxy were conspicuously missing: there was no "Marxism-Leninism," no "dictatorship of the proletariat," no "proletarian internationalism," and no "struggle against anti-Sovietism." The Italian formula of "international solidarity" had been adopted, as well as the Eurocommunist thesis that the various Communist parties were to develop, "basing themselves on the great ideas of Marx, Engels, and Lenin, but strictly preserving the equality and sovereign independence of each party: noninterference in each other's internal affairs and freedom to choose their different roads in the struggle for progressive social change and for socialism."[23]

More decisive than the document were the speeches by Santiago

Carrillo, Enrico Berlinguer, and Georges Marchais. These set the tone. These leaders, asserting that socialism, freedom, and democracy were interdependent, defined democracy in a way that left no room for Soviet orthodoxy. Even on coexistence, Marchais declared that it "should not be identified with an acceptance of the status quo in our country, nor with the division of the world into spheres of influence under the domination of more powerful states."[24]

Of the Eurocommunists, Carrillo was the bluntest. "Once Moscow was our Rome," he declared, "but no more. Now we no longer acknowledge a guiding center, an international discipline. . . We cannot accept any return to concepts or structures which belonged to a previous period of internationalism." Among "the greatest dangers that threaten us today," he listed both "imperialistic ambitions" (a swipe at Washington) and "the drive to hegemony" (a swipe at Moscow). It was necessary "to accept once and for all the diversity of our movement, and to renounce any attempt to intrigue against it."[25]

Thus was Eurocommunism firmly established as a major current in Marxist development, on a par with Leninism and Maoism. Berlinguer defended the word: "It [Eurocommunism] is not a term of our invention. . . but it is significant that several of the Communist and workers' parties of Western Europe have arrived at similar conclusions about the road to socialism and the nature of socialist society they wish to construct. These convergences of opinion have been expressed in the recent declarations which were made jointly with the comrades of Spain, France, and Great Britain."[26]

Right up to the conference, the Soviet Union and its supporters, particularly the Czechs and the East Germans, had been attacking the term "Eurocommunism." At the Berlin Conference they were obliged to swallow the concept.

In the spring of 1977 Carrillo's *Eurocommunism and the State* was published. For the first time Carrillo broached the subject whether, given its authoritarianism, the USSR could be considered a socialist state. The Soviet reaction was violent. Moscow's *New Times* excoriated Carrillo, and proceeded to distinguish between "good" Eurocommunism and "bad" Eurocommunism.[27] While the term "Eurocommunism" was an unfortunate one, said *New Times,* it could not be denied that "there is a common basis to the strategic theses of several of the West European parties, and, more generally, of parties in those capitalist countries with a high level of economic development." But, said *New Times,* there was nothing new in this; Lenin had been sensitive to national peculiarities. In sum, while there were errors in "good" Eurocommunism, there was room for argument as among comrades.

But "bad" Eurocommunism of the Carrillo kind was beyond the

pale. *New Times* attacked Carrillo, distorting his book: "Its first aim is to set the Communist parties of the capitalist countries of Europe against the Communist parties of the socialist countries. Its second aim is to denigrate the reality of socialism in those countries that have already created a new society, particularly the Soviet Union. Its third aim is to reject the joint conclusions of the European Communists. . . to struggle for the interests of the working class and of all toilers, in the cause of peace, democracy, and social progress. To this [Carrillo] juxtaposes a completely different program which amounts to maintaining the division of Europe into military blocs, and even worse, the reinforcement of the aggressive NATO bloc."

Moscow did not limit itself to words. It had already tried to set up a rival Communist party in Spain under the leadership of General Enrique Lister (a famous Civil War figure), but the attempt had fizzled. Now it tried to isolate Carrillo. At the sixtieth anniversary of the Russian Revolution, held at the Kremlin in November 1977, Carrillo was snubbed and prevented from speaking.* Despite all its signatures to documents, Moscow was still not reconciled to Eurocommunism.

But the movement could not be contained, and the tactic of distinguishing between "good" and "bad" Eurocommunism ended in a further retreat for Moscow. The tactic not only entailed the acceptance of the term, but necessitated approval of "good" Eurocommunists such as Berlinguer, who was asked to speak at length.

Berlinguer seized the occasion to define its meaning in a hard-hitting speech which Carrillo wholeheartedly endorsed. From the rostrum of the Kremlin Berlinguer asserted that "democracy today is not only the terrain on which our class adversaries can be forced to retreat; it is also the historically essential value on which a new socialist society must be founded." He went on to enumerate the characteristics of democracy, including all civil liberties, freedom of the press, pluralism of parties, etc.[28] The very next day Brezhnev praised Berlinguer and the work of the Italian Communist party.[29] "Good" Eurocommunism was officially accepted. This acceptance flowed in part from the strength of the PCI—it might enter into the Italian government at any time—in part from the PCI's genuine deference to Soviet achievements—revolution, industrialization, defeat of Hitler, etc.—and in part from Soviet political savvy: If you can't lick 'em, join 'em.

Moscow has been fighting a losing battle as Eurocommunism has won support within the Communist countries—Yugoslavia, Romania,

---

* Carrillo facilitated the snub by arriving a day late.

Hungary, and, more cautiously, Poland. East Germany, too, seemed to be affected. There, in January 1978, a document was issued by anonymous party officials announcing the formation of a "League of Democratic Communists." It said: "A creative and undogmatic humanist communism is developing. The Communist feudal system is yielding to a renaissance and enlightenment which will enable us once again to win the confidence of the workers of Germany."[30] Although nothing more has been heard of the league, the point is that there are stirrings even in the most rigidly pro-Soviet governments.

The most important development strengthening Eurocommunism has been the shift in China's ideological position. Once reviled by the Chinese as an arch-revisionist, Tito received an extraordinary reception in Peking in the fall of 1977. A year later, in September 1978, Chairman Hua Kuo-feng returned the visit and was welcomed to Belgrade as a true friend of Yugoslavia. He stood beside Tito while the Yugoslav leader bracketed the two countries as having achieved authentic socialist revolutions.[31] Much to the annoyance of the Russians, Hua also stopped in Romania for a state visit, and a couple of months later, in December, Romania turned down Soviet requests to increase its arms budget or place its armed forces under Warsaw Pact control. In October 1979 Hua again visited Europe and, in Rome, twice met with Berlinguer. In mid-April 1980, Berlinguer went to Peking for a warm welcome and praise for the PCI's policies.[32]

Soviet hegemony is being further undermined by the policies of the Vatican under John Paul II, as shown in the reciprocal support of Church and state in the papal visit to Poland and in the pope's neutrality in the Italian elections of June 1979. There is little doubt that the erosion of Soviet hegemony is irreversible and that the rejection of the Soviet model by Eurocommunist parties is both genuine and permanent. Moreover, whatever the *political* developments of Eurocommunism may turn out to be from country to country, the ideology of Eurocommunism is bound to grow.

A great explosion of Marxist thought and Marxist studies is taking place. In area after area it is shaking up received dogma— whether of Mao, Stalin, Lenin, and even Marx and Engels. Eurocommunism cannot but be nourished by this ferment, and, in the long run, it is bound to penetrate Soviet society. This was apparent in the conference that took place in Venice a week after Berlinguer spoke in the Kremlin. The conference, on the theme "Power and Opposition in Post-Revolutionary Societies," was held under the auspices of *Il Manifesto*. The *Manifesto* group is composed of individuals, many of whom were longtime party members. Luciana Castellina, one of its leaders, and a deputy, had been in the party twenty-five years and had worked closely with general secretary Berlinguer. For years these comrades had been demanding a more aggressive line. When active as individuals, the party gave them freedom of speech within and without. When they organized themselves into a functioning faction and put out the magazine *Il Manifesto*, the party expelled them. The group formed a party with a daily paper, both taking the name of the magazine. In 1976 they formed an electoral alliance, *Democrazia proletariana*, with *Lotta Continua\** and other groups, and polled 1.5 million votes, electing six deputies. The *Manifesto* group has maintained good relations with the PCI. All the participants were Marxists, some of world renown, such as Louis Althusser, Fernando Claudín, K. S. Karol, Andreas Hegedüs, Charles Bettelheim, and included representatives of dissenters from various socialist countries: Carlos Franqui of Cuba, Jiri Pelikan and Ludvik Kavil of Czechoslovakia, Dejan Poznavic of Yugoslavia, Leonid Plyush of Russia, Istevan Meszaros of Hungary, and Edmund Baluta of Poland.[33] The Soviet Union attacked the conference in the sharpest terms; the Italian Communist party mildly disapproved of it, but well-known party members—Bruno Trentin, Lombardo Radice, Giuseppe Boffa—were speakers.

*The conference was a short distance from my hotel and I attended as many sessions as I could. It was a pleasant walk, over the Ponte dei Scalzi on the Grand Canal, around two watery alleys stippled with tiny bridges, rowboats gently rocking, water lapping at doorsteps— Venice, the fairyland. The meetings were held at the Institute of Architecture, an ancient palace of stone staircases around a shadowed courtyard full of literature tables and busy young people. There were perhaps a thousand people in the audience, about four hundred in the meeting hall itself, the rest spilling over into the anterooms and staircases where they could watch the proceedings over closed-circuit television. In the hall there was simultaneous translation via earphones in French, Italian, and German. For an ultraleft splinter group, the* Manifesto *people had done a remarkable job.*

*The range and quality of the papers were extraordinary. Here were socialism and communism from the inside, ranging from the extreme anti-Marxist position of the French philosopher André Glucksmann to the somewhat pro-Soviet position of the Italian historian Giuseppe Boffa (PCI). Hard questions were on the table:*

---

\* *Lotta Continua* (Continuing Struggle) and the *autonomi* (autonomous, i.e., independent ones) are the largest of the extremist groups to the left of the Communists. They both draw from students and some young workers. *Lotta Continua* is better organized, has its own paper, and is nonviolent in theory, although its paper can be construed as a constant incitement to violence—disavowed when it takes place. The membership is intelligent, but fanatic. The *autonomi* use violence (to break up demonstrations, etc.), but are not terrorist. However, they provide a recruiting ground for terrorists.

*Was totalitarianism inherent in socialism? Were the existing socialist states "really" socialist? Was a "new class" and a new economic system evolving in those states? Was the concept of "class struggle" as the motor of history adequate? Was Eurocommunism a disguised form of Social Democracy? And so on.* Many speakers referred to a "current crisis in Marxism," but it was the philosopher Louis Althusser who argued that the crisis was there from its beginning. "It was in the thirties that Marxism was 'fixed' and blocked in a few formulas, and a line imposed by Stalin," but it would be an error just to blame Stalin, for "every time we study Marx, Lenin, Gramsci, to uncover the Marxism stifled by Stalin, we must surrender to the evidence: our own theoretical tradition [including Lenin] is full of gaps and contradictions," which must be faced "to give Marxism its liberating role."

The contributions of the dissidents from the East were equally self-critical, yet none rejected Marxism or socialism. The main self-reproach was that the party leadership had not sufficiently involved the mass of the people. Kavil of Czechoslovakia said that the "Dubcek spring" had originated with party intellectuals and that they had made great progress within the party (40 percent of the party, or six hundred thousand Communists, had to be expelled after the Soviet intervention), but had not reached into the mass of workers outside the party. This observation was given point by the Polish Edmund Baluta, who had been head of the strike committee that shut down the shipyards of Stettin and forced the head of the Communist party, Edward Gierek, to come knocking at their doors to settle the strike.

Although most of the participants were skeptical of Eurocommunism—criticizing it from left positions—there was none of the bitter hostility that for forty years had characterized the relations among left groups. Any rancor toward the powerful Italian Communist party was soothed by its participation and friendliness, demonstrating both its independence from Moscow and its respect for differing ideas. The result was to reinforce the image of Eurocommunism as a Marxist philosophy committed to democracy and free speech.

Perhaps the most significant bit of new information was given by Jiri Pelikan, minister of information in the Dubcek government. "After Khrushchev's secret report to the Twentieth Congress," he said, "we understood and rejected the Stalinist distortions. But we couldn't think clearly, couldn't develop a positive line, until we began to study Gramsci."

Antonio Gramsci is, of course, the Leninist precursor of Eurocommunism.

# CHAPTER 2

# Eurocommunism, Democracy and the State

EUROCOMMUNISM rejects Soviet hegemony. But so do Titoism, Maoism, and Castroism, none of which is considered Eurocommunist. What distinguishes Eurocommunism from these other variants of Marxism is its stress on democracy, both on the road to power and in the building of a socialist society.

After Stalin and Mao, to speak of democracy in connection with communism sounds like black humor; in connection with Marxism, it sounds incongruous. Yet Eurocommunism stakes its future on the double assertion that it is Marxist *and* it is democratic, arguing that this is the original position of Karl Marx and Frederick Engels. Eurocommunist historians see Lenin as ambivalent on democracy and Stalin as rigidly reductive. For them, Antonio Gramsci is the link between Lenin, in one of his aspects, and Togliatti, but a link which must be carefully interpreted. For Gramsci was a Leninist: he accepted completely the dictatorship of the proletariat and shared Lenin's contempt for "bourgeois democracy." However, by his emphasis on the autonomy of culture, of the political process and of the state, he provided open channels for the development of Eurocommunism. This is what makes him its precursor. The best way to understand Gramsci is first to examine Marx and Lenin's ideas concerning democracy. Such an examination will also clarify current Eurocommunist concepts.

For Marx and Engels, socialism and democracy were interdependent, and democracy, as conceived in the American Bill of Rights, was a major weapon of working-class emancipation—an unqualified good. In fact, they held at one time, as did the English Chartists, that universal suffrage, wrested from the bourgeoisie in mighty struggles, would be more than a democratic advance—it would be a socialist measure:

> Universal suffrage is the equivalent of political power for the working class in England, where the proletariat forms the large majority of the population. . . . The carrying of universal suffrage in England, would, therefore, be a far more socialist measure than anything which has been honored with the name on the Continent.[1]

Not only were Marx and Engels in favor of democracy, but they wished to see it extended from the political to the economic field. They criticized capitalist or "bourgeois" democracy as limited and distorted. Women had no vote, laws were applied according to property, power, and status, so that, in practice, there was one law for the rich and another for the poor, one law for the white and another for the black, one for the Gentile and another for the Jew. The founders of Marxism fought to extend "bourgeois" democracy into the economic sphere and transform it into a "proletarian" democracy.

But Marx and Engels also recognized that capitalist democracy, with all its flaws, was a vast improvement over previous systems. They urged the working class to participate in the democratic process so as to achieve needed reforms. In 1864 Marx praised the Ten Hour Bill in England: it was "not only a great practical success" but "the victory of a principle; it was the first time that in broad daylight the political economy of the middle class succumbed to the political economy of the working class."[2]

The issue which has divided Marxism for the last hundred years has not been concerned with the fight for reforms, but with whether such reforms could transform capitalism into socialism. Could this "transition to socialism" be effected through existing institutions—parliaments, trade unions, courts, etc.—or would the working class and its allies have to abolish these institutions before new ones could be created. Inside this general question is a narrower, and sharper, question: Could the transition to socialism be effected peacefully, or would the group in power, the capitalist class, use its control of the army and the police to destroy the legal power of the working class? Proponents of the latter theory believed the party should prepare itself for armed struggle. On these issues Marxism split into a "reformist" wing and a "revolutionary" wing.

The potential of this split was inherent in Marx's analysis of social change; both he and Engels were ambivalent on the subject. They were not pacifists, but they did not idealize violence; and they fought against the many movements of the nineteenth century that did: the disciples of the anarchist Mikhail Bakunin in Spain, Auguste

Blanqui in France, the nihilist Sergei Nechayev in Russia. Marx and Engels opposed terrorism, and they were against the armed coup d'état advocated by Blanqui. Marx and Engels thought of violence as the expression of a people in arms as exemplified in the French and American revolutions. In all previous history, said Marx, major transitions from one epoch to another had taken place through force, through wars and bloody revolutions. Violence was the midwife of history, and the change from capitalism to socialism would not be exempt. "The workers," said Marx, "will have to overthrow the old politics which bolster up old institutions." But he went on to say, "we do not claim that the road leading to this goal is the same everywhere":

> We know that heed must be paid to the institutions, customs, and traditions of the various countries, and we do not deny that there are countries, such as America and England, and if I was familiar with its institutions, I might include Holland, where the workers may achieve their goal by peaceful means. . . . [But] in most continental countries the lever of the revolution will have to be force. . . .[3]

This judgment of Marx's, made in 1872, flowed from conditions prevailing in those countries; on the one hand, a deep-rooted democratic tradition and a strong local self-government; on the other hand, a comparatively small bureaucracy and tiny standing armies. As conditions changed, Marx revised his judgment, believing that force would be required in all countries. Then, in Germany, conditions changed. The German Social Democratic party became legal and grew steadily at the polls. By 1895, after Marx's death, Engels could write:

> Its [SDP's] growth proceeds as spontaneously, as steadily, as irresistibly, and at the same time, as tranquilly as a natural process. All government intervention has proven powerless against it. We can count even today on two and a quarter million voters. If it continues in this fashion, by the end of the century we shall conquer the greater part of the middle strata of society, petty bourgeois and small peasants, and grow into the decisive power of the land, before which all other powers will have to bow, whether they like it or not. To keep this growth going without interruption until it, of itself, gets beyond the control of the prevailing governmental system, not to fritter away this daily increasing shock force in vanguard skirmishes, but to keep it intact until the decisive day, that is our main task.[4]

This passage from Engels's Introduction to Marx's *Class Struggles in France* is somewhat ambiguous; although it stresses gradualism, the words "decisive day" imply a revolutionary break. Moreover, Engels complained that the Introduction had been expurgated to make him appear a "peaceful worshiper of legality *quand même.*" Nevertheless, as Professor Ralph Miliband cogently argues, even in the unexpurgated version Engels clearly saw "bourgeois" democracy as a working-class weapon.[5] He did insist on the *right* to revolution, but added that "whatever may happen in other countries, German Social Democracy occupies a special position and therewith, at least in the immediate future, has a special task."[6]

World War I hardened the Marxist stance. As conditions changed, theoreticians, Lenin in particular, modified the theories. Before the war, he had a keen appreciation of "bourgeois" democracy in comparison to tsarism. In 1908 he was referring to America and England as countries "where complete liberty exists," and in 1913 he wrote that "advanced countries, Switzerland, Belgium, Norway, and others, provide us with an example of how the free nations under a really democratic system live together in peace or separate peacefully from each other."*[7]

The war, with its obscene killing and repression, swept away his reservations: "Both Britain and America, the biggest and the last representatives of Anglo-Saxon 'liberty' *in the sense that they had no militarist cliques and bureaucracy,* have completely sunk into the all-European filthy, bloody morass of bureaucratic-military institutions." (Italics added.)[8]

The italicized passage emphasizes the conditions under which, in Lenin's mind, a "bourgeois" democratic state might have been used in a peaceful transition to socialism. After 1917 these conditions were gone. Now, no countries were excepted from the necessity of "smashing" the state, that is, destroying capitalist institutions: banks, armies, bureaucracies, police corps. The October Revolution in Russia reinforced Lenin's theories; since then, the requirement of "smashing" the state has been unchallenged in orthodox Marxism. Both Stalin and Mao completely accepted it.

Eurocommunism has forced a deeper study of this theory. For example, closer examination of the Russian Revolution indicates that the "smashing" of the state was a bit of hyperbole. True, the bureaucracy lost a layer of high-ranking officials, yet six years after the revolution a huge number of the bureaucrats were holding the same jobs they had held under the tsar.†[9] Even the army was not,

* Norway and Sweden separated peacefully in 1907.

† These bureaucrats formed part of a state bourgeoisie which, as one scholar has noted, "was mainly composed of members of the old bourgeoisie."[10] This class was an important source of support for Stalin in his rise to power.

strictly speaking, "smashed." It disintegrated under the German impact because it was badly led and badly equipped. As defeats mounted, soldiers deserted by the hundreds of thousands, "voting with their feet." The Bolsheviks rebuilt the army, using thousands of tsarist officers under the control of political commissars. For Eurocommunists, this raises the question of whether an existing *democratic* army, one in which soldiers have a say, cannot be subject to *new* forms of control, as happened in Republican Spain. In the Netherlands today, soldiers are forming unions; in Italy, they are forming elected bodies with authority over their living conditions. And at a lesser, but still relevant level, the police in Italy are forming bona-fide trade unions.

As Eurocommunists examine the arguments around the issue of "smashing" the state, they have had to clarify the Marxist theory of what a state is. This theory has always been complicated and unclear, a fertile ground for disparate interpretations. Marx and Engels are as much to blame for the confusion as anyone.[11] At times they saw the state as the executive committee of the ruling class; at other times, as a power above classes—the arbiter between the bourgeoisie and the proletariat. At yet other times, it was the defender of the "national" interest—meaning not only the interests of the ruling groups but of the nation, for example, in a war of independence. There was also the state as a framework for economic measures.[12]

It was in relation to the state as the "executive committee of the ruling class" that its coercive apparatus of bureaucracy and armies had to be eliminated—this was *the state* "smashed." Here, too, confusion was confounded. As we have seen, at one time Marx and Engels thought the working class in Britain and America could use the bureaucracy and other institutions to advantage. Then, as conditions changed, they modified their theories. Lenin followed a similar trajectory and concluded that existing institutions must be destroyed, thereby closing the door on peaceful change.

Eurocommunists have reopened the door, analyzing the state in advanced capitalist nations. While the capitalist state is seen as a defender of the capitalist system, its every action conditioned by that system, Eurocommunists do not accept the idea that its component parts cannot be drastically modified *if democracy is maintained and extended*. For example, in Italy, the agencies of health, welfare, and employment benefits, hitherto controlled by the central government, are now being decentralized into the regions, the cities, and the neighborhoods and administered by local councils, thus weakening the central bureaucracy. Another instance of democratic power is the police in Italy, now in the process of unionization.

Closely related to the role of democracy and the issue of "smashing" the state is the question of what happens after the working class achieves power, the so-called "dictatorship of the proletariat," a phrase which the bourgeoisie constantly throws at Communists to "prove" their dictatorial intent. It is one of those phrases which, like "people's democracy," Stalinism has sullied. The Italian party was the first to stop using it: the French, Spanish, English, and other parties followed them. As used by Marx, with his penchant for sonorous Latinate words, it meant simply that once the great majority of the people had taken power, the people—the proletariat—would prevent the old ruling groups from subverting the new society. But Marx rarely used the phrase, and the clearest definition was given by Engels: "Do you wish to know what this dictatorship looks like? Look at the Paris Commune. That was the dictatorship of the proletariat."[13] The Commune of 1871 was, of course, an example of participatory democracy.

To Gramsci, in 1919, the phrase did not imply the kind of dictatorship that Stalin was to develop. "The dictatorship of the proletariat," said Gramsci, "is the installation of a new state, typically proletarian, into which flow the institutional experiences of the oppressed class, in which the social life of the worker and peasant class become a system, universal and strongly organized."[14]

Lenin picked up the phrase, narrowed it somewhat, and it became the *sine qua non* of Marxism-Leninism, the hyphenated philosophy invented by Grigori Zinoviev, promulgated by Stalin, and discarded by Eurocommunists. Rosa Luxemburg, criticizing Lenin, argued that with his kind of party, the dictatorship *of* the proletariat would end up as the dictatorship of the party *over* the proletariat. As an acknowledged Marxist leader, her views carried authority. She admired and praised the Bolsheviks for their courage, audacity, and revolutionary fervor, but she objected to their "cold disdain for the constituent assembly, universal suffrage, freedom of the press and of assembly; in short, the gamut of basic democratic rights of the mass of the people."[15]

Her writings are full of observations that could have been written by Thomas Jefferson:

Freedom only for supporters of the government, only for the members of one party—however numerous they may be—is no freedom at all. Freedom is always and exclusively for the one who thinks differently.[16]

Her warning was prophetic:

In place of the representative bodies created by general popular elections, Lenin and Trotsky have laid down the soviets as the only true representation of the masses. But with the repression of political life in the land as a whole, life in the soviets must also become more and more crippled. Without general elections, without unrestricted freedom of press and assembly, without a free struggle of opinion, life dies out in every public institution, becomes a mere semblance of life, in which only the bureaucracy remains as the active element.[17]

Luxemburg was murdered in 1919. In the stress of Allied intervention and civil war in Russia her warnings were forgotten, and Stalin went on to consolidate his power and make her fears a reality: the dictatorship of the proletariat became the dictatorship of one man. After Stalin's death and the erosion of Soviet hegemony, the phrase either fell into disuse (in the Italian party) or was expressly repudiated (by the French in 1976, the Spanish in 1979).

The document issued at the end of the Berlin Conference omitted the phrase entirely. That a phrase is no longer used does not mean, of course, that the reality it represents no longer exists. Critics to the right and left of Eurocommunism have made this point a major polemical issue. The right maintains that while the phrase "dictatorship of the proletariat" has been dropped, Eurocommunist parties once in power will be as dictatorial as those already in power. Left critics argue that the dropping of the phrase does not eliminate the reality of the class struggle. Just as capitalist governments represent bourgeois interests and controls—a more or less veiled "dictatorship of the bourgeois," any socialist government would represent working-class interests and controls—a more or less veiled "dictatorship of the working class." Whatever the name, the problem persists.[18]

The Eurocommunists answer that phrases such as "dictatorship of the bourgeoisie" and its obverse, "dictatorship of the proletariat," are deficient both in language and in content. They are far too simplistic. To deny meaningful difference among capitalist governments, to lump them all—from Hitler's Nazism to Roosevelt's New Deal—under the rubric "dictatorship of the bourgeoisie," is to abdicate political analysis. The Eurocommunists quote Lenin back at the Leninists:

There are bourgeois-democratic regimes like the one in Germany, and also like the one in England; like the one in Austria and also like those in America and Switzerland. He would be a fine Marxist, indeed, who in a period of democratic revolution failed to see the difference between the degrees of democraticism and the differences between its forms. . . .[19]

Eurocommunists contend that the term "dictatorship of the bourgeoisie" should be reserved for regimes such as those of Adolf Hitler, Benito Mussolini, Francisco Franco, Augusto Pinochet, et al., and that the term "hegemony of the bourgeoisie" should be used for democratic governments. "Hegemony" a word constantly used by Gramsci—is defined in *Webster's New International Dictionary* as "leadership; preponderant influence or authority." The word was for a long time a code word of Eurocommunism, but the Chinese are now using it against the Russians and it has crept into American diplomatic usage. In fact, Henry Kissinger claims he introduced the word and the Chinese copied him.[20]

When the Italian Eurocommunists say they are on the way to achieving "cultural hegemony" in their country, they are saying that values traditional to class-conscious workers are permeating society. *Pari passu*, they are working toward a "political hegemony" wherein working-class parties will guide Parliament to institute such economic reforms as will open the door to socialism: the economic hegemony of the working population.[21]

Violence is neither inherent nor desirable in such hegemony; rather, the goal is an ever deeper and more active democracy. The democratic coalition has no reason to resort to violence; on the contrary its problem is to prevent the violence of a desperate and discarded class—the present power elite. This is particularly true of the Italian Communist party, which has been developing the theory for thirty years.

*Democracy is seen by the Italian Communists as the major lever in the restructuring of the country. I was struck by this on a visit to the Palmiro Togliatti Institute, located thirty miles from Rome, near a town called Frattochie. Frattochie (the name has become a synonym for the school) is the graduate school of the party, with four full-time professors and a housekeeping staff.[22] Several impressive modern buildings with classrooms, dormitories, and dining rooms have been built on spacious, beautifully kept grounds once belonging to a well-to-do Italian Jew. He sold the villa and grounds to the Communists because "only they would resist commercial temptations of development and maintain the grounds as he would wish."[23]*

*The director of Frattochie is Luciano Gruppi, a man in his early fifties, as spare in speech as in physique. Gruppi is a member of the PCI Central Committee and head of its cultural commission. He brings to his studies the training of an academic philosopher, a thorough knowledge of Marxist classics, immersion in Gramsci's writings, and considerable practical experience as a Communist functionary. His book,* Togliatti e la via italiana al socialismo *(Tog-*

*liatti and the Italian road to socialism), published in March 1976, triggered an angry reply from Moscow, which issued a pamphlet attacking Gruppi directly. The PCI's paper,* L'Unita, *replied sharply that the attack on Gruppi was really directed "against the fundamental policy choices of the PCI and other Western parties," adding that the Soviet author's "grotesque formulations" had twisted Lenin's thought "into a system of immutable dogma."*

*I told Gruppi that I had been struck by the Communists' efforts to democratize trade-union structures, and to democratize politics by decentralization. I had also noted the creation of neighborhood councils, and the democratization of schools, giving a voice to teachers, parents, and students. But what most impressed me was the "style" of Communist work–the free and easy way they dealt with each other as well as Catholics and other non-Communists, the lack of pomposity and pretention in the leadership.*

*Having been to PCI meetings, I had found an American flavor that was unusual in Europe. Europeans, after all, have never known democracy in the way Americans know it—not only as parliamentarism but in their daily life and mental habits. England, for example, is caste-ridden to this day, whereas Americans are more egalitarian.*

*Gruppi both agreed and demurred: "There is little doubt that the American style of personal relations is influencing our people through your films, magazines, and books, but at the same time we are conscious of your racism, your imperialism, your intervention in Vietnam, Chile, etc. We consider your Bill of Rights as one of the great achievements of the Enlightenment. We view it as a point of departure, something to build upon. We know that in America it is often violated—in regard to blacks, women, Indians, Mexicans, Puerto Ricans, and the poor generally—but we believe the remedy is to extend its provisions and to add economic democracy."*

*I asked Gruppi if the Italian party's adherence to "bourgeois democracy" was not a revision of Marx and Lenin.*

*"We are trying to extend and decentralize the bourgeois democratic state, and in that process we are using bourgeois democracy and Parliament against the bourgeoisie. We are not revisionists of the class struggle. We are revising Lenin's position that the bourgeois state must be 'smashed,' but we must remember that this position in* State and Revolution *was developed in a polemic against the Social Democrats who subordinated the workers' struggles to parliamentary maneuvers. Today we have an unmistakable strength in Parliament which we can link to mass struggles outside of Parliament. Moreover, as the modern state becomes more authoritarian, as in Gaullism or Nixonism, restoring the prestige of Parliament may, in itself, be a democratic step forward. This is an important aspect of PCI strategy.*

*"Furthermore, at the very time Lenin was writing his book in 1917 he was also writing an article in which he said that, alongside the oppressive apparatus of the state, there was an economic apparatus which should not be smashed; rather, it should be taken over and used by socialists.*[24]

*"Let me put it another way. The reformists say: With reforms we can solve problems without destroying the system. The orthodox revolutionaries say: The struggle for reforms is not revolutionary because it does not change the system. Both overestimate the strength of the bourgeoisie; both separate the fight for reforms from the fight for power; and both sides end up as variants of opportunism."*

*As we parted, Gruppi gave me copies of the curriculum used at Frattochie and an annotated bibliography on democracy in the Marxist classics, including the writings of Luxemburg and Gramsci. He said: "The extension of democracy is the key to winning socialist power, and the Communists must be the teachers and organizers. Mao had said that Communists are the fish sustained by the sea of people; that is what we teach."*

The issue of the "smashing" of the state has been used by left critics of Eurocommunism, such as *Monthly Review*, to argue that the Italian Communists, by abandoning this concept and the related concept of "the dictatorship of the proletariat," have "sold out" to the capitalist system, much in the manner of the British Labour party. Whatever side one takes, the battle of quotations now raging may be, in the deepest sense, irrelevant.[25] For, as I have tried to show, one point is irrefutable: Marx, Engels, and Lenin changed their minds, and their theories, as the reality around them changed. Marxism has always insisted that events be examined in their detailed concreteness;[26] a battle of quotations does not alter that requirement. The issue, posed in its simplest terms, is this: Is Eurocommunism making a serious attempt to change capitalism so fundamentally as to open the way to socialism? If so, will it succeed? The first question requires us to look at what is happening; the second can only be answered in the future.

Italy provides a good testing ground for the first question, since the Italian Communist party has been devising tactics to carry out the Eurocommunist strategy and the results will be examined in the second part of this book. There is a danger, a danger stressed by left critics, namely, that in making its policies palatable to the middle class, the party undermines its working-class basis. That this is a real problem was shown in the setback to the PCI in the elections of June 1979. Professor Ralph Miliband has discussed the danger in his excellent critique, *Marxism and Politics:*

The basic point is that bourgeois democracy and constitutionalism generate considerable constraints for revolutionary movements and lead them towards what might be called reciprocal constitutionalism. . . .

Parties with serious electoral ambitions, however genuine their ultimate intention to transcend capitalist structures, are inevitably tempted to try and widen their appeal by emphasizing the relative moderation of their immediate (and not so immediate) aims.[27]

Italian party leaders are well aware of this danger and are searching for a solution. They may fail, just as the Paris Commune failed, but it cannot be proved, at this point, that they are *destined* to fail. Miliband, who is no exponent of Eurocommunism, ends his book precisely on that note:

Such a strategy is full of uncertainties and pitfalls, of dangers and dilemmas; and it may in the end turn out to be unworkable. But it is just as well to have a sober appreciation of the alternatives and not allow slogans to take over. . . . Bourgeois democracy is crippled by its class limitations, and under constant threat of further and drastic impairment by conservative forces, never more so than in a period of permanent and severe crisis. But the civic freedoms which, however inadequately and precariously, form part of bourgeois democracy are the products of unremitting popular struggles. The task of Marxist politics is to defend these freedoms; and to make possible their extension and enlargement by the removal of their class boundaries.[28]

Miliband's book has not been without critics,[29] but the thesis which most concerns us, the theoretical possibility of a peaceful transition, has been considered in depth by him and found to have merit. The finding should lay at rest many polemics. What the appropriate Communist strategies should be, is, of course, a matter of debate and verification. For example, many Marxists have suggested that the Labour party in 1945 could have followed a strategy of using the reforms it instituted as steppingstones to a changed society.[30]

Whether such a strategy would have worked is impossible to say. Surely the Labour party could not have done worse than it did in the elections of 1979, when many of its followers voted for Margaret Thatcher. It is interesting to note that British Marxists, whose national tradition is heavily tinged with empiricisim, should find common cause with Italian Marxists, whose national tradition has been, via Benedetto Croce, neo-Hegelian. In no area has this been so clear as in the argument over base and superstructure.

In Marxist thought, the concept of the superstructure embraces not only politics, with which we have been concerned in this chapter, but art, religion, jurisprudence, sociology, psychology, etc.—all the activities that are outside the province of economics and production, known as the "economic base"—relations of production, technology, natural resources, ownership, etc. The economic base sets parameters for the superstructure; it conditions everything in society. As the decades went by, this insight has tended to be vulgarized into a straitjacket: that the economic base *determines* the superstructure. This determinism vitiated Marxist analysis of the state, of religion, of culture. Gramsci, who broke with this deterministic vision, restored autonomy to the various components of the superstructure and began to analyze them in their own terms.

Antonio Gramsci was born in Sardinia in 1891. He became a socialist and a Marxist around 1910 and was one of the founders of the Italian Communist party in 1921, becoming its general secretary in 1924. His was an exceptional intelligence that was fascinated by Marxism; his writings are suffused with a sense of intellectual excitement.

This intellectual excitement is a commonplace among those who are touched by Marxism—even among those who later deprecate it. Clifford Odets once said to me that Marxism hadn't done much for him; it "just gave me a spin." Thinking of the passion of *Waiting for Lefty*, with its final appeal to "stormbirds of the revolution," I couldn't help laughing. "I know, I know," I said. "A *little* spin—right into a galactic orbit."

The little spin of a Marxist awakening is rarely transcended. Whatever the weaknesses of the *content* of Marxist philosophy, there is no doubt anywhere, the Vatican included, that its method is a superb achievement of Western culture. A surprising number of prelates in Italy are as well versed in the dialectic as they are in Thomist philosophy. The insights provided by Marxist analysis are so arresting that theory is held in the highest regard among Marxists—a regard sometimes bordering on fetishism. This is why arguments over theory play such a weighty role among Eurocommunists and their opponents. This high regard explains as well the tenacity with which Antonio Gramsci pursued his theoretical studies in Mussolini's jails.[31]

Gramsci was arrested in November 1926, and died, still under surveillance, in April 1937. In those ten years he wrote over a million words in thirty-three notebooks which his sister-in-law Tatiana

Schucht took from Gramsci's room while making the funeral arrangements. The notebooks were sent to Moscow.

These notebooks establish Gramsci as a major Marxist theorist, comparable to Mao Tse-tung in the post-Lenin period. (In 1917, Mao was twenty-four, Gramsci twenty-six.) Both were shaped by the Bolshevik revolution and both were Leninist, but both resisted "Russification," developing their Marxism in consonance with the national characteristics of their countries.

Gramsci is considered the "theoretician" of Eurocommunism, and it is a fitting definition, provided it is used with caution. For Gramsci, who died forty years before the flowering of Eurocommunism, died a Leninist, accepting the concept of the dictatorship of the proletariat, the discipline of the Comintern, and the rejection of gradualism. Nevertheless, he is a precursor of Eurocommunism. His writings adumbrate the broad lines of its development: a rejection of theoretical rigidity and the authoritarianism of the Comintern, and an emphasis on national cultures, on democracy within the party, on freedom of speech and research for intellectuals.

Gramsci's studies on the nature of the state, as well as on religion, science, the mediating institutions between the economic base and the social superstructure, were original and penetrating. His unusual talents were widely recognized. At his trial, when he was age thirty-one, the fascist public prosecutor told the judge, "We must prevent this brain from functioning for twenty years."[32] It is one of the recurrent ironies of history that jail gave him the leisure to put his brain to work.

Perhaps the most productive of Gramsci's ideas relates to the role of armed force in working-class strategies. In classical Marxism, whereas revolution was seen as essentially political and social, armed force was considered a necessary ingredient. Political power grew out of a gun barrel and force was the midwife of history. Basically, this meant civil war. With the advent of thermonuclear war, civil war in advanced industrial nations has become extremely dangerous, since it is likely to provoke a confrontation of the superpowers and "the ruin of the contending parties" envisaged in the *Communist Manifesto*. With capitalism on the defensive, this situation gives ruling classes a blackmailing edge that is bound to stultify any advances by the working classes. It is at this juncture that Gramsci's thought provided the seeds for Eurocommunist strategy.

Gramsci analyzed the problem of the seizure of power by distinguishing two methods of struggle in the transition to socialism—the war of movement and the war of position.[33] By war of movement Gramsci meant the techniques of Lenin and the Russian Revolution, what Miliband calls "insurrectionary politics." Others have called it the "Jacobin approach" of the French Revolution. In this variant, a disciplined organized party, in a time of social disintegration and of a disoriented ruling class (often the result of losing a war), can seize power by armed force. The revolutionaries are supported by a sympathetic, *but not necessarily class-conscious,* population. Such was the October Revolution.

By war of position, on the other hand, Gramsci meant the steady erosion of bourgeois institutions with the concomitant development of working-class consciousness. As the problems of capitalist society become increasingly insoluble, the working class sheds its sense of inferiority at being a subordinate class, learns to be a *governing* class, and establishes its hegemony. Gramsci, however, still believed that force would be necessary for the final assault on the capitalist citadel: a major revolutionary break was inevitable, and the bourgeois state would have to be broken by revolutionary blows. Yet if conditions are such that no one dares to use force, a peaceful transition becomes a *sine qua non* of survival; the Gramscian war of position then leads to the Eurocommunist concept of a peaceful transition.[34]

Gramsci establishes the Marxist legitimacy of Eurocommunism; he is the link between Marx and Lenin on the one hand and Togliatti and Berlinguer on the other. Togliatti, while still in Barcelona during the Spanish Civil War, received the photocopies of Gramsci's notebooks and, working by candlelight in the midst of bombing, began the work of studying the material with a view to publication.[35] The project was finally realized after World War II, the last volume appearing in Italy in 1954. Gramsci's thought, both in content and in methodology, has been invaluable to the Italian Communist party.[36]

As important to Eurocommunism as the new concepts developed by Gramsci is his legacy of humanism and devotion to Western culture in general and to the Enlightenment in particular. Gramsci believed that the working class should be the inheritor and custodian to the best achievements of the past. He argued for freedom of thought and creativity—utterly and unconditionally— in contradistinction to the Stalinist (and Maoist) control of intellectuals and artists.[37]

Gramsci is a Marxist in the great European cultural tradition of Marx himself, a thinker with an open mind, disciplined in the search of truth. The masthead of *L'Ordine nuovo,* edited by Gramsci, carried the motto "To Tell the Truth Is Revolutionary." Today when Marxists throughout the world suffer the consequences of a lack of probity, Gramsci's austerity is fresh and invigorating:

We must not conceive of a scientific discussion as if it were a courtroom proceeding in which there are a defendant and a prosecutor, who, by duty of his office, must show that the defendant is guilty, and therefore should be put out of circulation. It is a premise in scientific discussion that the interest lies in the search for truth and the advancement of science. Therefore the most "advanced" thinker is he who understands that his adversary may express a truth which should be incorporated in his own ideas, even if in a minor way.

To understand and evaluate realistically the position and reasons of one's adversary *(and sometimes the adversary is the entire thought of the past)* means precisely to have freed oneself from the prison of ideologies (in the bad sense of blind fanaticism). One has then arrived at a critical frame of mind, the only fruitful stance in scientific research. [Italics added.][38]

To Gramsci, creativity and realism were essential for the future workers' state. He writes:

From the moment when the oppressed class comes to power, creating a new type of state, it becomes necessary to create a new moral and intellectual order, that is to say, a new type of society. This entails the development of more universal concepts, of *more refined and decisive ideological weapons*. [Italics added.][39]

And again:

In the phase of struggle for hegemony, [before taking power], the science of politics is primarily developed; in the phase of *state* power *all* the superstructure must be developed, *or the state itself may disintegrate*. [Italics added.][40]

Gramsci was fully aware that in a transitional society old ideologies are powerful and operative and will take generations to disappear.* The temptation is strong to get rid of them by proscription and censorship (as the Catholic Church has done wherever it could) and for the state to set limits to free discussion. Gramsci is unequivocal:

It seems to me that, of necessity, the search for new truths . . . must be left to the free initiative of the individual scientists—even if scientists continually re-examine those very premises which seem most essential, fundamental, and settled once for all.[41]

Gramsci's ideas, particularly in Italy, have profoundly conditioned the party's relations with women, workers, priests, and

---

* In many Christian areas, traces of paganism are still powerful despite centuries of repression and extirpation.

professionals. Whatever their differences, everyone in Italy, left or right, agrees that Communists are serious people.* Gramsci's ethic has strengthened that approach:

> What is needed for revolution are men of sober mind, men who don't cause a bread shortage in the bakeries, who make trains run, who provide the factories with raw materials . . . who ensure the safety and freedom of the people against attacks by criminals . . . who do not reduce the people to despair. Verbal enthusiasms and reckless phraseology make one laugh (or cry) when a single one of these problems has to be resolved, even in a village of a hundred inhabitants.[43]

Gramsci lived up to his own standards, working hard and tenaciously as tuberculosis ravaged the organism, suffering insomnia, hemorrhages, faintings, deliriums. The enormous effort is reflected in the handwriting: the early notebooks are neat, written in clear and regular calligraphy; near the end the hand wavers, wanders, is erratic and weak. But the thinking remains lucid, vigorous, trenchant; the style poised and professional, spiced with humor, irony, and a genial twist of phrase.

Gramsci died on April 27, 1937. He died as fascist troops and Nazi squadrons were pouring into Spain. Nazism and fascism were marching forward, everywhere triumphant. Eight years later, as spring came round again to Italy, the carcass of Mussolini hung by its heels at a gas station in Milan.

Gramsci's thought remained, Gramsci's example. First in Italy, then in Europe, and slowly around the world, his open, creative Marxism is liberating minds. If Eurocommunism should fulfill its promise, much of the credit will go to Mussolini's jailbird.

---

* In English "serious" has a nuance of "austere"; in Italian the nuance is more toward "responsible" or "reliable." This evaluation of the PCI is commonplace in Italy and is a constant refrain.[42]

# CHAPTER 3

# Eurocommunists... and Eurosocialists

MOST CRITICS of Eurocommunism, whether from the left or the right, consider that its major problem lies in the confrontation with the capitalist class and the capitalist state: Will employers sabotage the economy? Will the army be neutral? Will the bureaucracy split? Will workers stay submissive? And so on. Without minimizing any of these, I believe the fundamental problem lies within the working class itself: Can class unity be achieved between Socialists and Communists? Class unity is the magnet that can attract allies from other groups—professionals, farmers, small businessmen. If workers cannot get along, other people aren't going to go along. In the twentieth century, this lack of unity has exacted a fearful price; among many catastrophes, it was a major factor in the rise and rule of Hitler.

The importance of working-class unity has not escaped the policy makers of the capitalist world; they have been past masters at applying the old Roman maxim of divide and rule. Since Socialist parties are less subject to discipline, they have been easier to influence, although Communist parties have not been immune to penetration.

As Eurocommunism has grown, a countermovement has developed—Eurosocialism, whose aim is to maintain socialist hegemony within the European left. Subject to many qualifications, it used the first direct elections to a European parliament (June 1979) as a test of strength. Current relations between Socialists and Communists in each country are extremely varied and complex country by country.

Historically, twentieth-century Socialist and Communist parties stem from a common ideology—Marxism—and a common organizational heritage—the First and Second Internationals.* The First International, a loose association of small radical groups, was torn by conflict between Karl Marx and Mikhail Bakunin, the anarchist leader; it was interred, in effect, in 1871.[1] In the following two decades Marxism became pre-eminent within socialist thought. Socialist parties were growing throughout Europe, and in 1889 the Second International was organized with the German Social Democratic party as the leading party. Friedrich Engels, then sixty-nine, was its acknowledged theoretician and elder statesman.

The Second International still survives,[2] although after World War I its left wing broke away to form the Third, or Communist, International, colloquially known as the Comintern. Conceived by Lenin, it was formed with great urgency in the expectation of revolutions throughout Europe. Several factors contributed to its shape and rules: the betrayal of the Second International, the imminence of the German revolution, the success of the Leninist party in the Russian Revolution. The birth and vicissitudes of the Comintern are an integral part of the development of Eurocommunism.

The betrayal of the Second International at the inception of World War I was unexpected and devastating. The International had enormous power at the time, its parties having millions of members and hundreds of deputies in the various countries. At the Stuttgart Congress (1907), the International leadership spoke out resolutely:

> Should war break out in spite of everything, it is the duty of Socialists to bring about its rapid conclusion and to work with all their strength to utilize the economic and political crisis provoked by the war to rouse the people, and thus accelerate the abolition of the rule of the capitalist class.[3]

Similar resolutions were adopted by the congresses of Copenhagen (1910) and Basel (1912). Jean Jaurès, the French leader who was not a left Socialist, said at Basel: "We will not go to war against our brothers! We will not open fire on them! If the conflagration breaks out despite everything, then there will be war on another front—there will be revolution."[4] But when World War I broke out, most Socialist parties backed their governments.

The second element that shaped the Comintern was the imminence of the general European revolution that seemed inevitable to

---

* The English Labour party is the most notable instance of a party considering itself socialist but not Marxist. Although influenced by Marxism, it has had an independent development going back to the Chartists. Recently, Bettino Craxi, leader of the Italian Socialist party, has tried to claim Pierre Proudhon, rather than Karl Marx, as his ideological ancestor, but the foray was recognized as a polemical ploy, deserving more compassion than derision.

Lenin. As Kaiser William II fled defeated Germany, Lenin wrote (October 1918) to Y. M. Sverdlov, chairman of the executive committee of the Soviets: "The international revolution has come so close in *one week* that it has to be reckoned as an event in the *next few days*. By spring, we must have an army of three million to help the international workers' revolution." (Lenin's italics.)[5]

The third element in shaping the Comintern was the prestige of the Russian Revolution which Lenin had guided—the first revolution in the history of mankind led by professional revolutionaries. They had consciously trained themselves for that task and dedicated their lives to it.[6]

Unquestionably, the decisive element in the formation of the Comintern was the betrayal of Social Democracy as war broke out, followed by a second betrayal at the war's end, when the revolution in Germany was skillfully channeled into the Socialist government of Friedrich Ebert. Ebert had made a secret deal with General Paul von Hindenburg; the army would support the Weimar Republic and the Republic would liquidate revolutionary activities. One of the consequences of this deal was the double murder of Rosa Luxemburg and Karl Liebknecht.[7] The blood spilled in the double betrayal nurtured the hatred of the left Socialists who formed the Comintern. The main enemy became not capitalism but Social Democracy.

The Comintern was flawed from its inception, the elements that influenced Lenin providing the flaws. The urgency made it premature; the hatred of the Social Democrats made it a divisive force in the workers' movements; the concept of a party made it too centralized. The Russian model was to prove a block rather than an inspiration. Rosa Luxemburg had foreseen the problem: "The Bolsheviks," she wrote, "by their determined revolutionary stand, their exemplary strength in action, and their unbreakable loyalty to international socialism . . . have contributed whatever could possibly be contributed under such devilish hard conditions." Then the warning: "The danger begins only when they make a virtue of necessity and want to *freeze into a complete theoretical system all the tactics* forced upon them by these fatal circumstances." (Italics added.)[8]

Although a strong proponent of centralism and discipline, Lenin had a deep sense of the specific conditions of the October Revolution. Before his death, at the Fourth Congress of the Comintern (1922), he warned against an uncritical acceptance of the Russian experience and urged Communists to study: "After five years of the Russian Revolution the most important thing for all of us, Russian and foreign comrades alike, is to sit down and study . . . and to study *from scratch*."[9] Writing sixty years later, the Spanish historian Fernando Claudín quotes Luxemburg and Lenin approvingly and regrets that their advice was not followed: "At the moment when critical thinking was most necessary, the October Revolution introduced *theoretical complacency*."[10]

With hindsight, the worst flaw of the Comintern was its stress on a strong centralized organization. In the fires of war a military state of mind and army jargon had become commonplace. Class war transmuted army jargon from metaphors into real concepts. Since imperialism was world-wide, Lenin argued that the working-class movement should be organized globally, under the leadership of a general staff that would command unquestioned obedience.

The betrayals of the Second International strengthened the drive to centralization. The influence of Social Democracy had to be cauterized at any cost, and the twenty-one conditions drawn up for membership in the Comintern were so stringent as to repel many socialist groups that admired the Bolsheviks. Under these conditions the various parties were to be *sections* of the International, its executive committee empowered to remove leaders and intervene in the internal policies of each section, with the presidium of the executive committee empowered to take action on its own.[11] Military discipline was mandated by the rules: "In the present epoch of acute civil war, the Communist party will be able to fulfill its duty only if its organization is as centralized as possible, if iron discipline prevails, and if the party center . . . has strength and authority and is equipped with the most comprehensive powers."[12]

From its inception, the Comintern saw as its main task the defense of the Russian Revolution; but it never entered the minds of its founders, including Lenin, that the tactics for that defense should be laid down by the Russians or that the Comintern should become an adjunct of Soviet foreign policy.* By 1930, such was the case. Stalin, dominant in the USSR, completely controlled the Comintern and made it a tool of his foreign policy. By the mid-thirties, he was disposing of foreign Communist leaders at will. Finally, in 1943, he dissolved the Third International. He wanted to reassure his capitalist allies that he had no intention of fomenting postwar revolutions.

There is little doubt that the experiences undergone in the Comintern by leading Communists—the Russification of the International, the stultification of Marxism, the physical liquidation of opponents—subverted their loyalties to Stalin. Well before his death, many of them resented and silently repudiated Stalinism, an attitude which was a far from negligible stimulus to the birth of Eurocommunism. It is easy today to criticize those men and women for their silence and subservience, but it was an age when discipline and esprit

---

* Lenin looked to the day when the headquarters of the Comintern would be in Berlin. But as it turned out, Moscow was the only safe place, and within a short time the Russian influence became paramount.

de corps were paramount, the days of counterrevolution and fascism: Mukden, Abyssinia, Vienna,* Guernica, Munich. Throughout the twenties and thirties the Comintern fought and had creditable achievements—the International Brigades in Spain, the formation of Communist parties in the colonial world, the training of Communist leadership from Asia and Africa.

In the twenty-four years between 1919 and 1943, relations between the parties of the Second and Third Internationals ranged from open enmity to suspicious co-operation. Until 1935 the enmity was unremitting and, in Germany, decisive in opening the door to Hitler. His rise had a sobering effect on the fratricidal struggle. The Italian Socialists and Communists arrived at a Pact of Unity in 1934, the French Communists made overtures to the Socialists, and finally, in 1935, the Seventh World Congress of the Comintern swung around to a policy of co-operation, which resulted in the Popular Front in France and in Spain. Togliatti was a major architect of this Congress, which elected Georgi Dimitrov, a Bulgarian, as its head.†

On the whole, given the role of the Second International in World War I, no group or party comes blameless before the bar of history. While Stalin is *sui generis,* Socialists made their contribution—by their leniency after the Kapp putsch of 1920 and the "beer-hall putsch" of Adolf Hitler and Erich Ludendorff in 1923, toward Franco in Spain in 1934, toward Dollfuss in Austria. The French Socialists, with Leon Blum at their head, had a particular responsibility for non-intervention in Spain and the betrayal of Czechoslovakia at Munich.‡

The hatred between the Internationals had that fanatic quality common to friends who feel betrayed by one another. It was exacerbated by the Communist tradition of invective, initiated by Marx and formalized by Lenin. Marx was a passionate man, and his vituperations were scorching. Lenin transformed this trait into a political weapon:

I purposely choose that tone calculated to evoke in the hearer hatred, disgust and contempt. . . . It is a tone, a formulation, designed not to convince but to break the ranks; not to correct a mistake of the opponent but to annihilate him, to wipe him off the face of the earth.[14]

---

* In February 1934 Austrian Chancellor Engelbert Dollfuss instituted a semifascist regime, using artillery against embattled Socialists and Communists besieged in their housing projects. The left was smashed; then, in June, the pro-Hitler wing of the fascists assassinated Dollfuss, paving the way for Hitler's takeover of Austria.

† Dimitrov was the hero of the Reichstag Fire trial, where he had reduced Hermann Goering to a state of near apoplexy.

‡ Blum said he accepted Munich "with shameful relief."[13]

Epithets such as "lickspittle," "vermin," and "running dogs of the bourgeoisie" are not soon forgotten. Such language, coupled with even more unforgivable acts, has left a legacy of mutual distrust that varies from country to country. It is most virulent in Germany, most quiescent in Italy. Even where dormant, it can flare up suddenly on either side, as happened in Portugal in 1975, France in 1978, and Italy in 1979. Ostensibly, Socialists mistrust the Eurocommunists' commitment to democracy. So astute an observer as Fernando Claudín considers this a central issue between Socialists and Communists.

*In October 1977 I sat in a bar behind the Prado Museum in Madrid, having a snack with Fernando Claudín, the Spanish historian of the Comintern. Claudín has written four books, including one on the Comintern and one on Eurocommunism, each emphasizing inner party matters and the relation between theories and policies. He is a deeply philosophical man, and his writings are special in the way Trotsky's* History of the Russian Revolution *is special; theory and practice are fused into a compelling whole by authors who were participants in the events they analyze.*

*Claudín was for years a leader in the Spanish Communist party. He was expelled in 1965 for "premature Eurocommunism." This, as he said ironically, gave him "the time and freedom of mind to search out, as far as my knowledge and experience allowed" what sort of Marxism it was that could produce Stalinism.*

*We had met to discuss Eurocommunism, and he had brought me the third edition of his book on the subject, just off the press, with a chapter updating the book to September 1977—a thoughtful gesture typical of the man. We are about the same age, of a somewhat similar cast of mind, and we were immediately at ease with one another. He has a sweet, wise humor, often directed at himself. We did not, and do not, see eye to eye on many issues. (I think he's a little too left and he thinks I'm a little too "American"—his polite way of saying "naive.") But he was extremely helpful, and his book on Eurocommunism is the best in English from the standpoint of the internal developments of the Communist movement.*

*Claudín emphasized the importance of the Comintern to the understanding of Eurocommunism. In his view, only by seeing the stultification of Marxism in those years can we evaluate the modifications that are now taking place. It was the autocratic nature of the Comintern which had damaged Communist parties; hence the issue of democracy was crucial in establishing the credibility of Eurocommunism. The major failing of Eurocommunism, in Claudín's eyes, is its failure to condemn sufficiently the Soviet Union's lack of democracy.*

*He saw the credibility of Eurocommunism as requiring three developments: the acknowledgment that the Eastern European regimes are not socialist; the rejection of Communist claim to hegemony over Western Socialist and allied parties; the democratization of the internal structure of the Communist parties, i.e., abandonment of so-called "democratic centralism."*

*I thought the first condition irrelevant to close working relations between Socialists and Communists; the second condition essential, that is, Communists cannot claim to be more "Marxist" than the Socialists; and the third condition probably unnecessary, depending on how one interprets "democratic centralism." Our discussion made it clear that Claudín is less dogmatic on these questions than his writings would indicate.*

Since talking to Claudín, events have further convinced me that co-operation between Socialists and Eurocommunists does not depend on two of his three conditions. To most rank-and-file Socialists it is a matter of indifference whether Eastern European regimes are considered socialist or not. Moreover, many of them see that these countries are being influenced by Eurocommunism toward an internal liberalization.

Socialists *are* irritated by Communist pretensions of hegemony, but the importance of this issue varies from country to country. The French party is still the most rigid, claiming to be *the* party of the working class. In Italy and Spain, where Communists are more attuned to Socialist sensibilities, opposing arguments are presented objectively in the Communist press, the books of their antagonists are fairly reviewed, and there is a notable lack of pomposity or condescension.

The issue of "democratic centralism" is more complicated. Socialists *do* attack it, but such attacks seem to be in the nature of electoral polemics rather than principled doubts about the democracy of Eurocommunism. Intermittently, many Socialist parties have had democratic centralism. Democratic trade unions, of whatever ideology, operate on a basis of democratic centralism—that is, after a free discussion and a free vote the majority decision is binding on the minority. This principle gives muscle to consensus: enough diversity for fresh ideas, enough continuity for stability. Political parties are generally diffuse, and the introduction of disciplined democratic centralism into a party was one of Lenin's contributions to politics. It has been reaffirmed at the last congresses of the major Eurocommunist parties: Spanish, French, Italian, and Japanese.

In the final analysis, it isn't slogans, statutes, or structures that determine a party's inner democracy; it is the daily work and the style in the work. Antonio Gramsci, a profound libertarian, saw it clearly nearly fifty years ago, writing in his prison notebooks: "Besides, the way in which the party functions provides discriminating criteria. When the party is progressive, it functions 'democratically' (democratic centralism); when the party is regressive it functions 'bureaucratically' (bureaucratic centralism). The party in this second case is a simple, unthinking executor. It is then technically a policing organism, and the name of 'political party' is simply a metaphor of a mythological character."[15] What a succinct insight into a Stalinist party! And is this insight to be given up because a Bettino Craxi or a Sir Harold Wilson bay at the moon? Eurocommunists find resonance in this thinker and cherish his meditations:

> Democratic centralism offers an elastic formula, which can be embodied in many diverse forms; it comes alive insofar as it is interpreted and continually adapted to necessity. It consists in the critical pursuit of what is identical in seeming diversities and yet distinct (or even opposed) in seeming uniformity. . . . This continuous effort to distinguish the "international" and "unitary" elements in national and local reality is true political action in the concrete, the only activity productive of historical progress. . . . It requires an organic unity between theory and practice, between intellectual strata and popular masses, between governors and governed.[16]

Democratic centralism is increasingly being interpreted in Gramscian terms within the Eurocommunist parties,* more so in Spain, least so in France. In Italy, freedom of expression among PCI artists and writers is complete; among other party members it is considerable and increasing. One example among many: In October and November of 1979 there was a sharp polemic in the public press between Giorgio Amendola, elder statesman of the PCI and Enrico Berlinguer, the general secretary, on trade union issues.[17] The controversy aroused considerable interest in Italy, but no one was surprised or scandalized. In my opinion, it is not likely that any Eurocommunist party will give up democratic centralism, but I also do not see that it provides an insurmountable problem for Socialist-Communist collaboration.

The issue of working-class unity is extremely complex, involving constituencies with different economic and social interests, power groupings within the parties, conflicting ambitions of leaders, and so on. Unless this problem of unity is resolved, the goal of a peaceful transition to socialism via existing institutions remains utopian. Critics on the left, such as Fernando Claudín, Ernest Mandel, the editors

* See, for example, the discussion of democratic centralism in *Rinascita*, August 10, 1979.

of *Monthly Review,* and others, doubt that Socialist-Communist unity, on a principled basis, can be achieved. Hence they have every reason to doubt the feasibility of a peaceful transition.

This is indeed a knotty problem. In theory, both Eurocommunists and Socialists want to *eliminate* the capitalist system; in actual political practice, a substantial number of the Socialist parties wants to *manage* the system, not abolish it. Put more precisely: while in both the socialist and Eurocommunist movements there are left and right currents, the disagreements within Eurocommunism have to do with the *speed* of economic change; within socialism, with the *nature* of such changes.[18] Thus, for example, in the French national elections of 1978, the Union of the Left ostensibly foundered on the question of how many industries were to be nationalized.

The obstacles to working-class unity are rooted in capitalist mores and are not easily eliminated or by-passed. They will not be solved by doctrinal disputes as to whether Eurocommunists are sufficiently democratic or the Socialists sufficiently radical. Nor can the solution be found in a jurisdictional agreement: Eurocommunists to organize workers, Socialists to organize the lower middle classes. There are workers who wish little change, professionals who are extremely militant. The task of the left leadership is twofold: on the one hand, to convince a *worker* in a small factory that his employer is a potential ally; on the other, to show the *factory owner* that a wage increase (which he fights) is not cutting into his profit margin as much as the price of monopolized raw materials (which he cannot fight). Both must understand the degree and nature of their exploitation to be able to compromise and become allies. In particular, the middle classes must learn that while they benefit from the system in some ways, they suffer in less obvious, but important, ways, which can only be remedied in alliance with the working class.

Not the least of the obstacles is the active disruption of the capitalist class. The ambivalence of some Socialists toward capitalism, the flaws of existing socialist states and the jockeying for political power among parties and leaders of the left open the door to intrusion by capitalist forces. These forces exert their influence in myriad ways—not excluding bribery, intimidation, slander, and economic manipulation, e.g., locating an industry in a given town. In the struggle, unpredictable, and sometimes paradoxical, strategies emerge in each country. A brief study of Communist-Socialist relations in Spain, France, and Italy will, I think, illuminate the problems of unity and the intrusion of ruling elites.

We begin with Spain.

In Spain today, the politics of the major left parties are conditioned by three historical events: the civil war, forty years of quasi fascism, and industrialization. The civil war was a traumatic experience (half a million dead) which still affects the middle and older generations, making it a major, if unspoken, emotional component of political life. Except for young people, Spaniards are reluctant to talk about the war, and I saw firsthand how they instinctively shrink from any reminder of it.

*In the winter of 1977 my wife and I went to Spain and visited the battlefields of my youth, the villages along the Ebro River—Pina, Caspe, Osera, where we had dug our trenches and from which we could see Saragossa, twelve miles distant, the lights of the city twinkling, as George Orwell put it, "like the portholes of a great long liner." The trenches had long ago eroded, and weeds filled the banks of the river. The headquarters of our forces, the anarchist Durruti Column, had been at Bujaraloz, a small town of white walls and unexpected arches. I remembered the headquarters as a large villa on the main square. When I finally located the square, there was no villa, just unbroken façades of three-story buildings with widely spaced doorways.*

*It was ten o'clock of a Sunday morning during the two-week Feast of the Virgin del Pilar, and people were either home or at church. I was looking for older people who would remember the war, and three times I approached what I thought were likely informants—a woman and two men. As soon as they heard the words* civil war, *they shook their heads and scuttled away. I got a sense not of fear but of distance: they didn't want to think about it. Finally, pursuing the third person, a man in his sixties with a dour face and a blue beret, I said in exasperation: "Por favor, señor, soy norteamericano . . . I'm an American and I beseech your aid . . . por favor, caballero." That held him long enough for me to tell him I had been with the Durruti Column and would he by chance know where the headquarters had been. "The house by the arch," he muttered and scurried away. What I remembered as a villa was one of a row of houses.*

*"Are you going to ring the bell," said my wife, "and introduce yourself as one of those bums who requisitioned their home?"*

*"No," I said, "I'm going to introduce myself as the man who saved their elegant furniture." In truth, it was Buenaventura Durruti who had locked up the furniture and turned the second floor into a dormitory.*

*The door was opened by a young man of about thirty. Was he the owner? No, the owners were in Madrid; he was the caretaker. When I explained my interest, he immediately invited us in, calling his wife and children. The entrance hall was as I remembered it; mosaics on the floor, decorated walls, a sweeping staircase of marble. On the second floor, the dormitory had vanished; in its place there was a luxurious apartment of three rooms—bedroom, dining room, and sitting room—with elegant gilt furniture of the eighteenth century, oriental rugs, brocaded draperies.*

*I sought out the kitchen, which I remembered as a huge room with a projecting brick hood over a raised hearth, six feet square. There we had huddled around a spitting fire of brush and branches, sipping our black coffee. The kitchen had vanished, overtaken by shabby modernity. It had become the caretaker's apartment, divided into three little rooms, one of them with a sink, a refrigerator, and a butane gas stove: clean, cramped, and dull. In the bedroom was a television set and a sewing machine.*

*In the apartment I met the caretaker's wife, a seamstress, and I could see they were devout Catholics—a crucifix over the bed, medallions of the Virgin over the sink and stove, withered Easter palms over the refrigerator. On the dresser was a photograph of two little girls dressed in white—"their communion," said the mother with a smile.*

*We drifted back into the hallways. After we had talked a bit, the caretaker said suddenly: "Didn't you have an ex-priest in the Column as secretary to Durruti?" We certainly did, and I remembered him well: a plump, shy man who avoided looking people in the eye and seemed perpetually to be expecting a kick. Understandably, for Durruti was a fierce anticlerical who, before the war, had gunned down the bishop of Saragossa. Durruti had spared the priest's life on condition that he get married—which he did.*

*When I said I had known him, the wife lit up: "He was the parish priest of my village. After the war, the marriage was annulled, and he came back to the village as our priest. He just died last year. He wrote a book about his life in the Column." Her husband laughed: "He couldn't get it published in Spain, even though the book was anti-Durruti and anti-Republican. It was published in Andorra."*

*They plied me with questions about the civil war; they wanted their children to listen. They couldn't get enough details. Despite their Catholicism and forty years of Franco rule and indoctrination, it was clear that they still saw the Republican Army of the Ebro through the eyes of their fathers and uncles. It was, of course, their age: the civil war had an aura of romance and high deeds. Later, in Madrid, as I saw young people clustering around bookstalls which overflowed with books on the civil war, I thought of the eagerness of the caretaker and his wife. I became conscious of the difference in attitude between the old and young, and how much those attitudes condition Communist policies.*

Of the Eurocommunist parties the Spanish is the most moderate in language and action, largely because it is trying to erase the image of violence and intransigeance that is the legacy of the civil war. The present general secretary of the Spanish party, Santiago Carrillo, was a member of the committee in charge of defending Madrid (he was then twenty-one), and the right-wing press still accuses him of complicity in atrocities perpetrated by irresponsible elements on the Republican side.

The memory of the civil war is also responsible, in part, for the intemperate language that Carrillo uses toward the USSR. Thirty years of Francoist propaganda have left their impression, and there is a general feeling that the Soviet Union manipulated the Spanish war for its own purposes. Even people who do not believe this accept another facet of Franco propaganda; namely, the USSR is bent on world revolution. What the Spaniards want is peace and quiet.

The Spanish party is right-of-center in Eurocommunism by virtue of its internal democratization, which gives wide latitude to dissenting opinions by party members. James M. Markham, the *New York Times* correspondent in Madrid, wrote about the last PCE Congress: "Already the tentative measures Carrillo has introduced have made the PCE the most open, and thereby the most interesting, Communist party around. Its disputes, and dirty laundry, hang openly: like most political parties it is seen to be a coalition of divergent forces, not a monolith."[19]

A measure of freedom within the PCE is provided by the internal opposition at the highest level, centered in the semiautonomous Catalan party. Its leader, Manuel Sacristan, has savagely attacked Carrillo's political orientation: "Eurocommunism, to the extent that one can take it seriously, is not a strategy toward socialism. On the contrary, it is the latest retreat reached by the present Communist movement since the defeat of 1917–21."[*20]

The long period of fascism also tends to work against the left. Although the repression has made people eager for freedom and democracy, it has also produced a strong sense of fear and passivity. Even now there is widespread fear of the military, which is held in check by a modernizing King Carlos I. He is aware that economic progress demands considerable freedom. Spaniards who want change tend to vote Socialist rather than Communist (the PSE has 124 deputies compared to 24 for the PCE), and within the Socialist party right-wing forces are in control, as was proven in 1978 by the showdown between Felipe Gonzales and the left.[21] Gonzales dislikes Communists and prefers the centrist Adolfo Suarez, but he has found it necessary to work with the PCE in the municipal elections. The

---

* "The defeat of 1917–21" refers to the failure of the Russian Revolution to spread throughout Europe.

Spanish Communist party therefore does not have the weight of the French or the Italian parties; yet it is not completely helpless and does have a bargaining position. This is because two decades of industrialization have resulted in a strong trade-union movement. The Communists play a dominant role in the unions and, secure in this base, can compete with the Socialists in extracting concessions from the government of Adolfo Suarez.

The future of Eurocommunism in Spain is not bleak. At the grassroots, Socialist-Communist unity is growing, in part because local issues are sharper in class terms, in part because regional decentralization (also on the rise) weakens national rivalries. In the first free elections since 1933, which took place on April 4, 1979, Communists and Socialists made a clean sweep of the major cities and larger towns, winning 42 percent of the popular vote. "The victory," said the *New York Times* in reporting the vote, "appeared to presage moves toward closer collaboration between the two parties."[22] A further impetus to Socialist-Communist unity in Spain will be forthcoming from Spanish admission to the European Common Market, where the Italian Communist party and the German Social Democratic party are moving toward a degree of collaboration.

Turning to the French scene, we find that some aspects of French Eurocommunism seem almost the opposite of the Spanish. For example, if Carrillo has been the gadfly to the Russian bear, then Georges Marchais, general secretary of the *Parti Communist Français* (PCF), has been the soothing ointment. The PCF was supportive of the Soviets during the long wrangling prior to the Berlin Conference; it was the last Eurocommunist party to disavow the dictatorship of the proletariat; and it has remained the most rigid of the three parties under consideration. More important, while the Spanish and Italian parties are thinking of multiparty center-left governments, the French party looks to a government of the left. This policy has its historical roots: the class structure in France is more clearly defined, and the middle classes are more deeply rooted in the capitalist system. From the time of the Dreyfus affair to the regime at Vichy, there have been two Frances, the France of the right and the France of the left.[23] In the fight against Vichy and the Germans, the resistance, such as it was, was largely of the left.* At a deeper historical level lies, of course, the revolution of 1789, which put a Jacobin imprint on the nation, whereas Spain—and, in a more complicated way, Italy—remained backward for a century and a half. Symbolically, the leading French historian of the events of 1789 is also a leading Communist intellectual, Albert Soboul.[24]

Soboul is in his sixties, a vigorous, mild-mannered, tough-

---

* There were two resistances in France, the Gaullist and the Communist, and while both were weak, numbering in the thousands, the Communist was the stronger and more active.

minded man. He accepts the Eurocommunist strategy, though not without skeptical reservations, thinking the Italian tactics too yielding and Carrillo's attacks on the USSR unwarranted. In the fall of 1977 he was kind enough to see me at his apartment and give me his appraisal of Socialist-Communist relations.

"We've had a checkered history," he said sardonically. "Leaving aside the rancor of the 1920s, we did unite against the fascists in 1934 and were the first country to work out a Popular Front. There were strains over Spain and a quarrel over Munich; we drew close again against Vichy and the Germans, only to quarrel again in the Cold War. Finally, by 1972 both sides seemed to have gained some mutual understanding, and we formed the Union of the Left with a Common Program as the basis of an electoral alliance. Each party would support the other in the second round."*

He poured us a dram of Polish vodka and spoke reflectively.

"There is no doubt that unity of the working class is a political magnet. It draws votes from our natural allies, the poor peasants, the artisans, the shopkeepers, the government workers. In 1973 the combined left vote went from 34 to 40 percent, and in the municipal elections of 1976 up to 45 percent. The polls predicted 55 percent for the left in the coming elections—a sure government . . . until this damn split over the Common Program."

"Well," I said mildly, "it was the Communist party that opened up the question of the Common Program."

"Of course," said Soboul impatiently. "The program was five years old and had to be updated. Mitterand agreed to do so. But he's a slippery fellow . . . as you must know."

I did know. The Socialist party leader, François Mitterand, was a haughty, conservative man who had come late to socialism. As minister of overseas territories in the 1950s, he had been a staunch defender of colonialism. During the Algerian war he had been minister of justice. He was distrusted in his own party and distrusted by the Communists. Although he couldn't reject the Communist proposal to update the Common Program, he maneuvered to restrict its discussion. At the Socialist Congress at Nantes in June 1977, he said: "It took only two weeks to negotiate the program in the first place, and I see no reason for taking months to bring it up to date. . . . These talks should be over and done with before the summer holidays."[25]

The reaction of the Communist general secretary, Georges Marchais, was immediate: "We are not prepared to give Mr. Mitterand a

---

* Under the constitution, as shaped by Charles de Gaulle, there are two rounds of voting, a week apart. In each district, if any candidate gets a majority on the first round, he is elected. If there is no majority, the two top candidates have a run-off on the second round. This means, in practice, that a left candidate and a right candidate fight it out, seeking the support of other groups.

blank check. The workers of this country are entitled to know, right now, what a government of the left will do for them, and when."[26]

Not only were the talks not concluded by the summer holidays, but they continued through September, climaxing with a breakdown at midnight on September 22, 1977. The principal obstacle was the definition of companies to be nationalized. The Common Program of 1972 had envisaged the nationalization of nine industrial groups. The Socialists maintained that only subsidiaries which were 98 percent owned by the parent company should be nationalized; the Communists argued for 51 percent ownership; otherwise, the companies could divest themselves of some shares, evade nationalization, and yet retain control. The first criterion would nationalize 200 subsidiaries; the second, 1000. The Communists offered a compromise of 729 companies, but Mitterand was adamant. Polemics sharpened, delighting the right and enraging the left. I had occasion to see both attitudes at work.

*In an elegant office near the Quai d'Orsay, I talked with Jean-Claude Servan-Schreiber, a World War II resistance hero, now working in government television. Jean-Claude is a cousin of Jean-Jacques Servan-Schreiber, the well-known journalist and politician. Jean-Claude and I had been classmates at Exeter College, Oxford, in 1937–38, and we reminisced a bit before we got down to politics. A Gaullist, he was running for deputy from the southern city of Nîmes. His opponent was the present mayor and deputy, Emile Jourdan, a Communist. "I lost to him in 1973 by just two hundred votes," said Jean-Claude jovially in faultless English, "but this time, with the split, I'll beat him. He is a good man, Emile, honest and able, and we are friends–but Nîmes is my town; my grandmother was a senator from that district."*

*I asked him if he thought the Communist-Socialist split would heal. He leaned over his desk and answered with assurance: "It's like this: Mitterand wants a free hand if elected; Marchais wants him tied down to an agreement beforehand. Irreconcilable. I go to Nîmes every weekend, politicking. I talk around—the Communist cadres dislike Mitterand intensely. They say he's using the PCF as a* marchepied *[a sidewalk] to his own victory. The quarrel will worsen, people will get disgusted, the left vote will fall, and I will be elected.* Voilà!" *As it turned out, Jean-Claude was right about everything except his own election; he lost by about the same number of votes as in 1973.*

*A few days later, I had an opportunity to assess the attitude of the Communist cadres, visiting the home of the Communist mayor of Colombes, a working-class town of seventy thousand people adjacent to Paris. In his modest living room, Dominique Frelaut, a burly*

*ex-machinist, now a Communist deputy as well as mayor, declaimed
against the Socialists: "They are insatiable," he said. "They are a
minority in our council, yet they want half the jobs, half the patronage, half of everything. And now that* flic *Mitterand won't agree to
our share of ministries!" ("In short," said a disgruntled ex-
Communist, "Socialists are behaving like Communists.")*

The elections of March 1978 penalized the Socialists. Their share of
the vote fell to 22.5 percent. The Communists held at 20.5 percent.
Each party blamed the other, but there is evidence that both miscalculated. The Communists, it is now known, did not expect Mitterand
to be so intransigeant—after all, he wanted to be premier. Mitterand,
on the other hand, was the one who disrupted the negotiations and
overplayed his hand: he thought the Communists would back down
for the sake of victory. Instead, they said to themselves, if this is the
way Mitterand behaves *before* becoming premier, what won't he do
*after?*[27]

The Socialists blamed the Communists for the defeat. On television, Mitterand hinted that the Communist party was still obeying
Moscow, which wanted President Valéry Giscard d'Estaing
strengthened, presumably as a counterweight to German-American
dominance. The editor-in-chief of *Le Monde,* Jacques Fauvet, supported Mitterand's hypothesis of "the hand of Moscow."[28] Another,
and more popular, speculation was that the Communists were fearful
of becoming an even weaker number two party of the left as the polls
showed increasing Socialist strength. Neither of these explanations
seems adequate, the first because it is contradicted by the evidence
that Mitterand broke off the negotiations, and the second because the
Communists were well aware that the Union of the Left would attract
many more vacillating voters to the Socialists than to the Communists. In fact, a year later, when Socialist-Communist unity was
re-established for the municipal elections, the combined parties
scored a huge victory, gaining 54.6 percent of the votes, with the
Socialists getting 33 percent, the Communist 17.3 percent, and
smaller groups the rest.[29]

The basic issue was not the expected Socialist increase but the
relationships of power between the two parties. Nationalization
became the crux of the problem, because the Communists counted on
nationalization to redress the Socialists' electoral strength. Wider
nationalization would strengthen the unions (Communist-led), provide patronage and organizational channels, and so compensate the
Communists for Mitterand's political hegemony.[30] Both parties
deliberately obscured this issue by presenting it purely as an economic issue. In fact, there were good reasons to agree: the most
asked by the Communists represented only 8 percent of the French

labor force and 5 percent of the French gross national product—way below nationalization in Austria, for example, or the percentage of companies controlled in Italy via "state participation."[31]

The issue of power was too subtle for many people. Mitterand as premier would probably preserve for his party the prestigious or sensitive ministries—foreign affairs, defense, interior, finance—relegating the Communists to the economic ministries—transport, agriculture, energy, public sector, and the Communists could best "valorize" these ministries through nationalization. However, in the popular mind, the French Communist party was held more responsible for the split and defeat. The fact that the French party *is* rigid and aggressive in many ways made the accusations more plausible. I had a taste of that mentality when I went to party headquarters on Place Colonel-Fabien in Belleville.[32] Belleville, one of the "red districts" of Paris, has a reputation for militancy going back to the Commune of 1871.

*The new headquarters is soaring modern building designed by Oscar Niemeyer, some twenty stories high, with a curved facade of blue-tinted glass windows that reflect the trees and the clouds. It is an extremely elegant building, more like a Hilton Hotel or a corporate headquarters. I thought of Thorez and Frattochie and how he would be turning in his grave at such splendor. Construction was still going on in front, and I went in through a side service entrance that overlooks the garage entrance ramp. It is a frowning, forbidding entrance, with a fortresslike bridge of monolithic concrete, gray and massive, so that the words "Maginot Line" came unbidden into my head. At the elevators the scene changed to a cool, aseptic elegance. But this, with the long curving corridors and closed doors in pastel colors, gave me such a feeling of size and concentrated administration that I was reminded of the Pentagon. I was wryly aware that images of Maginot Lines and Pentagons are hardly comradely, but I needn't have worried... the Communist official I met, Gerard Streif, had no need of comradeship.*

*In Madrid and Rome I had been welcomed in a friendly, not to say comradely, manner by Manuel Azcarate and Sergio Segre, Central Committee members in charge of foreign affairs. Their French opposite number, Jacques Sandys, was not available. His assistant, a prim, academic type, treated me as if I were an emissary of the CIA under an exceptionally clever cover: utterly polite, cool, correct, and distant.*

*When I asked Streif whom he considered the more interesting critics of the Communist position, he replied stiffly: "Monsieur, we do not make publicity for our adversaries." In Rome and Madrid I was given such names with appraisals and thumbnail sketches as a cheerful matter of course.*

*It happened that* Le Monde *that very morning had carried an analysis of the split by Fernando Claudín. It had struck me as balanced and objective, putting the Communist position in a rather favorable light. I asked Streif if he included Claudín among the party's adversaries. He was momentarily put out, but soon rallied. "No," he said haughtily, "but we find his analysis inaccurate."*

It is a sign of the influence of Eurocommunism that the rigidity of the French party provoked an explosion of criticism and disaffection within its ranks. The Socialists, too, were affected by the disillusionment following the failure at the polls. At a party convention held in Paris on April 29, 1978, Mitterand was forced to move to the left to block the attacks of the ambitious leader of right-wing Socialists, Michel Rocard. But acrimony among Socialists was nothing new; not so among the Communists. *Le Monde* opened its pages throughout April to a series of letters and articles from Communist intellectuals, students, and rank-and-file members, including four critical articles by Louis Althusser. The most scathing attack came from historian Jean Ellenstein, who demanded the end of sectarianism and a renewed alliance with the Socialists.[33]

Marchais at first was scornful. To Ellenstein's proposals he answered, "Falsifications! Ignorance!" But the pressure for liberalization became too great: the intellectuals were deserting the party, the cadres were apathetic. Marchais began to shift even as the Socialists did. A fragile reconciliation took place, vindicated by the victory in the municipal elections in March 1979. By the time the Twenty-third Congress of the Communist party took place, in mid-May 1979, Marchais was again courting the intellectuals (including Ellenstein) and top functionaries such as Henri Fiszbin of the Paris Federation, who had quit in January. Marchais stated unequivocally that change in France was only possible by a renewed alliance with the Socialists. Mitterand, speaking at Anglet, on August 21, seemed to respond favorably. By September Marchais was personally telephoning the "ignorant falsifier" Ellenstein to ask for his participation in the annual *Humanité* festival to raise funds for the newspaper.[34] Nonetheless, the French party has become more rigid, and it will take some time for the *Zeitgeist* of Eurocommunism to assert itself. In this process, the first direct elections to the European Parliament in June played a warning role by showing the left everywhere how far Europe was drifting to the right.

When we turn to the third of the countries under discussion, we find that the Italian experience is totally different from that of the

French or the Spanish. Since Italy will be discussed at length in the second part of this book, we will limit ourselves to a brief résumé.

The Italian Socialist party (*Partito Socialista Italiano,* PSI) had been against World War I and was not tainted by the betrayal of Social Democracy. Both parties, Socialist and Communist, suffered under fascism and early recognized the necessity of working together against it, as shown by the Pact of Unity of August 17, 1934. The Spanish Civil War had further drawn the exiles closer, both Pietro Nenni and Palmiro Togliatti participating directly, each coming to respect the other. Of Nenni, it was said in the Brigades that he was the most honest and reliable of the Socialists. Of Togliatti, Nenni said, "He was the only clear-sighted man among those who walked blindly."[35]

In addition to this favorable historical background, there has always been a quality of tolerance among Italians. To say that they are cynics would be a slander—a turnout of 90 percent of the voters is hardly an index of cynicism—but one can say that Italians are allergic to claims of infallibility. For one brought up in the milieu of the Comintern, Togliatti was comparatively tolerant. For example, he readmitted into the party in 1962 Alfonso Leonetti, for many years a Trotskyist after his expulsion in 1930. Togliatti also had published the early correspondence of top party leaders containing passages very critical of Togliatti—an action unprecedented in the history of Communist parties.[36] As Oriana Fallaci testifies, tolerance in the PCI has increased as the concepts of Eurocommunism have flourished.[37]

More important than all these reasons, however, was the armed resistance movement against Germany during World War II. In Italy, unlike France, this was no peripheral phenomenon: the armed formations of the partisans amounted to hundreds of thousands, intermingling Catholics, Socialists, Communists, and other groupings. Although there were more units led by Communists than Socialists, there were no invidious comparisons. The fraternal relations cemented in battle have left a strong legacy in contemporary Italian politics. Nenni, the leaders of the Socialist party, once said that he never felt completely at ease with any political figure who had not been in the resistance.[38]

After the war, Nenni and Togliatti renewed the Pact of Unity, and it survived the American pressures of the Cold War, the split in the Italian trade unions, and even a split within the Socialist party. Only Khrushchev's revelations of Stalin's crimes broke the pact. Outraged, Nenni turned over to the Red Cross and other charities his Stalin Peace Prize money and began making overtures to the Christian Democratic party (*Democrazia Cristiana,* DC). The PCI did not blame Nenni for his revulsion (which it shared), but felt that he was politically naive not to see that the capitalist world had seized on

Khrushchev's report to beat down and isolate Communists throughout the world. As Pietro Ingrao has pointed out, Nenni unwittingly played into capitalist hands.[39]

At the time, however, Nenni thought he was being politically perspicacious. He moved the PSI into an accommodation with the Christian Democrats, entering a center-left government in 1963. The Socialists began well, forcing the nationalization of the electrical industry and laws for regionalism, but then got inveigled into the system. Instead of fighting against corruption and patronage and reforming the ministries they controlled, the Socialists, with the exception of Nenni and a few others, became indistinguishable from other venal politicians. Voters expressed their disgust with the center-left government, and the elections of 1972 were a disaster for the PSI. Their share of the vote dropped from 14 percent to 9.6 percent. The Communist share went up to 27 percent, gaining two points.

The Socialists then left the government and moved toward the Communists. Trade-union unity was achieved, and though difficult to measure, this unity and the amity between Socialists and Communists contributed heavily to the overwhelming left victory in the referendum on divorce in 1974. In the regional elections of 1975 the Socialists, running in co-operation with the Communists, increased their vote to 12 percent, while the Communists increased theirs to 32 percent. Confident that they were gaining momentum, the Socialists precipitated the elections of 1976. Their vote dropped back to 9.6 percent.[40] The Communist vote reached its highest point: 34.5 percent, within four points of the Christian Democrats.

The 1976 defeat undermined the authority of the PSI general secretary Francesco De Martino. He was attacked from the right as being too friendly with the Communists, from the ultraleft for not being more radical than the Communists.[41]

At the July 1976 Congress of the Socialist party, a new coalition was formed. Bettino Craxi, a firm anti-Communist, was elected general secretary. Craxi's first concern was to weed out De Martino's followers and build up his political machine, giving jobs to rightists and ultraleftists impartially. The last important Socialist post, the editorship of the party's paper, *Avanti!*, was taken over by Craxi himself in the spring of 1978. Thereupon Craxi mounted a sustained offensive against the Communists along two main lines: first, the PCI Eurocommunist stance was a sham—the party was still Leninist and antidemocratic; second, the PCI was selling out workers to curry favor with the Christian Democrats.

Craxi is not a pleasant personality—narcissistic, shallow, vainglorious. He embarked on a campaign of self-aggrandizement, taking opportunistic positions that would gain him the public eye, such as his stance on the Aldo Moro kidnapping (March 16, 1978), the maneuvers following Moro's assassination (May 9), and his intrigues in the election of a new president (July 1978). For a while he seemed to make headway as a coming young leader (at age forty-five), but in the end he outsmarted himself and was blocked from the premiership in early 1979. He offended the left wing of the DC in the Moro affair. And the poor showing of the Socialist party in the national elections of June 1979 further dimmed his prestige.

Craxi is currently being supported by the right wing of the DC and being enticed to enter a DC-PSI government, thus isolating the Communist party. Craxi would like to enter such a government, but there are risks, for it would be an even more conservative grouping than the center-left government of the sixties that failed so abysmally.

Yet Craxi, though weak electorally, is as powerful politically in Italy as Mitterand is in France. He holds a keystone position in the political arch from DC to PCI. No coalition is conceivable that does not include the Socialists. In addition, Craxi, like Mitterand, has the support of the United States, which sees Eurosocialism as an important component of its strategy against Eurocommunism, and recognizes that these two leaders are the only ones who can make Eurosocialism palatable to workers.

The Second International, after its rebirth in 1951, has been completely dominated by the German Social Democratic party, and that party has dropped any pretensions of changing capitalism. Like the British Labour party, they say they can manage the capitalist system more efficiently because they can get the support of the workers. For this last purpose, the Second International needs Craxi and Mitterand because they are ostensibly anticapitalist.

Hitherto, German Chancellor Helmut Schmidt has been the channel through which the United States has operated. He was a key figure at the 1977 Puerto Rico Conference in which Carter decided to put economic pressure on Italy if the Communists entered the government. Schmidt was the key figure in the Guadaloupe Conference of December 1978, from which Italy was pointedly excluded. At the DC Congress in Rome, February 1980, the German SDP continued its subservient role. Washington had reiterated its opposition to the PCI in the government in January, and the SDP general secretary, Helmut Kohl, who was a guest speaker on the first day of the Congress, expressed his sharp opposition to DC-PCI collaboration.[42]

Whether Eurosocialism can be made viable as an anti-Eurocommunist bastion is problematic. Chancellor Schmidt is not well liked in Europe, and even within his own party his policies are under attack. More important, in the June elections for a European Parliament, the German Social Democrats were overtaken by the German Christian Democrats, 40.8 percent to 49.2 percent. The CD is led by Franz Josef Strauss, and he is, if not a neofascist, a passable facsimile thereof. This was quite a jolt, particularly in view of the over-all shift to the right in the Community, with the left now in a three to five minority—155 seats for Social Democrats, Socialists, and Communists to 255 for all the others.[43] Given such weakness, continuing American support for the SDP is problematic, and as the German SDP looks around for strong, reliable allies the obvious one is the Italian Communist party. Berlinguer has made it a point to extend a hand of friendship and collaboration to the SDP.[44] The Italian party is committed to working inside the Community to make Europe more independent of both the USA and the USSR. It is willing to trade economic hegemony to Germany (which Germany has anyway) for European political independence in general and a solid shift to the left in particular.

As I discussed the results of the European election with friends in Rome in June 1979, my mind went back to a conversation in Belgrade in October 1977. Alexander Grlickov, a member of the Yugoslav Central Committee and its expert on foreign affairs, was dealing with the problem of Socialist-Communist relations in Europe.

"There is an ebb and flow to socialist politics" he said. "Social Democrats have just as many difficulties as Communists have. We see ours clearly, at close range, but we forget that their problems are as great as ours, if not greater. All over Europe, socialist members are deeply alienated from the capitalist system: they want change and they want it badly. Despite their reluctance, socialist leadership will need to move left, or be left behind."

In 1980 his words seem prescient. The debacle of the British Labour party has resulted in a decisive shift to the left, as shown in the changes in party structure mandated at Brighton in September 1979. At the same time Wedgewood Benn in England and Georges Marchais in France, the bitterest opponents of the Common Market, seem to be changing their strategy and coming closer to the Italian views. The admission to the Common Market of Greece, Spain, and Portugal will strengthen anti-American economic tendencies in Europe.

Eurocommunism is alive and kicking, and Italy remains its testing ground. Although the issue of the European Community is still a very minor one on the left, it is going to loom ever larger and may ultimately be decisive for the success or failure of the Eurocommunist strategy. Already it is forcing a re-examination of one of its basic tenets—the sharp separation from one party to another. The revulsion from Comintern centralization is understandable, but a degree of co-operation, of mutually worked-out policies on matters of common interest, is clearly necessary. The split in the Union of the Left had its repercussions in the Italian elections, and the PCI was very critical of the PCF's strategy.[45] Both the French and the Italian elections of 1979 had their repercussions on the June 9 elections to the European Parliament. The admission of Spain to the Common Market is another example of policies at cross-purpose. The Spanish Communist party wants in, the Italian party supports admission, the French party fights it. The PCI sees admission as strengthening the European left and furthering the Eurocommunist strategy of making Europe neutral between the two superpowers, whereas the PCF, more nationalistic, is worried that Spanish competition will hurt French agriculture. (It will hurt Italian agriculture even more.)

The proof that Eurocommunism is moving from adolescence to maturity lies not only in the greater roles the various Communist parties are playing in their respective countries, but also in the effects their policies, activities, and problems are having on the Socialist parties in Europe, thus influencing, to a growing extent, the nature of European development. In the decade of the eighties, whatever detours and setbacks may take place, Eurocommunism will be a felt presence.

# CHAPTER 4

# The Vatican and Eurocommunism

SOME THIRTY-FIVE YEARS AGO, in what seems another era, Stalin asked contemptuously: "How many battalions has the pope?" He was speaking within a select club having but three members, and the entrance fee was an army of several million soldiers.

It was a tasteless and sardonic remark, for, as Stalin knew, the Catholic Church did not need battalions to play a substantial role in winning World War II. The Vatican's endorsement of the Allied powers (including the USSR) carried great weight among the anti-Communist peoples of Poland, Hungary, and Romania. Today the power of the Church is incontestable. It plays a major role in the third world—more than half of the 700 million Catholics live in Asia, Africa, and Latin America. It has played an important role in the second world (the socialist world), and with the election of the Polish pope, its importance will increase. It is therefore imperative to recognize that since 1962 the Church has been undergoing changes so profound as to constitute an ecclesiastial revolution. The scope of the revolution can only be appreciated in historical perspective.

Until the Edict of Milan of Emperor Constantine (A.D. 313), the Catholic Church had been the church of the catacombs and the martyrs, the underground church of the poor and the oppressed— antislavery, subversive. This period is known historically as the Primitive Church, the Biblical Church, the Apostolic Church. For sixteen centuries after the edict, the Church was increasingly concerned with pomp and power, increasingly hierarchical and centralized. Despite many changes and challenges it remained an imperial Church and scholars dubbed it the "Constantinian Church." Then, on Christmas Day 1961, Pope John XXIII convoked Vatican Council II, and the Church has not been the same since.

There had been hints of activism. Shortly after his election in 1958 John had thrown open the casement windows of his Vatican apartment with the sibylline remark: "Time to let a little air in." Later, he translated his remark into blunter language: "We must shake out the imperial dust accumulated on the throne of St. Peter since Constantine."[1]

This reforming pope was a complete surprise. Angelo Cardinal Roncalli, patriarch of Venice, had been elected at the age of seventy-seven as a transitional pope—bland, kindly, unobtrusive—one who would keep the throne warm for his successor. Roncalli was not the most eminent of his peers: he had been born of poor, devout sharecroppers in the tiny village of Sotto il Monte (province of Bergamo) in the far north of Italy. Books were a rarity in his home. At age six he was helping his father in the fields; at age ten he was walking twelve miles to school and back—a tormented journey in winter, with chilblains on his cold fingers.*

Not that Roncalli didn't have excellent qualities. Monsignor Louis Capovilla, his secretary as bishop and pope, defined him as *un prete all'antica*, a priest of olden times—pious, wise, traditionalist.[2] His peasant origins were not a disadvantage: the Church usually chooses its popes either from sturdy stock or from the trained upper classes: either Percherons or thoroughbreds. Roncalli had a reputation for diplomacy under the exacting Pius XII, and as patriarch of Venice he had become legendary for his compassion, his populist appeal, and his finessing of social issues without compromising traditional values. All in all, he was eminently *papabile* and was easily elected as a transitional pope.†

The calling of Vatican Council II was a thunderbolt. The new pope had to overcome the resistance of the Vatican bureaucracy, and then the lethargy, conservatism, and outright opposition of the top ranks of the hierarchy. Despite his authority, Pope John could never have accomplished his task by *force majeure;* he did it by the moral force of his personality, the qualities that had made him *papabile*. He literally converted Giacomo Cardinal Lercaro by the example of his gentle humanity.

Lercaro, bishop of Bologna, a power in the hierarchy and a fierce traditionalist, was turned 180 degrees and became the pope's strong right arm in Vatican Council II. An unreconstructed anti-Communist, for years bitterly opposed to the red government of his own city,

---

* The movie *L'Albero degli zoccoli* (The tree of the wooden clogs), which was filmed in Roncalli's province with local peasants as actors, gives a vivid and accurate picture of John's harsh childhood.

† *Papabile* is a word full of nuances. It means "fit to be pope," but fit not only as "worthy" or "capable" but as politically feasible; that is, one who by his career, his qualities, his personality—and his political leanings—would attract the votes of the other cardinals.

Lercaro was so changed by the new pope that, returning to Bologna, he was welcomed at the station by a Communist-led demonstration. They cheered as he accepted the honorary citizenship of the city at the hands of the Communist mayor, Giuseppe Dozza. Significantly, Lercaro had appointed as his auxiliary bishop, his "vicar" in the Council, the forty-year-old Bishop Luigi Bettazzi, who is today one of the greatest forces for progress within the hierarchy.

Pope John prepared the ground thoroughly, appointing prepatory commissions and creating thirty-three additional cardinals, for a total of eighty-five, thereby breaking a tradition of four centuries.* Among them were men such as the German Jesuit, Augustine Bea, an outstanding progressive theologian, and Laureen Rugambwa of Tanganyika, the first black cardinal. As a canny politician, John had put the people and issues in place to make this ecumenical council the vehicle of *aggiornamento*—the bringing of the Church up to date.

*The enormous weight of the ecumenical councils in the life of the Catholic Church is proportionate to their rarity. Prior to Pope John, there had been only two in five hundred years, a total of twenty in two thousand years. The last two had been convened to meet deadly crises in the Church: the Council of Trent (which ended in 1563) was the nineteenth ecumenical council—the Council of the Counter Reformation, called to check Luther and Protestantism.†*

*Vatican I, the twentieth council, was convened to deal with the papal loss of temporal power when Victor Emmanuel II took Rome in 1870. Pope Pius IX shut himself into the Vatican, a self-declared prisoner, proclaimed the doctrine of papal infallibility at Vatican Council I, and prohibited Catholics from participating in the Italian Parliament under pain of excommunication. Then was a time of crisis.*

*No such crisis was apparent in 1960, yet there was a definite malaise within the Church. There were acute problems, such as contraception, abortion, and divorce. The tides of secularization, socialization, and industrialization were rising. The number of nuns and priests was steadily diminishing.[4] Despite all efforts, socialism and communism were spreading: Catholic countries, such as Poland and Hungary, had Communist governments. John's predecessor, Pope Pius XII, a strong opponent of communism, had felt at a loss: "I*

---

\* In 1586 Pope Sixtus V had set the number in the Sacred College at seventy.

† The Council of Trent was masterminded by Carlo Cardinal Borromeo, later canonized. Saint Carlo Borromeo was a favorite of Pope John, who owed the start of his career to research on the saint. This brought the young priest into contact with the archivist of the Biblioteca Ambrogiana, Achille Ratti. In 1922 Ratti became Pope Pius XI, and he brought Roncalli to Rome. (At a less historical level, San Carlo Borromeo is this writer's patron saint.)[3]

*am poorly adapted,"* he said to the French ambassador, *"to solve the problems posed to the Church by the existence and expansion of communism. I can only wish that I'm called to God and that a younger successor takes my place."*[5] The pope was then well over eighty, nearing the end of his pontificate. Pope John was of the same generation, minted by the same Church, yet he marched to a different hymn.

*Vatican II convened on October 11, 1962. An imposing procession wended its way into St. Peter's Church where the Council was held, and that night—a soft lovely night—the pope spoke from his window. The multitude in the square listened amidst a sea of torches flaring in the wind, the pediments of Michelangelo and the colonnades of Bernini gleaming in the spotlights, the twin fountains cascading their sparkling waters. The pope's message was simple but compelling: "Let us continue to be loving of each other . . . to pluck what unites us, leave aside whatever may create difficulties.* Fratres sumus *[We are brothers]." He ended on a characteristic note: "When you return home, you will see your little children. Caress them and tell them: this is a caress from the pope."*

*As the council was deliberating, John issued two encyclicals which set the tone:* Mater et Magistra, *which brought up to date the social doctrines of the Church, and the epochal* Pacem in Terris, *which was a significant factor in defusing the Cold War. Though John XXIII died in 1963, the Council was continued by his successor, Paul VI, and concluded on October 28, 1965. The final conciliar document,* Gaudium et Spes, *which in effect summarizes the Council and is binding on the Church, is suffused with the Johannine spirit.*

It is impossible to overestimate the importance of Vatican Council II within the Church or the magnitude of the shift that has taken place against entrenched opposition. Bitter internal struggles have ranged from flaunted hostility to clandestine sabotage. Two papal elections in 1978 served to decide the struggle, and the emergence of John Paul II signifies that the reforms of Vatican II are irreversible.[6] The sixteen years preceding his election, back to the Council's opening, have as much weight now as the previous sixteen hundred. The very words in constant use, the *Constantianian* Church of the past and the *Conciliar* Church of the present, testify to the power of Vatican II.

This book is primarily concerned with the political repercussions of Vatican II, but it should be noted that the greatest impact has been ecclesiastical. For example, Vatican II wiped out the ancient slander that Jews had crucified Christ—the guts of religious anti-Semitism.[7] It admitted that Catholics had not been blameless in the schism of the Reformation.[8] It modified a basic doctrine of the

Constantinian Church that there is no salvation outside the Church. It modified the old attitude on women. Pius XII had wanted women in the home and subordinate to men.[9]

*Pacem in Terris* was forthright, asserting that within the family there should be "parity of rights and duties between men and women." Further, it welcomed "the entry of women into public life. . . . In a woman the consciousness of her own dignity is ever clearer and operative. She will not permit herself to be considered and treated as an instrument; she demands that she be treated as a person."[10] The continued sexism within the Church (as exemplified most recently in the speeches of John Paul II in the U.S.A.) should not negate the enormous advances of *Pacem in Terris*.

That sexism is being fought from within, particularly in the United States. Sister Joan Chittister, for example, is leading a fight to eliminate the sexist language in hymns, rituals, and documents. She is past-president of the Leadership Conference of Women Religious, an organization of executives of more than a hundred Catholic female religious orders in America.[11] Her efforts are uphill, particularly after John Paul's American visit. The episcopal conference of U.S. bishops, meeting in November 1979, rejected a proposal to change the liturgy from "all men" to "all people."[12]

But probably the most liberating impact of the Council was in its challenge to ancient obscurantism and political reaction. This was the theme of the last speaker, Michele Cardinal Pellegrino, archbishop of Turin, who was characterized by *Civiltà cattolica* as "*the* bishop of the council." The importance of his speech was underlined by *Le Monde:*

> It is not by accident that a prelate so young and so brilliant . . . was chosen to close the debates of Vatican II. This authorizes us to see in that choice a symbol: that of a Church on the road to renewal, trusting its more dynamic members. . . .[13]

What Pellegrino had to say was earthshaking within the Church. He affirmed the necessity of *complete freedom of thought and research* not only for lay people but for clergy: they should be spurred to greater intellectual efforts to see things not only "in the light of faith . . . but also with a clear vision of current problems and the historical reality in which these problems reside and must be resolved."[14]

From a political standpoint, the heart of Vatican II lies in two documents: *Pacem in Terris* and *Gaudium et Spes*. The first opened the door to a dialogue between Catholics and Marxists; the second (under Paul VI) reaffirmed the necessity of the dialogue and made it acceptable. The Italian road to socialism, rocky and thorny as it has been, would have been impassable without those documents. The role of *Pacem in Terris* in world politics is pre-eminent.* Much credit is due Pope John but equal credit must go to one who prepared the way for the great shift in the Church. That person was Palmiro Togliatti, one of the founders of the Italian Communist party and its general secretary after Gramsci's death.

Roncalli and Togliatti may go down in Italian history as the shapers of a new country, like the two men who made the nation, Garibaldi and Cavour, the man of the heart and the man of the head. The analogy must not be stretched too far, but in Italy this comparison did not elicit scorn.†

John and Togliatti had deep similarities. Both were mavericks within an authoritarian system; both were pillars of the system, unconsciously rebelling and biding their time: John, the traditionalist who became the modernizer of an ancient institution; Togliatti, the Stalinist who became the initiator in Italy of participatory democracy.

Both had to change. Roncalli, despite his distaste for fascism, had vacillated, supporting Mussolini and blessing the Ethiopian war: "From this war will come benediction and prosperity for our dear country."[16] He had also supported Pius XII in his appeasing diplomacy toward Hitler.[17] In 1946 he had campaigned for the monarchy: "For the people, I believe the monarchy is preferable to the republic."[18] As late as 1956, an orthodox Roncalli was laying down the law: "We must resist socialist ideas . . . freedom of thought is very well . . . but within limits . . . everyone then to his post: to command, those who should command; to obey, those who should obey."[19]

Just as Roncalli was totally a man of the Constantinian Church, so Togliatti became a man of the Comintern.‡ His submission to Stalin had been unconditional: "If you feel that you are worthless before the will of the Party and of the International, then do what the Party and the International ask of you: say 'I accept, I am humble before the will of the International and of the Party: I shall keep quiet and sign.' "[20] He participated in some of the worst excesses of Stalinism, such as the extermination of the Polish Central Committee.[21]

Rarely have two men been so thoroughly conditioned, yet both men *did* change. The process of change is recondite, perhaps unfathomable, but obviously early influences are significant. For Ron-

---

* The influence of *Pacem in Terris* in the U.S. has been grossly underestimated; it merits, and awaits, a doctoral thesis. Not only on its impact on a Catholic President, but the way it protected his fledgling steps on détente from the hierarchy.[15]

† The historian Giorgio Bocca would accept this estimate of John and reject that of Togliatti. Yet his biography of Togliatti, despite many petty and snide remarks, ends in an unqualified praise that supports my judgment.

‡ Togliatti, of course, came to the Comintern already formed in a more libertarian mold. His submission to Stalin was political rather than intellectual.

calli, the city of Bergamo was such an influence; he attended its seminary from age ten to nineteen, at a time when Bergamo was called "the most Catholic of all cities" by *L'Osservatore romano*, and even two decades later Gramsci was using it as an example of militant Catholicism.[22] From 1870 to 1904 the city was the center of an epic conflict between the "intransigeants" and the "conciliators" within the Church—almost a preview of the fight between "integralists" and "conciliars" now taking place sixty-five years later.*

The struggle in Bergamo originated in Pius IX's response to the unification of Italy in 1870: There was to be no participation by Catholics in the elections—no voting and no candidates. Bergamo was most obedient; in the elections of 1890 fully 80 percent of the eligible voters refused to vote. But if their obedience was strong, so was their criticism of a policy that left the political field to secular and anticlerical forces. Bergamo led the fight within the Church, shaping arguments and sending representatives to three successive popes, Pius IX, Leo XIII, and Pius X, seeking the lifting of the prohibition. The final persuasive plea was made by a Bergamo emissary just before the 1904 elections, and Pope Pius X surrendered. A few days later, Bergamo sent to Parliament the first "official" Catholic deputy.[23]

The arguments of that period parallel the present ones. Then, as now, each side of the political argument has itself split between the "hard" and the "soft" on social matters. Thus in Bergamo there were conciliators in politics who were "hard" against socialists, accusing the "soft" intransigeants of subversion. For example, the bishop of Bergamo in 1900 was an intransigeant, bitterly defending papal politics and dogma against Marxists, yet giving a free hand to conciliators in his diocese who organized progressive social agencies on a large scale. Whereas in other regions the masses were pro-Socialist, in Bergamo Catholicism pre-empted the field.

Roncalli left Bergamo for Rome in 1900, when the controversy was at its hottest. He was deeply influenced by the arguments of the time, which have now reappeared with analogous crosscurrents: there are "conciliar" theologians who are "integralists" in politics, and vice versa.[24]

*While in Rome in October 1977, I was exposed to the complexity and nuances of the crosscurrents. Pope Paul VI appointed Valerio Volpini editor of* L'Osservatore romano, *the official Vatican paper. A news item in* Corriere della sera *gave Volpini's background: literary*

---

* An "integralist" is a fiercely traditionalist Catholic, usually resentful of Vatican II. A "conciliar" is one who accepts Vatican II wholeheartedly. The latter term should not be confused with "conciliator" of Bergamo days.

*critic, teacher and journalist, mentioning that his recent book* I
sporchi cattolici *(Dirty Catholics) had pleased the pope and may
have influenced the appointment. As its satirical title implies, the
book turned out to be a spirited defense of Catholic policies,
thoroughly integralist. It was puzzling: the pope had kept himself
carefully neutral in the struggle between integralists and conciliars.
Nevertheless, he was clearly a pope of the Council, faithful to the
vision of Pope John. How could he appoint such a hard-liner? I
concluded that the pope was going to move leftward and was protecting his flanks.*

*I mentioned my Machiavellian analysis to Guido Bodrato, a
brilliant and charming man who is one of the younger leaders of the
Christian Democrats and a man "of the dialogue." He laughed out
loud and said, chuckling affectionately: "Carlo, you are becoming
more Roman than American. That's Roman thinking—only it isn't
true. Volpini is a hard-line integralist in his ideology and polemics; he
despises Marxism, but he is very open to working with Communists,*
camminare insieme *as Pope John used to say.*\*[25] *Volpini is the son of
a sharecropper and was a well-known partisan in the resistance: he
has worked with Communists and shares many of their social
positions. Also, my dear Americanized Roman, you must learn that
the pope doesn't need to protect his flanks—ever."*

What Bergamo was to Roncalli, Turin was to Togliatti. Right after
World War I, the Torinese workers were the most militant and
class-conscious in Italy. They occupied the Fiat factories and established "factory councils"—Italian "soviets." The workers' discipline and self-management showed the enormous power of
participatory democracy, the most extensive Italy had ever seen.
Togliatti, then in his mid-twenties, never forgot the experience.

In addition to the workers, there was Gramsci's influence on
Togliatti, two years his junior. Gramsci and Togliatti met as teenagers
in the summer of 1911, as they were both cramming for scholarships at
Carlo Alberto College. They both won, and for fifteen years, until
Gramsci was jailed in 1926, they studied and worked together. The
continued presence of Gramsci within the younger man cannot be
overestimated: under the worst pressures of Stalinism, Togliatti
kept that margin of detachment that saved him from stultification.
"He was a man of long views," writes a biographer, himself strongly
opposed to communism. "In the arc of his life, one senses his
incessant effort, often tragic, to salvage his intellectual dignity."[26]

---

\* *Camminare insieme*, "walking together," might be translated by a Henry Kissinger as
"fellow-traveling," although the Italian implies that the travelers are equal. Pope John was very
fond of the concept and used it in many ways.

On Catholicism, the two Marxist co-workers saw eye to eye. While Gramsci was to examine the Catholic question in depth in his prison notebooks, he had begun the analysis before his imprisonment. Gramsci discerned similarities between Christianity and communism, not by looking at communism as a secular religion, but rather by looking at Christianity as "a revolution in the fullness of its development . . . the creation of a new and original system of moral, juridicial, philosophical and artistic relations."[27] From 1919 onward, Gramsci saw the solution of the Catholic question both in theory and in practice as a *political* necessity to forge the alliances between the Marxist working class and the Catholic peasantry. Togliatti had shared this judgment completely; when he returned to Italy in 1944, he came with a firm and considered policy: under no circumstances would the Communist party attack the Vatican.

Soon after Togliatti's arrival he sought a direct channel to the Curia (the administration of the Vatican) and became friends with Don Giuseppe De Luca, as adviser to the Holy Office. Critized later for his contacts with the militantly anti-Communist reign of Pope Pius XII, Togliatti retorted that "a sterile opposition was a form of political desperation . . . the attitude of those who see no way out of a given situation." Further: "While it is true that the Church has doctrines [on Church and state] set out in fundamental documents, some of which go back to the distant centuries of medieval times, [and while] it is understandable that the Church itself presents these doctrines as something immutable and absolute . . . it is the role of the historian and the politician to show that, in new and different historical circumstances, that same doctrinal wrapping can, and does, cover, entirely different positions. . . ."[28]

His channel to the Vatican opened, Togliatti began a campaign of writings and speeches on the Catholic question to influence the hierarchy, train his party, and educate the population. For example, in an essay, "Communism and Catholic Conscience," published on January 1, 1945, Togliatti wrote: "We believe in the possibility of a broad and enduring collaboration with Catholic workers and intellectuals . . . in the struggle for a new order and the fulfillment of the aspirations of those who live by their labor. If anyone believes there is something in the Catholic conscience which is contrary to those aspirations, let him say so openly; but do not say that our wish to work with the Catholic working class . . . is part of a plan to injure the Church. Whoever says this not only wrongs us; he also wrongs the Church."[29]

To the dismay of liberals and socialists, Togliatti refused to attack the Concordat of 1929 between the Church and Mussolini. At the first party congress after the liberation (December 1945), Togliatti stated unequivocally: "We know that the Concordat is an instrument of international import . . . that it cannot be modified except by bilateral consent. . . . Ours is a clear and sharp position to avoid any misunderstanding which might poison relations between our party and the Catholic Church of Italy. Our party does not want a religious war."[30] At the same congress chairman Luigi Longo stressed that "anticlericalism has always been condemned, and is still condemned, by the Communist party."[31]

Two years later, with Communist support, Article 7 of the Constitution made Catholicism the state religion of Italy. The vote in Parliament was 350 for, 149 against. Since the Communists had 104 votes, their vote was pivotal. In the hall, prior to voting, Togliatti made a memorable speech to an angry group of socialist and liberal deputies: "We need religious peace, and we will not allow this peace to be disturbed in any way. I would add that our responsibility is greater than that of our Socialist colleagues. . . . You read this morning the results of a vote at the Trade Union Congress in Milan, where the Communists received 327,000 votes, the Socialists 152,000, and the Christian Democrats 106,000. Well, we don't want a rupture with those 106,000 workers."[32]

No one challenged Togliatti's sincerity. What he had done was to trade the Concordat for a progressive constitution. (In retrospect, Togliatti got a better bargain than the Church. After the 1974 referendum, the Christian Democrats themselves began negotiating for a revision of the Concordat.[33])

The party maintained its pressure on the Vatican. In 1954 Togliatti made a speech proposing to Catholics a common action program to defend civilization against the menace of atomic war.[34] The proposal was met with silence. A year later he repeated the appeal, and again there was no response from the Vatican.[35] On the contrary, in the decade of the fifties the Vatican had its own McCarthyite repression, such as the silencing and exiling of progressive priests and prominent laymen who believed in a dialogue with Socialists and Communists.* The result was a growing underground of resistance to the anticommunism of Pope Pius XII, a resistance nourished by the moderate position of the Communists.

With the accession of Pope John XXIII, in October 1958, the atmosphere changed rapidly and dramatically. The Communists at first hesitated to trust him. His encyclical *Mater et Magistra* (1961) was castigated as neocapitalist and its advocacy of social measures

---

\* For example, *Cronache sociali*, a group within the DC headed by the beloved Giuseppe Dossetti, was disbanded and Dossetti left public life; censorship was imposed by the Holy Office on the biweekly *Adesso*, which was then suspended and allowed to reopen without its editor, Don Primo Mazzolari; the youth section of *Azione Cattolica* was purged in 1954, with most of its leaders, including a priest, Don Gino Paoli, removed.[36]

interpreted as support for the welfare state.[37] But when the Vatican gave evidence of its neutrality, not interfering in the shift to the left at the congress of the *Democrazia Cristiana* in Naples, the party responded with a major ideological change.

The Tenth Congress of the PCI in 1962 marked a qualitative advance. An approved resolution, dictated by Togliatti, categorically asserted: "We must understand that deep desire for a socialist society not only can exist in those of religious faith, but may be stimulated by a tormented religious conscience confronting the stark problems of the contemporary world."[38] For the first time in history a Communist party had abandoned "the opium of the people" philosophy and recovered the less well-known part of Marx's paragraph, giving it resonance in modern terms.*

Though the Vatican did not respond officially, noted Catholic scholars and prelates paid attention. The dialogue between Catholics and Marxists, never wholly suppressed, now increased considerably. Three months later, on March 20, 1963, the party held a conference on Catholicism and Marxism in Bergamo, John's favorite city. Curiously, Togliatti's speech anticipated the flavor of *Pacem in Terris*, which had already been written but not published. Was it pure intuition, or had Togliatti received through his channels some sense of the encyclical's contents? No one knows, but the choice of Bergamo as the conference site seems too perfect to be wholly fortuitous. Togliatti spoke of the desirability of Catholic-Communist collaboration for achieving peace and social change. He stated: "Concerning religious conscience, we no longer accept the naive and erroneous idea that changes in social structures are sufficient to bring about social change. This idea, derived from the enlightenment of the eighteenth century, and the materialism of the nineteenth, has not passed the test of history. Reality is more complex: the roots of change are deeper; transformations take place in different ways. It is becoming clear that we must have a profound mutual understanding —hence, collaboration."[40]

*Pacem in Terris* appeared twenty days later. It modified the doctrinal posture of the Church even more drastically than the Communists had modified their own position. It extended to the political sphere the legitimacy of collaboration that *Mater et Magistra* had already granted to the social sphere. In addition, it made three major advances: it reinterpreted the traditional distinction between *errore ed erranti*, "error and those who err," to mean that believers

---

* Marx had written: "Religious misery is at the same time the expression of a real misery and *a protest against the real misery*. Religion is the sigh of the oppressed creature, the sentiment of a heartless world, the soul within a soulless world. It is the opium of the people." (Italics added.)[39]

and nonbelievers should seek the truth together.* Secondly, it made a distinction between "false doctrines on the nature, origin, and destiny of man and the universe," and those historical movements "originating in those doctrines and still drawing inspiration from them"; it extended the area of permissible dialogue from the international plane, where the Vatican had always functioned, to include differing political currents within a single country.[41]

Philosophically, and practically, *Pacem in Terris* threw wide open the doors to the dialogue. In fact, the thrust of the encyclical was to bring together "all men of good will" who worked for peace—not just Catholics, as in the past. The encyclical came only a few weeks before a general election in which the Communists were expected to gain. The pope was bitterly criticized for his timing: couldn't he have waited another month? Clearly, Pope John was distancing the Vatican from politics—a sharp departure from his predecessor.

John died in June 1963; Togliatti, a little over a year later, in August 1964. The day before he was fatally stricken, Togliatti finished the *memoriale* in which he urged tolerance and patience: "At the time of Pope John, there was a shift to the left in the Catholic masses and organization. Now *there is, at the top, a backlash to the right. But at the base, the conditions for a leftward shift still obtain.* We must understand this, and show our support for the base. Towards this end, the old atheistic propaganda is worse than useless." (Italics added).[42]

The funerals of these two architects of the dialogue and *camminare insieme* were marked by extraordinary outpourings of people. There were probably as many Communists who wept for John as there were Catholics weeping for Togliatti. Cardinal Lercaro, the converted reactionary, said: "If we don't examine seriously why and how we all left [John] so alone, our admiration can, quicker than we know, be veined with hypocrisy, become corrupt and sterile."[43] Of Togliatti, Giorgio Bocca, his socialist biographer and lifelong opponent, said: "The *memoriale* is a document of the highest stature, worthy of the whole life of Palmiro Togliatti—a lucid Italian called to lead a mass movement founded on sentiments which are rarely lucid. I refer to hope, justice, and solidarity among men."[44]

Time was to show that the two architects had built solidly, but in the short run the enormous resistance within the Church surfaced after the Council. During the Council, with the help of over one

---

* In the past, Catholic doctrine made the distinction between error and those who err for the purposes of converting those who err. It didn't mean they had any rights. Under John's interpretation, error still has no rights, but *those who err* have as many rights as those who criticize them. In politics, this meant that Catholics and Communists have equal rights in searching for truth and working together in that search—particularly the search for peace.

thousand bishops, many resentful of the Curia, both John and Paul and their supporters could make a great deal of headway. By persuasion, patronage, and papal authority, they could put together a coalition in support of any given point. But the sum of those points added up to a drastic new orientation, which made large sections of the episcopate uncomfortable.

As the reforms began to be felt, there was a stiffening of the opposition at every level of the hierarchy. In France, Archbishop Marcel Lefebvre's insubordination was so extensive that he came close to excommunication. Paul VI, fearing a fragmentation of the Church, became increasingly susceptible to conservative pressures. He was unable to reform the Curia, unable to reform the Code of Canon Law, unable to implement the principle of collegiality in the running of the Church.[45]

At the same time, however, he was prudently supportive of the main lines of the Council, both in theology and in politics. *Gaudium et Spes*, the last document approved by Vatican II, in December 1965, specifically uses the word "dialogue," endorsing it: "The Church, while absolutely rejecting atheism, nevertheless recognizes that *all men, believers and nonbelievers, must contribute to the building of a just world* in which all can live together: this certainly cannot happen without a frank and prudent dialogue." (Italics added.)[46]

A Church document of 1968, summarizing the advances of the Council, speaks of "dialogue that Christians intended to establish with men not of the same faith, whether to seek truth in various fields or whether *to solve, through collaboration, the most urgent problems of our times.*" This document actually expands conciliar meanings, saying that "dialogue is possible even when the interlocutors agree upon only a few things," and *"religious divergencies do not by themselves exclude convergence in the temporal sphere,* which is autonomous." (Italics added.)[47]

The Communists responded in kind. At the Eleventh Congress of the party, in 1966, Luigi Longo suggested that the idea of a positive religious stimulus could apply not only to the individual and his conscience but also to the Church as a whole: "We are watching and helping the transcending of conservative positions which had made of religion the opium of the people—a transcendence which is taking place through the aspirations, religious and Christian, flowing from the new way the Church faces the essential problems of the world. . . ".[48]

Paul VI's caution did ease strains within the lower Italian clergy, who saw him as a conservative pope, but it failed to satisfy the reactionaries, who saw in him a stout supporter of progressive positions. Two incidents in Rome may serve to dramatize this last point: one in my old school, the other in the Sistine Chapel.

*I had gone to visit my old school near the Colosseum, the Istituto Angelo Mai, which goes from first grade through high school. The semester hadn't begun and the porticoed courtyard seemed deserted. As I stood there, filled with childhood memories, I noticed a man in a corner of the far portico and went to him. He was a little, rotund fellow, dressed in a blue serge suit and a loud and tasteless shirt and tie. He looked like a janitor in his Sunday best. "Is the director around?" I asked.*

*"I am the director," he said. "Fra Ambrogio."*

*Taken aback, I blurted out: "What are you doing out of uniform?" He wasn't even wearing a clerical collar! I was shocked.*

*"Times have changed." He smiled, unruffled. "I put on my cassock when school starts."*

*I told him who I was, an American professor, once a student in this school. Instantly he was affable, whereas I, the Marxist, was recovering from a sense of loss–a piece of my childhood was gone. But there was more to my feelings. The truth was, he had lost dignity: what would have been humility in a cassock was a trademan's obsequiousness in a serge suit.*

*We chatted, and to draw him out I spoke about Pope John, how loved he had been by Catholics and Protestants alike.*

*"Yes, he had warmth. A pope of the heart," Ambrogio said, but his tone was cool and detached. "And what do you think of Paul [Pope Paul VI]?" he asked.*

*"He seems to us a little cold," I replied.*

*"Yes, a diplomat. A pope of the head." But his tone was warmer, and there was no mistaking the undercurrent: what the Church needed was a pope of the head. This director of an elite private school was not about to say so explicitly, but he clearly saw Vatican II as an egregious mistake.*

*Fra Ambrogio accepted Paul, but a hard-line layman will speak of him as a traitor, a veritable Judas Iscariot. Manlio Barberito, my oldest friend in Italy (we started kindergarten together), who loves the medieval Rome of Sixtus V, disliked Paul intensely. One day we went to visit the Sistine Chapel. Visitors approach the chapel through a labyrinth of narrow passages, cramped stone staircases, and majestic chambers known as* le stanze di Raffael, *from the latter's many paintings there.*

*The prominent color is a celestial blue, and I lightly commented that Pope Sixtus must have loved blue. "Happy were those days," said Manlio bitterly. "Now the pope loves red." "You mean Pope John?" I asked. "Yes, and Paul too." He spoke of the two popes with such hostility that I was taken aback; most Romans thought of Paul as essentially conservative. I asked Manlio how many Catholics shared his feelings. "Not enough," he said tersely.[49]*

Pope Paul VI died in August 1978, after a reign of fifteen years. Despite great pressures he had remained loyal to Pope John. Shortly before Paul died, Professor Gary MacEoin, author of *The Inner Elite*, made this assessment: "Pope John and the Vatican Council built a capital of goodwill that has been kept intact by Pope Paul VI, or, if dissipated in some respects, recouped in others."[50] The dissipation was in administrative matters; the recouping was in political and intellectual matters. During his papacy, Catholic thinkers had established a kind of conciliar hegemony and the dialogue between Catholics and Communists was in full swing.[51] Integralists could not challenge the trend, since Paul, going further than John, had legitimized such discussions in his encyclical *Octogesima Adveniens* (1971). This had put the integralists on the defensive: an integralist professor of the University of Bologna, Gianfranco Morra, said to me: "We must resist, even unto martyrdom." When I repeated this to a conciliar authority, Professor Luigi Pedrazzi, he laughed and said ironically: "It takes two to make a martyr. I don't see any executioners on the horizon."

Given the flourishing of the dialogue, it is not surprising that a rapprochement has taken place between communism and Catholicism to an extent undreamt of before Vatican II. For example, it became possible for a leading Catholic layman, Raniero La Valle, to run and be elected as an independent on the Communist ticket. Further, Paul VI tacitly approved the entry of the Communists into the legislative side of the government in early 1978, as well as subtly welcoming Berlinguer's presence at the pontifical mass for the murdered Aldo Moro. The papal tolerance, in turn, influenced the hierarchy: the 1977 synod of Italian bishops (about three-hundred members) was split evenly between integralists and conciliars. Before Vatican Council II, it would have been difficult to find two dozen bishops favoring the Communists.[52]

The integralists reacted with extreme bitterness. Writing in *National Review,* Malachi B. Martin, author of *The Final Conclave,* said of Paul that "his policy of rapprochement has had predictable results. One cardinal-elector, [Joseph Marie] Trin of Hanoi, stated last September that, in Vietnam, 'we are Marxists. We are impregnated with Leninism. And we are Catholics.' Last June, the four French cardinal-electors . . . insisted on the possibility of political and economic collaboration with the Communists." Martin accused Paul of preparing the way for a successor "ready to arrange an accommodation with Communist politicians [read: Eurocommunism] in the four predominantly Catholic countries of Western Europe."[53]

A more sober Catholic historian wrote that, although Paul "would be stupified if he were the pope of the transition to socialism; nevertheless, he is the pope that recognizes the legitmacy of such a transition."[54] For half the episcopate of Italy, this was anathema, and the pope's death in 1978 came as a timely relief. Here was a historical opportunity to reverse political trends, attenuate existing reforms, and write finis to any serious implementation of Vatican II. Professor MacEoin wrote forebodingly that "the gains achieved by the Council have not been consolidated; on the contrary strong counter-movements have developed."[55]

Upon Paul's death a titanic clash of ideas took place during one of the most dramatic episodes in the history of the millenarian Church: within ten weeks more than a hundred cardinals had gathered in two conclaves, elected two popes, one of whom died. Those 1978 conclaves were high drama, more sensational than such novels as *The Shoes of the Fisherman*, involving fierce battles cloaked in velvet courtesies. The future of the Church was being decided, and not the least important aspect was the Church's position on communism.

Though vastly different, the two conclaves and the two popes were both the creatures of Pope Paul VI. Of the 115 voting cardinals he had hand-picked 110.[56] Yet so ambivalent were Paul's policies and so careful was he to balance right and left that the same cardinals, on the same issues, came out with different results in less than two months. As a crowning irony, the two cardinals who most deeply influenced the elections in opposing directions were both protégés of Paul VI: Giovanni Cardinal Benelli, of Florence, and Michele Cardinal Pellegrino, of Turin.* By good luck, I had seen both.

*Michele Cardinal Pellegrino lives in retirement in Vallo Torinese, a pastoral village. His home is on a hillside having a fine view of the white-tipped Alps in mid-distance. A small villa, simply furnished, with a sun porch and a garden has been put at his disposal by the parish. He has a secretary, and a couple cleans, cooks, and gardens. There seems to be little money. For a prince of the Church, it is a modest but lovely setting. Pellegrino is a legend in Italy. He came to Turin to be its archbishop at a time of intense class struggle. To the dismay of the industrialists, he behaved toward workers with exemplary fairness. Not untypical was his speech to the Episcopal Conference of June 1973, where he told how, when a strike threatened, he had sent telegrams to the union, the ministry of labor, and to* Confindustria *(the federation of industrialists, analogous to the National Association of Manufacturers [NAM] in the U.S.) The first two had answered him, and the last hadn't bothered. Pellegrino had been compassionate toward workers, courteous to Communists, and detached from the Christian Democracy. Affectionately dubbed*

---

* Cardinal Pellegrino resigned from the Turin post early in 1977.

*the Red Bishop, he was beloved by the population, respected by all sides, with the enmity of none and the affection of many who disagreed with him. Thus did he come to be known as "the bishop of the Council," chosen by Pope Paul to play a key role in its deliberation.*

*Politically, Pellegrino is in the great tradition of Pope John: inflexible in doctrine, open to working with all men of good will. "With regard to ideology," he once said, "it is clear that our opposition to Marxism is radical. For the rest,* collaboration in everything that serves human progress is not only legitimate but an obligation. *However, any yielding to the thought of atheistic, materialistic ideology is incompatible with the Christian faith."*[57] *This, of course, is solid Council doctrine, endorsed by Paul VI and anathema to integralists who attack Pellegrino as surrogate for John and Paul. When I met him, I could understand the hostility of the integralists, for the cardinal not only thinks like Pope John, he has some resemblance to him physically and, to an even greater extent, mentally: the tranquil piety, the sweet simplicity, the goodness and the shrewdness, the open mind—a man of one season, spring.*

*He was tired when I saw him, and he politely refused to be drawn into discussions. He had retired, he said gently, and he had set down on paper whatever he had to say. He would send me copies. I took this as a dismissal and left after fifteen minutes of small talk, wondering why he had troubled to see me, given his physical condition. I put it down to courtesy, but I was wrong: as a veteran of the battles of Turin, Pellegrino had no use for amateurs. He wanted to see what kind of person I was, the seriousness of my attitude toward the Church and of my concern with the dialogue. Back in New York, I received a stream of pamphlets, pastoral letters, and copies of speeches, particularly his interventions at the Council. I was deeply moved; tired as he was, he was helping.*

*Giovanni Cardinal Benelli is the antithesis of Pellegrino. Pellegrino is a scholar and a man of wisdom, Benelli an administrator and a man of power. Both were protégés of Paul VI. They are of different generations—in 1978 one was seventy-five, the other fifty-seven. The older man was shaped by the European culture of the nineteenth century—thoughtful, reticent; the younger influenced by the Americanization of the twentieth century, aggressive, deceptively jovial—a go-getter. Yet of the two it is Pellegrino whose mind is open to the winds of change and who serenely faces the future, relying on the past as the soil of a new harvest. In contrast, Benelli is anxious, conscious of fighting a rearguard action, looking to the past for security.*

*Benelli revels in the pomp of a prince of the Church. I heard him speaking at a gathering of perhaps a hundred pious notables. Dressed in the full regalia of a cardinal, he stood on a raised platform at the center of the Duomo (that magnificent Florentine cathedral), behind a long marble table, and read from a lectern flanked by massive candelabra. Behind him, seated in a semicircle, were a score of priests and monsignors in lavender vestments, with the auxiliary bishop, in deep purple, seated in the center. The rich red of Benelli's garments, set off by the purple and the lavender, was stunning.*

*Benelli was commemorating the lives of defunct Florentine bishops, particularly the last one, Elia Cardinal Della Costa. The nostalgia was palpable. Benelli mourned not only the deceased prelate, but the passing of a time when hospitals, schools, and charity had been the cares of the Church, fulfilling Christ's teachings; now the state had pre-empted these functions and institutions, secularizing them. Godless materialism was creeping over the land; sports were replacing the Mass, television was replacing the Host. He was most despairing.*

*Some time later I met a young bishop, a fervent admirer of Benelli, who had worked with him. I mentioned the sermon, how old-fashioned it seemed. "No, no," he said. "It was only the occasion, the commemoration. His Eminence is very modern, very. He was Pope Paul's right hand for ten years, and he supports aggiornamento. But not at the cost of fundamentals; not at the cost of surrender to the Communists. That, no, never."*

*I asked him why Benelli was so much more bitterly anti-Communist than other cardinals. "Such as whom," he asked. "Such as Pellegrino," I replied.*

*"Cardinal Pellegrino is unworldly, a saint, like Pope John. Cardinal Benelli is a realist. It isn't a question of ideology; it's a question of power. His Eminence doesn't fear Marxism; he fears the state, the secular state. It is the secularization of society which is satanic, which is destroying civilization. Communism is only a symptom; the liberals are just as bad. Worse, because they are more anticlerical."*

*"Yet you do work with liberals, why not with Communists?"*

*"Because they are more effective. They are clever, diabolically clever. They can twist people around, arouse their worst instincts. I was born in a village in Tuscany; my father was the mayor, a Christian law-abiding man. When Togliatti was shot in 1948, I was eleven years old, and I'll never forget the mob that burned our house down, a mob inflamed by Communists."*

*"But that was thirty years ago. If the Communists and Catholics don't work together today, there is no way out for Italy . . . no way out of unemployment, unrest, terrorism. The society will be torn apart."*

*"I disagree," he said politely, "but if so, it is God's will."*

*"What about war and peace?" I argued. "Eurocommunism is a buffer between the superpowers . . . it helps détente."*

*"An illusion," said the bishop. "Détente is a Russian maneuver."*

*"Then you think war is inevitable?"*

*"I do not know; God's will be done."*

*"Do you think the Communists will enter the government?"*

*"Not if we can help it."*

*"But if they do, what then?"*

*"I do not know." He paused and spoke with great honesty, unforgettably. "The Church goes to the future without fear . . . but without much confidence."*

Giovanni Cardinal Benelli was the great elector in the first of the two conclaves of 1978. A man of great ability, he was considered too young to be pope. Despite his conservatism, he had made many personal enemies in the thirty-odd departments of the Curia during the decade (1967–77) when he had acted as Paul's executive officer. But he had two great strengths: he was bitterly anti-Communist, which endeared him to the Curia (provided he was not himself a candidate), and he had excellent relations with the third world cardinals, who had nearly all been elevated by Paul while Benelli was his assistant. These prelates were refractory to any member of the Curia as a papal candidate and were in favor of a pastoral, nondiplomat prelate. Benelli had a candidate who would please both camps, Albino Cardinal Luciani, archbishop of Venice.

As a candidate, Luciani had useful virtues: he was inoffensive and virtually unknown—a man of simplicity and piety, with a telegenic smile. Quietly and subtly, Benelli put together his combination: the Curia and the third world. He got the votes of the curialists by pointing out that no extreme right-winger could win, that the inexperienced Luciani would be no threat to them in running the Vatican and that Luciani was ardently anti-Communist. To the third world cardinals, Benelli offered Luciani of the kindly smile, the man of the people who had great compassion for the poor, the son of a Socialist bricklayer. Luciani disliked pomp and wealth and would turn the Church toward humility and austerity.

Benelli's combination, and the little-known Luciani, caught progressives by surprise. On the third ballot Luciani was elected. He took the name of John Paul I. That was a bit of demagoguery, since it implied that he would continue the policies of Vatican II, whereas at best he would limit the advances of the Council and at worst, as in the dialogue with Communists, reverse them. Benelli's delight in John Paul I was matched only by his expectations: "His happiness was as vast as a cathedral," said a priest in his entourage, and the veteran journalist Mauro Lancisi reported in *Panorama* that "Benelli has spoken about the policies of the new pope with a self-assurance which leaves no doubt that his influence over Luciani will be very great indeed."[58]

Within and without the Church, the right wing was exultant. Insiders knew how great was the conservative victory and boasted about it in flamboyant language. A good example was the editorial of *Il Borghese*, a magazine allied with the Italian Social Movement (*Movimento Sociale Italiano*, MSI), the neofascist party. *Il Borghese* considered both John XXIII and Paul VI appeasers (if not worse) of communism. But now everything would change; the election of John Paul, said its editorial, meant "the defeat of Catholic left-wing scum in all forms, from the collaborationist *filo-montenero* of the Pironios to the paraprotestant revisionism of the Suenenses." Even for Italians this ornate prose required translation: *filo-montenero* meant following the policies of Pope Paul (family name, Montini), and "paraprotestant revisionism" meant the ecclesiastical policies of Vatican Council II. The two cardinals attacked, Eduardo Pironio of Argentina and Leo Jozef Suenens of Belgium, had been leaders in Vatican II.

"Before the conclave," continued the editorial, "this left-wing coalition within Catholicism seemed exceedingly strong; some said it had become the arbiter of the Church. . . . But when the chips were down . . . the left has been revealed for what it is . . . a minority which was forced to surrender. . . . The disastrous consequences for our country of the policies of John XXIII are still too much with us . . . the election of John Paul I should now bring Catholics to a total commitment in this battle [against communism] as militant disciples of the Church of Rome . . . and not as followers of a pope ensnared in an *Ostpolitik* pleasing to *Pravda*."[59]

*Il Borghese* knew it could count on Benelli's ascendancy over Luciani. Then, after thirty-three days, Pope John Paul died. *Il Borghese*, bemoaning "those things that could have been and will not be," mourned the loss of a pontiff whose "popular culture is today deprecated because Marxism is its natural enemy and because intellectuals find it more convenient to be 'producers of consciousness-raising.' "

Despite its sorrow and a sense of missed opportunities, *Il Borghese* was still confident that the right-wing momentum would be maintained and that the policies of John XXIII and Paul VI would be rejected by the second conclave. "Coming after the Hamletlike policies of Montini* [Paul VI] . . . and the cavalier diplomacy of John, Luciani stood before the people as *a true believer*. . . . That his was a *true* pontificate is evidenced by the fact that *the thirty-three days of Luciani have literally canceled the fifteen years of Montini.* Today, in fact, no one says, 'Let us return to Paul VI,' while everyone says, 'We must find another Luciani.' " (Italics added.)[61]

The second conclave ended in a stunning reversal of the first; it didn't seem possible that the same College of Cardinals could have elected two such disparate individuals. In all respects, except piety and simplicity, Karol Wojtyla was Luciani's opposite: young, athletic, a man of strong will and independent judgment, a cultured intellectual versed in government and diplomacy. It seemed as if there were two Sacred Colleges, one sclerotic, the other iconoclastic—producing the first non-Italian pope in five centuries, the first pope from a socialist country, and the youngest in over a hundred years. The first election reflected parochialism, timidity, refuge in the past; the second, worldliness, audacity, confidence in the future. Yet while the Sacred College seemed oddly schizoid, in truth it was an accurate reflection of the divided soul of the Hamlet Pope and of the conflicts within the Church. In an act of decisive statesmanship, the Sacred College had made up its collective mind: Vatican II was to be irreversible. Wojtyla's youth and firmness guaranteed there would be no turning back, since he would probably appoint *all* the cardinals of the next conclave. The Conciliar Church had triumphed; someday, John XXIII would be canonized.

The rage of the right was palpable. As the new pontiff finished his first speech and benediction, one of the defeated electors, Giuseppe Cardinal Siri, strode to his limousine, a scowl on his face. When a reporter asked him what he thought of the speech, he snapped, "I don't know. I didn't listen!"[62]

*Il Borghese* was livid. Unable to attack a living pope directly, the editor devised an immortal ploy: it attacked the pope's country. "Poland," intoned the editorial, *"has always brought harm to Europe,* a Europe whose cultural, moral and spiritual frontier stops with Prussia [i.e., the East German Republic], which against natural law, has been severed from its German Fatherland." (Italics added.)[63] The nonsequitur poorly conceals a racist argument: Slavs are not fit to be Europeans.

Equally palpable was the rejoicing of the progressives. Father Andrew M. Greeley, the American authority on the Vatican, reported that Aloisio Cardinal Lorscheider of Brazil was "beaming with happiness. So was Michele Pellegrino, who was absolutely radiant. His warm, handsome face was alive with joy."[64]

---

* Pope John XXIII had characterized Montini as "our most eminent Cardinal Hamlet."[60]

Pellegrino had every right to be radiant. Just as Cardinal Benelli had been the architect of the first election, Cardinal Pellegrino had been the moving spirit behind the second election. With Leo Josef Suenens, Hyacinthe Thiandoum, Franz Koenig, and a few others he had orchestrated the politics of the second conclave. They had the votes to veto a right-wing election. At the same time, their reasonableness in the first election had gained them the respect and sympathy of the centrists for the second election. After the first flush of unity behind John Paul, many cardinals realized that Luciani would not be strong enough to withstand the power of the Curia: consciously or unconsciously, they felt they had been manipulated, and they blamed Benelli. Then the very death of John Paul had an adverse effect on Benelli. Few cardinals are without a touch of superstition; the sudden death seemed like a sign from the Holy Ghost, and Benelli was tarred with rejection. Wojtyla was known to be conservative on Church doctrine, though loyal to Vatican II, and very conservative on such matters as celibacy, proper dress for nuns, etc., which pleased many cardinals.* Finally, some of them had second thoughts about the wisdom of a head-on collision with Communist regimes in Eastern Europe and Communist parties in Western Europe. Undoubtedly, the moral stature of Pellegrino, his wisdom and piety, made themselves felt. All these factors, and others, combined to open the road for the first non-Italian pope in nearly five hundred years. As I wrote in an editorial in the *Nation* the night after the election of John Paul II: "Without Cardinal Benelli's quiet blitz that resulted in the election of the short-lived pope, the Sacred College might not have achieved the clarity that second thoughts often bring. Millions of Italians believe in both the dialectic and the Holy Ghost. They might find it fitting and proper that Cardinal Benelli's triumph in August should have ordained his defeat in October."[66]

Within a year of his election, John Paul II had shaped the contours of his pontificate: there was no significant issue on which he had not taken a stand. He has often distressed the progressive elements in the Church by his conservative stance on many social, religious, and theological issues.[67] On the anniversary of his election a leading Catholic theologian, the Swiss Hans Küng, wrote a long memorandum voicing his misgivings.[68] The Vatican did not evade the issues, but met them head-on. By the end of 1979 three theologians, including Küng, had been censored or punished, the Jesuit order had been sharply reprimanded and the pope was in the process of giving greater power to the authoritarian order known as Opus Dei.[69]

It is quite clear that Wojtyla has a strong authoritarian bent and is inclined to rigidly orthodox positions in Church doctrine

---

* The pope's conservative views when bluntly expressed during his visit to the United States shocked many American Catholics. But they had been well known to students of the Church.[65]

considered retrograde by progressive theologians. Whether he will maintain his positions remains to be seen, for he is a realist and the controversy may prove costly to the Church. Küng has already thrown down the gauntlet by refusing to resign from his teaching position. In a closely reasoned article in the *New York Times*, January 28, 1980, he defends his Catholicism against Rome's interpretations, "the ingrown Roman absolutist claims from the Middle Ages and later times." Indeed, he says sharply, " 'Roman Catholic' is a late and misleading neologism." Küng's arguments have resonance throughout the Church; he is not quite a helpless, isolated priest.

The controversial matters at issue are of the greatest importance, but they concern us, in this context, only to the extent that they impinge on the political stance of the Vatican within Italy and its attitude to Marxism and Eurocommunism in general. If, for example, the Vatican were to press for a referendum on abortion as it did on divorce, then Wojtyla's known personal feelings on abortion would become significant. But despite the pope's strong statements to the episcopate and Cardinal Benelli's diocesan crusade to push for a referendum, there is no indication of a Vatican crusade. Politically, the pope has been very prudent.[70] On some issues, such as the role of nuns and the ordination of women, there is resistance within the Church. This resistance surfaced during the papal visit to the U.S. in the many demonstrations by women in various cities, the picketing in Washington, and Mother Teresa Kane's dignified and courageous disagreement with the pope.[71]

However, though theologically conservative within the Church, in his relations with the outside world, particularly in politics, John Paul II seems to be receptive to change. On this score, the rage of reactionaries and the editorial lamentations of *Il Borghese* seem amply justified.

"Let us have no illusions," warned *Il Borghese*. "The smile, the optimism, the faith of Pope Luciani are gone forever. Pope Wojtyla brings us the Catholicism, persecuted but ambiguous, of those who have lived *in partibus infidelium* [among the infidels]. . . . *The most probable hypothesis, and the most worrisome, is that* [the conclave] *is convinced that it must come to terms with communism*. It considers ineluctable a further advance of Marxism in the world; it is preparing to deal with it. . . . If tomorrow Italy were to be Communist, a pope such as Wojtyla would know how to operate. . . . The perspective is far from cheerful." (Italics added.)[72]

The "probable hypothesis" of *Il Borghese* was soon confirmed by one of the participants, Hyacinthe Cardinal Thiandoum, archbishop of Dakar and president of the Symposium of African bishops. In an interview with *Il Messagero* shortly after the election of

Pope John Paul II, he expressed his satisfaction with the outcome. When asked "Was the choice of a Polish cardinal an anti-Communist action?" he replied: "Absolutely not. Had it been a question of finding an anti-Communist cardinal, the election would have been much quicker. But let us recall that the Council [Vatican II] and particularly *Gaudium et Spes* [its final document] demand a dialogue with all men of good will. The Council does not anticipate a struggle against a particular group of people, but rather augurs a loyal collaboration with everyone, everywhere, in order to develop the values of liberty, justice, peace, and progress. We live in this perspective, albeit firm in the defense of religious liberty."[73]

John Paul II is, of course, anti-Communist. But he is also a realist. He has appointed to the key post of Secretary of State, Agostino Cardinal Casaroli, architect of Paul VI's *Ostpolitik*. On his visit to Poland, June 1979, the pope let the huge crowds testify to the Church's power, while he behaved amiably and, on departing, kissed the Polish prime minister.* The televised kiss conferred a much-needed legitimacy to a grateful government, though, of course, a price was implicit. Within a year the Church obtained many important concessions (see *L'Espresso,* May 25, 1980).

But perhaps the most important political fact about John Paul II is his fierce commitment to social justice. This was exemplified in his speech to the United Nations during his visit to the United States. This commitment must be seen in the context of a significant current within the Vatican: namely, the *Catholic Church is slowly detaching itself from capitalism and its institutions as presently structured.* This is a startling idea, but I think it is true, and its first inklings were given to me by Monsignor Luigi Bettazzi. Without him I would have overlooked this trend, as all foreign observers have.

This is not to say that the Church is becoming socialist. Far from it. It is not even to say that the Church is anticapitalist. What it does say is that the Church has decided that the capitalist system is slowly sinking and the Church has no intention of going down with it.

In his book *Farsi uomo* (Becoming a man) Bettazzi states unequivocally: "The choice today is not between . . . communism and democracy—the one anti-Christian and the other Christian. . . . The choice is between a system that benefits some, suffocating others, and an orientation to greater equality. . . . In the light of the Gospels and

---

* An analogous legitimacy was tendered to the PCF and the PCI. The *New York Times,* of June 1, 1980, shocked its readers with a front-page photo of the pope in Paris shaking hands with Georges Marchais, who wore a sheepish grin, while Wojtyla had a sly, amused smile. Next day, on his televised return to Rome, the pope was shown cordially shaking hands with the Communist deputy mayor—a week before the municipal elections. His Holiness does not shake hands with the Devil's disciples or kiss the Antichrist, so the message was clear: Communists are acceptable people.

recent documents of the Church, the choice is clear; capitalism founded on absolute liberalism is not compatible with Christianity."[74]

In conversation Bettazzi said to me: "There are Church documents with very advanced positions. For example, there is a document from the Vatican commission *Justitia et Pax*, prepared for the International Assembly on the Rights of the Seas, which is working on a seabed treaty. It says: 'From the point of view of Catholic Christianity, the primary thing is not property rights; it is the distribution of earthly goods. If the system of private property does this, fine. But if it gives too much to some while depriving others, then private property must be superseded.' "[75]

Bettazzi told me to read other documents, for example, *Popolorum Progressio* of Paul VI ("it is very advanced, very critical of capitalism"), and particularly *Gaudium et Spes*, the last document of Vatican II and, in a sense, the constitution of the Conciliar Church. There one reads: "God has destined the earth and all it contains for the use of all men and all peoples. . . . according to just criteria . . . economic development must not . . . be left to the arbitrary judgment of a few men or groups who have great economic power . . . or a few powerful nations."[76] Without mentioning imperialism by name, it states: "Peace demands, first of all, the elimination of the causes of discord, beginning with injustices. Many are due to economic inequalities . . . and the spirit of domination."[77]

An accompanying declaration was more explicit. It condemns "the concentration of economic power in a small number of nations and multinational groups" which lead to "disequilibrium of commerce, disparity in prices between the products of industrial nations, impotence in combining economic growth and fair distribution both within nations and internationally, unemployment, discrimination in raw materials and in their consumption."[78]

There are strong and growing movements, such as Christians for Socialism, within the Church which resolutely reject capitalism. A Catholic historian, George Hourdin, writes: "Today there are not a few Catholics who wish to change society because they believe that the capitalist system is incompatible with the Christian faith."[79]

The nascent detachment from the capitalist system is nourished by strong roots in Italy and in the Church. The Italian peasantry, the core strength of the Church, has been essentially precapitalist in production, and its mores are those of ancient times: work, not profit, is the *summum bonum;* to this day in Italy work is considered good, speculation evil. The Italian Constitution opens with the words: "Italy is a republic, founded on labor." The Church has always identified capitalism with the liberal state of 1870 onward, and it has always considered protestantism and capitalism Siamese twins. A leading theologian, Gianni Baget Bozzo, adviser to Siri, one of the most powerful cardinals in Italy, published *Il partito cristiano, il comunismo, e la società radicale* (1976), a book which refurbishes the polemics of the past in this area. Not accidentally, he is a proponent of the dialogue.*

This insight into the Church, opened up by Bettazzi, prompted me to discuss it at length with one of the party's most knowledgeable men, Alceste Santini, Vatican correspondent for *L'Unità*, who is both a scholar and a first-rate reporter.

*Santini and I first met in 1977 at the* Ufficio Stampa *of the Vatican (the public relations agency), which is located at the head of the Via Conciliare, an imposing wide boulevard, with the piazza of St. Peter's Church at the other end. It is a majestic, almost formal, approach.* Ufficio Stampa *is next to a large* galleria *that sells religious objects, including rosaries blessed by the pope (which sell well above the price of unblessed ones). I found this hucksterism undignified and wondered why the pope lent himself to it. Manlio later told me: "You don't understand, Carlo. I'm sure the pope feels as you do, but Italians are poor and tourists have money. The Holy Father, as bishop of Rome, must pay attention to the material needs of his flock."*

*Santini turned out to be a well-dressed man in his forties, rather good-looking. He looked like a rising executive at middle corporate levels. When I told him of my feeling about the Church detaching itself from capitalism, he said I was right about the tendency but not to expect rapid development. The Church had very substantial relations with Big Business, both in Europe and in America. Nevertheless, the thrust was there, rooted in the very essence of Vatican Council II. The Church was returning to its origins of defending the poor, the sick, and the oppressed—it was becoming once again the Apostolic Church. He could give me hundreds of references to make the point.†*

*Moreover, he went on, the integralists were not against the trend; in common with the rest of the hierarchy they had always disliked the secular "liberal" state and had no firm ecclesiastical commitment to capitalism. Members of the hierarchy increasingly had their origins in the laboring mass. Fifty years ago, although the*

---

* Cardinal Siri is one of the fiercest integralists in the Church. That he should choose as his adviser a conciliar theologian is one of those anomalies that are constantly recurring in Italian life—to the confusion of foreign observers.

† Here is a typical example, from the speech of Paolo Evaristo Arns, of Brazil, at the Fourth Episcopal Synod, of 1974: "The Church must line up on the side of the exploited, support those suffering and in jail, and act to undo the oppressors and the jailers."

*Church had always recruited the bulk of the clergy from the urban and rural poor, the higher ranks were filled by the younger sons of the upper classes; only the exceptional ones among the poor, like Roncalli, made it to the top. Today the upper classes don't send their sons into the Church: their sons won't go. It was inevitable that people like Roncalli and Bettazzi were going to be more plentiful. This and the impact of the third world prelates meant that the hierarchy was bound to change for the better.*

*Nearly two years later, in June 1979, I saw Santini again, this time at dinner at his home. I reminded him of our discussion and asked what he thought of Pope John Paul II in that context. Santini was cautious but positive. "I was in his plane when he went to Mexico," he said. "And of course I heard him at Puebla and other places. He is a decisive man, but he is also a prudent one. For example, I think his religious conservatism is partly due to his wish to heal the wounds of the extreme right, people like Lefebvre, who can make serious trouble. As for capitalism, my hunch is he doesn't like it. He sees what it is doing to the poor, and he certainly wants to disassociate the Church from the obvious iniquities of the system. But it is still too early to tell."*

*I asked Santini about the pope and the PCI. "He has been very correct. You may remember that in his first speech he said that he had no intention of political interference, and he has stuck to his word. The Vatican kept hands off our June national elections—in fact, the pope was in Poland. On the plane he also said that 'Catholics who vote Communist are still Catholics and their choice may be coherent with the principles of faith and morals.'[80] Toward me, he was friendly, saying that he always read my paper first every morning. He knew very well he was giving me a small scoop.\* I must say he is very* simpatico—*direct, warm, charismatic." I told Santini that the reports from Puebla put the pope on the side of reactionary hierarchs who wanted to undo the Episcopal Conference of Medellin (1968), which progressives had dominated.[81] Santini demurred: "I know the press tried to give that impression, and it is true that Wojtyla put his foot down on the priests being guerrilla leaders and the use of violence. But it isn't true that he reversed Medellin. His stress on defense of the oppressed was powerful and serious, committing the Church to the fullest extent the left could wish. I heard him in Mexico say that systems which exploit men are unjust.[82] In fact, a new code word emerged, 'evangelization,' which the pope used repeatedly and which the left appropriated. They said: 'All we are doing in leading social struggles is evangelizing and the pope wants us to do that.' The*

---

\*　Santini cabled the paper, and the next morning it ran an eight-column headline: POPE READS "L'UNITA" FIRST.

*truth is, the progressive bishops were satisfied; there were rumors
that the pope had rewritten the speeches brought from Rome.''*


Shortly after speaking with Santini I met with Father Bartolomeo
Sorge, who is, with Bettazzi, the most advanced exponent of the
dialogue. Sorge was enthusiastic about the pope and confided that he
is often consulted. I asked him about the rumor that the pope had
rewritten his speeches in Mexico. Sorge shook his head decisively.
"Not at all," he said. "They were planned and written here, and
unchanged. I know. I helped to write them."[83] Sorge showed me a
book just off the press, *Il Papa dal volto umano,* * in which many
writers, including Sorge himself, talked about the pope. The first
chapter had been written by the pope, and it left no question that the
papal thrust was toward a continuation of the dialogue, as well as
disapproval of materialism and consumerism. In effect, this is a
covert way to criticize capitalism.

A week later I visited Monsignor Bettazzi in Ivrea. He was warm
and gracious, regaling me with excellent food and wine. Bettazzi was
at one with Sorge in seeing the pope as a powerful progressive force
despite his conservative stand on certain issues. He was sure that the
Church critique of the capitalist system as presently organized would
grow and widen, and that John Paul II would bend his mind and
energies toward transcending the present division between rich and
poor nations, "He has deep compassion, a first-rate mind, boundless
energy—and a long reign ahead."

My own judgment is that John Paul II will be a tough bargainer
and will extract many concessions from the socialist bloc. He will be a
constant pressure for liberalization, a pressure exerted with firmness
but amity, in contradistinction to the self-serving "human rights"
campaign of President Jimmy Carter. For the future of Eurocommunism, nothing but good can come of this pressure. The same
applies to the papal coolness toward the capitalist system and its
concern with the economics of poverty, both among nations and
within each nation. This powerful trend toward separation from the
capitalist system is furthered by Wojtyla's personal experience, but it
is also a reflection of the mass pressure from the Catholics of Africa,
Asia, and Latin America. This in turn affects such conservative groups
as the American hierarchy. Following the pope's visit, the American
episcopal conference was told by its president, Archbishop John R.
Quinn of San Francisco, that the pope's "real challenge to us as

---

* The pope with the human face. The title is taken from an essay by Gianni Baget Bozzo. No
one seems to have noticed the irony in the concept: the Dubcek spring was called "communism
with a human face."

American Catholics was the homily at Yankee Stadium. He called on us to go beyond conventional charity and to 'seek out the *structural reasons* which foster or cause the different forms of poverty' in the world and in our country."[84] (Italics added).

Throughout the third world, and particularly in Latin America, the distancing of the hierarchy from the capitalist system has become explicit. In March 1980 the general assembly of Brazilian bishops issued a document stating that the land problems "will be solved only when the mentality and structure of our society changes. As long as the political-economic system favors the profits of a small number of capitalists, there will not be a solution to the situation of injustice and exploitation of the labor of the majority." Father Orlando Dotti, head of the commission that drafted the document, used the phrase "capitalist exploitation" to describe existing conditions, adding: "The reaction of the sharecroppers, even when it is violent, is legitimate."[84a]

Even more dramatic is the pastoral letter of the episcopate of Nicaragua, read in all churches of that country in February 1980. It promises that "the Church must be on the side of those who fight to transform production with land and other resources to permit man to live and make of our country of Nicaragua a land of justice, solidarity, peace and liberty . . . if this means socialism, we [the bishops] have no objections." The bishops add: "If socialism implies a growing diminution of injustices and traditional inequalities between city and country, between intellectual and manual pay, if it means participation of the workers in the product of their work, thus overcoming economic alienation, there is nothing in Christianity to contradict this process."[84b]

Pope John Paul II supports these positions and went out of his way to make the endorsement public. On March 3, 1980, he received in audience two members of the junta governing Nicaragua, Violetta Barrios and Commander Daniel Ortega Avedra, and made explicit reference to the pastoral letter, wishing "the highest achievements" to the workers, peasants, and students of Nicaragua. Giving his blessing to the forthcoming campaign against illiteracy, he urged all Catholic "educators to participate in his enterprise" and went on to say that "the Church, in Nicaragua as elsewhere, encourages all efforts to promote the economic, social, political, and cultural well-being of individuals."[84c]

Many liberals, alienated by Wojtyla's doctrinal conservatism, will question my analysis as wishful thinking. I was pleased, therefore, to discover that an eminent French observer, André Fontaine, wrote for *Le Monde* a very similar evaluation of the pope. "When you leave this domain [of doctrine] to move into that of politics, John Paul

II's message [to the United Nations] confirms considerable progress on the part of the Holy See.'' He quotes James Reston on the pope's visit as having "brought us back to elemental things," and spells out what that means: "The elemental thing is that the world has to become reconciled with itself to share its resources instead of preparing for war over raw materials and energy. It was a masterstroke for the pope to have chosen the world's richest nation . . . as the place to denounce 'the abyss separating the minority of the excessively rich from the multitude of the destitute.' . . . Probably never before has anyone so strenuously insisted to the Americans, and through them to world opinion, on the absolute necessity and the possibility of bringing another world into being, a world less unjust and less absurd than today's.''[85]

A further confirmation of the validity of my analysis came from an unexpected source, *Commentary* magazine, a publication of the American Jewish Committee. *Commentary,* under cover of a pseudoliberal tradition, is one of the most reactionary publications in the United States; it can smell an anticapitalist heresy anywhere on the planet, including the Vatican. In December 1979 it published an article, "The Politics of John Paul II," by Michael Novak, which, though cloaked in deferential phrases, is a sustained attack on the papal view of world economics. The roots of war, said the pope at the UN, lie in "the systems that decide the history of all our societies." This phrase, says Mr. Novak, "is suspiciously impersonal, deterministic, vulgarly Marxist." Moreover, the pope's "proposing a more just distribution of the world's goods seems to invite extortion. Fidel Castro . . . cited the Pope almost verbatim while demanding a transfer of $300 billion from the Western nations. . . ." In short, the pope's "own observations and analysis fall short of reality."[86] *Pace,* Mr. Novak, they seem right on target. Moreover, the fact that the pope sometimes uses Marxist concepts only shows that he is a serious student of philosophy. For example, during the conclave that elected him pope, he was reading a Marxist theoretical journal.[87]

The Italian Communist party seems to be impressed by the papal stance. During a meeting of its Central Committee in November 1979, Luciano Gruppi pointed out, "Though this pope is conservative and traditionalist in matters of doctrine and discipline, nevertheless he has courageously posed problems of the rights of man and social justice. Hence, there is for us a wide area of understanding and of dialogue with the masses that look to him."[88]

While not dismissing the long-run evolution of the Church against capitalism, the PCI still takes a cautious attitude. As a high Communist official said to me, half joking, completely serious: "He *is* non-Italian and therefore to some extent less concerned with our national, and to him parochial, politics. He loves to travel. We shall encourage that propensity."

The PCI does well to be wary, given Wojtyla's style, at once headstrong and wily, including unabashed use of power within the Church: the latest example being the draconian edict forcing Father Robert F. Drinan the Massachusetts congressman, to abandon his career in politics. Yet, ecclesiastical matters aside, the pope continues to be progressive: He has been tough and unequivocal in championing the poor and the oppressed, in supporting the third world, in fighting to prevent thermonuclear war.

The pope is autonomous. During his visit to Paris in June 1980, he praised Giscard d'Estaing's summit with Brezhnev despite Washington's anger at the meeting. Although ferociously opposed to Marxism as an ideology, he is amiable toward Socialists and Communists (see page 85). He professes neutrality in politics, and kept a low profile in the Italian national election of 1979 and the local elections of 1980.

However, life is complex, and Vatican ideology is bound to impinge on politics. Abortion and divorce are obvious examples. A recent two-day sensation involved the sources of terrorism. The right blames Marxism and the PCI; the Communists blame unemployment and the breakdown of capitalist society. The truth, which most sociologists accept, is that the terrorists include fanatic Catholics as well as fanatic Marxists, a truth which is anathema to the Vatican, which went on the offensive. The official *Civiltà cattolica* editorialized on April 19, 1980, that "the bases of the cult of violence are the ideologies, in the first place, Marxist ideology. . . ." Simultaneously, the pope entered the fray. A papal speech in Turin had been mimeographed, in advance, for journalists, and next day all the newspapers (but one) headlined a key passage: "the ideology and practice of atheistic Marxism, joined, one may say, to the extreme consequences of its materialist postulates within the various denominations of contemporary terrorism. . . ."

*Unità* demurred. Its correspondent, Alceste Santini, asserted that the pope had dropped the word "terrorism" and actually said "within contemporary denominations." Santini was correct, as officially confirmed by the Vatican. It was later learned that Cardinal Pellegrino had urged the pope to drop the association as unfair and provocative: Turin had suffered heavily, and everyone knew that the Communist administration and the Communist-led unions had been leading the fight against terrorists.[89]

Without being overly sanguine, I think an accommodation is possible between the Vatican and Eurocommunism. The ideological conflict is deep, but there are substantial areas of mutual interest. After all, a basic tenet of Eurocommunism is independence from Moscow of all socialist states, a tenet which can hardly displease a Polish prelate.

# CHAPTER 5

# The Italian Contribution
# to Eurocommunism

On the morning of July 14, 1948, there is a routine session at Montecitorio, the imposing palace near the Corso (the Fifth Avenue of Rome) that houses the Chamber of Deputies. As the legislators disperse, Palmiro Togliatti and his intimate friend, Nilde Jotti—both Communist deputies—run into a cabinet minister, Ugo La Malfa, who greets Togliatti: "I'm going to Moscow on an economic mission." "Really," jokes Togliatti, "how did you manage to get permission of the American ambassador?" With a smile and a wave, the Communist leader exits through a side entrance, takes a few steps and is struck down by three revolver shots. Togliatti falls to his knees, sliding to the ground as Nilde Jotti throws herself over his body. Togliatti is murmuring, she recalls later, "something about "Andreoni's article." The assassin hesitates, fires a shot that misses, and flees. The hour is 11:30 A.M.[1]

Within a couple of hours the would-be assassin is arrested in his room in a cheap pension. He is a young Sicilian, Antonio Pallante, with home-town connections with the Mafia and well-known fascists. On his bureau is a copy of *Mein Kampf* and a diary of nationalistic outpourings. Under questioning he says he shot Togliatti because he "was the most dangerous element in Italian politics, who blocked the renewal of the country by his activity as a foreign agent."

No one knows to this day whether the assassin acted completely on his own; clearly, Pallante was responding to the anti-Communist hysteria of the Church and right-wing press as the Cold War threatened to turn into a hot war. The attacks on the Communists in press and radio had become ferocious. A Father Riccardo Lombardi had mounted a campaign in a series of meetings and radio speeches calling for violent measures against the "Communist-traitors." A well-known editor, Carlo Andreoni, called Togliatti "the Russian" and said he should be nailed to the wall.[2] It was this editorial that Togliatti presumably had in mind when he was shot.

Togliatti was taken by ambulance to the Polyclinic Hospital. He remained conscious and said to Mauro Scoccimarro, a veteran Communist leader, "Be calm; don't lose your head." He was operated on for two and a quarter hours while hundreds of well-wishers came to donate blood. Two were chosen, a cook and a Capuchin friar, Don Angelo Parini. The operation was successful, but the danger of death still remained.

As soon as the news of the attempt spread, with the first erroneous report that Togliatti was dead, people assumed there had been a conspiracy, and a spontaneous general strike paralyzed the country. It was "a general strike," says the historian Giorgio Bocca, "such as had never occurred in Italian history, a strike which suspended the government's authority in the major Italian cities, and opened an interregnum in which anything could happen."[3] In town after town, police stations were occupied by the people, in some cases the police chiefs reporting to Communist headquarters for instructions; factories were taken over, including the Fiat plants at Mirafiori, where the head of the company, Vittorio Valletta, and his staff were held hostage. Ex-partisans were everywhere in command; machine guns and bazookas once used against the Germans were taken out of their hiding places, cleaned of their protective grease, and mounted on buildings facing police and *carabinieri* headquarters. Armed patrols set up checkpoints in the cities and highways; armed miners seized Abbadia San Salvatore, the key communications center between north and south Italy.

There were numerous attacks on the offices of fascist parties and of the Christian Democrats. Functionaries of those parties were beaten, and in some cases their homes were burned down. Huge demonstrations in the major cities, some fifty thousand people and more, filled the streets and the squares, seething with anger and needing only a signal to march against the government. The country was on the brink of civil war: it waited for the Communist party to move.

Now, if ever, the party seemed to be in a strong position to take power by armed force. Twice before, ultraleft critics charged, the party should have tried. In April 1945, at war's end, the Communists controlled an army of battle-hardened partisans estimated at between two hundred and three hundred thousand. Considered the heroes of the resistance, they would have been supported—so it was argued— by the entire population.

The second occasion had come a year before, in June 1947, when the Communists had been dropped from the cabinet unceremoniously and, some maintained, illegally. Everyone knew they had been thrown out at the behest of the United States; Alcide De Gasperi later said as much: "Beside the traditional parties in Italy there is a fourth party . . . that can paralyze us . . . those who have money and economic power."*[4] This time, ultraleft critics argued, De Gasperi's high-handed behavior, his support by the fascists, and the insult to nationalist pride by American intervention, would all combine to give popular support to an insurrection.

On both occasions, the criticisms were puerile. There was no possibility whatsoever of an insurrection in 1945, given the presence of American and British troops in Italy: "Any slightly informed person," writes Bocca, "knows that an insurrection was not only impossible, but inconceivable."[6] As for 1947, American economic aid was not resented by most Italians, but welcomed, even if the price was a right-wing government.

But in July 14, 1948, the mood was different. The spontaneity, rapidity, and extent of the general strike surprised everyone, including the Communist leadership. Battista Santhià, the top Communist functionary in the Fiat plants, later recalled that both he and Valletta were taken by surprise. Santhià adds: "In those hours Valletta didn't say a word . . . he was obviously worried; let us admit it, he was scared."[7]

*Turin is solidly in the hands of the Communist paramilitary organization, as is true of the large towns throughout Piedmont. From the barracks of the army, the air force, and the* carabinieri, *the Communist cells telephone in: "We are ready; the weapons are ready." The aviators at the military air base at Casermetto are prepared to mutiny at a signal.*

*In Milan the Socialist mayor is met with hostility from the demonstrators; only the Communist Guiseppe Alberganti may speak on the Piazza del Duomo: "This strike will not end today—nor tomorrow." Two factories protected by police are invaded by "Red Squads" and the police taken prisoners. There are thirty wounded. In Genoa a police station is taken by assault, and all the police are made prisoners. Five police tanks are blocked by the crowds; young Communists jump up on them, open the turrets, and force their surrender. At five o'clock, a hundred thousand workers are in the streets, among*

---

\* The expulsion of the Communists occurred a month *before* the Marshall Plan was rejected by the USSR.[5]

*them many soldiers giving the clenched fist salute. That evening a column of the* Celere\* *and* carabinieri *tries to take control of the center of Milan; it is met with gunfire and retreats—three policemen are wounded, six* carabinieri *and their officers are captured. The slogans on the streets of Milan are the same as those in Turin: "Out with the government assassins!" An extra edition of* L'Unità, *on the afternoon of the fourteenth, carries the slogan on the front page and demands the resignation of the government. There are clashes throughout the north—in Milan province alone forty are wounded— and the army deploys three battalions of mountain troops at war readiness.*

*In Venice workers occupy the factories, the radio station, and the key bridges. There are clashes throughout Italy: Piombino, Taranto, Ferrara, Cagliari, Modena, La Spezia. In Rome all traffic is stopped, buses returning to their garages. A huge demonstration in Piazza Esedra shouts to the Communist speakers: "Give us the word! Let's go!" But Luigi Longo, second in the party, sees the police tanks lined up and is not ready. He suggests a silent march to the Polyclinic Hospital.*

In this context, at five o'clock, Togliatti opened his eyes and smiled at his son Aldo, who had arrived from Turin. Then four top leaders were allowed in: Luigi Longo, Pietro Secchia, Mauro Scoccimarro, and Massimo Caprara, the first three being hard-liners. *"Calma,"* said Togliatti. *"Mi raccomando, calma. Non facciamo sciochezze.* Be calm, I beg you. Let's not do anything silly." What else he said is not on record, but the next day Longo and Secchia explained to a hastily called meeting of the Central Committee why insurrection was not possible. The orders went out: quench the ardor, quiet things down, end the strike.[8]

Prime Minister Alcide De Gasperi, on his side, moved quickly to placate the left. He condemned the attempted assassination, and immediately released the transcript of the interrogation of the assassin along with whatever other information the police had. He did not declare a state of emergency, and troops were kept confined to their barracks, except in sporadic cases where local commanders acted on their own initiative. The word throughout the government was: Be calm, don't do anything silly.

Unquestionably, the decisive voice was that of Togliatti. Weak, hardly able to speak, his life hanging in the balance, he held firmly to

---

\*   The *Celere* was a special parliamentary police group set up by the DC minister of the interior, Mario Scelba, to deal with demonstrations. They used their armored jeeps like cavalry, racing around a crowd to contain it, then charging into it, breaking it into sections and driving around each section, containing it, so that the police on foot could deal with the smaller groups.

the political line he had developed since *la svolta di Salerno* of 1944: no insurrectionary strategy.* Togliatti's restraint, accepted by the party, marks a critical point in the rise of Eurocommunism, since it convinced *all* strata of Italian society that the PCI's commitment to democratic procedures was deep rooted and irreversible. If the Communists did not seize this opportunity to overthrow the government by force, when all the factors seemed to be in their favor, then it was clear to everyone that they would probably never make the attempt. Togliatti and other party leaders could see that they would probably never again have such a favorable conjunction of forces. They had no illusions about what would happen now; they would be disarmed. This, of course, is exactly what did happen.

When the emergency strike was over, De Gasperi cynically accused the party of insurrectional plans, and many militants were jailed for long periods. Then was initiated a witch hunt that lasted throughout the fifties: workers, teachers, and government employees were fired and blacklisted.[9] Ruling groups were deeply frightened and their anticommunism intensified by the militancy of the workers; yet, paradoxically, they were finally persuaded by the restraint of the Communists that they had no intention of coming to power by armed force. More important, ever larger sections of the population became convinced that the Communists could be trusted to govern constitutionally. In the months I spent in Italy, I never found one person—not one, including Bennelli, Morra, and Manlio—who didn't agree privately that Communists would operate legally once in the government. In public, of course, there was a good deal of electoral rhetoric from the right, which, unfortunately, some foreign newspapermen took at face value.†

Togliatti's rejection of insurrectionary politics had been gestating for a long time. While *la svolta di Salerno* was a specific reaction to a specific situation, it was influenced by a decade of momentous events. As far back as 1935, the fight against fascism had convinced Togliatti of the necessity for unity among all democratic elements. He was able to persuade Stalin, and the Seventh World Congress of the Comintern was the result. The Spanish Civil War confirmed Togliatti's judgment that democracy—even "bourgeois" democracy—was an indispensable ingredient in mobilizing people. Finally, the devastation attending World War II showed him that civil war would wreck a modern industrial country and would probably involve the superpowers. A showdown between them might well destroy Europe

* *Svolta* means "sharp turn." At Salerno in 1944 the Communist party line, which had been antimonarchical, turned toward temporary collaboration with the monarchy.

† This makes the more despicable Kissinger's line on an NBC Special News program that "when a Communist party has won power, it has never given it up." Since the issue *now* is PCI participation in government, exactly as in *1946*, he is deliberately making propaganda.[10]

physically, and the advent of the atom bomb turned the possibility into a probability.

When Togliatti had returned from Moscow, on March 27, 1944, he found a complex and insoluble political problem, inextricably intertwined with the fortunes of war: Italy's defeat, the Allies' progress, the German intervention. A few months previously, in July 1943, King Victor Emmanuel III had dismissed Mussolini, who was arrested and jailed. The new authoritarian government formed by the king, with Marshal Pietro Badoglio as premier, had little, if any, authority with the population.

The Badoglio government, following Allied directives, had reluctantly allowed the formation of political parties: Christian Democrat, Socialist, Communist, Liberal, Action, and Democratic Labor. By September all six parties had formed a coalition, the Committee for National Liberation (CLN). The CLN refused to accept the king, the crown prince, or any regent for the monarchy.

By Allied agreement, the British were in charge of military government in the liberated areas of Italy.[11] Churchill adamantly refused to jettison the monarchy. An ominous political impasse was created. Without the CLN, Badoglio could not govern Italy, could not control the partisan legions in the north, could not move to cobelligerency status—all crucial to Italian political independence. The British, for their part, would only relinquish their powers to a strong monarchical regime. Meanwhile, to further muddle the issues, a daring commando raid by the Nazi Colonel Otto Skorzeny had rescued Mussolini from his fortress prison and spirited him north to the town of Salò. There Mussolini set up a Nazi puppet government, the Italian Social Republic, with demagogic socialist slogans.[12] This was an added reason for a strong government in Rome.

The political stalemate was broken by Togliatti. He argued that the key issue was the regaining of political independence for the nation, freeing it from Allied military government and setting up a legal indigenous government. If the price was acceptance of a monarchy, that price had to be paid: let the issue be held in abeyance until after the war. *Within ten days,* he persuaded his own party and the other five parties of the CLN. After some negotiations, a new Badoglio government was formed, all parties participating. The king retired from public life and appointed his son, Crown Prince Humbert, lieutenant-general of the realm.

Abroad, liberals protested against the retention of a monarchy so deeply tainted by fascism. I remember the occasion well as I was about to go to Italy on an OSS mission and went up to Harvard University to say good-bye to an old friend and mentor, Professor Gaetano Salvemini. Salvemini, the outstanding antifascist in the

United States, was furious. He blamed Togliatti, who, as he saw it, was implementing Moscow's policies.*

In the Italy of 1945, on the other hand, I found complete acceptance of Togliatti's policy. He had not only persuaded his own comrades, but the tough, intelligent leaders of the other five parties—men like Pietro Nenni, Ferruccio Parri, Carlo Sforza, Giulio Rodino.† Togliatti's main goal was to get a new structure of government, a new constitution. Everything was subordinated to that end. One incident illustrates his alertness and tenacity. On April 6 Badoglio presented a text embodying the agreed compromises. Among various provisions it said that "immediately after the war, the Italian people shall elect a Chamber of Deputies." Togliatti had this changed to read: "Immediately after the war the Italian people shall elect a Constituent Assembly," thereby assuring that the first order of business in postwar Italy would be a new structure of government. In later years, Togliatti was asked what he felt his contribution was at the time. He replied, "I improved the grammar a little."[13]

The Italian Constitution that followed from Togliatti's grammar lesson is the most progressive in Europe and contains no barriers to socialism, in contrast, for example, to the United States Constitution, in which a business contract is sacrosanct. The sanctity of contracts has been the basic legal defense of capitalism and the ruling class understands very well the importance of legalisms, fighting aggressively for them, even for single words. For example, one of the major fights in the Italian Constituent Assembly was over the word "indissoluble" in reference to marriage. The Catholic Church and the right wanted the word in; the Communists led the fight to eliminate it. The left won, and when civil divorce became the subject of a law almost twenty five years later (1970), there was no constitutional obstacle.

Under the Italian Constitution all contracts are conditioned by the state; any contract can be declared illegal if it can be shown to be socially harmful.‡ Placing human rights above property rights undermines capitalism and facilitates a transition to socialism. When the Vatican takes a similar position, then imperialism and capitalism have suffered a heavy blow and the politics of Eurocommunism are to that extent made easier.**

---

* *La svolta* did correspond to Stalin's foreign policy (he had made an agreement with Churchill placing Italy in the capitalist camp), but was the result of Togliatti's independent analysis. Still, Stalin's line made Togliatti's task easier. It is ironic that the gestation of Eurocommunism should owe something to Josef Stalin.

† Nenni's famous remark on Togliatti's vision was made at this time. See page 57.

‡ This is not as "un-American" as it sounds; a contract to commit a crime is invalid in the United States.

** Provided, of course, the Vatican carries out this policy, as Bettazzi seems to think it will.

In Italy today there are no constitutional barriers to taxes on wealth as such or to laws, however drastic, affecting investments. The control of investments is the linchpin of Eurocommunist economic thinking because it is the heart of the capitalist process.

Marxists and capitalist alike have called capitalism the profit system, but the description, while true, is misleading, because it sounds as if the realization of profit is the point of decision. It is not. The point of decision is investment, which is indeed made on the *expectation* of profit. If the profit does not materialize, the capitalist goes bankrupt—and many do. PCI economists are not greatly concerned about profits; powerful trade unions, on the one hand, and the taxing power of the state, on the other, will enable a progressive government to deal with profits. They are vitally concerned in the control of investment: they want to say to a corporation, you may not invest in a high-rise apartment house on the Emerald Coast of Sardinia (which might return 20 percent), but you may invest in a shoe factory in Sicily (which might return 6 percent). This, of course, also means control of investments abroad.

*you wanna see a quick capital strike?*

This economic position has considerable political consequences, because the small businessman usually invests in his own business: he doesn't have a huge surplus of capital. It is Big Business that has a lot of capital and investment choices at home and abroad. Therefore laws controlling investments do not greatly offend small businessmen, who can be won over as allies to the working class; they are anathema to Big Business, which remains a bitter enemy of the PCI.[14]

The importance of the Italian Constitution is generally overlooked by foreigners, but for the Communists it is a crucial asset, socially, politically, and economically.[15] For example, the decentralization of the country into regions, which is perhaps the strongest force reshaping the country, was mandated in the Constitution. So is the equality of men and women before the law and the right of women to vote. *so why do the majority of ♀ vote DC?*

*The church has much influence w/ ♀*

The framing of the Constitution was no small matter: it owed a great deal to the unity forged in the resistance and a great deal also to the support of the Vatican. This in turn was due to the skill and perspicacity of Togliatti, who shaped a tacit deal between the Vatican and the PCI whereby the 1929 Concordat was maintained in Article 7. Togliatti's long-range views on Catholicism and his contribution to democratic politics made a profound impression. Two revered Catholic leaders of *Democrazia Cristiana*, Giorgio La Pira and Giuseppe Dossetti, who were working with Togliatti at the time, have testified: "Article 7 was not the result of tactical or manipulative considerations. . . . to understand the profound genesis of Article 7 one must keep in mind the entire Gramscian background in history, culture, and politics wherein Togliatti has his roots."[16]

Other Communist opponents paid tribute. Piero Calamandrei, a liberal historian, wrote of the years 1944–1945: "If, in those two years . . . national unity and the Republic withstood deceits and provocations [of the right], much of the credit is due to the stability, moderation, and yes, we must say it, the patriotism of the Communist leaders." Bocca, whose enmity to communism has been noted, and whose dislike of Togliatti is as obvious as his respect, quotes Calamandrei approvingly, adding his own judgment: "The Communists represented a progressive force, capitalism was conditioned for the better by their presence, and democracy [in Italy] made stronger."*[17]

When one examines what is going on in Italy today, one is impressed by the patience and prescience of Togliatti in making of the Constitution the climax of the resistance and the war of liberation, which Gruppi says "can be defined as an antifascist, democratic, and popular revolution." As a result, continues Gruppi, "the Constitution and its principles are profoundly rooted in the consciousness of the great bulk of the people. The Constitution has become a unifying legal platform of democratic struggle; in a certain sense, it has become a political force."[18]

It would be too simple to say that Togliatti in 1946 could foresee the developments of 1980, too simple to see a linear connection between *la svolta di Salerno* and Eurocommunism. Yet the *organic* connection is there. We have the testimony of Edvard Kardelj, theoretician of the Yugoslav party and, until his death in 1979, Tito's closest collaborator. His memoirs, published in February 1980, deal at length with Togliatti and his ideas.[18a] Kardelj met with Togliatti in Rome, October 16 and 17, 1944, and he recalls: "He had already developed those theses which today are called 'the historic compromise,' though not known then by this phrase. He maintained that the Communist party had to defend the democratic system not only in alliance with the Socialist, but with all other social forces, because only thus could Communists strengthen the position of the working class in Italy and make of it a real political force." Kardelj goes on to present Togliatti as a precursor of Eurocommunism. "When I think back to what Togliatti told me then [in 1944], I must conclude that he had expounded with great clarity those theses which later were to be called 'Eurocommunism.' "[18b]

Kardelj, with 20–20 hindsight, may give undue credit. The Italian road to socialism has not been, nor will it be, a paved highway, smoothly engineered; on the contrary, it has been full of twists and turns, of detours and gaps, sharp setbacks and discontinuities such as

* These sentiments, of course, bolster the contention of left Marxists that Eurocommunism is a subtle way to save capitalism. The only answer lies in the future, to see which side wins: "Who, Whom," as Lenin put it.

the Moro assassination and the 1979 drop in PCI votes. Nevertheless, one can say that there was a coherence in Togliatti's vision and development, which, a decade after his death, was given explicit formulation by Berlinguer.

The two most important gaps or discontinuities on the Italian road to socialism are those between Gramsci of the twenties and Togliatti of the forties; the second is between Togliatti's line before 1956 and his line from then to his death. The first discontinuity has to do with the dictatorship of the proletariat and the nature of the party. This has been discussed in Chapter 2: Gramsci was a Leninist, accepted the Comintern and the dictatorship of the proletariat. Togliatti in 1944 launched a mass party of a new type embedded in democracy and the plurality of parties. Togliatti was against civil war, but for many years he tolerated, if he did not encourage, a paramilitary network which was a residue of the resistance. It was formed by former partisans who had kept their weapons in hiding. The line has been called *"doppiezza"* by Italian historians such as Bocca.* The word literally means "duplicity," but the English translation is too strong, for there was nothing secret about the existence of the armed sector. *Doppiezza* can be best rendered as a "two-track policy"; on one side, a commitment to democracy, on the other, an ability to resort to arms. After American pressure forced the PCI out of the government in 1947 and it looked as if the Cold War might become a hot war, Togliatti gave an explicit warning to the government in a speech to the Chamber of Deputies on July 10, 1948: "If our country should be dragged into war, we know our duty. To an imperialist war the answer is a revolt, an insurrection in defense of peace, independence, and the future of our country."

Carlo Andreoni, a Social-Democrat, the editor of *L'Umanità*, had answered: "To the Russian Togliatti's speech of insurrection we say . . . that *before* the Communists can complete their treason . . . the government of the Republic and the majority of the Italian people will nail Togliatti and his accomplices to the wall . . . and we won't nail them metaphorically."[20]

After 1956, however, the *droppiezza* policy receded, and it finally disappeared completely. The PCI today envisages armed struggle only as an answer to a fascist coup, an answer given not by the PCI alone but by the population as a whole, a replay of the resistance. By the time Togliatti died in 1964 the line of a broad alliance between the Catholic masses and the left was firmly in place. Berlinguer, Togliatti's disciple, was only making explicit his teacher's long-range policies when he coined the phrase, *il compromesso storico*, in September, 1973.[21]

---

* Bocca, however, makes it clear that he does not use the term in a pejorative sense, as an epithet.[19]

The phrase, and the policy, of *il compromesso storico* ("the historic compromise") has been widely misunderstood in Italy and abroad. It has been interpreted narrowly to mean a parliamentary maneuver, a coalition cabinet of the Christian Democrats and the Communists—a power condominium which would control the country and to which other parties, particularly the Socialist party, would have to adhere, *faute de mieux*. Moreover, since the phrase was coined by Berlinguer in his analysis of the neofascist coup in Chile against the Allende government, it was colored by those events and interpreted as a defensive tactic of the PCI against potential right-wing and CIA destabilization. The PCI's emphasis on the parliamentary coalition, and its reluctance in 1978 to bring down the government despite the provocations, lent some credence to this analysis, so that when the PCI lost four percentage points in the election of June 3, 1979, almost all observers chorused: *il compromesso storico* is dead. *revisionism dies hard*

The reports of death were vastly exaggerated. In August 1979 in an editorial in *Rinascita* and in an interview with the German magazine *Stern* (reprinted in *Epoca*) Berlinguer made clear that *il compromesso* was very much alive and remained the fundamental strategy of the PCI. He tried once more to place *il compromesso* in historical perspective. It was not a parliamentary tactic: "The historic compromise," he told *Stern*, "is not a relationship between the PCI and the DC nor is it a formula of government. The historic compromise is a strategy that can go ahead without the collaboration of Communists and Christian Democrats within the government. We think of it as an understanding and a coming-together of the great popular currents in Italian life: the Communists, the Socialists, the Catholics. The Catholic component is only in part represented by Christian Democracy."[22]

In the *Rinascita* editorial Berlinguer recalled one of Togliatti's editorials in the same review thirty-three years before, in August 1946. "Togliatti defined the phrase of '*a precise compromise*' between 'the great wings' (the progressive and the conservative) of 'the antifascist front.' He promised that the war of liberation, the Republic, and the Constituent Assembly '*were objectives that must be reached at any cost, and before all else.*' . . . Togliatti asserted that this compromise had established and furthered the perspective '*of the democratization of the country in its entirety.*' . . . " (Berlinguer's italics.)[23]

*Il compromesso storico* is the latest expression, shaped by fifty years of struggle, of Gramsci's insight that the popular currents in Italian life—the Catholic, the Socialist, and the Communist—must be reconciled if the nation is to be unified, the welfare of the people assured, and reaction isolated.[24] That vision was given flesh by Togliatti in the forties and fifties and by Longo and Berlinguer in the sixties and seventies. Despite all detours and discontinuities, the red thread from Gramsci to Berlinguer, however frayed, is clearly discernible. And the hand of the weaver is Togliatti's.[25]

*and fading to pink*

Togliatti is an ideal prism through which Eurocommunism can be understood, refracting aspects and nuances of its origins and development. His political life was polarized between Stalin and Gramsci; as time goes by, these two—Stalin and Gramsci—emerge as the great antagonists within Marxism after Lenin. Togliatti, of course, was not alone: There was a party—often a cantankerous one—but he dominated the opposition by his intellect, personality, and political savvy. For example, he took steps to disseminate his ideas in depth. "Theoretical work," said Togliatti, "cannot and must not, be disassociated from political struggle." One of the first things he did after his return was to launch the theoretical organ of the PCI, *Rinascita* (Renascence), staffed by the brightest young minds in the movement.* Simultaneously, he moved to bring forward the younger generation, Eugenio Reale, Paolo Ricci, Pietro Ingrao, Giorgio Napolitano, including one young man who at twenty-five was made head of the Communist Youth—Enrico Berlinguer, today the general secretary of the PCI.

After 1948 the Italian people increasingly turned to the Communist party. The chart-line of its influence zoomed, from a vote of 19 percent in 1946 to 34.5 percent in 1976. The vote dropped in the 1979 election, but until that time, over a thirty-year period, it had increased with every election.[27] The increase reflected the growth of the Communist presence in every aspect of Italian life. There isn't a town or village, a school or a factory, a union local or a sports club, where there aren't some Communists. In all newspapers, magazines, radio and television networks, whether owned by the Church, state, or Big Business, Communists are treated with respect, their proposals discussed and given due consideration. Most of the artists and writers of Italy are either Communist or sympathetic to communism. At the very least, they vote Communist. The same is true of professors, doctors, lawyers, and other professionals. Cultural hegemony, so stressed by Gramsci, is becoming a fact; there are only two philosophies in Italy today, Catholicism and Marxism. As has been noted, everyone in Italy, from the pope on down, seems to have read, or is reading, Marxist writings. The hegemony goes hand in hand with the popular belief that the PCI is committed to the democratic process, as Bocca and Calamandrei acknowledge. The myriad ways in which the PCI is extending democracy are detailed in Part II of this book, but its power as a weapon of class struggle is an integral part of

*the point is not to understand history but to change it.*

---

*    According to Bocca, "the first four issues were exemplary and made an enormous impression: the cultural level was very high, higher than that ever reached by an Italian political journal, and the seduction it exerted on Italian intellectuals was very strong indeed."[26]

*democracy is the best possible political shell for capitalism—L*

Eurocommunism. I saw it through the eyes of a DC politician in the city of Bologna, a city which has been governed by a Communist mayor for thirty years.

*I walked into the courtyard of the Palazzo d'Accursio, an old archi- tectural gem in the heart of Bologna. It is the seat of the municipal government: mayor's office, ceremonial hall, and meeting room of the city council. The front door is bronze, modern, immaculate, its only ornamentation being the massive handles in the shape of the city seal. One enters and is in another world: outside, the ancient stone columns of the porticoes and the medieval cobblestones; inside, an elegant modern decor, a carpeted staircase with a graceful aluminium rail, soft lights, white plaster walls. Only the ceremonial hall has been preserved from the old days, a movie set of rich brocades, red carpet, and gilt chairs.*

*The day before, I had talked to Renato Zangheri, the Communist mayor, and he had suggested that, as an antidote, I should talk to Signor Colletta, leader of the DC opposition on the city council.*[28] *There was a council meeting scheduled for the following evening, and if I came a little early Colletta would talk to me.*

*Colletta appeared punctually and led me into the ceremonial hall, closing the doors. We sat at the corner of a long table in the vast space, like two diplomats wary of one another—he because Zangheri had made the appointment; I, because I hoped he would talk freely. My concern was unfounded. As soon as I mentioned that* Bologna rossa *had a reputation throughout Europe as a well-run city, he was off in a torrent of words.*

*"Of course, it's well run, and why? Because we, the DC opposi- tion, keep the Communists on their toes. We watch them like hawks, and so do the papers. They don't dare have scandals." I couldn't resist pointing out that other cities, and the national government run by the DC, also watched by people and papers, had an unending series of scandals—favoritism, nepotism, bribes, embezzlements, and frauds of all kinds. "Of course," he replied, "there are some scandals—just like you have in America, but they are vastly exagger- ated.\* Besides we are fighting corruption."*

*"But you've been in power for thirty years. Why haven't you done so before?"*

*He waved the question aside and went on. "The Communists will tell you all the wonderful things they have done in Bologna, but they*

---

\* Far from being exaggerated, DC scandals are huge and commonplace. *La Civiltà cattolica* called them *"chain scandals.* . . . The DC must not cover them up if it wants to recover the confidence of Italians, a confidence which is today so profoundly shaken." Peter Nichols used the same phrase· "From the end of the war onwards, Italy has continued to produce a chain of scandals."[29]

*don't tell you how much they have spent. The interest alone on our bonds is $60 million a year!* Because we try to keep expenditures down, be businesslike, we are attacked."*

*"But aren't other cities, with DC governments, in the same situation?"*

*"Of course. The Communists create it. Look, if a Communist town has a public swimming pool, then the next town wants one too, and if the DC mayor doesn't give it to them, they'll get a Communist mayor. If Communists give day-care centers, the DC has to give them too. It's a kind of blackmail."*

The idea that people pressing their city government for social services is akin to blackmail had a strange ring to American ears, but I said nothing. I did remark that this escalation of competition sounded like a good argument for a national coalition to achieve austerity.

*"Never. Once you let the Communists into the government, they'll never leave."*

I asked him if he thought they would use force to stay in power.

*"Oh, no, they're too clever for that. The people would turn against them; so would the army. No, they'll do it democratically. They'll pick an issue, like controlling investments—which means the end of private enterprise—and if we vote against it, they'll say we're for Big Business, thereby getting more votes for themselves."*

*"Well, then, what should the DC do?"*

*"Keep them out at all costs. They are nibbling at us all the time. I know them well, and they are diabolically clever."* For an instant he lost control, and his hatred flashed. *"They burned my father's house in the general strike of 1948 because he was the DC mayor of the town."*†

Colletta belongs to the right wing of the DC, which, although losing ground, is still extremely strong in the middle echelons of the party. Church and patronage are the twin pillars of the *Democrazia Cristiana,* and these middle layers are deeply influenced by the integralists. To the extent that integralists lose within the hierarchy, people like Colletta will undoubedly move to a more conciliatory position. And the integralists are on the defensive. Willy-nilly, because of the cities and regions the Communists govern, the prelates have to deal with them. This makes them think, and as I talked to men on both

---

* Mayor Zangheri had given me the same figure the day before. He admits they have spent a lot of money, but so have other cities run by the DC. "The difference," he said, "is that we have something to show for the money and they haven't. It's been frittered away through corruption and bad management."

† Two other people told me of beatings and burnings in their families in 1948. One was the integralist bishop I've already mentioned, the other a railway stationmaster. Both, of course, are bitter anti-Communists.

sides—Professors Adriano Bausola, Gianfranco Morra, and Augusto Del Noce on the integralist side and Cardinal Pellegrino, Bishop Bettazzi and Father Sorge on the conciliar side—I was struck by the high level of their arguments.

While the two world views of Marxism and Catholicism, one immanent and the other transcendental, are *in theory* irreconcilable, in practice the profound wisdom of Pope John has made a distinction between doctrines and historical movements. *Pacem in Terris* states: "Doctrines, once elaborated and defined, remain forever the same; but the movements mentioned [historical movements], acting on historical situations incessantly evolving, cannot avoid the influence of the times, hence cannot help but change—even unto profound mutations."* Then the great self-fulfilling prophecy: "It may happen that an event or an encounter of a practical nature, which yesterday was considered inopportune or not fecund, may today, tomorrow, become so."[30]

Tomorrow is here today, and so we read in *La Civiltà cattolica,* the major theoretical journal run by the Jesuits, in a report by its editor, Father Sorge: "It is urgent to clearly define what relation Catholic expectations have to other, particularly Marxist, expectations. . . . Certainly Marxism appears to many the greatest expectation man has ever conceived to free himself by his own efforts. . . . Marxism has helped to develop in the world the hope of liberation, in itself truthful and good, that must not be deluded. The fatal error is in its methods and solutions. . . . The hope of a new society, a participating and tolerant society that refutes the individualism of bourgeois liberalism, is in itself good and true."[31]

Such abstruse verbiage may seem placid and tepid to most Americans, but to Italian Catholics it was earthshaking. Imagine granting any validity to Marxism, however circumscribed!

Sorge's attitude is anathema to the integralists, in part because his editorial position gives his views prestige and influence. Furthermore the Jesuits, the intellectuals of the Church, have always taken the long view and realize that the strength of the Church, and its future, lies in adaption—the opposite position of the integralists.[32] The integralists motto could be: I break but I will not bend, whereas the motto of Pope John and the Jesuits could well be: Bend but don't break.

Professor Morra said to me in sharp tones, "Father Sorge is the only person who scrambles all the various positions within the Church—according to the traditions of his order, the Jesuit order. In Father Sorge you will find everything, and its opposite. Forgive me if I speak frankly."

* Compare this passage with Togliatti's almost identical observations made years before. See page 70.

Professor Morra is forty-seven years old, a brilliant, erudite man, often on the Vatican Radio, embattled in speeches and writings. He smells defeat. He gave me a copy of his book, *Il Marxismo e la religione* (Marxism and religion), saying: "There, the book analyzes everything—the change in ACLI, Christians for Socialism—all these things which have brought about the present situation." He saw the future in apocalyptic terms, writing in the book, "The destiny of religion appears difficult and tragic. It faces an agonizing *aut-aut:* either it comes to terms with the modern epoch, setting aside its religious character, thus obtaining a small, ineffectual, sterile space in the culture . . . or it remains firm to its own supernatural vocation, paying for its faithful and heroic coherence the price of emargination and persecution."[33]

The *opposition* to Communism is adamant. But the *hatred* is directed against the Enlightenment of four hundred years ago and the Reformation which culminated in the lay state of 1870. Much like the American South, which was still fighting the Civil War until recently, these men are fighting anew the battles of the past. The secularization of society is the modern evil, of which Marxism is only a product.

The sense of actuality in talking about the Enlightenment among integralists is startling. One can almost hear them arguing with Voltaire and Rousseau in the same terms they argue with the liberal anticlericals of today—men like Senator Eugenio Reale of the Republican Party. The integralist bishop I've mentioned said to me: "It isn't the Communists that worry us; it's the liberals. One can always reason with the Communists."

Despite his unyielding stand, Morra was very helpful, giving me introductions not only to other integralists, like Bausola and Del Noce, but also to his opponents like Luigi Pedrazzi, Giuseppe Lazzati (rector of the Catholic University of the Sacred Heart), Cardinal Pellegrino and others. This intellectual chivalry was usual throughout Italy: Communists opened doors to Socialists and Christian Democrats and vice-versa. Manlio, the conservative, praised Luigi Spaventa, economist and deputy on the PCI ticket; Napolitano, the Communist, praised Del Noce, the integralist: "A brilliant man, well worth seeing."

*Augusto Del Noce is the acknowledged intellectual leader of the integralists.[34] He lives in the Parioli district of Rome, the upper-class area, and his apartment is right out of the eighteenth century, with gilt chairs and an ormolu clock. A plump, bouncy fellow, he reminded me of Professor Alfred Whitehead. When I told him that Napolitano had praised him, he shook himself delightedly, like a tomtit. "Did he really? Well, well, did he really?" I thought to myself: "Carl, my man, you are witnessing cultural hegemony in action."*

*Over a neat whiskey we locked horns. How could one work with Communists, he wanted to know, given their Gramscian substitution theory? Gramsci had thought that just as Catholicism had become the world view of the people, embedded in their common sense, people would also absorb Marxism through their daily struggles to live decently. Some day, he argued, Marxism would become embedded in the popular wisdom.*

*My response was that what Gramsci believed was immaterial: "If there exists a God and He is reflected in man's soul, then it doesn't matter what the Communists think. They can never wipe out God or men's souls. Martyrdom will only strengthen belief. In a sense, it's Pascal's wager in reverse: the Church has nothing to lose."*

*"True, true, I agree," he said. "But if they come into power, they will use coercion—and why should we risk martyrdom?"*

*"Come now. They have not come to power. They want a joint government of all parties. They have said they reject violence and dictatorship. Do you doubt them?"*

*"I don't doubt their sincerity. No, I don't. But I doubt their intelligence. I think they will be forced into coercive means to straighten out the economy, etc."*

*"Then the Christian Democrats will throw them out."*

*"And if they don't go?"*

*"They went in 1948, when they had arms. Besides, you have the army, the* carabinieri, *and the police."*

*"The police," he snorted. "They are organizing a left-wing union."*

*I laughed. "You should have paid them a living wage."*

*We got nowhere, but we had a good time. When I left, he gave me a copy of his book* L'Eurocomunismo e l'Italia *(Eurocommunism and Italy), inscribing it: "To Carlo Marzani, with a lively friendship that has exploded during a most agreeable visit on December 13, 1977."*

*Leafing through it, I saw it was composed of articles published throughout 1975 in* Il Popolo, *the DC paper. Del Noce said, "Fanfani suggested they be published as good propaganda for the 1976 elections." I thought to myself: These professors, left or right, know what they're doing.*[35]

On the conciliar side, the most impressive men are Michele Cardinal Pellegrino and Luigi Bettazzi, bishop of Ivrea. They are neighbors, some fifty miles apart, and the day I met Cardinal Pellegrino I also visited Bishop Bettazzi.

Ivrea is the original home and present headquarters of Olivetti, the far-flung corporation which began by manufacturing typewriters and went on to calculators, computers, and much of modern electronic wizardry.[36] Its first factory, a grim nineteenth-century brick building, is still in use. The town, heavily industrialized, retains an aura of the past, and the diocesean office is in a centuries-old building, accessible through a walled courtyard, behind a church. On the first floor are the bishop's living quarters. We met in his study, a spacious, elegant, airy room, tall windows reaching from ceiling to floor.

In appearance, speech, and manner, Bettazzi is wholly modern, just as Pellegrino recalls another epoch. His speech is more direct than allusive, his gestures more vivid than serene. He exudes more friendliness than kindliness, and tends to the hearty laugh rather than the slow smile and gentle chuckle. Yet he and Pellegrino, a generation apart, share an openness of mind, an audacity of concepts, and a fearlessness towards the future rooted in the conviction of God's presence and His love, mercy, and grace. Now in his mid-fifties, Bettazzi was forty when he was greatly influenced by Pellegrino. He continues to build on the work of his elder. A shrewd man, with brilliant political savvy, he is totally dedicated to his church, committed to its salvation through *aggiornamento*.

Theologically, he is as intransigeant as Morra, who, in fact, quotes him in his book: "The bishop must say to Communists—or at least to the Christians who sympathize with the Communists—that it is an absurdity to believe in God and yet profess materialistism, an atheistic doctrine."[37]

Bettazzi walks confidently where orthodox angels fear to tread. It was he who precipitated the great continuing debate between Communists and Catholics, a debate which is clarifying positions and putting pressures on *both* the Communist party and the Church. His unlikely partner in this daring venture was Enrico Berlinguer, general secretary of the PCI. What Bettazzi did was to write an open letter to the party immediately after the 1976 elections—a long, closely reasoned, courteous letter asking critical questions; what Berlinguer did, a year later, was to reply—a long, closely reasoned, courteous letter giving critical answers. It was a duet reminiscent of the exchanges between Pope John and Togliatti, except that Bettazzi and Berlinguer were addressing each other directly. Willy-nilly, it forced both the Church hierarchy and the party to re-examine and rethink their positions. Furthermore, it involved the general population.[38]

*In the space of a few days I attended two debates on the subject: one at Conigliano del Veneto and the other at Fabbrizzo, in the province of Piedmont. At both the speakers were a Christian Democrat, a Communist, a Socialist, and a member of ACLI,\* and the audience*

---

\* ACLI: *Associazioni Cristiane dei Lavoratori Italiani* (Christian [read: Catholic] Associations of Italian Workers). Originally developed to hinder unionization, it is now chiefly social in purpose. Its history is traced below, in Chapter 6.

*was about evenly divided, left and right. The exchange of letters provided a springboard for discussing the Communist intentions. The meeting at Conigliano turned into a fascinating duel between the DC deputy, Onorevole (Honorable) Lino Innocenti, a dapper, skilled parliamentarian, and Rino Serri, PCI regional secretary and member of the national directorate of the party, a man in his late thirties, lean and sharp. The deputy used the letters as springboard for a disquisition on Marxism, full of quotes from Marx, Engels, and Lenin, to show that Marxism and religion were not compatible; then he went on to say that, of course, if the Italian party was abandoning Marxism, then Catholics could in theory work together with Communists. From this position he moved to a political question: 'What guarantees could the party give that, if voted out of office, it would go peacefully?*

*The Socialist senator answered the theoretical arguments of the DC speaker—matching quote for quote, then took up the question of Communist sincerity. He had fought with them in the resistance, he said. They were serious people and unquestioned patriots. As for leaving the government peacefully, they had already proven that in 1947.*

*The Communist Serri brushed aside the issue of guarantees. What guarantees could the party give except its performance over thirty years, which must be persuasive, inasmuch as one third of the people were voting Communist. He then spent considerable time on Law 382, mentioned in the letters,\* and went on to stress the crisis in the country and what the PCI would do about it in specific detail.*

*Finally, he touched on the fact that the party was changing. It is true, he said to Innocenti, who was sitting next to him, that the party had changed on many issues, as Innocenti had pointed out, but now he wanted to say to him directly: "We have changed and we are changing, but you, you of the DC, when are you going to change?"*

*The audience, whose applause had been partisan up to this point, now exploded in a flurry of hand-clapping and foot-stamping that was a clear political demonstration uniting Communists, Socialists, and Christian Democrats.*[39]

*Later, Serri and some twenty men and women, local party leaders, got together around a table in the back room of a restaurant for wine, bread, bean soup, and cold cuts. It was midnight by then, and Serri hadn't eaten all day. He was tired, but frisky and exuberant. "You're like an old war horse," I said to him. "An evening like this recharges you." He grinned like a street urchin: "It does, it does. We made a dent here tonight. Did you hear that clapping?" When I said*

---

\* Law 382 continued the process of decentralizing the nation, giving to the regions control of education, health, and welfare institutions. There was a good deal of bargaining going on as to which institutions, previously administered by the Church with state subsidies, should now pass to the regions.

*that I judged at least half of the audience to be Christian Democrats,
everyone agreed.*\*

*Serri asked me if I thought he had been too rough on Innocenti,
and I said no, he had been sharp but not hostile. He nodded, pleased:
"I held back, you know—I didn't want to offend him. He's a decent
man, and his coming to the debate tonight shows it. If he feels his
people are ready, he'll be more open toward us."*

*The impromptu gathering broke up at three in the morning, and a
comrade drove us back to Venice, a forty-five-minute drive. I dozed
while they talked party matters, and once I heard the driver say with
pride: "I did six weeks at Frattochie." In Venice, Serri and I took a
vaporino to a landing near my hotel, which was also near Serri's
home. "Come to my headquarters at noon," he said on the ferry.
"There's a man you ought to meet. He's a devout Catholic, still on
the national council of ACLI, and he has just become a party
functionary." As we were saying good-night, I asked him: "Bettazzi's letter has been a great help to the party, hasn't it?" When he
nodded, I said, "Why did he do it?" "Because," said Serri quietly,
"he's a good Catholic and a good Italian."*

Bettazzi's letter gave full credit to the Communist party for its
honesty and dedication, noted the presence of "Catholic" candidates
elected on Communist tickets, and referred to the hierarchy's prudent
reaction to this new phenomenon. He was impressed by the party's
independence from "foreign experiences" and hoped it would continue. Somewhere in the middle of the letter he inserted a casual but
important paragraph in which he asked the party not to hold hostage
Catholic institutions (schools, hospitals, etc.): "I do not ask this as a
bishop, but I do as a citizen who loves his country." By "hostage"
Bettazzi was referring to Law 382, by which the regions could control
Catholic charities.

Berlinguer replied a year later, clearly having waited for a
propitious political situation, such as developed in Italy during after
July 1977 when the "six-party agreement" had been developed.
Furthermore, Law 382 was going into effect, making urgent a
clarification of positions. Matching the prelate in courtesy, Berlinguer
asserted that Article 2 of the party statutes from the Fifth Congress of
the PCI (1946) explicitly stated that a member need accept *only* the
political program of the party and *not* its ideology: "Does the Italian

---

\* The Communists are constantly assessing the mood of the population and its trends.
Sometimes the occasion is spectacular: in September in the city of Modena took place a week-long
festival for *L'Unità;* at the same time, by coincidence or competition, the Church held a week-long
Eucharistic Congress in the city of Pescara. On the Saturday climaxing the events, Berlinguer
spoke in Modena and the Pope in Pescara. Berlinguer drew a crowd of 400,000 people; the Pope
150,000. The figures do not provide a fair test, however, because the weather was balmy in Modena;
it rained all day in Pescara.[40]

Communist party, as such, that is, as a political organization, explicitly profess Marxist ideology—an atheistic, materialist philosophy? Precisely because of the explanations given above, I would answer no."[41]

On the key question of "hostages," he gave an unequivocal answer: The old liberal state had been so remiss in caring for people's needs that many private institutions, lay and religious, had filled the gaps in education, day-care centers, hospitals, clinics, old-age homes, welfare aid of all kinds; but the democratic state envisaged by the party would assume in full those responsibilities. Ergo, there was no place for private institutions.* However, he added, state institutions would be run democratically (full participation of teachers, students, medical staff, patients, etc.), and within them both the faithful and the hierarchy would have full expression and participation.

The exchange created an enormous stir. *L' Osservatore romano* cautioned that Berlinguer's reply, ostensibly directed at Bettazzi, was really directed to the episcopate, which should therefore be the one to answer. Bettazzi commented to me on this: "I couldn't agree more; it is just what I had hoped." The Vatican paper pointed out that while Article 2 said anyone could be a party member without accepting Marxism, Berlinguer hadn't talked about Article 5, which urged members to study Marxism-Leninism," an omission so glaring that it cannot be dismissed as a simple oversight."[42]

The reference to the nature of the party membership by the papal organ illustrates the symbiosis between the Church and the PCI. Just as Communists influence the Church, the Church influences the party. The party had already dropped the phrase "Marxism-Leninism" from its writings; the Fifteenth Congress, in May 1979, dropped both the phrase and Article 5 from the statutes.[43]

The present Communist party of Italy is a mass party, as much a part of the population as fishes are a part of the sea. In the creation of a mass party, Togliatti most clearly shows the influence of his country on his thought: he irradiated one hundred years of Marxism into two thousand years of Catholicism, a piece of alchemy that no one but an Italian could have achieved. It was no accident that Togliatti survived Stalin's wholesale exterminations, no accident that he kept within himself a hard core of detachment, criticism, and judgment.†

Togliatti was the heir to three thousand years of uninterrupted political life by Italians under all kinds of circumstances—at various times the subjugators and the subjugated, empire builders and miser-

---

* Berlinguer did not mean, of course, that institutions *paid for by the Church*—seminaries, for example—could not exist: he meant institutions open to the public and subsidized by the state.

† This is fully recognized by Giorgio Bocca, no friend to Togliatti.[44]

able emigrants, mountebanks and geniuses. Italian skepticism, curiosity, and love of beauty gave Europe the Renaissance, and since then Italy has not been the least civilized nation in regard to art. It is in the art of politics that she has established a clear primacy, whether in Roman law or political theory—Caesar, Machiavelli, Vico, Pareto, Gramsci. Italian history has made politics a national pastime.

Three thousand years of vicissitudes have created a race of hot-tempered, warm-hearted *realists;* there are few Don Quixotes in Italian history—and few Sancho Panzas. Together with this realism goes a profound admiration and appreciation of intelligence, "perhaps the only form of popular chauvinism in Italy." The observation is Gramsci's, and one can understand why the Englishman Nichols says that Italy today *"may renew its historical function of deeply influencing the rest of the West."* (Italics added.)[45]

This historical function was envisaged by Gramsci as a continuation, in modern terms, of the universalism of the Roman Empire and of the Catholic Church. Writing forty-five years before Nichols, he said: "The Italian people is the one which 'nationalistically' is most interested in internationalism. Not only the worker but the peasant, particularly the peasant of the south. To collaborate in shaping the world economically in a unified manner is in the tradition of Italian history and the Italian people. . . . The civilizing mission of the Italian people is to renew Roman and medieval cosmopolitanism, only in its modern and most advanced form. Let it be as a proletarian nation; proletarian because it has been the reserve army of foreign capitalists. . . . Precisely for this reason, it must insert itself in the front of the modern struggle to reorganize also the non-Italian world."[46]

*I stood with a dear friend, Paula, in the Roman Forum of a soft September afternoon, a slight breeze gentling the warmth of the sun. We were standing on a landing of the iron stairs leading down to the tomb of Romulus.\* At the landing, my head was at ground level, and I could gaze all around where the Forum spreads against a hill that keeps going up, beyond the Forum's limits.*

*Looking down some fifteen feet below the landing I could see the rough-hewn black tombstone, circa 700 B.C., and then glance up at the tufa brick of the Senate house of the Republic (still B.C.). A few feet higher are the marble columns, pediments, and other remnants of temples from the days of the Caesars. Progressively higher up the hill I could see a circling cobblestone road from the Dark Ages, a dark brown medieval church, an eighteenth-century palace, and, way on top, a modern villa, straight out of Corbusier.*

---

\* That's what it's called; but experts think it is the burial place of Romulus's foster parents.

*Within the compass of a glance, a whole civilization could be felt almost physically. When London, Paris, and Prague were mud villages, Rome was a proud city. I felt within me, arising irresistibly, the pride of birth:* Civis romanus sum! *As I looked at the Senate where Cicero denounced Cataline and thought of the continuity—even that of its seal\*—I said to my friend that I could see a direct line between Cicero and Gramsci.*

*Paula is a New York woman married to an Italian. She has a substantial knowledge of Italy, its language, art, and history, so she laughed sympathetically and said:* "Now, that's a charming literary conceit."

"No, no," *I said.* "I mean it seriously."

"Oh, come off it; it's nonsense."

"It is not."

*We had been walking along the Via Sacra of the Forum, and as we came to the end, going up the old brick steps, Paula was a few steps ahead. She stopped and turned and spoke down at me with a hint of anger.*

"Don't be stubborn, Carlo! You are so wrapped up in Gramsci, you'll find a direct line between him and Jesus Christ."

"That, too," *I said,* "although not so direct. But you listen to me—and don't be so stubborn yourself. There could be no Gramsci without Vico, Pareto, and Machiavelli, you agree to that?" *She did.* "Okay, now you couldn't have had Machiavelli without all the city-states and their politics going straight back to Dante and De Monarchia—even the Divine Comedy is a political tract."

"Some tract!"

"Well, you certainly couldn't have Dante without the Church, and that takes you right to Constantine, then back through the emperors to Julius Caesar, and there you are with Cicero."

*My friend laughed.* "You are a Jesuit."

"Not at all," *I said.* "A Roman."

*(Padre, I confess I've sinned, the sin of excessive pride. Not pride of tribe but of culture, not of family but of birthplace.)*

---

\* The Roman Senate seal "S.P.Q.R." has remained the seal of the city of Rome, and is stamped on all city property—manhole covers, park benches, water-main valves, and so on. It stands for *Senatus Populusque Romanus*, The Senate and the People of Rome.

# PART TWO

# The Italian Road
# to Socialism

# CHAPTER 6

# When Women Counted

WOMEN in Italy have always been second-class citizens.[1] In the south particularly, a woman was a man's chattel. In bitter contrast, the more the woman bore the burden of poverty and unemployment, the more she scrimped and slaved to hold the family together and raise the children, the less she counted. She had no influence on the laws and mores of the country. Until 1947 she had no vote, and for decades thereafter that vote was controlled by men, by father, brother, parish priest.

For centuries, for milleniums, it was a male world, with male-made laws stretched by male judges to the limits of absurdity. As late as 1966, for example, the Ninth Section of the Civil Tribunal of Milan—a modern northern city—decreed that a woman who made her husband wash dishes and do other domestic chores offended his dignity so deeply that the offense was proper ground for legal separation.[2] The laws were pitilessly one-sided: Adultery was a crime for women, not for men. Although legally separated, the woman could be charged with adultery by her absent spouse and sentenced to three months in jail. The separated husband still had the right to read her letters and to prohibit her from seeing people of whom he disapproved. He could live openly with another woman.

A woman had no property rights: she couldn't even take her own wedding dress if she left home. Under certain conditions, she had no right to life. Under Article 587 of the Penal Code a man could kill or wound with quasi impunity a wife, a sister, or a daughter caught with another man.[3] Male judges interpreted this statute in incredibly permissive terms. For centuries women accepted these dispositions as natural, proper, and just.

119

It is history's sardonic jest that this oppressed half of humanity, which for so long had counted for so little, should administer a profound shock to the male-dominated politics of Europe and the world, opening the door to the greatest contemporary challenge to the West's status quo, namely Eurocommunism. Eurocommunism will stand or fall with the Italian experience; it is there that many of its concepts were developed, it is there that a political strategy embodying these concepts has shown promise, and it is there that the tactics and organization for that strategy have been tested in action.

The long-term strategy of Eurocommunism is to extend democracy to its furthest limits, moving from politics to economics, in the process effecting a peaceful transition from capitalism to socialism. In Italy, this strategy was envisaged by Togliatti as far back as 1944, in *la svolta di Salerno,* and carried through with skill and tenacity. Through an extension of democratic participation in every field and an involvement of masses of people, Togliatti believed that an inimical Vatican and its political ally, *Democrazia Cristiana,* could be brought willy-nilly to an alliance with the Communists and Socialists. This alliance would govern Italy, transforming its institutions to fit a changing world. Progress was slow but persistent, and it could be gauged by the popular vote in national and local elections. By 1972 the Communist vote rose to 27 percent but the Christian Democrats could still put together a majority solid enough for them to govern with right-wing allies. In 1976 the Communist vote reached 34.5 percent to the Christian Democrats 38.8 percent; neither party could now govern without the acquiescence of the other.[4] Peter Nichols, Rome correspondent of the London *Times,* called this vote one of the most important, if not *the* most important of postwar elections. It impelled him to write *The Italian Decision,* in which he says, "I have tried to give a picture of an extremely complex country at a particularly complex moment of its history, a moment which may renew its *historical function of deeply influencing the rest of the West."* (Italics added.)[5]

The event that triggered the enormous gains of the PCI in 1976 was the referendum on divorce of 1974. In that referendum the women played a decisive role. If and when Communists enter the Italian government and thereby set up a crucial test for Eurocommunism, the referendum of 1974 will always be considered the point of departure, and the election of 1976 the hinge of Italian politics. The women, one might say, provided the pin of the hinge.

After the election, the Communists won the presidency of the Chamber of Deputies as well as the chairmanship of several important parliamentary committees, partners in a broad coalition of six parties, three major (DC, PCI, and PSI) and three minor (PLI, PRI, and

PSDI).* The Communists did not take a place in the cabinet, but they supported the government by abstaining from voting against it on motions of confidence.† The architect of this semialliance was Aldo Moro, president of the DC. With Premier Andreotti and secretary Benigno Zaccagnini, he was leading a recalcitrant party to closer and closer collaboration with the PCI. In March 1978, to Washington's chagrin, the DC-PCI entente was strengthened, and the PCI became an equal partner in Parliament, no longer abstaining. Newsmen called the new government *la maggioranza*—literally, "the majority"—a code word for a coalition of parties within Parliament but one in which the executive power is not shared. The cabinet was wholly DC. This was the penultimate step before the PCI would enter the cabinet, presumably in early 1979. It was generally understood that this scenario had the approval of Pope Paul VI.

On the day the *maggioranza* Parliament opened, Aldo Moro was kidnapped by the Red Brigades and later murdered. The assassination was intended to wreck Moro's strategy and to convulse Italian politics. It succeeded in doing both. The right wing of the DC precipitated a series of maneuvers which finally led to the elections of June 1979. These will be examined in detail in Chapter 12, but essentially they showed that the right failed. The historic compromise was still alive, and the consequences of the referendum on divorce remained the matrix of Italian politics into the 1980s.

The role of women in the referendum has never been properly appreciated. Even Peter Nichols, married to an Italian woman, sympathetic to feminism, knowledgeable as he is, obscures their contribution. The women were led, informed, and organized by the Union of Italian Women (*Unione di Donne Italiane*, UDI).‡ Hardly known to the outside world, ignored by the Vatican, disparaged by the Christian Democrats and underestimated by the Communists, UDI can rightfully claim major credit for the outcome of the referendum. It is the historian's duty, and delight, to evaluate that claim.

---

* The six parties were the *Democrazia Cristiana* (DC), the Catholic party, Vatican-supported; *Partito Communista Italiano* (PCI); *Partito Socialista Italiano* (PSI); *Partito Liberale Italiano* (PLI); *Partito Republicano Italiano* (PRI); and *Partito Socialista Democratico Italiano* (PSDI).

Acronyms are constantly used in the Italian press, as they are throughout this book. Outside the coalition were, on the left, small groupings coalesced for electoral purposes into the *Democrazia Proletaria* (DP) and the Radical party (PR), a catch-all for ecologists, hippies, some feminists, anarchists, and so on. On the right was the neofascist *Movimento Sociale Italiano* (MSI), headed by Giorgio Almirante.

† Typical of Moro's subtleties: The prime minister no longer called for a vote of confidence (*fiducia*) on important issues, for the PCI would vote against. To get the PCI to abstain, the prime minister called for a vote of *fiducia e non-sfiducia;* that is, a vote of "confidence and no nonconfidence."

‡ There was also a small but aggressive organization. Woman's Liberation Movement (*Movimento di Liberazione della Donna*, MLD), which was affiliated with the Radical party.[6]

Divorce has always been a dirty word in Italy. Except for a brief period during the Napoleonic Era, divorce has never been countenanced by Italian law, in deference to its prohibition by the Catholic Church—for all practical purposes a state religion. This status of state religion, inherent in the Lateran Treaties and Concordat of 1929, was reaffirmed in Article 7 of the Italian Constitution of 1947. Besides the legal stipulations, the Constitution had given the Church a powerful political instrument: woman suffrage. The ascendancy of the parish priest on a woman's mind was formidable, and it was taken for granted that the vast majority of women would be influenced by the Vatican.

On divorce, church influence was reinforced by custom and the weight of the social structure. Not only was marriage sacred and indissoluble by Church teachings, but it was the only honorable status conceivable to a woman, the only way she could achieve a measure of identity. Her condition in life, her destiny from birth, was to be wife and mother. So powerful is the status of marriage as a symbol of identity that even the so-called white widows do not usually apply for a divorce. (White widows are women whose husbands have emigrated and made new families in foreign lands with no intention of returning.)

Divorce is seen as a shame, marriage as a necessity, whatever the cost, whatever the humiliations or beatings by the husband. It is not uncommon in the south for a man who wishes to marry an unwilling woman to rape her and let the fact be known. Being "dishonored," she can expect no marriage, and therefore she has to marry her rapist. He is abetted by the law: Article 544 of the Penal Code states that marriage between the violated woman and her rapist nullifies the crime![7] Rape itself is not taken too seriously by the law. It is not considered a crime against the person, but is placed in the lesser category of an offense against public morals.[8]

Such powerful customs reinforced the political power of *Democrazia Cristiana* so that it seemed unlikely divorce would ever come to Italy. Indeed, from 1948 to 1968 the DC easily controlled Parliament, with women voting heavily DC. The Communists joked that if they hadn't given the women the vote, they would have been in power all along.*

In 1968, however, the DC lost its supremacy. The elections resulted in an equilibrium of left and right forces and the DC could not prevent Parliament from enacting several progressive laws (reform of

---

* Woman suffrage is one of the many instances of the long-range perspectives on which the Vatican operates, but in which it has found a match in the Communist party. The Church was against votes for women because, while beneficial to the Church in the short run, it would tend to draw women into national life and educate them; for the same reasons the Communists supported the vote, paying the political price in the short run.

pensions, agrarian rents, workers' rights, etc.), including a fiercely debated law on divorce. It was passed in an all-night session on December 2, 1970, by a vote of 319–286.

The divorce law was hardly permissive. Its principal condition was a period of legal separation for a minimum of five years or a maximum of seven years if an innocent party objected to a divorce. Divorce was permitted if one of the couple was serving a long penal sentence or had committed immoral acts on members of the family. This last was an important clause, aimed at men who violated their daughters, a not uncommon by-product of unbridled male supremacy. Wives, broken-hearted but fearful for their lives, actually connived at such violations.

*I stood outside a courtroom in Reggio Calabria, at the toe of Italy, in December 1977 and watched two men and a woman, manacled, chained together, and escorted by* carabinieri *into the court for sentencing on charges of rape and murder. The older man was in his late thirties or early forties, a strongly built peasant ill at ease in his cheap suit, a lined, intelligent face with stubborn jaw and veiled eyes. The woman was his wife, probably younger but looking twenty years older, in a black dress and black shawl, hips out of kilter, with a martyred face and swollen, red eyes that had been weeping for weeks. The couple had four children, all girls, ages 17, 15, 13, and 10. The husband had violated the three older daughters whenever he was drunk, which was fairly often, and finally got the eldest pregnant. The baby was born alive. It was strangled by the father-grandfather, who forced his wife to help bury the tiny corpse. Its accidental discovery opened the case and led to the trial and sentencing. The other man was the fiancé of the seventeen-year-old; he had participated with the father in violating the other girls. He was twenty years old, solidly built, with a stupid, sullen face.*

*At the trial the wife had testified, choked by tears, to how she had been terrorized by her husband, often beaten, her life threatened—an infernal household of hate, fear, lust, guilt. "What could I do?" she repeated as she wept, "What could I do?"*

*The judges gave the husband life at hard labor and the young man ten years (he had not been implicated in the murder), and the wife got five years—suspended. Our group\* approved of the sentence as properly harsh on the man and properly merciful to the woman. Discussing the case, we agreed that many people in the village must have known what was going on, but no one had alerted the authorities. One of our group, deputy police commissioner said: "What*

---

\* Our group consisted of Communists, unionists, lawyers, and a deputy police commissioner who were involved in the next trial—a Mafia attack on a union organizer.

*would you? In part it's fear, but deep down it is* omertà, *the folk law of silence: you don't squeal to the cops."*

In view of such crimes and feminine subjugation, one marvels at the Church's resistance to divorce. The Vatican is not insensitive to the injustices involved, but marriage is a sacrament, holy and untouchable. Pope Paul VI was in Australia when the new law was enacted, and he expressed at once his "profound pain"; the Church, fully aware that a shift of seventeen votes (3 percent) would have defeated the law, immediately began scheming to wipe it out. Speed was of the essence. If the law were in force for any substantial length of time, people would become accustomed to it, appreciate its benefits, and realize it did not promote the epidemic of divorces predicted by the Church. (In fact, in the next twenty months there were only 71,678 requests for divorces, of which 40,830 were granted.[9] In over half of those divorces, the couple had been separated for more than ten years.)

There was an additional reason for the Church to have the law abrogated. Defeating the pope on his own grounds would tend to encourage secular forces in the society. A leading newspaper, *Il Messagero,* said as much: "For a country like ours which has not had the experience of the Reformation but rather has suffered all the negative effects of the Counter Reformation, the approval of divorce means above all that the Italian Parliament has been able to. . .affirm the autonomy of the Italian state against all absurd interpretations of the Lateran Treaties."[10] A prescient editorial: within four years the DC itself had initiated a revision of the concordat.

The DC government found itself in the anomalous position of enforcing a law that it abhorred. Foreseeing that the divorce law might pass, the Christian Democrats a few months previously had enacted statues to regulate the national referendums prescribed by the Constitution. (It took twenty-three years—and a fear of the divorce law—to bring enactment of the statutes.)

Now various Catholic groups,* supported by a majority of bishops, embarked on a campaign for a popular referendum to wipe out divorce. They easily obtained double the signatures required; and in January 1974 the referendum was set for May.

Informed opinion, on the right and on the left, agreed that the voting would be close but that the antidivorce forces would probably win. This general opinion was based mainly on the received wisdom on the backwardness of woman, particularly in the south, and on their total subjugation to the Church. There was also the fact, however,

---

*    Including Italian Center for Women (*Centro Italiano Femminile,* CIF), which was Catholic-DC oriented.

that the country seemed to be shifting to the right with the election as president of Giovanni Leone, a conservative Christian Democrat, and the clear majority obtained by *Democrazia Cristiana* and the parties of the right in the 1972 elections.

Behind the question of divorce lay deeper political implications. Speaking two months before the referendum at a huge meeting celebrating the International Woman's Day, Berlinguer warned that religious war might threaten the democratic foundations of the state. "We are dealing with a reactionary maneuver, of an initiative which heartens and unleashes the most backward and obscurantist forces in our society, and in the Church itself." Berlinguer was here hinting at those forces within the Church which were hostile to Vatican Council II and continuing to press for its covert repudiation. He went on: "The confrontation of the referendum introduces by definition a logic of diversion, division, and even provocation in Italian political life. . .with Almirante* allowed to become the protagonist of this political confrontation."[11] He concluded by reminding the audience that the Communists had tried hard to avoid the referendum and had offered many compromises.

It was a reminder the audience of women did not need. They had objected strenuously to the proposed Communist compromises as further weakening an emaciated law. "I was very angry with the comrades," recalled Anita Pasquale, herself a Communist in the leadership of UDI. "They were practically grovelling at the feet of the DC. We women felt we would win, and in any case the posture was too abject. It was disgusting. We gave them hell and stiffened their spines a little."

However abject the PCI, the DC rejected all compromises. The Church was adamant: the law had to go, and there might never be as good an opportunity. The campaign confirmed the gloomy predictions of the Communists. The tone was set by Almirante, who acted as the sharpest spokesman of the antidivorce coalition and was accepted by the DC as such. He said that the issue was the destruction of the family by atheistic communism. The Communist party was out to dominate the country and only a yes vote would stop them.‡ *Il Popolo,* the DC newspaper, ran excerpts from Catholic authorities, past and present, including St. Thomas Aquinas, on the inviolability of marriage and used the slogan DIO LO VUOLE (God wants it), meaning both indissoluble marriage and a yes vote. DC posters thundered: GOD IS WATCHING YOU—VOTE YES![12]

On the Communist side the emphasis was on the protection of the

---

* Giorgio Almirante, leader of the *Movimento Sociale Italiano* (MSI), was a powerful orator.

‡ The government had deliberately worded the referendum to ask: Should the divorce law be repealed? A yes vote would mean repeal; a no vote was a yes to divorce. This must be constantly borne in mind.

children and the constitutionality of the law. The major slogan was: WE MUST NOT TURN BACK. The party also attacked the hierarchy. One poster said: "The Church has always reserved the right to annul and dissolve failed marriages. WHY SHOULDN'T THE STATE?" It also made the point that ecclesiastial annulments do not protect the children or the weaker partner, the woman. It ended: "IN THE REFERENDUM—ANSWER NO!"[13]

The Church mobilized all its forces, from bishops to parish priests. In an unusual move, the Vatican came out openly onto the political arena and its official organ. *L'Osservatore romano,* filled its front page with antidivorce propaganda and exhortations to vote yes. The Conference of the Italian Episcopate (CEI), made up of some three hundred bishops, issued a *notificazione*—an order of the day against divorce. Squads of priests in loudspeakers' vans were sent out to reinforce the DC precinct workers—the populace dubbed them *preti volanti* ("flying priests"). Parish priests reminded their congregations that whoever voted Communist—that meant whoever voted no—would be excommunicated. In many confessionals, lists of proscribed organizations (including unions) were posted: no one belonging to them would be permitted confession unless he or she resigned and expressed remorse.[14]

In rural parishes women were told that divorce meant that wives and children could be abandoned by the man of the house. Anonymous leaflets pounded the same theme. Nichols agrees that while the prodivorce groups, fought a clean battle, relying on information and education, the antidivorce groups used fear, slander and falsifications to win votes. Above all, the central theme of these forces was anticommunism.* With British understatement, Nichols called their efforts "a virulent, extremist campaign, backed by the ecclesiastical hierarchy."[15] The propaganda of the DC and the MSI made great inroads on the popular mind, and the referendum became, to a considerable extent, a vote of confidence in the Communist party.

There were many instances of fraud by the government forces in charge of the polling booths, but as it turned out they were irrelevant.[16] The no votes carried by nearly 60 percent in a referendum in which close to 90 percent of the eligible voters participated.[17] Everyone was astounded, including UDI, whose headquarters I visited soon after arriving in Rome in September 1977. The headquarters is a modest five-room office on a little street, Via Colonna Antonina, just off Piazza Colonna in the heart of Rome. There I had a long interview with Anita Pasquale of the UDI leadership.†

---

* The Communists used this attack as a way to mobilize the northern workers—"Vote no to block the neofascists."

† A collective leadership of twelve women: five Communists, three Socialists, and four Catholics. Catholic, in this context, means they had been (and often still were) members of Catholic organizations.

Anita Pasquale is an attractive woman in her late thirties, attractive physically and psychologically—sensuous, organized, articulate. It was she who stressed the role of women in the referendum and pointed out that the left victories of 1975 and 1976 had flowed from the campaign on the referendum. "It was a political earthquake—surprised everybody. And the women did it, particularly the women of the south. They stood up to their men and they voted their hearts. They will not lie down again, not ever!" She spoke with pride and a fierce insistence. "They counted! For the first time in their lives, they *counted!"*

*Later, as I went around the country, the word "earthquake" was used again and again, as people reminisced in awed tones. An ACLI militant in Venice told me in December: "I voted no, of course, but I never thought we'd win. Then I heard over the radio that Treviso had voted 48 percent noes and I knew there had been an earthquake—they had never given more than a third of their votes to the left. I ran down the street yelling: 'Treviso, Treviso, 48 percent noes' and everybody knew it was an earthquake."*

*A sophisticated Roman lady, exquisitely couth, told me with touching remorse: "I didn't believe it could happen, not with all those ignorant women in the hands of the priests. People like me look down on those women; we shouldn't, I know we shouldn't. I'm a Communist and I shouldn't. But I do—I mean, I did. No more. Somehow those poor women, alone and isolated, did learn, they worked things out in solitude and silence. They made me so ashamed. . .and so happy, so very, very happy. I haven't cried for years and years. But that night I cried.*

UDI was the only organization which had been sure of victory. "Was it womanly intuition?" I asked Anita. She accepted the provocation good-naturedly. "Hardly," she said. "We knew, of course, our opponents were relying on the women to swing the votes their way, but we also knew they were wrong. We *knew* this in a way they couldn't know, because politicians don't even talk to their wives sometimes. And priests, what do they really know about women? A few piddling sins at the confessional . . . petty matters of gossip, small lies, illicit thoughts, weak attendance at mass and so on . . . What could they know of the deep angers that women don't even acknowledge to themselves? But we . . . we knew a lot." She tapped her chest, and then rapped the table. "We know about ourselves in our UDI and we talk. How we talk! We have our magazine *Noi donne* [We women] and receive hundreds of letters month after month. We recruit steadily and we have over a hundred thousand members. It doesn't sound like a lot, but we're well organized, with groups in all the cities and large towns. Since the late sixties we sensed that women were changing, becoming more aware of their problems, less fearful of their men, willing to speak up."

She looked at me sharply. "I sound vague and talk in generalities, don't I?" I started to deny it, but she had got up from her desk and crossed to a bookcase. She brought back a paperback book. An off-white cover, ever so slightly tinted in pink, embossed in the center with the male-female genetic symbols; and a title in dark red: *Sesso Amaro* (Bitter sex). Below it, a subtitle: "Thirty Thousand Women Respond on Maternity, Sexuality, Abortion."[18]

"There," she said, "that's documentation. Right after the referendum we decided to move immediately on abortion—use our momentum, our sense of victory and strength to pressure Parliament. We decided that the best way to dramatize our needs was to have the women speak—women of all ages, all conditions of life from all over the country—cities, towns, and mountain villages."

She pointed at the book.

"We came up with that. We didn't think a poll, scientific sampling and all that, would give us the flavor we wanted. So we used our members to get interviews, or get groups together to talk, small groups where possible, large meetings when the women preferred them. Take it, the details are in there.[19] We taped when we could, or we took notes. We worked all through 1975, then it took us a year to edit and print. It came out early this year, and it has had an enormous impact."

Her hand swept the air like a scythe. "I know personally more than a dozen deputies who were so moved and so ashamed for their fellow males that they voted for the abortion law despite their party and Church pressure. We got it passed in the Chamber and then it got defeated in the Senate by a few votes—some of our best friends didn't show up, like Giuseppe Saragat." She spat his name out contemptuously, the leader of the Social Democratic party (PSDI), which had presumably backed the law. "But we're not through yet," she said grimly, "not with him, nor the law, nor the Senate."*

"Read," she said. "You'll see the bitterness, the pent-up anger, the growing sense of revolt. Again and again you'll see a woman saying, 'Two years ago I began . . .', 'Three years ago I began . . . ,' and so on—'the ripening of the grapes of wrath,' as your great Steinbeck wrote." She had pronounced the phrase in very good English, and I complimented her on it. "I only know a few words—to be chic." She smiled mischievously. "In Rome, English is the chic language and whiskey the chic drink. But thank you, Carlo."

---

* She was right. In April 1978 abortion was legalized.[20]

"And politics," I added, "the chic occupation."

UDI's claim of a special role for women in the referendum was not accepted by most observers. Paolo Vittorelli, of the national executive of the PSI, said the left Catholics had been most responsible for the victory; Ugo La Malfa of the PRI said no, it was the popular front of left and lay forces—old-fashioned politics.[21] The usually profeminist Nichols advanced a novel theory to explain the results: Italians don't like to make decisions, and when forced to do so, resent it. The referendum forced them to make a decision for or against divorce; hence the landslide vote of noes.[22] The socialist writer, Giorgio Bocca, has a somewhat similar theory: The vote was a punishment to the DC meted out by electors tired of scandals. DC leaders opted for the idea that the conspicuous neofascist presence in the campaign had turned people against them.[23] Catholic thinkers blamed the secularization of society. Anything to avoid giving the women credit. But, in fairness, it must be said that these male analysts never refused to give credit to women. The thought never entered their minds.

Even among Communists the recognition of the women's role seemed rather grudging. For example, the PCI official analysis of the voting states: "Women have demonstrated that they are a great force in the struggle for democracy and civic progress."[24] Pallid jargon for their decisive role. One aspect of the voting is so charming that it must be singled out: in many places *nuns* voted overwhelmingly *for divorce*, and so did the women under their immediate influence. Their no vote reached a higher percentage than that of the general population—in some cases as high as 90 percent![25]

All commentators agreed that the women of Italy had shifted left. The question was: Had they shifted only on the divorce issue or had they shifted politically? Was the UDI right in asserting that women would not lie down again? And if so, what did this portend? All politicians understood that a shift in the women vote would reflect and further influence the male vote. The heart of the question therefore was: Had the political landscape of Italy changed?

A month later to the day, on June 12, 1974, Sardinia held its elections for the regional assembly. For the first time the left got a majority, 51.02 percent, up from 43.4 percent in 1969.[26] Five months later, in two provincial elections, the left registered notable gains.[27] By the time the administrative elections (regional, provincial, municipal) of June 15, 1975, took place, the extent of the shift was astounding; the left won practically all the major cities and half the regions with a total of some 60 percent of the entire population. The Communist vote was 32 percent.[28]

The national elections of June 20, 1976, affirmed the trend. The Communist party got 34.4 percent of the vote, *Democrazia Cristiana*

38.8 percent. The Communists had increased their votes by 7 percent since 1972, while the *Democrazia Cristiana* had remained stationary.[29] But the right had lost, so that the DC and MSI together could only muster 45 percent of the votes. There was no possible way for the DC to govern without the assent, implicit or explicit, of the Communists.

Contemporary politics from 1976 to 1980 has revolved around this central fact, with the DC stubbornly refusing to accept the PCI into the government, while the Communists were inexorably checkmating the DC into the historic compromise. A Communist functionary in Turin, Zuccotti, put it this way: "We have brought the DC horse to water, we must now make him drink." What brought the horse to water was the referendum. Nichols, after noting that "even the most ardent supporters of divorce were stupified by the extent of their victory," goes on to state unequivocally: "If ever in the life of a country a single event may be considered decisive, then such an event was the result of the referendum on divorce."[30]

For the Church the referendum was a profound shock. The most immediate, and unintended, penalty of the results was the fillip they gave to the anticlerical forces—from the Socialist leader Pietro Nenni to the Republican Senator Eugenio Reale— who promptly called for a revision of the concordat, a revision that many Catholics had long wanted and that many Christian Democrats, resentful of the political defeat forced on them by the Vatican, no longer opposed.[31]

Within the hierarchy the prelate who paid a high price for the defeat was Cardinal Benelli of Florence. He had been the strongest instigator of the referendum,[32] thereby alienating many progressive prelates; and the defeat alienated others who had supported him. In the conclave of October 1978, Benelli seemed within reach of the papal crown. But cardinals have long memories.

The Church still feels the wounds inflicted by this defeat, which accelerated divisions between the clergy and the laity. Less visible, but deeply significant, were the strains it caused within the hierarchy. These strains built up a huge potential for change in the Church, for carrying through the reforms of Vatican II, and for increasing the dialogue between Catholics and Communists.

From the time of Vatican Council II, there had been sharp divisions within the Church and its theologians over old doctrines on conjugal love, marriage, birth control, and sexuality.[33] Paul VI was adamantly traditionalist on these issues, but many high prelates disagreed with him.*

In this context, when the Conference of the Italian Episcopate, in

---

* Pope John Paul II is even more adamant. While Paul eased annulments and allowed priests to give up their vows and marry, John Paul has clamped down on both escape mechanisms. For this he has been heavily criticized by progressive theologians.

February 1974, issued its *notificazione*, which openly threw the weight of the Church on the side of the antidivorce forces, there was a sharp reaction from the more liberal clergy.* The revolt was small in numbers, but when bishops and cardinals come out in the open against established Church policy, no revolt is small.

The common denominator of the revolt was the assertion that the Conference's declaration was not juridically binding on individual bishops and priests. Bishop Bettazzi of Ivrea, Cardinal Pellegrino of Turin, Monsignor Antonio Fustella of Saluzzo, Bishop Aldo Del Monte of Novara—all were from the Piedmont region—immediately pointed out that the Conference had restated the teaching of the Church but had no binding authority on the various dioceses. The secretary of the Conference, Monsignor Gaetano Bonicelli had to admit in the press that "everyone at the local level may act freely." Cardinal Pellegrino, who had not attended the Conference, made public a long, reasoned statement of his position: "In our diocese, while fully recognizing the doctrine of indissolubility [of marriage] and actively supporting this fundamental value, there is no desire to range ourselves on the side of those who wish to abrogate the law." He explained this position was taken for "motives of liberty of conscience and social peace."

Bishop Aldo Del Monte, who had attended the meeting and voted for the announcement, made it known that the document he had voted for had been censored before publication: "Three lines were taken out of that document, precisely those three lines in which I supported the right of choice of Catholic consciences."[35]

The revolt of lay Catholics was explicit, whether speaking as individuals or via the innumerable associations, charitable, social, sporting, that form a dense network in parishes and dioceses. In the Piedmont region alone scores of parishes saw appeals to vote no issued by Catholics and signed by priests, DC mayors, deputies, and various organizations. One appeal said: "We maintain it is politically just and proper to vote no." Another appeal invited citizens to "reject with a no the attempt to impose the choice of a personal faith on a pluralistic society."[36] Of crucial importance in this rebellion is the fact that not only individuals, but organized groups, began to work with Socialists and Communists, getting to know, respect, and influence one another.

On a national scale the Christians for Socialism (CS) movement engaged itself wholeheartedly in the "no" campaign. This movement

---

* Times have changed. Now, only five years later, despite Pope John Paul's personal feelings on divorce and abortion, it is not likely that the Italian episcopate will again meddle so blatantly in political affairs. One of the few appointments Wojtyla has made is that of Alberto Cardinal Ballestrero to be president of the episcopal conference, a post sought by Benelli. Ballestrero, who followed Pellegrino as archbishop of Turin, is noted for his aloofness from politics.[34]

had grown up in the late sixties all over the country, composed of small groups of devout Catholics who had come to see the class struggle as central to the development of society and of their personal religious impulse. In September 1973 they had their first national congress in Bologna and went on record against the proposed referendum (at that time only an eventuality).[37] By May 1974 the CS had considerable influence in the voting. More important by far than the role of the CS, however, was the shift of a key catholic organization the *Associazioni Cristiane dei Lavoratori Italiani* (ACLI).

*ACLI is a powerful organization with local chapters everywhere, regional secretaries, and a national executive. Its roots go back to fascist days, but it was reshaped in 1944 as the trade-union arm of the Church, corresponding to the* Democrazia Cristiana *(Christian Democratic party), the political arm, and* Azione Cattolica Italiana *(Catholic action), the social arm. It was well financed by special measures of the Vatican, including contributions from the United States made via various channels.*

*The importance of ACLI is measured by two facts: its president was chosen directly by the pope, and its "protector" in its formative stage was a "comer" in the hierarchy—Monsignor Giovanni Battista Montini, later Cardinal Montini, the Secretary of State for Pope John XXIII, and finally Paul VI, the vice-regent of Christ on Earth. Most of the important leaders of the DC—Rumor, Scelba, Fanfani, Gronchi, Andreotti—were connected with ACLI during their careers.*\*[38]

*ACLI had always had a militant component, and it gathered momentum during the student and workers' upsurge of 1968, shifting the organization leftward. The referendum on divorce provided a climax to this increasing militancy. The majority of ACLI's leaders and constituent groups went on record for a no vote, and this sharp break with its past proved irreversible.*[39]

*For example, in the debate at Conigliano del Veneto, one of the speakers was the regional secretary of the ACLI. He had voted Communist in 1976, having first shifted from the DC in the referendum. Throughout Italy, from Turin to Palermo, again and again I found ACLI members voting Communist, assuming posts in Communist-led organizations and, in some cases, becoming functionaries of the party itself.*

It is difficult to convey the depth of feeling aroused among devout Catholics by the referendum, its devastating impact amounting to a

---

\*   Mariano Rumor, Giulio Andreotti, and Mario Scelba have all been prime ministers. Giovanni Gronchi was the second president of the Republic.

crisis of conscience, and by the political consequences as Catholics shifted left, often permanently. This was vividly brought home to me in Bologna, where I met Professor Luigi Pedrazzi of the University of Bologna. He and others on the faculty had established a Center for the Documentation of Religious History, which has also become the unofficial center for the Democratic League, a left faction within the DC. The Center is housed in an old palace (how many unions, Communist headquarters and left-wing organizations are housed in ancient quarters!) where I was interviewing a young administrator, and Pedrazzi showed up unexpectedly to pick up some papers.

He was in his forties, a stocky man with a cheerful face and an open manner. After we were introduced, I said I'd like to talk to him. "Willingly," he said. "But now I have an appointment. What about tomorrow?" Tomorrow I had to be in Ferrara, and after that, Venice. He grinned and said, "Then we'll have to talk now, won't we?" After he had made a telephone call, we sat talking for two hours. He had many original and penetrating ideas and observations on politics and religion, including one relevant to the referendum. He had never belonged to any party, he said, but for twenty years he had voted regularly for the DC. "The referendum shifted me." He asked the administrator for a book of clippings to show me his interview in *Il Popolo,* the official DC paper, titled "Religion and Politics in Praise of Catholic Commitment." I read: "At a certain point, for reasons which still seem to me correct, my own decisions diverged more and more from those of the DC: thus I abstained from voting in 1972. I voted no in the referendum, then Socialist in the administrative elections of 1975, and for the PCI on June 20, 1976."[40]

*I saw Pedrazzi again in June 1979. He invited me to his home, high on a hill above Bologna, and as we shared a pot of coffee he told me he had voted PCI again. He was concerned about the decrease in the party's vote but not unduly worried. He pointed out that the real losers of the election had been the DC. In a local election after Moro's death, the DC had increased its vote considerably. Believing that a national election would bring them 42-44 percent (as the polls showed), giving them and their allies a majority,\* the DC had forced the Communists out and precipitated the elections. But the DC miscalculated: it increased its vote by only 0.1 percent, and while the Communists had lost, their votes went to the left, particularly to the Radical party. All the DC accomplished was to push the PCI into the opposition, alienate workers still more, and in the long run hurt itself.*

*"What's going to happen?" I asked. "Things are pretty bad."*

\*    The Liberals (PLI) and the Republicans (PRI) got 7 percent between them in 1979.

*"Caro Carlo," said Pedrazzi. "There is much room for things to get worse."*

If the most important consequence of the referendum was the emergent role of women in politics,* and the next important was its impact within the Church, then the third was its effect on the popular image of the Communist party. The PCI emerged as a sober, responsible party, mindful of the national interest, a party fit to govern. This was emphasized by Professor Sylos Labini of the University of Rome. He told me: "The referendum wrote finis to redbaiting in Italian politics. It was the grave of overt neofascism, a grave dug by the right itself, including the DC right, when it made the PCI the issue in the campaign. The DC can never ally itself with the MSI again. As Berlinguer has noted, redbaiting has lost its edge.[42] Conversely, of course, the PCI's sober campaign overcame the reservations of many in the professional and middle classes. With its UDI, the party reached millions of women."†

The next day I happened to have lunch with Anita Pasquale and told her what Sylos Labini had said. She reacted sharply to the implication that UDI was tied to the party. "That's loose talk, Carlo, and he knows better. Our collective [leadership] has a majority of non-Communists, seven to five, and we have never divided on a party basis. Not once! Generally we reach agreement, because if even one person has a strong objection to any proposal, we lay it aside for the time being."

"It's true that when UDI began, the party helped with advice and money—Togliatti was very advanced on the woman question—but we pushed for complete autonomy and the party didn't resist[43] The referendum marked a complete break: we were very angry with the party, and I for one made life miserable for the comrades, but they are good people and they came around. Now our relations are friendly and correct. We like it that way, and so do they."

Professor Labini had also said that the PCI, which had tried to avoid the test of strength, refused to crow about a victory over its adversaries in the DC or to take undue credit. Berlinguer had immediately made a statement: "It is not the victory of a single party," and listed all the prodivorce forces. Then he went on to stress the

---

* In the 1976 Parliament there were 61 women. Of these, 47 were Communists (compared to 21 previously), and 11 DC (compared to 9 before). Nevertheless, women were only 6.5 percent of the total.[41]

† Professor Labini is a noted sociologist whose analysis of social classes in Italy has influenced the PCI's electoral strategies. His judgment was vindicated in June 1979, when, despite the fact that *all* parties, left and right, attacked the PCI, the redbaiting, except for the extreme right, was muted. The attacks were on issues: the right on the grounds of socialism, the left on the grounds of revisionism. However, in the June 1980 elections there was again considerable redbaiting.

Catholic input: "The results of the referendum also point up the support of militants and of voters from the Catholic world and from *Democrazia Cristiana* itself who did not yield in the face of great pressure."[44]

I asked Labini whether he was a Communist. He said no, he was in "the socialist area," but had great respect for the party and its leadership.* "I have never become a member, though I've been asked several times. I don't really know why. I think it is still the influence of Salvemini, who always blew hot and cold about the party."

"Salvemini? Why, he was one of my dearest friends—friend and teacher."

"No? Me too! We, a group of students, have established a fund in his memory, to print important essays."[45]

*Suddenly, in that bookish, cluttered study on Via Nomentana the image of a beloved teacher took shape, the white spade beard, the twinkling eyes, the earthy expression, the voluble gestures of the incessant talker—how dear, how very dear and very real he was. In that study we became friends, Sylos Labini and I; he, twenty years my junior, held in fraternal bonds through a teacher twenty years my senior.*

*"I know what you mean about blowing hot and cold over the party," I said. "In 1937, after I came out of Spain and was at Oxford, Salvemini brought Rosselli's widow and eleven-year-old boy to my house for a week of peace and quiet.‡ When I told him I had joined the British Communist party, he was delighted. Then, in 1942, I needed his recommendation to enter the OSS, the wartime intelligence service. And he said to me: 'I don't want any ethical discussions. If you are a member of the Communist party, I won't give the recommendation. Are you?' I said no, I had left the party many months before. 'Fine,' he said, 'I'll give you a letter.' Then I asked him how did he know I was telling the truth—after all, Communists are supposed to lie, steal, murder, to get their way. Salvemini snorted impatiently. 'Don't be ridiculous,' he said, 'We are both honest men, are we not?' "*

"Perfect, perfect, just like him," said Labini.

We went to lunch and kept talking. I told him of Anita's claim that the women's vote had been decisive. Labini frowned. "Decisive . . . I wouldn't say. Important yes, but decisive. . . ."

---

\* A small, but not wholly irrelevant, reason is that he and Berlinguer are neighbors in Sardinia.

‡ Carlo Rosselli, an Italian Socialist and antifascist, was assassinated in France by Mussolini's secret service.[46]

"Wasn't it?" I challenged. "Particularly in the south, the woman vote was unexpected—by everybody. Wouldn't you say it was a unique contribution? Decisive to the *quality* of the victory?"

He sipped his wine thoughtfully, quirked his head and finally nodded firmly. "Hmm, perhaps . . . I had never thought of it quite that way, but yes, you could say it was decisive. But in a deeper sense than Comrade Pasquale sees it. True, women are changing . . . but the point is the whole society has been changing. The referendum was like a flash of light in the dark; it showed suddenly how much our social landscape had changed."

Labini's mobile, gamin face was intent. "True, the impact of the changes has been greatest on the women, and they in turn accelerated the changes. You could say that in the referendum, they were the vanguard. But the party counted. Without its reputation, its earned image of honesty, of caring, anticommunism would have won out. Moreover, the big troops were the trade unions. You've got to study the growth of union militancy since the late sixties, and their impact on the society. And, of course, the American contribution."

He caught my startled expression and laughed. "Yes, of course, the American influence on our society. In every way. The war in Vietnam, for example. Practically everyone hated it, hated the atrocities of napalm, the obscenity of those incredible bombings—a huge, powerful nation bullying a small rural country. The pope spoke against the war; the Church was scandalized. *Pax Christi** sent two delegations to Vietnam—one north, one south—and organized a huge congress in Turin in September 1973.[47] You should read the proceedings, especially the speech of Raniero La Valle. The congress made big news: Cardinal Pellegrino welcomed the congress, and what he does is always news. The journalists love him, he's such good copy."

We were now on our coffee, and Sylos Labini went on. "The Vietnam war hurt the DC, hurt it badly. *Democrazia Cristiana* had deliberately identified itself with the United States. For twenty years it had stressed its close relationship with Washington. When American loans came, the DC had got them; when food came, the DC took credit. And when equipment came and films and the rock music—all the things Italians liked—the DC shone in the reflected light of American popularity. With the war the opposite happened. Now the DC had to share in the reflected hostility. The disillusionment with

---

* The Peace of Christ, an international Catholic organization for the promotion of peace, founded by a French prelate after World War I. By its statutes, the international president is a cardinal, the presidents of the national sections bishops. Bishop Bettazzi of Ivrea has been president of the Italian section for nine years, a position which has nurtured his contacts abroad, particularly with the third world. The president of the American section is Bishop Thomas J. Gumbleton of Detroit, who at Christmas 1979 went to Teheran to comfort the Americans being held hostage there.

America went deep—there were thousands and thousands of meetings in support of Vietnam. I am convinced the hatred for the war was a significant factor in the results of the referendum—in essence, a vote against the DC's kowtowing to Washington.

"But the war was only the most obvious case of how America has affected our politics. Of more profound significance is its impact on our whole society as it shifted from a rural to an industrialized economy. We copied you. We made the automobile king. We call our economy 'the American model.' We imported your consumerism. Your films showed how well one can live, and we tried to do the same. You eroded our old values, secularized our society, made small families and whiskey chic, woman's freedom a natural and proper thing. You are the one influence that constantly challenges the Church—as on marriage and sexual matters. Our young people love your domestic ways, your free-and-easy relations, the undercurrent of irreverence to authority. Believe me, what's best in America was reflected in the vote, as well as the less good—your consumerism. Our growing middle classes aped your customs and your attitudes. America is chic! How in the devil could Italy be against divorce when it is a great American custom?"

He was laughing, partly to tease me but more as a professional sociologist.

"Listen to me, Carlo, go talk to the Church, the priests, the bishops. They'll tell you about secularization. Talk to the Communists—they'll tell you about democracy. Above all, go talk to the unions—about how they split in '48, and how they came together in '72, just in time for the referendum. With all due respect to the women, you couldn't have gotten the landslide of noes without the mobilization of the unions."

I did. I went to Turin to the metal workers, who are a combination of auto and steel workers. Turin, of course, is the ancestral home and modern fortress of Fiat.

# CHAPTER 7

# The Hard Years at Fiat

On a chilly afternoon in mid-November, I stood before a storefront whose dusty windows displayed old election posters. It was the Communist party headquarters in the Mirafiori district at the edge of Turin.

The Mirafiori complex is the heart of the Empire FIAT,* and in Turin Fiat is God. In the middle distance was the administrative building for the complex—some twenty odd stories, gray, rectangular, ungainly. It squatted there, a somber feudal presence, dominating the low structures around it. On its roof stood the tall letters F I A T, illuminated at night: *Fiat lux*. In the far distance stretched the factories with their serrated roofs, acres and acres of them. Every day they took in an army of sixty thousand workers, one third of the entire Fiat force in Italy.

The district had an unfinished look, with a sprinkling of vacant spaces, a tall housing project and a large playground, a rash of single houses and two-story apartment buildings. It seemed very un-Italian, more like the outskirts of Los Angeles. I took in the surroundings half-consciously; I was thinking of the stepped-up activities of the Red Brigades. The day before, Carlo Casalegno, vice-editor of *La Stampa,* had been shot in the face by four terrorists.[1] Up to now, the Red Brigades had been seizing people or shooting them in the legs, kidnapping or knee-capping them, as the Italians put it. I shivered; I had no overcoat and both my thoughts and the weather were cold. A man came up.

---

* Fiat stands for *Federazione Italiana Automobilistica Torino*, words never used in print or speech, their sense eroded over eighty years. The acronym has become standard.

"Marzani?"

"That's me."

"I'm Riccio, the secretary. A pleasure." A burly man in his fifties, with tousled red hair and a no-nonsense face with friendly eyes. He wore a red-checkered shirt and a nylon windbreaker like a Canadian logger.

"Cold wind," said Ricco, opening the door. Inside, it looked like any party headquarters in the Bronx—or Chicago, Bombay, Hong Kong—everything in functional disarray and that "masculine" cleanliness that leaves most of the dirt undisturbed. On the walls were charts on the current recruiting drive, with headings laboriously lettered: Foundry, Body, Assembly, Maintenance, etc. They showed last year's figures, this year's target, and the score to date. On a shelf in the hallway was a clutch of loudspeakers and amplifiers; a circular stairway led downwards into pitch darkness.

"Make yourself at home" said Riccio expansively. "The region called me about you—said a comrade professor from America. . ."

"I know," I said. "I was there when he called you."

As he hung up the phone, the regional secretary had said to me: "You're in luck. Three o'clock tomorrow at party headquarters at Mirafiori, and I'm sure they'll discuss the work stoppage protesting Casalegno's assassination. A meeting like that is unusual, we don't have a Communist caucus. . .too divisive. Our comrades meet in their own separate union halls, but once in a while we like to get them all together. . . .to remind them they are party members." He grinned. "Union comrades tend to forget. Well, I've got to run along, help organize tonight's meeting. Be sure to come, Piazza San Carlo."

*The Italian trade-union movement has had a complex history in the last thirty years. It is now "unitary"\* with a Federation of Trade Unions comprising practically all unions. This is not a merger, as with the AFL-CIO, but a true federation having a directorate of the leaders of the three confederations, each of which is allied to a party or parties: the Communist-oriented CGIL* (Confederazione generale italiana del lavoro), *the Catholic-oriented CISL* (Confederazione italiana sindacati lavoratori), *and the UIL* (Unione italiana del lavoro),† *which is a melange of Republicans, Social Democrats, and Socialists. While the leadership tends to be aligned politically, every union has workers from all parties. These confederations are made up*

---

\* "Unitary" is a word constantly used in Italy to indicate a concept basic to Communist policies. It is difficult to translate: "united" is too strong; "working-together" too weak. So I've used "unitary" as in the Unitarian Church.

† CGIL, General Confederation of Labor; CISL, Confederation of Workers' Syndicates; UIL, Union of Labor. These are the usual English renderings with the word Italian dropped. I've used the Italian acronyms throughout.

*of industrial and craft unions—miners, carpenters, textiles, auto, etc., much as in our own AFL and CIO unions. In Italy they are called* sindacati di categorie *("unions by categories"), or* categorie *for short.*

*In 1944 all union leaders, Catholic, Communist, and Socialist, decided on a united labor movement. Mindful that their old division had helped fascism come to power, they formed the CGIL, the* General Confederation of Labor. *During the negotiations, the biggest disagreement had been on the degree of democracy within the unions, and it had been the Communists who had fought for the* widest extension of democracy. *Their opponents, honestly concerned to have a strong organization, wanted a single highly centralized organ, appointment of union organizers, co-option in the higher bodies, and, above all, the union shop and the checkoff.* \*

*Giuseppe Di Vittorio, the Communist leader, argued that the antifascist workers were sick of regimentation and should be free to join the union, or not join. They should pay their dues individually and elect all their representatives, from the lowest to the highest bodies.[2] At that time, the CGIL comprised 95 percent of all unionists, and as a counterforce, the Vatican organized the ACLI.*

*In 1948, with the Cold War in full swing, the Catholics split away from the CGIL in collusion with the ACLI, the Christian Democrats' government and the Americans—CIA, State Department, and the AFL.[3] The pretext was Communist control of the general strike called in July 1948 to answer the shooting of Togliatti. In fact, the strike was spontaneous and the Communist leadership moved to contain it. The newly formed pro-Catholic union was the CISL;[4] the ACLI became more of a social and sports organization. At the time of the split, the CGIL got 79 percent of the workers; the CISL, 21 percent. The following year, Social Democrats and Republicans organized the UIL. Over the next decade, the repression of government and man- agement at Fiat reduced the CGIL to 21 percent of the workers, with the Catholics and unaffiliated unions sharing the rest more or less evenly.[5] In the sixties, workers' militancy began to rise and the proportions shifted, with the unaffiliated dropping and the CGIL increasing. Today the CGIL is again the strongest federation with 4.5 million members, the CISL has 2.5 million, UIL under one million, and the unaffiliated unions a few hundred thousands.[6]*

*In 1972 the three confederations came together again under the umbrella of the Federation of Trade Unions.[7] The unitary federation was the result of three major factors: the callousness and exploitation*

---

\* Co-option means that an existing leadership brings new leaders in by fiat, without election by, or consultation with, the membership. In a union shop a worker must join the union after he is hired. The checkoff is the system whereby management deducts union dues from the workers' pay and transmits them to the union in bulk payments.

*of management, the rapid increase in militancy of the workers, and the leadership of the Communists in pressing for more democracy and greater autonomy of unions vis-à-vis the political parties.*

As I hung around the party headquarters, workers were gathering, greeting each other, chatting, joking. A prim old man, spare, white-haired, with steel-rimmed glasses—a miniature Harry Truman—was talking to Riccio. He motioned me over. "This is comrade Marzani, a professor from the United States. He's doing a book on the party." To me, he said, "Comrade Zuccotti used to be an engineer at Fiat. He was the first Communist fired in 1952, after twenty-two years in Fiat." He grinned. "You wouldn't think it, but he's seventy-four years old—a charter member of the party." There was pride and affection in his voice.*

We shook hands, Zuccotti courteous but detached. Riccio raised his voice: "Put the lights on, somebody, and let's get going." From below, the circular staircase was abruptly illuminated and men began to go down. The spiral was tight; the iron steps narrow. We went down gingerly, the bigger men squeezing. We ended up in a big open area perhaps forty by sixty feet, lit by fluorescent lamps, with a table at one end and some eighty-odd folding chairs. Riccio and Zuccotti sat at the table, and Riccio motioned for me to sit next to him. I angled the chair to the side so I could see Zuccotti as well as the audience.

Latecomers straggled in. The place was jammed, all chairs taken, a few people on the lower steps, a dozen or more along the walls. It was three o'clock, and they had all come directly from the morning shift. I was struck by the absence of women.

The majority of the men were in their late twenties and thirties, though there was a substantial sprinkling of old-timers. They came in all sizes and shapes, brawny and skinny, alert and phlegmatic, irreverent and prim, voluble, taciturn, dogmatic, wisecracking, ponderous, mercurial. Some were fourth-generation Fiat workers, others only a few years distant from the Calabrian mountains and the Sicilian plains. You could guess their origins from their speech—the clipped phrases of the Piedmontese, the harsh consonants of the Romans, the slurred accents of the southerners. But there was one distinct flavor—a flavor typical the world over—the flavor of party seriousness. When Riccio rapped the table for order, there was quiet at once.

Riccio introduced me as a trustworthy comrade from the United States; all could speak freely. He went on to say that while the meeting had been called originally to discuss the rent-control laws, recent events had to be covered first. He gave the floor to Zuccotti,

---

* I wasn't able to verify that Zuccotti was a charter member of the PCI. He could have been—he would have been eighteen at the time (1921).

who shuffled his notes, set them aside, put his elbows on the table, crossed his fingers, and rested his chin on them. He spoke quietly as his eyes swept the audience.

"Two days ago, just about this time, Carlo Casalegno was shot in the head; he is hanging between life and death in the hospital. Last evening there was a demonstration in Piazza San Carlo to answer the terrorists, sponsored by all the parties and all the unions. The demonstration was chaired by our mayor, our own Communist mayor whom we put in office, Comrade Novelli. Now, the piazza can hold fifty thousand people; at the most there were fifteen thousand. I call it a disgrace. How many of you were there?"

One man, toward the center, put up his hand. Zuccotti nodded. "Good for you, Hannibal, and how many of you asked other people to go?"

An older man against the rear wall put up his hand.

"You must have a friend who lives on the piazza," said Zuccotti sarcastically. There were a couple of short-lived titters; the hall was quiet; they could sense the scolding coming.

"No," said the man mildly. "My daughter and her fiancé."

"At least you'll have a good son-in-law," retorted Zuccotti. He went on, still in a conversational tone: "The federation called for a one-hour strike this morning. A simple work stoppage, yet only some five hundred workers turned out—five hundred out of sixty thousand. The metal workers are supposed to be the vanguard of the working class." His tone was not sarcastic. "Mirafiori is the heart of the *metalmeccanici.** Nevertheless, the strike was a complete dud. How do we explain that? You tell me."

*There are three metal workers unions, three* categorie *affiliated to the CGIL, the CISL, and the UIL. They are the best organized, the most militant, the most political of all the workers—a formidable force dominating the economy. The Fiat workers are the heart of the metal workers, and Mirafiori is the core of the Fiat force. Cradle of Fiat, Mirafiori has the longest history of struggles of all Italian workers, going back to the turn of the century. In 1900, 50 workers produced 24 cars; in 1973, 160,000 workers produced 1,500,000 cars.*[8]

*If the 56,000 Mirafiori workers and employees are the cream of the metal workers, the Communist unionists among them are the cream of the cream—a coherent, shaping force. In this room were* their *leaders, from all three unions, the brains of the Mirafiori complex—chief shop stewards, chairmen of the grievance committees, heads of the factory councils. There was power in this hall: the power of knowledge, organization, and discipline.*

---

\* The *metalmeccanici* are a combination of steel and auto workers.

Zuccotti, after a moment or two of silence, raised his voice insistently. "Come on, tell me why the strike failed . . . and the meeting last night. You all have ideas."

The man who had attended the meeting, Hannibal, an older man with a northern accent, spoke up: "I was at the meeting. Agreed, it wasn't good, but I didn't see any Demochristians around or any of Casalegno's friends—doctors and lawyers and such. Almost all young people; most of them ours. A lot of comrades, too, not from Mirafiori, but comrades from town. It was supposed to be a demonstration of the whole city, wasn't it? But only we Communists put out. If they don't care when one of theirs gets hurt, why should we?"

Here and there, men nodded, and now several wanted to speak, their hands up. Riccio pointed at one, a young man with a dark intent face, seated in the rear. He didn't stand up, but spoke vehemently.

"Hannibal's absolutely right. There were newsmen at the gate, like vultures, wanting to know why we didn't strike. And my buddy, a good Catholic militant from the CISL, said to one: "Hey, Mr. Newspaperman, if tomorrow they shoot me, will you go on strike?"[9] Besides, we all know Agnelli* owns *La Stampa,* our own boss, and we know him, what a turd he is! So if one of his gets it . . . "

"Hey, *aspetta,* just a minute. . . " The remonstration came from the side, but the speaker swept on. "Okay, okay, I know about Casalegno, a hero of the resistance and all that—a real democrat. But he fought us just the same. He did work on Agnelli's paper, didn't he? And took Agnelli's money didn't he? We got so much work, so damn many meetings—how can I ask a worker to give up his free time to fight for his boss's stooge?"

Before Riccio could intervene, the first speaker had cut in. "Yeah, and I heard Levi [editor of *La Stampa*] talk, . . . about how he was for the democratic state and how he was a Jew and wasn't discriminated against. Hell, if you're working for Agnelli, who's going to discriminate—even if you're a Turk. All the crap about Casalegno being a servant of the state, how noble and all that. But whose state, Agnelli's? Levi did a little redbaiting, too." He held up a restraining hand as some of his comrades muttered. "Oh, yes he did! In his quiet way—about how terrorism comes from breaking down old values . . . from fighting in the streets and so on. He meant *us,* that's who. Our fights, our strikes, we are responsible. Not *their* unemployment, *their* high prices, *their* thievery and corruption!" His voice dripped scorn. "You can have Levi. And Casalegno too." He waved a deprecating hand. "Naturally, I'm sorry he got shot. I hope he makes it."

I listened in amazement. I had been at the demonstration the

---

* Giovanni Agnelli, president of Fiat.

evening before and the square seemed half full. If Piazza San Carlo held 50,000, there were at least 20,000 present—a good turnout on twenty-four hours notice. A speaker's dais had been set up, and on the balconies above it hung a huge streamer professionally lettered in yellow on a blue background, the city's colors: TURIN RESISTS THE TERROR. Other streamers, more amateurish, were stretched across the equestrian statue in the center of the square: NON MOLLARE; NO ALLA PAURA; ABBASSO LA VILTÀ.* The dais was alive with the municipal banners of Piedmont towns and villages, old-fashioned standards like those of early British trade unions, embroidered in gold letters on red or blue backgrounds, with tassels and ribbons, the staff held by each town's uniformed police. Their police cars, with the names of the towns on their doors, were parked on the far side of the square. Considering that the city had been plastered with printed notices of the meeting, that speakers had to be gotten together, loudspeakers set up, and so on, the organizing job on such short notice had seemed to me more than credible.[10]

Moreover, I thought Arrigo Levi had made a good speech. The Red Brigades had announced that they had "executed a servant of the state," and Levi played upon that. Casalegno's daily column was titled "*Our* State," and Levi stressed that that meant the democratic state born of the resistance, a people's state to be defended against reactionaries, to be cleansed of the corruption that was helping the terrorists. Irreproachable sentiments, I had thought.

The reference to being a Jew was made in passing. Levi had been talking about Casalegno's attempt to resign (he was seventy) and how Levi had persuaded him to stay on—at this point Levi's voice broke. Recovering, he said: "Excuse me, Carlo would not have shown such emotion. He was a Piedmontese, but I'm an Emiliano and a Jew and can't control my feelings as well as he." He then made a small reference to the lack of discrimination against Jews. To me, the incident was moving; in this hall the reaction was anger. How they hated Fiat!

Riccio pointed to another man, two chairs from me. "You, *Ciccia.*"† This one was a plump pigeon with a concave face, slicked-down hair, and a tie—one of the few ties in the hall. He was young and very earnest: he had made notes.

"Well, comrades, I think the reason for our failure is fear. With good reason. I'll give you an example. I'm in Maintenance, Section 12, and everybody struck this morning, including the supervisor. Well, an hour later, there was a leaflet in the washroom, handwritten." He pulled it out and read: " 'The morning shift in Maintenance

*Handwritten margin note:* CPI. conceives of the state as a popular front in its own right, without vanguard necessary as USCP did w.r.t. Democratic party in 1930's

---

* "Don't Give In," "No to Fear," "Down with Cowardice."

† *Ciccia* is slang for "juicy flesh," roughly comparable to "fatso" in American, though more affectionate.

12 is a nest of Communist collaborators with Fiat. Warning: The Red Brigades are watching you.' A little later two of the men came up to me: 'Look, we got wives and kids. We're sticking our neck out. What are you going to do about it?' So I said to them, 'What are *we all* going to do about it? If we don't fight, it'll be like having the Mafia in the shop.' I know I said the right thing, but, believe me, those men aren't going to strike again.''

Zuccotti leaned over and whispered to Riccio. "One more," Riccio decided. "You, Amadeo."

Amadeo was sitting on the far side, and he stood up to speak, a tall, scraggly man with muscular hands. He took off from the previous speaker and at once you knew this was a pro, a veteran of many an inner party struggle. His sentences were measured, his timing accurate.

"Comrades," he said, "of course workers are afraid. You've seen it, I've seen it. But why? That's the question! Is it really because they are afraid of terrorists? They haven't been afraid of firings and discrimination on the job. They haven't been afraid of arrests and jailings, of police and company goons. They've faced the motorized squads of the *Celere,* Scelba's armored jeeps and guns and tear gas. So what's an occasional terrorist?''

Amadeo stretched out a sinewy hand and, tendons tense, slowly clenched into a fist. "Fiat workers are like that; men, not cream puffs. They got guts: they took the hard years at Fiat, and beat the management. They're not afraid—they are puzzled. They cannot express their feelings well, they use words like fear, but that's not what's in their minds. They said to Ciccia there, they said: 'What are you going to do about it?' But that 'you' didn't mean Ciccia; it meant the party. What was the *party* going to do about it? I tell you comrades, behind that question is a political critique.''

He paused for a moment, tall, austere, dominating the audience of his peers. "Comrades, attention must be paid. The workers are saying the party has become soft, has lost its aggressive spirit. We rely on deals and maneuvers—just like all the other parties. We shun fights and play footsie with the DC, word games like *non sfiducia.* For a year we keep them in power and finally force them to an agreement to do something—the pact of six parties—and what happens? The DC government hasn't carried out a single one of its promises. We have nothing to show for our support, nothing. Cost of living is up, unemployment is up, taxes up, bus and trainfares up, gas and electric up—the only thing down is our morale. The government is wiping out rent control, and the bosses are cutting our real wages, cheating on the *scala mobile.** The kids get frustrated; and it's back to the Church

---

* *Scala mobile* means "escalator" and refers to the clauses in contracts whereby wages are adjusted periodically to match inflation.

and the DC. Fiat workers aren't scared; they are disoriented! Disoriented by us!"

Amadeo drew himself up and took a deep breath, his whole body in an attitude of defiance: Luther nailing his theses on the church door. "Comrades, *we* are disoriented. Our tactics are not paying off. Our enemies are laughing at us. We've got to change our political line. I don't mean revolution, nothing silly like that. I mean an aggressive line. We say to the government: execute the laws, stop sabotaging agreements, or we'll go out in the streets; we'll stop production. We've got to put a little fear of God into them. Let them run scared, not us. We have to speak up so our party leaders in Rome will hear. They are good comrades, and they know we are on the front lines. But we have to speak loud, real loud—so they can hear us right through the walls of Parliament."

Amadeo sat down. He had not shouted: he had occasionally raised his voice slightly, expertly, yet my head rang from his leashed passion, as if he had been thundering, so powerful was the impact of his conviction. Heads had nodded as he spoke, not every one, not on everything he said, but he had obviously said much that had been often thought by many present.

My mind was racing at all the implications of this meeting. These were not ordinary functionaries in quiet rooms, no chair-borne staff officers; these were the combat colonels, the tank commanders of the class struggle, the very guts of the Communist party arguing over the most basic issue facing the party—collaboration with *Democrazia Cristiana*, the historic compromise.

*In Rome, a month earlier, in the deserted bar of my hotel, I had talked with Lisa Foa, a leader of* Lotta Continua, *a Marxist group to the left of the Communists. About fifty, her ascetic body dressed in austere black, she had sat erect, her hands folded quietly in her lap— Whistler's Roman Mother.*

*"The Communist party has betrayed the workers, and the workers are leaving the party. The 'historic compromise' is a betrayal. The PCI has become a social-democratic party, subordinated to the DC, acquiescing in a police state." She spoke in matter-of-fact tones. "I am not exaggerating; the government is operating with police laws enacted under fascism, with methods and procedures sanctioned by Mussolini. Workers no longer trust the PCI; the PCI has sold out to Agnelli and Confindustria. The Communist party has become a collaborationist party, a capitalist party, like the British Labour party."*

I thought of Lisa Foa as Amadeo was speaking. A man of his caliber would not speak with his passion, and his words would not find resonance in his peers, if the workers in the shops were not restive. I looked at the little Zuccotti: what could the poor man say to the conviction in Amadeo's mind? Zuccotti was so frail, so old—what chance had this seventy-four-year-old man, whose mature life had been one unending beating?

Zuccotti began to speak, slowly, authoritatively.

"Comrades, it is clear, is it not, that our bad showing was not due to fear, or Casalegno's politics. No, it was primarily due to our lack of enthusiasm. After all, Ciccia got a unanimous strike in his section, and there isn't a man here who thinks Ciccia is a better organizer than he is. Clearly, there are doubts about the party line—a political issue of the first magnitude."

Zuccotti polished his glasses, rested his folded arms on the table. "Amadeo is right when he says Fiat workers don't scare. They led the Turin strike in 1943—the first strike under fascism. A couple of you were in it, and so was I—already an old man of forty. We have quite a few of those workers still around and if they weren't afraid of Hitler and Mussolini, they aren't going to be scared by a few terrorists. No, Amadeo is right, and he knows Fiat workers. Incidentally, for some of you youngsters, Amadeo was in the resistance in his teens and came into Fiat in 1947. How old were you then?

"Nineteen," said Amadeo. "I was in the ACLI, and then in CISL."

"Right. And you came into the party in 1952. I remember, we met on the picket line after I was fired. We kept his joining quiet, had him drop all activities. It wasn't easy. Amadeo was always such a hothead." Zuccotti threw him a friendly smile and Amadeo grinned back. "How Fiat missed him on that picket line, I'll never know. But we knew the repression was coming, and we kept the little-known comrades under cover. Amadeo has been in Mirafiori continuously for thirty years. He knows the workers, and they know him."

Zuccotti, paused for a moment, then picked up Amadeo's challenge.

"That, of course, doesn't mean he is right. Amadeo has talked about the hard years at Fiat, throughout the fifties. And they were hard. Year after year, the battle of signatures went on. Anyone signing our CGIL cards was sure to be fired.* Once fired, you were on a blacklist and no company would give you a job. Thousands of our comrades emigrated, others worked as laborers picking up a few lire here and there. Some of our people broke under pressure. I remember Comrade Pautasso—fired at the Lingotto plant. He hadn't wanted to sign, his wife was against it, he had five children, and he knew he'd get fired, but the party made him, literally forced him—I know, I was on

---

* The signer agreed to be a candidate for CGIL committeeman—a kind of shop steward.

the committee, and we were merciless—and so he signed and afterwards he got fired. And he went through the routine; get a job elsewhere one day, fired the next. Week after week. I got him a job once, cleaning up the shit in the square after the circus left town. He worked all night, and in the morning they gave him five hundred lire. Five hundred lire! He came to me to tell of the injustice. He said, 'It's true, we have to keep going and not give in. We must not surrender to anyone, not even our family. But one must have strength to do it.' Half an hour later he committed suicide—he threw himself in the Po River. I told you: I was on the committee that made him sign."[11]

Zuccotti spoke evenly, a schoolmaster, as if suicides, emigration, hunger, family hatreds, were small matters. "They were disastrous years. In 1951 we had 70 percent of all committeemen, 103. Eight years later it was down to 30. To get them we had to get 300 signatures, half for candidates and half for poll watchers.[12] Those not elected would get fired, plus anyone caught soliciting signatures. Every year we paid a price of twenty or thirty comrades put out on the street for each committeeman elected. We got badly hurt, but we didn't get knocked out. We never went below thirty committeemen, and we had our 'sleepers'—comrades like Amadeo—that the informers didn't know and who hung on until the workers began to move again. Now, why am I going over all this ancient history, which most of you are too young to have known. Is it an old man reminiscing? No, comrades, no!"

His voice, hitherto calm, suddenly had a bite to it. He leaned forward, his sentences lashing the audience. "No, comrades, it's to make a point. The point is that the party made a political decision: whatever the cost, whatever the suffering, our presence in the shops had to be maintained. It wasn't easy. Every cadre, without exception, had to 'sign' although he knew he'd end up on the street. We had to work four months to get 300 signatures out of 40,000 workers. Four months! Until 1962 we couldn't get more than a few hundred workers out on the picket line.[13] But we still called the strikes, still put out the picket lines, still collected the signatures—in blood and anguish. Why? Because the party's political line demanded it and the political line mattered! We had internal struggles over that line that makes this afternoon's argument look like a kissing lark. We had splits and fights. Many comrades thought we ought not to contest the elections, work inside the Catholic unions until the storm had passed. That was a sensible *trade-union* approach but it was a narrow approach. The storm wouldn't pass: it would get worse. The only hope for the Fiat workers was a *political* solution—the unity of the workers and the support of the population. We had to fight for a unitary line, and that meant our party had to be present, to be visible, to be speaking up—choosing the right issues and pointing up the cost of collaboration with management. Of course, organizing was important, that was the job of the 'sleepers,' but without both activities going on we would never have won. And we did win. That's the point: our political line was correct. Without that line we would not have been able to deal with the upsurge of the sixties."

Zuccotti had changed. His gestures were still restrained, but his voice was engaged, resonant, assertive, as he hammered his points home.

"Without our presence, our leadership, that upsurge would have been dissipated. The anger of our southern brothers would have been frittered away in sporadic outbursts—violent, counterproductive. Instead, all those things led to working together on local contracts, then unity, then as the unitarian tactics paid off, pressure by the CISL and UIL militants on their own leadership.* This led to joint industry bargaining throughout the sixties, then nationwide co-operation, until we achieved the federation of the three confederations in 1972. This was a vindication of our political line, of our struggles, our sufferings."

*The story of Communist tenacity for twenty-five years in achieving the unitary federation of 1972 tells a great deal about the present. The PCI strategies within the trade unions and toward the Catholic Church are the sources of Communist success today and are pioneering examples for Eurocommunism. Several factors were involved. In the late fifties, there took place a technological revolution. Throughout industry—auto, steel, textile, petrochemicals—more advanced machinery was introduced, more intricate methods of production. One example: Fiat's fixed capital investment for machinery, buildings, and research soared astronomically, from 90 billion lire in 1951 to 927 billion in 1966—a tenfold increase![14] Even by American standards it was stupendous. With the CISL and UIL collaborating with management, the great increase in productivity, and profits, was accompanied by practically stationary wages and a clear deterioration of working conditions—fragmentation of the work process, tougher labor discipline, tighter supervision and, above all, the speedup. The satire of Chaplin's* Modern Times *was not too far removed from Italian reality.*

*Concomitantly, the labor force doubled and tripled. Again, taking Fiat as example, its total work force doubled from 1952 to 1966 and tripled by 1973—to 70,000, then 140,000, and 200,000.[15] The bulk of the workers came from the south, facing working and living conditions which were traumatic. Rural work is harsh—long hours,*

---

* A CISL organizer in Ferrara told me that, as early as 1958, CISL leaders in his region were paying attention to the advantages of a unitary approach.

*unremitting, backbreaking toil—but it is varied, with natural rhythms and traditional tempos. Village life is protective. Personal relationships, scaled to human dimensions, leave time for gossip and a glass of wine. In the north, the southerners were at first disoriented and terrorized, but soon resentful and rebellious.* Rocco and His Brothers, *a film made in 1960, gives the viewer a direct feel for the trauma of these workers: their grim life in the ghettos, their alienation and despair, their violence and rebellion.*

*In this period, peasants abandoned the land in huge numbers— some five millions migrated north and abroad. The Establishment didn't mind; industry was getting its required labor force, ignorant, docile—and very, very cheap.*

*While docile at first, these men soon rebelled. They were hot-tempered, easily moved to anger and action, and they didn't frighten.* They didn't know enough to be frightened! *The combination of their militancy, the speedup, and the contemptuous foremen was explosive. The Communists were there to provide the spark. Older workers took courage from the newcomers; the newcomers got history, knowledge, and organizational knowhow from the old-timers. Throughout all sections Communists, the "sleepers," were organizing, while the committeemen, showing the face of the party, were publicly leading and explaining. Wildcat strikes began to increase; CISL and UIL workers became more militant, struck in solidarity, pressured their leaders. Factory councils were activated and moved toward unity under the leadership of the Communists, whose unions steadily increased their membership at the expense of the other two. Meanwhile, contract negotiations became increasingly unitary, and the union-approved strikes began to roll: 1968, five days of general strikes; 1969, six days of general strikes plus some two dozen days of departmental strikes (two hundred hours in all). In 1970 the first political input: six days of general strike to back the reforms before Parliament.*[16]

*The unitary federation was achieved by 1972, just in time for the referendum on divorce. To avoid offending their more backward members, the federation and the three confederations took no official positions. But innumerable union leaders came out for divorce, as individuals. The majority of unionists, thoroughly politicized in the past decade, threw themselves enthusiastically into the campaign. While UDI provided the spirit and the peaks of the victory, the unions provided the massive base.*[17]

The history of those years was of course common knowledge among the unionists in the hall. Zuccotti reminded them of the importance of the federation.

"Comrades, without the unitary federation we wouldn't have had a political agreement in the referendum—thousands of local unions could not have spent the money and the manpower to set up the meetings, the debates, the demonstrations, the leaflets, and the factory bulletins that reached millions and millions in factories and housing projects to vote no. Union unity was a major factor in the referendum, but the unitary federation was the result of the *correct* political line of the party in the hard years."

Zuccotti's tone changed again, became less authoritative, more argumentative, at times almost cajoling.

"The party now has a political line for the whole of Italy, as far-reaching and as long-range as its political line on industry twenty-five years ago; the line of the 'historic compromise'—a working together of Catholics, Communists, and Socialists for the salvation of our country. Casalegno accepted that line.

"What's the alternative to our policy? Go into opposition and block legislation? But that's exactly what the right wing of *Democrazia Cristiana* wants us to do—and those infantile leftists of *Lotta Continua* and the *autonomi*. Even the *Manifesto* isn't asking us to do that; certainly Amadeo isn't. Therefore the party's strategy is not in question, only its tactics. Amadeo says we're too soft; we are getting nothing for our support. I think he's wrong on both counts. Number one: how tough should we be? The right-wing Demochristians don't want to work with us; they want us to be in the opposition. If our conditions are too tough, the liberal and center wings end up on the right. Certainly Zaccagnini and Andreotti* are exercising a kind of political blackmail: if you want too much, they say, we'll be defeated inside the DC. So, inherently and inevitably, we have to be more accommodating than perhaps is warranted. Number two: Amadeo says we are getting nothing out of this. That's simply not true. Amadeo gets carried away and he exaggerates—he was always a bit of a hothead—but the fact is that the working class of Italy, and its unions, with the Fiat workers at the head of them, have had no major setbacks either in wages or working conditions in a *period of depression!* Our working class has suffered less than any working class in Europe!"[18]

He paused dramatically. His fist crashed the table, and he repeated: "Less than any working class in Europe! We have held the bosses at bay—and they are yelping! Read Agnelli, read Carli!† The escalation clause is still functioning; layoffs in big industry have been

---

\* DC secretary and DC prime minister, respectively.

† Agnelli, president of FIAT, is a former president of *Confindustria;* Guido Carli, president of *Confindustria,* is a former head of the Bank of Italy, where he was more liberal than in his present job.

blocked. Most of the unemployed are youths who can't get jobs—no one minimizes that problem, least of all our party—but the basic fact remains that *Big Business has not been able to use that unemployment to beat the unions down.* Think of it: it may be for the first time in the history of capitalism!

"And why, comrades, why? Not because of our union strength: there are more powerful unions, with more money and more manpower, in France and Britain—or America for that matter. But they have lost ground, they haven't been able to achieve what our unions have achieved. And why? Because of our political framework, that's why! The political framework—our party in Parliament, wheeling and dealing; our mayors in cities, just look at Bologna—*Bologna rossa*—the best-run city in Europe; our comrades in the regions—we run half of the regions of Italy! We govern, comrades, we *govern,* 60 percent of the population—that's a political framework such as exists nowhere else in the capitalist world! The parliamentary maneuvers that Amadeo scorns—playing footsie he calls it—is what politics is about, wheeling and dealing, the art of compromise. As Togliatti kept saying: *fare politica.**[19] We have stopped many bad measures— created space for the unions to flourish. Our strength in cities and regions gives our unions support and protection. Workers grumble— it's a depression and times are bad and they expect miracles from us—but the fact is, and it's our job, your *job,* to remind them—the party is still the first and best line of defense of the working class!''

Zuccotti's voice had steadily risen, fulminating like a prophet of old. One wouldn't have thought that frail body had the strength. The truth is, I thought whimsically, age has little to do with energy: when you're hot, you're hot. He now dropped his voice and made a placating, wait-a-minute gesture.

"Take rent control. Amadeo says it's being wiped out. Now that's formally true and actually false. True, the Supreme Court has held the present rent control law to be unconstitutional—ergo, it is being wiped out. If the Communist deputies were in opposition perhaps it would stay wiped out. But we're not, and we've been working with the DC on a substitute law, which is being passed, and I'm here today to explain it to you.[20] It's not the best possible law, a lot will depend on who's administering it, but it's one we can live with. I know, since I'll be the one administering it in Turin. But that's only the beginning. We are going to get a trade union of police, affiliated to the federation—our unions! Imagine! We are getting democratic procedures in the army—elected representation in the regiments, the divisions, the army bases. Imagine! Most important of all we have

---

* Literally, "make politics," i.e., be a professional, be as good as the ruling class, beat the politicians at their own game. *exploiting the workers?*

Law 382* passed, sealed, and delivered! Do you realize what that means? It is potentially the most powerful instrument for restructuring the country, for introducing elements of socialism in daily life and in the economy. Don't forget, we now run half the regions and practically all the major cities. With Law 382, *Democrazia Cristiana* will have to reform or die.''

I was puzzled: Why, then, had the *DC* agreed to the law. DC leaders were not stupid—far from it! Why agree to a law that undermined them?

''Why did the DC agree to the law?'' Zuccotti had been reading my mind. ''Because that's the price they had to pay for our support. The alternative would be the fall of the government, new elections on the issue of regions—which the Constitution demanded and the DC has evaded for thirty years! How wrong can Amadeo be?''

Zuccotti was now rolling his speech fast and forceful, reveling in the party's skill.

''Look, comrades. Peasants say: You can lead a horse to water but you can't make it drink. Through our voting power in the referendum and the elections† we've brought the DC to water: now we have to make them drink. They *don't want* to drink, comrades, but they *are* drinking, gagging, a sip at a time! And they'll have to sip again and again, at closer and closer intervals. Amadeo says our enemies are laughing: I don't hear them. What I do hear is Agnelli saying clearly: 'At issue is the class hegemony in the country. The stakes are very high.'[21] If Agnelli understands, why don't we? Our party has achieved cultural hegemony in the country; we are on the road to political hegemony. Along that road we're also taking steps toward economic hegemony . . . five, ten, twenty years—whatever it takes. This is the meaning of the 'historic compromise.' This is our strategy: it needs a historical perspective, tenacity, will power, clarity. Above all, *perspective,* which gives us courage and stamina, strengthens our will at difficult moments.''

*[handwritten margin note: Program of the Left Social-Democrats in Sweden]*

Zuccotti was in his element, zestful, sparkling, the audience in the palm of his hand, mesmerized as much by his exuberance and youthfulness as by the strength of his arguments. My God, I thought, and he is seventy-four! And I had felt sorry for him. The little chicken had become a rooster, his voice relishing the irony in the predicament of the DC.

''How do we make the DC drink? By our tactics, by relying on the needs of the people, by helping participate in politics, *by de-*

* Law 382 was the enabling statute spelling out the powers of the regions. At the minimum it gave regions power over health, schools, welfare programs, social security, and agriculture. Since half of the regions were Communist-led, this was a great deal of power. For the text of the law, see Barbera, *Governo locale* . . .

† The referendum on divorce, 1974; local elections, 1975; national elections 1976.

*mocracy, and more democracy and still more democracy!* By analyzing every situation, no matter how complicated, by picking key issues, no matter how small, and so presenting them that the DC, at every level, has no choice but to vote our way. For example, the central government is holding back money that now belongs to the regions, so what do we do? We organize *all* the regions, red and white, and send a joint delegation to Rome.[22] The DC regions *need* the money, *want* the money, as much as the red regions do—so what is the DC in Rome going to do? Stall their own supporters? That's tricky and dangerous—so, sure, they still drag their heels, but while they would stall us for two or three years, they can only stall the DC regions (and us) a few months. But, inevitably, they have to give in; they have to drink. That is óur job as trade unionists—to create conditions to make the DC drink. We are Communists, are we not? We have studied dialectics, and talk dialectics—but we must apply dialectics, think dialectically, search out the contradictions in the DC's positions and make those contradictions work for us." *until the fascist coup*

He looked around at the faces, smiling like a benevolent grand-father, enjoying the role.

"And that, comrades, brings me to Casalegno. It's true what Hannibal says, he works for *La Stampa,* Agnelli's paper, the Fiat paper. But that's not all there is to Casalegno. He is an honest man, a man of the resistance. He has integrity. Like Levi, he is an indepen-dent man, he doesn't feel bought by Agnelli. To us, that's a con-tradiction, but that's only a part of a greater contradiction, the one Agnelli is locked into. That's where we must think dialectically. Consider: for *La Stampa* to be effective to be useful to Agnelli, it must have credibility, it must seem to be independent. That's hard to fake, so Agnelli has to pick editors who do have a degree of independence —men of known integrity, such as Levi and Casalegno. We all know they watch out for Fiat's interests: any idea of Agnelli's gets plenty of space; anything derogatory to Fiat gets buried on page seven with one paragraph. But that paragraph *is* published. Any major DC scandal involving Fiat, something *L'Unità* would headline on the front page with three columns of copy, *La Stampa* puts on page 3 with half a column of copy. But it is there, and Agnelli doesn't like it, but the credibility of the paper demands it. Of course, the paper supports the DC. But from time to time a key issue arises, like the referendum, where the combination of their integrity and credibility forces Levi and Casalegno to go *against* the DC, *against* Agnelli, *against* the Church. *La Stampa* came out strongly for no. It influenced thousands and tens of thousands of votes, don't think it didn't. Casalegno, comrades, is an ally, an ally not an enemy, a man whom we must respect, must protect, must cherish. You read Fortebraccio* this morning, his tribute to Casalegno, how Casalegno has never baited reds. It was a moving tribute.[23] Millions of Catholics vote Communist; thousands of Communists go to church: I hope they are all praying for his life today.''

Zuccotti paused, momentarily spent. His tongue gentled, became pedagogic.

"Comrades, there are thousands, hundreds of thousands, in the middle and professional classes, inside the Church, inside the DC, yes, and inside management too, who again and again find themselves agreeing with us on different issues. We need them, if we are to make the DC drink. We need them as friends and allies if we are to make Italy *socialist!* If we want to make the working class into the governing class, then other classes must believe in us, trust us to defend *their* interests! This is crucial, comrades: if we want to govern we must learn to govern, must be fit to govern! Gramsci has taught us: a governing class must take into account the interests of all groups in society, must reach a certain equilibrium of compromises and must be ready to sacrifice some of its immediate interests.[24] He's talking about us unionists, comrades. He's warning us against what Lenin called the economism of the trade unions, and what we call corporativism—the hangover from our origins within the capitalist system where everyone grabs what he can. If Casalegno's friends don't show up at meetings, the more reason for us to show up. When workers don't show up on a picket line, we don't say: If Titus and Caius don't show up, we won't either. Not at all, we say: They're backward, we must educate them. It's the same with the middle class and the professionals. There is one more thing.''

His voice hardened.

"When Casalegno gets hit and the Red Brigades say they've executed a servant of the state, that sounds very revolutionary doesn't it? He's the servant of the state, which is the state of Fiat, so even though it's not nice to go around killing people, and we certainly do not believe in assassination as a political weapon, still it's one less of them, right, and no great harm is done. There is a kind of sneaking sympathy for these tough reds, these half bandits, like there was for Giuliano.† But that sympathy is misplaced. When fascist terrorists shoot Communists, their purpose is obvious. When left terrorists do the shooting, their purpose is not so obvious. They say they want to

---

 * Fortebraccio ("the strong arm," the Italian name for Popeye) is the *nom de guerre* of the satirist who does a daily column for *L'Unità*, a skilled writer of sardonic wit and mordant phrase. His real name is Mario Mellone.

 † Salvatore Giuliano, a Sicilian bandit with a reputation as a Robin Hood who robbed the rich and gave to the poor. He did rob, but he also shot workers, and the Robin Hood reputation was undeserved.

expose the fascist character of *Democrazia Cristiana* by forcing the DC to take repressive measures. What they are doing, in fact, is frightening people, making them susceptible to fascist demands for repressive measures. They are trying to destabilize society, make it chaotic, disorderly—just as the American CIA planned in Chile. If these Red Brigades are so revolutionary, why didn't they shoot management when it was grinding workers into the dirt? Why not? Why today when the unions are strong, the party is strong and advancing? Because comrades, they are fighting us, just like the fascists are fighting us and our line. Push the DC to the right, toward fascism, so we cannot work with them, so our strategy fails. When they strike at Casalegno, they strike at us! We must understand; we must resist. So far, we've blocked them. Unlike Germany, our country has not swung to the right.* If we teach the people, if we mobilize the people, we'll win.

"Comrades, our party has a great goal: socialism. We will enter the government as the first step in the great battle to restructure our country. We've won many battles, and we'll win this one, the hardest and longest of them all."

He stopped. Then the half-conscious afterthought came out, with great simplicity. "And I, comrades, am not getting any younger."

He was finished. The room exhaled. No one spoke, but Amadeo threw him a warm, rueful smile that said, "Well done, comrade. But I'm still only half-convinced." *perhaps because its half-true*

When the meeting was adjourned, I went up and shook Zuccotti's hand. "A magnificent performance," I said. *"Magistrale e madornale."*† He smiled, appreciating the phrase, and ran a deprecating hand alongside his nose.

"One does what one can," he said.

"What are you going to do about Amadeo?" I said.

He looked at me bewildered: "What's to do about what?"

"Well, he's disruptive isn't he? He must be a thorn in your side—a defeatist. . . ."

"He's not a defeatist," Zuccotti said sharply. "He's a good comrade, mature, experienced, and he has a right to his opinion— sometimes he's right, and we'd be fools to cut him off."

I nodded in agreement. "Still, there has to be a limit—or else what's the meaning of democratic centralism. You sound more like a debating society."

---

\* The impact of terrorist assassinations and kidnappings in Germany has strengthened the right-wing forces to such a degree that the country is in the grip of McCarthyite hysteria. The police have been given enormous powers, and civil liberties have been seriously eroded.[25]

† "Magisterial and a lulu." *Madornale* verges on slang and is used to indicate something extraordinary. We'd say, "terrific, enormous, stupendous—a lulu!"

He bristled. "Nonsense, the party is not a debating society; we do run on democratic centralism. When the *Manifesto* people organized a faction, we threw them out. That's centralism. But when Amadeo speaks—that's democracy. The two go together. Our comrades must be free to speak. Must. Otherwise how can we work out a line that's correct, that corresponds to reality. Gramsci said there's a kernel of truth in what your opponent says, a kernel that you must understand and incorporate."

"I know the quote," I said, unable to resist, and as he raised a skeptical eyebrow, I intoned: "We must not conceive of a scientific discussion as if it were a courtroom proceeding . . ." His eyebrow—and his jaw—dropped. I grinned at him. "I translated that quote," I said. "I was the first to translate Gramsci into English—enough Gramsci to get started on him."

He grasped my biceps and gave me a little shake. "You should have told us sooner," he said warmly. "I'm sorry I was so cool before, but most American professors don't know very much; they are something of a nuisance. They want to know about the Italian road to socialism and they've never heard of Gramsci. Anyway, forgive me . . ."

"Not at all. Look at me, taking up your time . . ."

"Don't mouth stupidities," he said using the familiar *tu*. Ask anything."

"*Okay*. How come there were no women here? Doesn't Fiat hire them?"

"In administration, yes, but very few in production. None in the foundry, of course. Still, we do have women in production, and you are right—there should be some here. But all these people here were elected, and I'm afraid our workers, including many comrades, are still very backward on this issue. Don't forget, the people here are the ones who deal with foremen and managers—and there are no women among them! On the contrary, a lot of sexism. Still, you are right."

I asked him what was a good book on the Fiat. "There are several," Zuccotti replied, "But I like *Gli anni duri alla Fiat* [The hard years at Fiat] by two comrades, Emilio Pugno and Sergio Garavini. I gave them a lot of material; it's full of incidents, statistical tables, chronology and, for me, excellent analysis. You'll find it very useful."

I thanked him and took a streetcar back to downtown Turin, thinking of Zuccotti, what an able man he was. He was not even a provincial leader, but a relatively minor functionary, like hundreds of others. What most impressed me was his emphasis on democracy— the understanding of what democracy means, not as parliamentarism, the way most of Europe understands it, but the way Americans understand it. . . .the expression and participation of the people in their own associations—what Tocqueville saw a century ago and what is still scarce in Europe. *retch*

*That evening I had dinner with Claudio, a newspaperman on La Stampa, a devout Catholic, almost mystic in his religion, and a staunch supporter of the DC ("But on the divorce, I voted no—such a DC stupidity!"). Pedrazzi, in Bologna, had given me his name, describing him as "an intelligent man close to Cardinal Pellegrino. The cardinal has just retired and doesn't see many people, but Claudio can arrange it."*

*Claudio greeted me buoyantly. He has a saturnine face, reminiscent of Ed Murrow, and he has something of his style as well, factual, astringent—the opposite of the discursive, literary style prevalent in Italian journalism.*

*"Good news, my friend! Cardinal Pellegrino, three o'clock tomorrow, Vallo Torinese. He tires easily, but he will see you. He couldn't resist an American who was baptized in San Pietro on Vincoli."*

*"But tomorrow I see Bishop Bettazzi—way out in Ivrea."*

*"Vallo Torinese is on the way. You'll simply have to hustle, American style. What time is your appointment?"*

*"I take a bus at nine o'clock. The appointment is for eleven."*

*"Take a taxi instead. The driver will wait in Ivrea an hour or so—Bettazzi won't spare you more—and drop you off in Vallo on the way back. He goes home, you eat lunch, see the cardinal and make your way back by bus. Shouldn't cost you more than twenty thousand lire. A bargain: to pluck a cardinal and a bishop in one day for only twenty-five dollars!"*

*We went to eat in cheerful camaraderie, anticipating the rewards of the morrow. Over the Barolo and Bologna fettucine I told him of the afternoon and of Zuccotti.*

*"I see he made quite an impression on you. I know him well—for years he was the local martyr. Not a bad fellow, a little stiff—you say uptight, yes? The right word?"*

*"Yes, very up-to-date."*

*"Good, but you mustn't take everything he says as gospel, you know."*

*"You mean he wasn't fired? Or blacklisted? To me it sounded like the McCarthy years in the States; government helping management against left unions, FBI hounding Communists. . ."*

*"No question—our fifties were like your fifties. But," Claudio held up an admonishing finger, "that's not the point. Zuccotti has left things out. The point is that in 1948, after the Catholic split, the CGIL still had 80 percent of the union vote. Ten years later they had 20*

*percent. An enormous drop! Granted, the government helped man-*
*agement, and management was tough. . .but that's not enough to*
*explain the drop. No, workers just walked away from the CGIL*
*because the CGIL was against the Marshall Plan. The Communists*
*called strike after strike in opposition to the plan. It was a huge*
*mistake: Can you imagine Fiat workers being against American*
*loans, American food, American orders? Nonsense! It was the*
*costliest mistake the party ever made, and they know it. Russia made*
*them do it, and they know that, too. Between you and me, I think this*
*had more to do with Togliatti's moving away from the Russians than*
*did Khrushchev's speech about Stalin.*

*I asked about American pressure.*

*"It's always been there, everybody knows it. They pressured De*
*Gasperi against his better judgment to throw the Communists out of*
*the cabinet in 1947."*

*I told him that Pedrazzi thought that De Gasperi and Togliatti*
*were unwitting partners: De Gasperi resisting the Americans and the*
*Vatican, Togliatti the Russians and the PCI hard-liners. What did he*
*think?*

*"Oh, there's much to be said for it. De Gasperi, for example,*
*blocked the Vatican plan to bring the fascists into the municipal*
*government of Rome in 1952. Pope Pius XII was so angry he never*
*again granted an audience to De Gasperi.*[26] *As for the Americans,*
*what could we do? We needed the loans and contracts. The book on*
*Fiat that Zuccotti mentioned documents a meeting between the U.S.*
*ambassador, Clare Boothe Luce, and the head of Fiat, Vittorio*
*Valletta. She tells him outright: American orders depend on Fiat's*
*anti-Communist work, and Valletta gives her a memo on what Fiat*
*was doing against the Communists.*[27] *Just the same, the Communist*
*eclipse was due largely to their mistakes—just as, ironically, their*
*comeback was due to Fiat's mistakes."*

*He paused and raised an eyebrow. He was showing me he was*
*objective. "Tell me about the mistakes," I said, and he nodded,*
*obligingly.*

*"So many. Not only Fiat, all of the big industrialists, well,*
*almost all. They were antediluvians, shaped under fascism, and they*
*came out of the war having learned nothing—regular Bourbons, their*
*minds fixed on the past: they forgot nothing and learned nothing.*
*They were terribly greedy. Profits zoomed and they wouldn't even*
*give a few crumbs to the workers. This undermined the CISL and the*
*UIL. You see, how stupid that was. The same thing with the speedup*
*and tight supervision. Because the non-Communist unions were*
*supine, management could get away with worsening conditions. But*
*in the long run it was fatal, destroyed the credibility of those unions.*
*Bodrato warned them, but they wouldn't listen."*

*"Bodrato?"*

*"Guido Bodrato, a DC deputy from Turin. A good friend of mine, extremely intelligent and well read. He's very high up in DC councils, close to Zaccagnini. A likable man too. You should meet him. I will arange it."*

*"Sounds like one of the men that's helping the DC drink,"* I said, recounting Zuccotti's metaphor. Claudio laughed appreciatively.

*"Not bad, not bad.* Se non è vero, è ben trovato.* *Anyway, the Communists made a comeback in the unions, and that led to the combined federation, and that paved the way for the victory on divorce, and that paved the way for everything since. Italian politics in a nutshell—a series of DC defeats—well earned and fully merited by DC arrogance, Fiat callousness, capitalist greed, and general ruling-class ineptness. I was delighted."*

*"Tell me, Claudio, why aren't you a Communist?"*

*"I like them, you know; some of my best friends are in the party. But not for me. They're utopian; they think human nature can change, as you do. You are a Marxist, the summit of the Enlightenment and secularism, and for you man is the measure of all things. But for me, God is the measure. Man is born evil, a beast, civilized only by religion, made human only by the grace of God. So, you see: how could I be a Communist?"*

*"Then why do you work with them?"*

*"Because they are serious, and their policies are good for the country. Besides,"* he grinned wickedly, *"more and more Communists are joining the Church, on the one hand, and on the other their competition is forcing a renewal in the DC and a renewal in the Church. At this stage, Communist influence is all to the good. It may well be God's design. You smile and you are polite, but inside you laugh. But Pope John was as abreast of his times as Togliatti. Tomorrow you will see Pellegrino and Bettazzi—a generation apart, yet both deeply religious, both deeply modern. You will learn how complex Catholicism is."*

*"Fiat lux,"* I jested, but Claudio was unperturbed.

*"Exactly. You will see the light,"* he said, urbane and serene. *"You will see the light because you are a Roman, genetically and by environment. You see?"* He patted my arm affectionately. *"How else could an American understand us?"*

The meetings with Pellegrino and Bettazzi have been recounted, but Claudio's detour on original sin didn't make me forget Zuccotti or Amadeo. Two years later, when the PCI lost four points in the

---

*    "If not true, well invented"; i.e., it may not be the literal truth, but it expresses a deeper truth.

election, I remembered Amadeo's misgivings. Yet in the same two years, there was a vindication of Zuccotti's confidence in the metal workers' class consciousness.

Two weeks after the Mirafiori meeting, the metal workers staged a demonstration in Rome (December 3, 1977), which, in effect, brought down the government. The resolution of that crisis was the government of *la maggioranza*, which took office March 16, the day Moro was kidnapped. This, as we have seen, set in train a series of events which eventuated in the elections of June 3, 1979. The PCI decline was recognized immediately by the unions as an incentive for employers to mount a counteroffensive. A huge demonstration of the metal workers in Rome on June 22, 1979, was turned into a major political warning: NO TURNING BACK! The suspicions of the unions were soon confirmed in a bitter fight for the renewal of expiring contracts, particularly at Fiat which is the pacesetter of all industry. The Fiat attempts to erode the power of the unions via the contract negotiations failed, but Agnelli did not give up. He widened the offensive by playing on the public's revulsion against terrorism. On October 9, 1979, Fiat fired sixty-one workers for lack of "diligence, propriety, and good faith on the job." The next day, Alfa Romeo in Milan fired four workers.* At the same time, Fiat announced that it was suspending hiring because the factories had become "ungovernable."[28] While the workers were not directly accused of terrorism, the timing of the firings five days after attacks by Red Brigades,† and the phraseology imputing violence to the fired workers, made the implications obvious.

One commentator said that the firings "could be the beginning of the counterrevolution in Italian labor relations. . . . The emergency atmosphere created by terrorism has apparently convinced Fiat that it can take on its workers in a test of strength and start to unravel the solidarity and combativity that have made them so formidable."[30]

Through the unions the PCI is under attack. Fiat has shrewdly set its trap: if the federation and the PCI defend the workers, they will be accused of complicity in terrorism; if they accept the firings, they will be accused of class-collaboration, weakening their hold on the workers and stimulating independent unions.‡ Fiat has suggested indirectly that the firings were made with union consent.

---

* They were fired for "absenteeism," but it was generally accepted that they were fired in retaliation for terrorist graffiti that were inscribed on the factory walls.

† There have been 128 acts of violence against Fiat executives in four years: 3 have been murdered and 17 wounded; 58 have had their cars set on fire; 30 have suffered aggression of various sorts; and 18 have had fires in their offices. Five days before the firings, Cesare Varetto, in charge of union relations at Mirafiori, had been "knee-capped"; next day a Fiat consultant, Pier Carlo Andreoletti, had been shot in the legs.[29]

‡ Independent unions are growing. Although their strikes tend to be more disruptive, they tend to be apolitical, and therefore less dangerous to the system.[31]

The unions and the PCI responded vigorously with complete support for the workers, all the while reiterating their opposition to terrorism and collecting statements from each of the fired workers that he disapproved completely of terrorism. At the same time the PCI, in major statements by top leaders such as Gerardo Chiaromonte and Adalberto Minucci, tied the Fiat offensive to the economic and political crisis facing the country. Minucci paid particular attention to Fiat's economic position, asserting that while the present Fiat offensive was comparable to that of the 1950s the power relations had changed. Not only were the unions united, but Fiat was facing contracting markets. Since 1970 the proportion of Fiats in Italy had gone from 75 percent of all autos to 53 percent, and in the European market from 8 percent to 3 percent. The company was gambling on government support to tame the unions.[32]

The DC maneuvered to inveigle the PCI into supporting the government, spreading rumors that the PCI was tacitly going along, thus sowing mistrust of the party politically just as Fiat was sowing mistrust within the unions. Berlinguer met the maneuver by asserting the party's opposition and its immediate fight in two directions: first, the defense of the poorer sections of the people in regard to pensions, housing, cost of living, and second, in a fight for peace, specifically around the issue of emplacing the new American missiles within NATO countries.[33]

On November 16, an arbiter declared the firings illegal and sentenced Fiat to retroactive payment of wages as well as fines. Fiat paid, but it refused to reinstate the workers and issued new charges against them.[34] The federation declared a general strike for November 21, in part, said Luciano Lama of the CGIL, to answer Fiat's campaign.[35] A considerable part of the press supported the goal of Fiat, namely, the re-establishment of a managerial free hand inside the factories, but had misgivings on the way Fiat was going about it, as provocative and counterproductive.[36]

The misgivings were well founded. Less than three months after Fiat disregarded the arbiter's findings, the PCI used the Fiat offensive to counterattack both the company and the government. It fought on two fronts: on the issue of terrorism and on the issue of Fiat's economic efficiency. On the first front, it launched a series of meetings in all the departments of Fiat in Turin to fight terrorism. To these meetings within the factories the workers systematically invited the representatives of the police and police unions, magistrates, representatives of the mayor and regional politicians, lawyers, and, as one paper put it, "men of culture."

The correspondent of La Repubblica, Guido Neppi Mondona, was practically euphoric in his reportage: "I don't usually visit Fiat, but I certainly can say on the basis of my experience and of those who have participated at these meetings, that there was a climate of composure and participation . . . demonstrating that the coming together of the workers' movement and of the democratic institutions has become a reality.

"There was an instinctive, and I would say almost visceral, awareness of the danger of mass repressive measures . . . the rooted conviction that terrorism seeks to induce an authoritarian response, thus creating conditions for a frontal clash between the workers' movement and the state.

"This means that the massive consensus necessary for a political line that connects rigor and efficiency to democratic procedures in the fight against terrorism are to be found precisely in the working class."[37]

In the same newspaper, another columnist, Massimo Riva, described the other prong of the PCI counterattack, namely a clear defense of the importance of Fiat and the auto industry to the economy of the country. Riva referred to Minucci's article on the difficulties of Fiat and its contracting markets and lauded the PCI proposal for a major production conference at Fiat. The PCI argued that the road to profitability was not to cut down on union strength and salaries, but to reinvigorate productivity and technology. Agnelli had no option but to agree. Said Riva: "Credit is due the PCI for its initiative, and Agnelli for not closing the door in their face."

The lesson of the counteroffensive was not lost on Riva: "On the Fiat issue, the Communist party intends to demonstrate its irreversible passage from a culture of opposition to a culture of government. The stakes are high, both at home and abroad. . . . The leaders of the PCI wish to prove concretely, in Turin, their thesis that the working class is sufficiently mature to become a national governing class."[38]

As of March 31, 1980, the problem of the 61 dismissed workers had not been resolved. Fiat had tried to save face by offering to reinstate some but not others, while the unions remained adamant. Whatever the outcome, it is clear that the Fiat offensive has been blunted and is disintegrating, with significant repercussions in Italian politics.

# CHAPTER 8

# Why the DC Horse *Is* Drinking

POLITICS is the search for consensus, but the craft turns on differentiation: to regard *Democrazia Cristiana* simply as the party of Big Business and the Vatican is misleadingly reductive. The DC is the party backed by the Vatican today, but it is not the party the Vatican wanted at the end of the war. To understand what it is the Vatican wanted and what it got, we need to go back to 1919.

When the 1870 papal policy of nonparticipation in elections failed, Pope Pius X reluctantly allowed Catholics to vote. The first "Catholic" deputy was elected from Bergamo in 1904, but nine years passed before the Gentiloni Pact of 1913 acknowledged Catholic power and another six years elapsed before a Catholic party was formed—the Popular party *(Partito Popolare)* of Don Luigi Sturzo of 1919.[1] Although Don Sturzo was a priest, the Vatican did not feel it had enough control over the party, in part because it had misgivings about direct political action by Catholics. Thus it decided to support Mussolini, who suppressed the *Partito Popolare* and other parties.

The Church's support for Mussolini paid off at first. The Lateran Treaties and the concordat made Roman Catholicism the state religion, granted sovereignty to the Vatican State, gave substantial payments to the Vatican as well as subsidies to Catholic schools, hospitals, and welfare agencies of all types. In exchange, the Church co-operated with Mussolini, blessed the Ethiopian War, Italy's pro-Franco intervention in Spain, and the war against the Soviet Union in 1941. There were frictions, of course: for example, over youth organizations and education in general. Then, too, Mussolini did not want the works of Jacques Maritain published in Italy. It was Monsignor Giovanni Montini (later Paul VI) who secured their translation and publication. Also notable was the Church's resistance to the anti-Semitic laws of 1938.

The defeat of fascism heavily compromised the Church. By 1942 the Vatican was beginning to think about the shape of the postwar world and to recognize the uses a Catholic party could be put to. The Church could easily create such a party, since it was the only social institution that had retained power under fascism—money, buildings, networks of people and agencies. One such agency, Catholic Action *(Azione Cattolica),* had been formed, ostensibly, as a social organization, but actually as a defense against fascist encroachments on the Church. Its leaders, such as Luigi Gedda, had obtained favors and concessions by working wholeheartedly with the fascists. They were virulently anti-Communist, as was Pope Pius XII, who saw Catholic Action as the natural nucleus of a Catholic party under full control of the Vatican. In August 1943 Gedda wrote to Marshal Pietro Badoglio, offering him the support of Catholic Action in exchange for access to communication media, then under censorship, and for other political favors.[2] That was the first step toward the creation of a new party.

Pope Pius had reckoned without Alcide De Gasperi. De Gasperi had been an irredentist deputy in the Austrian legislature before World War I,* and then a member of *Partito Popolare.* During the war he worked at a minor job in the Vatican. A shrewd politician, he saw events more realistically than the Vatican did. He knew there were many Catholic groups that would never accept the tainted Gedda—factory workers and Catholic partisans in the north, unionists who hated fascism, intellectuals and priests grouped around Giuseppe Dossetti, Giorgio La Pira, and the periodical *Cronache sociali,* who were contemptuous of Vatican compromises with Mussolini. De Gasperi rallied these groups and amalgamated them with older elements—the old leadership of *Partito Popolare,* and a strong group in Milan of conservative but antifascist Catholics. The new party was called *Democrazia Cristiana,* which had great resonance, as it had been the name of the left wing of the *Partito Popolare* in 1919.

With consummate skill, De Gasperi avoided a conflict with either Gedda or the reactionary sections of the hierarchy. At the same time, he secured the support of prelates, such as Montini, who appreciated the Church's need to overcome its profascist record. De Gasperi managed to be a man *for* the pope without being the man *of* the pope. Thus when the Committee of National Liberation was formed in 1943, the DC was able to join it as one of the six antifascist parties.

In the spring of 1945, according to the Catholic historian Pietro Scoppola, the Vatican accepted the DC as the party for Catholics.[3] Since De Gasperi was already one of the principal leaders of a

---

* De Gasperi was a native of the Trentino, a part of Austria-Hungary until it was annexed to Italy at the end of World War I.

government recognized by the Allies, he had, in a sense, imposed his kind of party on the Vatican. In a deeper sense, a large segment of Catholics politicized by the struggles against fascism, by the partisan war against Germans, and by the disasters of fascism and Vatican acquiescence had imposed a new kind of party on the Vatican via De Gasperi.* The social current represented by La Pira and Dossetti at one time controlled as much as 40 percent of the *Democrazia Cristiana.*† It was to this segment of the DC that Togliatti addressed his unitary line; the payoff was the referendum on the monarchy held on June 2, 1946. The Republic won by a narrow margin: 12.7 million for, 10.7 million against. That margin was provided by the left of the DC, which had split 2 million for a republic, 6 million for the monarchy.[4] The Vatican wanted the monarchy desperately: so did Big Business and the Anglo-American high command. They did not get it because of the defection of 25 percent of the DC—the party all supported—a defection facilitated by the Communist policy of antifascist unity and amity with the Church.

As with the Vatican, the DC relations with Big Business are very complicated. To call it, as *Monthly Review* does, "par excellence the party of the Italian bourgeosie"[5] is also reductive. Guido Carli, the president of *Confindustria,* calls it "the party of the petty bourgeoisie," and if he and Giovanni Agnelli of Fiat support the DC, it is not *par excellence,* but *faute de mieux.*[6] The truth, and it is an important truth, is that *Big Business has not been able to form a mass party* in Italy.‡ Agnelli and Carli do not live easily with the DC; they mistrust its left wing and resent the cost of corruption. In the late sixties, during the period of DC-Socialist governments, Agnelli and Carli toyed with the idea of shifting their support to the Republican party headed by Ugo La Malfa. Before the 1976 elections again there was gossip that Agnelli and Carli would run as deputies on the PRI ticket, but finally withdrew; the operation was too risky.[8] At least one astute commentator told me that La Malfa felt betrayed and swung left. Whatever the truth of that particular event, men high in the leadership of the DC, I later learned, do not feel dependent on the big industrialists.

*I sat in Guido Bodrato's office at the headquarters of* Democrazia Cristiana, *4 Piazza del Gesù. He is a deputy and an intimate advisor of*

---

* There is for Americans an interesting analogy between Franklin D. Roosevelt and De Gasperi. Each acted against the short-range wishes of the ruling groups (business in the case of FDR, the Vatican in the case of De Gasperi) for their best long-range interests. Each had to impose solutions which had been forced on them by the masses; in FDR's case the unemployed, the unorganized workers, the trade unionists, etc.

† This was the figure given to me by Luigi Pedrazzi. This current was liquidated in the fifties.

‡ Gramsci argued that Big Business usually does not *want* its own party.[7]

Benigno Zaccagnini, at that time the general secretary of the DC and a former disciple of Dossetti. I knew that Dossetti had had many anticapitalist feelings, and I was curious about the present leadership's commitment to the big corporations. I told Bodrato it was my opinion that the key issue in the "historic compromise" was not whether Marxists and Catholics could get along, but whether the DC was prepared to fight Big Business over state control of investments. His answer was indirect and provocative. He said, "[German] Chancellor Schmidt told me once that he thought Democrazia Cristiana had achieved three great goals in postwar Italy: it had made Christianity democratic, it had made democrats liberal, and it had sustained an antifascism that isolated the neofascists." Now, as Bodrato knew perfectly well, the DC had flirted with the neofascists in the government of Ferdinando Tambroni and worked with the neofascists in the referendum on divorce. He also knew that I knew. His little speech was a diversion that I met with silence. After a long pause he added: "The fourth thing we have to achieve is to make the Communists see the light on democracy." I said, "That's what the Communists say about you," and we both laughed. Then I added, "Including, as we were saying, the problem of investments."

At that, he sat forward on his swivel chair, toyed with a letter opener, and spoke in a quiet, abstract tone. "There is a checkered history in our relations with heavy industry. In the early years, De Gasperi and Costa of Confindustria were very close—in fact, one speaks of the De Gasperi-Costa era.[9] In my judgment, however, as far as De Gasperi was concerned, he was making political, rather than economic, decisions. He knew that Italy needed American help and that people like Luigi Einaudi and Angelo Costa were acceptable to the Americans. De Gasperi, like Togliatti, was not well versed in economics. He just went along, primarily to get American aid.

"Then there came a time in the sixties when the center-left government pushed nationalization further, particularly in the electrical power sector. The Confindustria resisted; we had big battles. Today "—his voice trailed off—"today, we are friendly. We need them and they need us. I believe they need us more than we need them. However, as I said, relations are friendly; I wouldn't say they were cordial."

He refused, gently and courteously, to be drawn out further. We returned to political questions. I said things seemed to be happening very fast, that in the three months I had been in Italy, the center and right leadership of the DC had moved left, that is to say, moved toward Zaccagnini's position: the pact of six parties of July 1977 should be regarded as a point of departure rather than as the limits of co-operation. He agreed, but pointed out that large parts of the middle-level leadership were not ready for further steps. "If we move *too fast, if we make a mistake, it will be disastrous for us—and for the country." I thought the Communists seemed to recognize this (he nodded in agreement), but events were hemming them in. The unions were restive; terrorism and unemployment explosive. Again he agreed.*

*It was apparent that he had an open mind, and understood that the problems facing the nation were so complex and critical that any step should be seriously considered—provided it was politically feasible.*

Bodrato's concern with the anticommunism of middle-level DC leadership was well founded.* I had already noted it in talks with people like Colletta of Bologna and Alberto Garocchio, the DC regional secretary in Milan. Garocchio's counterpart in Turin, Silvio Lega, though a strong supporter of Bodrato, was reluctant to work with the PCI. This middle-level leadership strengthened the irreconcilables at the top: Amintore Fanfani, Emilio Colombo, Mariano Rumor, Donat Cattin, and others—who were held in check by the prestige of Aldo Moro backed by Andreotti and Zaccagnini.† But Bodrato was well aware of the precariousness of the equilibrium in the DC. An index of right-wing strength was given in the bitter internal debate in the winter of 1977–78. A DC deputy from Milan, Massimo De Carolis, led a group of some ninety deputies who wanted an anti-Communist showdown.[10] They were outmaneuvered by Moro, and a new government of *la maggioranza* was formed.

The government was installed on March 16, 1978. On the same day the Red Brigades kidnapped Moro. His subsequent assassination destroyed the equilibirum in the DC and derailed all political plans. The right in the DC grew stronger; the Socialists, under Craxi, hardened against the PCI. The breakup of the coalition, postponed because of two papal deaths and a presidential resignation, finally took place, and new elections were held on June 3, 1979.‡

The great surprise for the PCI was the decline of the vote in the industrial areas such as Turin, and I remembered Amadeo's warnings. The drop in the workers' vote came primarily among southerners, who were not yet as class conscious as their fellows. The PCI's

---

* Sandro Magister in *L'Espresso*, February 3, 1980, reports on a Doxa poll showing that hostility to the PCI is strongest in DC organizers and in activists over forty years old. In the DC membership 26 percent are against the PCI in the government, while 46 percent are in favor of it, and 28 percent are undecided. These figures explain the vacillations of the leadership at the DC Congress in Rome, February 1980 (see page 277).

† The "irreconcilables" had about a third of the DC deputies but the support of perhaps 40 percent of the middle-level leadership—mayors, councilmen, assessors, regional assemblymen, school principals, welfare administrators, etc.—whose power of sabotage was formidable.

‡ For details of the pre-election maneuvers and an analysis of the results, see Chapter 12.

share of the youth vote also dropped from the 40 percent obtained in 1976 to around 25 percent.[11] The share of the women's vote held, in part because of the fight made by the PCI on passing the abortion law. But while many reasons can be adduced, I felt that an underlying cause, suffused throughout the social structures, was the dilution of party cadres and organization through the huge successes of 1975 and 1976.

Communists were spread thin. Twelve million votes (one in three) sounds enormous, and a membership of nearly two million is imposing. But those votes and that membership come in good part from the less educated, less trained, and less self-confident sections of the population: 25 percent of the members are agricultural laborers and housewives; another 45 percent are factory workers.[12] Only 20 percent are students, technicians, professionals, public employees, and artisans. That is enough to influence every strata of society, but not enough to provide the experienced administrators a modern society requires. In contrast, a greater proportion of DC membership comes from managerial and professional groups.

The Communist victories in the municipal and regional elections of 1975 strained their personnel to the utmost; they had to provide mayors, councilmen and women, municipal and regional administrators of all types: the mayor of Turin is a former newspaperman; the mayors of Bologna and Rome are former college professors; the regional president of Umbria is a former surgeon: the regional secretary of the party in Naples is a former psychiatrist. The PCI has strained for cadres at both ends of the age scale: Zuccotti, in charge of rent control in Turin was over seventy; the leader of the co-operatives in Calabria was twenty-three. It was a commonplace to find men and women in their middle twenties occupying responsible positions, working long hours, learning on the job.* A newly elected section organizer in Bologna, age twenty six, drove me to a party meeting where he was to give a report. He had notes and began well, but within a few minutes he lost the thread of his argument and floundered, his face froze, and he sat down in despair. A comrade criticized him, kindly but firmly, for not having prepared himself better.

On the way back, the new functionary said bitterly: "He's right. But it's easy for him to talk—he's in the trade unions and he's been at it a long time . . . an old hand." The "old hand" was thirty.

The party is constantly training cadres. The school at Frattochie handles about fifteen hundred students a year in courses ranging from seven months to one week. Students live in the school and study

---

* A comparable situation existed in the States in the building of the CIO in the thirties: Julius Emspak, James Matles, James Carey of the UE; Walter Reuther, George Addes, Maurice Sugar, Mortimer Wyndham of the UAW; Joseph Selly of ACA; James Curran of the NMU; Michael Quill of the TWU—all were in their twenties. At thirty, Harry Bridges was the old man.

intensively. At least half come directly from the factories, men and women of considerable practical experience who learn how to study and write coherently. Some have never read a book in its entirety until they come to Frattochie. Six similar but smaller schools are scattered throughout Italy. The students are working adults whose wages have to be paid to support their families while studying—an expensive proposition. Frattochie is increasing its teaching staff from four to six people as are other schools, so that the expected "crop" for 1978 was four to five thousand cadres, a substantial number, but a great many fewer than needed.[12a]

While Communist cadres are increasing, the "irreconcilables" within the DC are decreasing. Events are changing their opinions. For example, the region of Friuli, in northwest Italy, was subject to a series of terrible earthquakes in 1976–77. Millions of dollars in cash and supplies were rushed in from all over the world. A DC functionary in the Rome ministry was caught using that money to help building speculators. The scandal made the front pages, and in order to divert attention from the ministry, some of the newspapers accused the local authorities of breaking the law and conniving to keep supplies from the needy. The DC mayor of one of the towns became so enraged that he was about to resign. He was dissuaded by the Communist deputy for the area, who urged that he confront his accusers. The two men held a press conference in which they jointly assumed complete responsibility for giving supplies and relief without investigation or proper record-keeping.[13] The mayor raged: "Certainly I broke the law! If someone came and said he had six children, I gave him six blankets! I didn't have him sign an affidavit, and I didn't keep records in sextuplicate, and I didn't send a policeman to check on him. Yes, I broke a hundred laws a hundred times—but I didn't make a penny—not like the ministry in Rome." This DC mayor, and his friends, were no longer distant toward the PCI.

Another DC mayor in a small town in the center of Sicily told me that in 1975 two Communists were elected to the town council of twelve people. One of them was an engineer for the state-owned television system, a well-educated man who was always at the disposal of the mayor for paper work, consultations, and so forth. The mayor came to rely on him, and whenever he had business at the regional office (controlled by the DC), he always took along the Communist councilman. The two formed a united front against the DC bureaucracy. These two mayors mentioned had many hard-line supporters who couldn't help but be swayed by the effective DC-PCI collaboration. Moreover many DC functionaries are impressed by PCI honesty in the municipalities. When one considers that there are over thirteen hundred PCI mayors and that, together with Socialists, they govern most of the large cities and towns, or some 53 percent of the population, one can see that the pressure on the DC is unremitting.[14]

The erosion of enmity to the PCI within the DC is both direct and indirect, as people shift leftward in response to events. A dramatic example is the cholera scare in Naples in the summer of 1973. After many cases of cholera had appeared, and several people had died, an epidemic was feared. People flocked to hospitals, clinics, and doctors, clamoring for anticholera inoculations. Instead of moving swiftly to obtain supplies, organize the inoculation campaign, and reassure the population, the DC mayor and administration simply abdicated responsibility.

"It was incredible" said the Communist regional leader Renzo La Piccerella, a thin former psychiatrist of fifty with a careworn face. "The mayor disappeared, and so did the health commissioner. Directors of hospitals didn't report for work—the administration had dissolved in fear. Terrible. Only we, the left, didn't panic—the Communists, the Socialists, the trade unionists.

"We took over, mobilized our doctors, and got them to mobilize their colleagues. We sent carloads of comrades to Rome to buy, beg, and lobby for serum. We kept the clinics open, used other municipal buildings, and manned them with comrades to administer them, got the police working, mobilized the nurses and nurses' aides to give injections. In a matter of hours the city knew there was a hand at the helm. We broadcast what we were doing, got the unions to put out leaflets and hold meetings, and soon there were long lines of people everywhere, getting anticholera shots. In a few days everything was under control, the mayor and the administration surfaced—everything seemed unchanged."

La Piccerella smiled grimly. "Only it wasn't; the people didn't forget. A year later, in the divorce referendum, Naples voted 55 percent for divorce! Naples! One of the most reactionary strongholds in the country, which had voted 80 percent for the monarchy in 1946; which had voted 20 percent for the *fascist* party in 1972! I tell you, it was an earthquake!"

There was hardly a major city or region where some event hadn't shifted the people leftward. In Umbria it was the fight against closing down the steelworks at Terni. In Ferrara it was the fight against closing down the sugar refinery and the mobilization of the sugar-beet growers around that struggle. In Turin it was the fight against Fiat. The big national struggles—the divorce referendum, the general strikes, the regrouping of trade unions into a unitary federation—all had local and regional aspects which moved the people steadily left. Even the 1979 elections did not change this trend, for PCI's lost votes went to the Radical party and other left groupings. The DC remained stationary (it lost 0.4 percent), and, in fact, was also a loser, since it had anticipated an increase to 42 or 43 percent. The neofascists lost one percent. The population was growing more sophisticated and, in the deepest sense, the force of democracy has been at work pressuring, spreading, bursting the structures of the past. Democracy has been the key lever of Communist strategy, the vision of the Italian road to socialism. The greatest single step forward in spreading democracy has been the ongoing decentralization of government. Its impact on hard-liners within the Church and within the DC cannot be overestimated.

Today, Italy is divided into fifteen *regioni ordinarie* (ordinary or standard regions) and five special regions. The latter comprise Sicily and Sardinia and three border regions along the Alps (from east to west, Val d'Aosta, with a French minority; Trentino-Alto Adige, with a strong German minority; Friuli-Venezia Giulia, bordering Yugoslavia, with a Slav minority).

The setting up of the regions was mandated by Italy's republican constitution, but it was only implemented in the seventies under strong Communist and Socialist pressure. Its implementation culminated in Law 382, passed July 22, 1975 (after the DC defeat in the administrative elections). The decree putting the law into effect, however, was not passed until a year later, on July 24, 1976, after the DC defeat in the national elections. The decree was part of the price demanded by Communists and Socialists for supporting the Andreotti government.

Passage of Law 382 was the most important event in Italy since the shaping of the Constitution of 1947. Peter Nichols, giving full credit to Nenni, calls the institution of regions "potentially the most important measure enacted by the center-left coalition."[15] It is already an important consideration for the Vatican, affecting the renegotiation of the concordat (which has gone on since the divorce referendum) as well as all the Church establishments of health and welfare.[16] Law 382 may turn out to be the most important single reason why the DC horse, brought to water by the referendum and the elections, and until now reluctantly sipping, will finally begin to drink in earnest.

The importance of the law was explained to me by Dr. Germano Marri, a surgeon who is now the Communist president of the *giunta* (the executive committee) of the region of Umbria. Its capital, Perugia, is halfway between Rome and Florence.

*Umbria has two great historic claims: it was a part of Etruscan civilization, that extraordinary flowering of craftsmanship predating Greek civilization; and it is the land of Saint Francis of Assisi, the great "heretic" of the thirteenth century (he thought the Church should be poor) who was tamed by a shrewd pope who got him to start a new order, the Franciscan order.* \*

*Umbria is a poor region of 780,000 inhabitants, and it suffers a small but steady decline in population from year to year. Although it is north of Rome, it has more in common with the southern areas, as it is chiefly agricultural, with a sharecropping system of production until the last decade. (Sharecropping is surpassed only by slavery for poor productivity.) Umbria has steel mills in Terni, built around 1915 to supply armor for warships, but they have not been modernized and have reduced operations. There has been an incessant battle to maintain employment against managerial desire to close down the mills. The same problem exists in the lignite mines, which cannot meet the capitalist competition of oil, but could be socially produc-tive.*

*Because of these struggles, and its poverty, Umbria has shifted steadily leftward. By 1970 it was controlled by a coalition of Socialists and Communists commanding close to 60 percent of the votes. The region has pioneered in regional economic planning. As early as 1953 the left CGIL and the Socialist UIL worked together in strikes; by the late fifties the Catholic CISL had joined them. By 1963 the unions had developed an economic plan for the region, and it was accepted by all the parties, including the DC.* [17a]

*Despite its being a "red" region, or perhaps because of it, the Umbrian clergy is strongly integralist, as I found out when visiting relatives in Perugia.† Paul, a twenty-year-old cousin (his grandfather was my uncle), who had just received a Fiat for his birthday, offered to drive me to La Scheggia, a village some forty miles northeast of Perugia, where two generations of our ancestors are buried.‡*

*On a beautiful fall morning we drove through the foothills of the Apennines. Paul, a philosophy student in his third year at the univer-sity, was a bright, alert youngster, and we were soon deep in argument. Given his youth, I was amazed to find that he was to the right of the hard-line integralists I had talked to. When I asked him if many students felt as he did, he said no, very few: most were being corrupted by secularism, by American books, movies, and music.*

*He was viscerally anti-Communist, and I later learned that he blamed the Russians for his father's death. His father, my first cousin, had fought in World War II, in the Italian divisions near Stalingrad. The Italian troops had been short of food, ammunition,*

---

\*   Gramsci, among others, has pointed out how the Church controlled its mystics and popular upsurges by channeling them into various orders.[17]

†   The Marzanis are parvenus in Italy, having come from Austria in the late eighteenth century. On my mother's side, the Gorgas have been Roman for over thirty generations—six or seven hundred years.

‡   The region was part of the Papal States, and Perugia was a favorite fortress of popes when in trouble.

*clothing. He had been wounded and repatriated. This was in 1943. In 1960, when Paul was three years old, his father died of a heart attack. The family was convinced that it resulted from his wartime privations: "He couldn't get the cold out of his bones," said Paul. It never occurred to Paul, or to his family, to blame Mussolini for having sent Italian troops to Russia.*

*La Scheggia is a tiny agricultural village, set in a tiny valley a few miles from the town of Gubbio, where Saint Francis tamed a ravenous wolf into a gentle Brother Wolf. We found the cemetery, an idyllic place guarded by tall poplars, but it had been bombed and rebuilt, with records lost, gravestones shifted, and inscriptions eroded. However, in the municipal offices, housed in an ancient tower, we found complete records of births and deaths going back to 1700. For two hours we dug through entries written in wretched Latin with indecipherable abbreviations and crabbed script. We found entries for my grandfather and his brothers and sisters, but time ran out, and we left reluctantly.*

We returned in good time for my appointment with Dr. Marri. Paul dropped me in the main square, before a beautiful old palace that houses the regional *giunta*. There I met Dr. Marri and Gino Galli, regional secretary of the PCI and a member of its Central Committee. Galli was a man of rough-hewn features, with that relaxed listening attitude that many good organizers have. Marri was a lithe man in his early forties, with a handsome, thoughtful face. His job was comparable to that of an American state governor, requiring political and administrative skills. I asked him if he regretted giving up his profession of surgeon and he said no, his present work was exciting and rewarding.

His office was a huge room with a high ceiling adorned with a painting of the biblical Judith. Tall windows reached down to the marble floor, a large desk was barricaded with papers, folders, booklets, and a "talking" corner was arranged with modern chairs of chrome and black leather around a coffee table. Despite the size of the room, the soft lighting created a sense of intimacy. The combination of ancient buildings and modern furnishings—at once assertive of tradition and change—is carried out with that quiet elegance that one comes to associate with Italian taste.

I gave Marri a copy of the *Monthly Review* containing my article in defense of the Italian Communist party, and he gave me a copy of a documentary history of the Umbrian region from 1944 to 1970.* He knew English, as did Galli, but we conversed in Italian.

---

* Umbria also has a theoretical monthly *Cronache umbre*. The PCI puts out an enormous amount of literature, some at the highest intellectual level. Only the Church surpasses the party in output—and only in certain regions.[18]

I said that I wanted to put flesh and blood on the theoretical arguments, advanced by Giorgio Napolitano in *The Italian Road to Socialism*.[19] Among the matters discussed was regionalism, and everyone had told me of the importance of Law 382. I was here to be instructed. Marri laughed softly, settled himself, and began.

"You must understand," he said, "the enormous diversity of Italy and the power of regional differences resulting from their origins, their geography, and their history—the many, many invasions that have produced a fierce protective parochialism among Italians. Our first loyalty is to the family, even unto second and third cousins. Then our loyalty is to our village or our town. Then to our province. And finally, not very strong, loyalty to our country. Even to this day, Italy is not truly a united country: the Sicilians, the Romans, the Piedmontese, are almost centuries apart. The Sicilians will brag they were conquered by the Normans A.D. 1060, six years before England was; they are as proud of their conquerors as the Romans are of their conquests."

Marri leaned forward, his hand cupped as if to hold a concept he wanted me to see in the round. "This diversity is reflected in everything—in language, customs, folklore, administration. Turin had an efficient civil service two hundred years ago; Naples still doesn't have one. In Palermo there are twenty-five hundred street cleaners, three hundred more than in Milan, which has twice the population: Milan is clean, Palermo is disgraceful."

Galli cut in, smiling. "I'll give you an amusing illustration of regionalism in politics. We had three premiers during the period of center-left governments: Fanfani, Moro, and Rumor. Fanfani is from Tuscany, energetic, sarcastic, brilliant, self-assured. Moro is from Apulia (around Bari), tall, slow-moving, with a sad face and slow to smile. Rumor is from the Veneto, friendly, hospitable and very pious. Their administrations were so colored by regional traits that an English correspondent wrote an article suggesting that there was a Tuscan center-left, a Pugliese center-left, and a Venetian center-left. Everyone thought it was very clever of him."[20]

Marri laughed. "I remember that: a good example. Regional folklore and customs are powerful. *Omertà* in Sicily and Calabria is still the major weapon of the Mafia. Turin still considers herself the artistic capital. The Palio festival of Siena is world-renowned.* The Marche, north of Umbria, is still supposed to produce the best accountants, because in the Papal States the *marchigiani* were the assessors and tax collectors. Though the Papal States ceased to exist over a hundred years ago, they still have a proverb in Rome: 'Better a corpse in the house than a *marchigiano* at the door.' We talk glibly of

---

* The Palio is a horse race around the main square of Siena in which each horse represents a different district of the city. The race has been run twice a year for more than three centuries.

Dante and the formation of the Italian language, *lingua toscana in bocca romana* [Tuscan speech from Roman lips], but the fact is that Dante was a Florentine and Tuscan his regional dialect. For centuries, most Italians have spoken dialects which are incomprehensible between regions, sometimes between villages twenty kilometers apart. That's true to this day, though it is changing because of universal education, superhighways, and television.''

Marri held up an admonishing hand. "Don't misunderstand, I am not against this regional diversity. On the contrary. I think it is a good thing that our culture is still shaped by the regions, that the best newspapers are from a dozen cities, that our best writers are rooted in their native places; Moravia in Rome, Bassani in Ferrara, De Filippo in Naples, Quasimodo in Sicily. Our regional and municipal traditions are a source of strength: Bologna, with the oldest university, Florence with Dante and the Medici, Rome with Julius Caesar and Sixtus V, Parma with its Duchy, Milan with the Sforzas, Urbino with Raphael, and so on, dozens, hundreds, of towns each with its own peculiar history. The regionalism is so ingrained that it was easy to get a consensus to write it into our Constitution in 1947.''[21]

Marri got up and went to his desk, returning with a small book. "I'll read to you from Article 117, which, thirty years later, culminated in Law 382. The region is given the power to *legislate*—legislate mind you—sovereignty within its competence, and its laws are as valid as Parliament's laws. What is their competence? It covers almost everything that affects the daily life of people, such as, and I quote: 'election districts, urban and rural police, fairs, and markets; public welfare, health, and hospitals; trade schools, professional schools, and educational assistance; local museums and libraries; problems of urbanization; tourism and the hotel industry; streetcars and regional bus lines; building and maintenance of aqueducts and regional public works; navigation and harbors on lakes; mineral and thermal waters; quarries and peatbogs; hunting; fishing in inland waters; agriculture and forestry; artisans.' That's Article 117, and Article 118 says the state may delegate other functions to the region and municipalities. This,'' said Marri, closing the book, "is decentralization the way you Americans have long had it in states and cities. If you take police powers, welfare, health and education, you cover 90 percent of matters in which the average citizen comes into contact with government. But this is only the beginning.''

Marri was intent, caught up in his own vision of the future. "Although not spelled out, the door is wide open to economic planning by the region and to *executing* those plans. Manufacturers and nationalized industries have to co-operate with us because their plants need roads, water, sewers, electricity—all under local or regional control. However, the most powerful lever we have is our jurisdiction over agriculture. For example, in our region, the Alto Tevere [Upper Tiber River] is a tobacco growing area. For centuries the prices paid to peasants for tobacco were fixed by big companies. In the last two years we have organized the peasants into co-operatives, and now *they fix prices.* Ordinarily, the tobacco companies would have turned to the state for help in fighting, or braking, the co-operatives, but not in this case. *State power was in our hands!*"

Galli had been watching me. "It may seem like a small matter to you," he said, "But it is a taste of things to come. A *million* such small events will give a different structure to society, a different orientation. This is what Giorgio Napolitano means when he speaks of introducing elements of socialism into the capitalist economy."

Marri added another argument. "The ruling class is very conscious of this potential: the government is sabotaging the law, transferring functions slowly, holding back money that belongs to us. For example, we now control the clinics. Last year, run from the center, those clinics got 5 billion lire. So far, the government has given us 1 billion. They are cheating. Either the ministry is using the 4 billion to pay staff that should be laid off, or it is simply keeping the money. By holding back money, we can't function. Thus the idea of regionalism gets discredited."

"You have no taxing powers?" I said.

"Practically none. Regions and municipalities get a percentage of the national budget. In addition, as functions are transferred, we are supposed to get the money that used to be spent nationally. Further, we are supposed to get the money allocated to useless agencies slated for elimination. For example, there is an agency which is supposedly taking care of widows of soldiers killed in Somalia in 1894. What it is, of course, is a pocket of patronage, a few people getting paid for doing nothing."

Marri went to his desk again. He handed me a large-format pamphlet headed "OFFICIAL BULLETIN—Region of Umbria—Perugia, 7 September 1977." "We reprinted the decree effecting Law 382, July 1977. On page 32 there are listed sixty-two agencies which everyone has agreed to eliminate. Mind you, this is only the start. No one knows how many useless agencies and offices there are. When Ugo La Malfa, a republican, was minister of the treasury, he reported over three thousand of them in his ministry. Recently, the undersecretary of the interior, a DC man, put the figure at fifty-four thousand. Pure clientism, and an incalculable waste. That money belongs to us."

"But how are you going to get it?" I asked. "Why should the DC government eliminate agencies which are part of their political machine? Isn't this political suicide?"

Marri and Galli laughed delightedly, as if I were a bright pupil.

"*Ecco,*" said Marri. "You have grasped the crux of the problem. *Democrazia Cristiana* cannot go on the old way; it has to reform itself. It is resisting, but it is moving."

"But why? How? Why pass Law 382 in the first place? I can see that it might have been passed pro forma, as a demagogic gesture. But why pass the decree putting it into effect?"

"We made them," said Galli. "Our party made Law 382 part of the price for supporting the Andreotti government."

*It was not the whole answer, as I was to find out. I found the answer in an obscure Catholic journal that was attacking Law 382. While sitting in the anteroom of the rector of the Sacred Heart University in Bologna, Giuseppe Lazzati, waiting to see him, I saw on a table a score of journals and reviews. I happened to pick up* La Rivista del clero italiano *[Review of the Italian clergy] and an article caught my eye: "An Evaluation of Eurocommunism." Just then the attendant called me, and I made a mental note of the date, November 1977. After talking to the rector, I passed by the university bookstore, run by nuns. I was lucky; they had the review.*

*The article on Eurocommunism was mediocre.*[22] *But there was an invaluable article on Law 382 and its genesis, explaining that, at the turn of the century Vatican intellectuals took up regionalism as a weapon against the secular state fathered by Cavour, and this policy became embedded in Catholic political tradition.*[23] *By the time of the Constituent Assembly the original reasons and the traditions were part of the DC; and since the Socialists were strong regionalists, Title V of the Constitution, establishing the regions, was approved.*

*However, when the 1948 elections gave an absolute majority to the* Democrazia Cristiana, *De Gasperi had no intention of weakening his own central government. As the years went by and Communists and Socialists gained in "the red belt" (the central regions of Emilia-Romagna, Tuscany, Umbria), the DC government saw less and less reason to institute the regions. Many Communists were slow to see the potential in regionalism, except the Umbrian Communists.*

*Most credit belongs to Pietro Nenni, the veteran Socialist leader.*[24] *He made regionalism a condition (along with the nationalization of the electric power industry) for joining the center-left government of the sixties. After much procrastination, a law was passed, Law 281, on May 16, 1970, setting up the regions. The law was rather vague, and in January 1975 a new law, 382, was passed to* "complete *the transference of administrative functions"—which had not even begun. Instead, a commission presided over by Professor*

*Massimo Severo Giannini was appointed to study how the transfer-
ence would take place.*[25]

*By this time the Communists and Socialists had gained a major-
ity in six regions and had considerable influence in three more, and
they were pressing the government to act. The elections of 1976 gave
them the power to force the government to give meaning to Law 382.
When Gino said, "We made them," he was correct tactically; but the
implication of a long-term Communist strategy was not correct.*

Marri discussed the problems the regions had with the national
government. For example, the regional assembly is a legislature,
similar to an American state legislature, and can enact any law,
provided it is not in conflict with other national laws, the laws of other
regions, or the Italian Constitution. To prevent the first a commissioner of regions in Rome rules on these issues. The second and
third are the prerogatives of the cabinet, whose decisions can be
appealed to the Constitutional Court. What had happened, said
Marri, was that the cabinet had arrogated to itself the power to pass on
the *merit* of the regional laws rather than on their constitutionality.
Since jurisdictional problems abounded, hundreds of appeals were
pending, and the transference of powers was slowed down.

Another major conflict was financial. The national government
demanded a plan from each region before telling it what its financial
allocation would be. Clearly, this was putting the cart before the
horse. Meanwhile, without a plan, when the money came, it could not
be spent and became *passivi* (passive, i.e., unused balances): in
effect, the region would never get them. Marri told me that in Umbria
they had worked hard to present plans and spend their allocation.*
Their *passivi* were only some 20 billion lire (about $22 million),
whereas the accumulated *passivi* of Sicily ran into the hundreds of
billions of lire.

The inefficiency and apathy of the national bureaucracy infuriated Marri. "You know," he said, "the extent of bureaucracy in
Italy is vastly exaggerated. If you examine the statistics, you'll see we
are very considerably below other European countries in per capita
government workers.[26] But the productivity of our bureaucrats is
abysmal—because of nepotism."

Gino broke in. "Mind you, we Communists are not against giving
jobs to relatives. In Italy, this would be blasphemy. If we have jobs we
prefer them to go to Communists or Socialists rather than Christian

---

* This general problem was dealt with by Communists in various ways. See Chapter 10 for an
example in Calabria.

Democrats. *But they have to qualify.* \* The DC gives jobs to people who don't bother to come to work, not even on payday. They send a relative to pick up the envelope."†

"On top of inefficiency is arrogance," Marri put in. "A petty clerk represents the government, represents authority. If you make a fuss over service, he'll tell you: Curb your tongue, or I'll call a policeman. And he can. There's still a law from fascist days which makes it a misdemeanor to show disrespect to authority."

I asked: "How do you know your bureaucrats in the regions and towns won't act the same as in Rome?"

"A fair question," said Marri, "and there is a danger. But so far the trend has been the other way. Our people work, and when I say our people work, I don't mean the left people only. I mean everybody. Other things being equal, we do give the jobs to the left, but if a DC engineer is better qualified than a Communist engineer, he gets the job. And everyone works because we set the example. I work hard, so does Gino. In a typical agency the top man is a political appointee who does nothing. He has an assistant to run the place, and that assistant has an assistant who actually does the work. Three men for the work of one. This demoralizes the rest. We try to create an esprit de corps."

Gino broke in eagerly. "We Communists have shown what can be done. Bologna has had a left administration for thirty years and is considered the best-run city in Italy, if not Europe. *Bologna rossa* (Red Bologna) is a byword in Italy, the pride of the left and the envy of the right. Not a breath of scandal in thirty years! I don't believe that can be said of any comparable city in the world, not even in Scandinavia. We evoke the best in people around us; selflessness, service, the human connection. I know we sound like a troop of Boy Scouts, but you know," said Gino wryly, "there is nothing wrong with Boy Scout mores."

"I was a Boy Scout," I told him, "in Rome. And our Communist party has been kidded on the same basis."‡ But I went on to clarify a puzzle: why would a DC government help red regions in a development that would undermine its own political machine. "Why should Rome give you money," I asked. "You said they are trying to discredit the regions; you said they are cheating you. How are you going to make them change?"

---

\*   In practice, since there are hundreds of applicants for every job, there are apt to be dozens of people with the same civil service grades, and so some choice is possible without breaking the rules.

†   In the *New Yorker* Jane Kramer wrote from Rome that the Communists are as bad as the DC at clientism, "only their people work." This is like saying that since there are twelve hours at night and twelve in the day, the two are the same, "only you can read during the day."[27]

‡   An American writer has written: "To hear [Marzani] tell it, the CP on the Lower East Side during the thirties was like an enthusiastic Boy Scout troop: cheerful, hard-working, open, and honest."[28]

The look that appeared on Marri's face was straight from Mephistopheles, his eyes half-lidded, his nostrils flaring, his smile sardonic. "Oh," he said smugly, "we'll get the money. And very soon, too." Galli chuckled, and I could see the issue had been raised before.

"If the Christian Democrats in Rome," said Marri, "don't give up the money owed to the regions, the DC will be split down the middle. The regions are equally divided, six red, six white, a few in-between. Most of the problems of the white regions are the same as ours—money, jurisdiction, implementation, and so on. We of the red regions have made it an iron rule never to fight the government alone. Never. Always a unitary approach. On any given issue we work out with the white regions a set of demands which are acceptable to everyone; then we go to the government, *all* of us. What can the government do? They can stall for two or three months, but they have to give in or lose the support of their own people. They cannot afford the risk."

I asked if they had a council of *giunta* presidents.

"No," said Marri, "it's too early for that. Everything is informal. The president of the regional assembly in Bologna, Natalino Guerra, is a Christian Democrat—a reasonable, open-minded man of intelligence and integrity. He is a good friend of Renato Zangheri, the Red Mayor, and he understands that we all have to work together.* If I have a problem, I call him up: has he got a similar one? We exchange ideas, reach a tentative solution. He calls the DC presidents around the country. I call the Communists and Socialists. Informally, we reach a consensus. Then we go to Rome—together."

Marri tapped the side of his nose with his finger. "We smell the situation. There are many good men in *Democrazia Cristiana,* both in the party and in the higher reaches of the bureaucracy. They support our proposals. Some are ambitious; we make deals. There are political IOUs; we call them in. On any given issue we can work up a *combinazione* that the government can't block."

Galli reached for the history of Umbria that Marri had given me and leafed through it. "You must realize," he said, "that many able men in the Church and the DC want to reform the party. They see the regions as an instrument of DC renewal. Listen to this from the DC deputy from this area: 'We Christian Democrats of Umbria have been in a minority for fifteen years. With the region we can try to reverse the existing political equilibrium. But only with the region.' "[29]

---

\*   Guerra's commitment to working together was shown by his acceptance of the presidency of the assembly in a red region where the *giunta* was controlled by Communists and Socialists who also had a majority in the assembly. This action by a DC political figure was a major breakthrough on co-operation.

"That deputy is Francesco Maria Malfatti," said Marri, "an important man in the DC. He was chosen by the government to be president of the Executive Council of the Common Market when Italy's turn came. By the way, the Malfatti quote is from an article by Gino in *Rinascita* way back in the early sixties when the party was rather backward on the subject. You should read it."[30]

"Page five," said Galli. "I'll put it down on the flyleaf." He looked at his watch. "Shall we go?"

It was raining lightly as Marri drove me to my hotel. With the car bouncing over the cobblestones, he said, "One final point before you go. The biggest factor in forcing the government to act against its will is popular pressure, particularly from the unions. For example, there was a general strike in 1970 to push for reforms, including the first law on regions. There is also enormous pressure from neighborhood councils and mayors, irrespective of party affiliations. At the grass-roots, party labels don't mean much when needs are pressing—Christian Democrats are just as militant as Communists when it comes to clinics, schools, welfare. When you get to Bologna, you'll see what can be accomplished with unity and leadership—and this despite Rome's harassment, restrictions, and holding back on money. You must spend some time there; I'll call Zangheri [the mayor] tomorrow and tell him to expect you.

Bologna rossa *is probably the greatest advertisement for communism in Europe. Bologna has become a standard of municipal excellence throughout the continent, and the two words are usually said together like a brand name:* Bologna rossa. *The German weekly* Der Spiegel *wrote: "Bologna, a dream come true of city renewal"; the French weekly* Vie république: *"Bologna is incessantly making news." Across the Atlantic, anti-Communist media cannot resist a pinch of admiration: "Efficient and democratic," said the* New York Times, *and from* Newsweek: *"Everywhere, Bologna is considered the best-administered city in Europe."*[31] *However, the encomiums also tend to regard Bologna as exceptional, a red "island." The* Bolognese *reject this concept. In his elegant mayor's office, Professor Zangheri gave me tea and insights. "We are not an island," he said quietly. "We are as much a part of Italy as Turin or Rome or Naples. We are not pioneers; we've initiated some things, copied others. In our region, Emilia-Romagna, we have developed our* leghe dei braccianti *[leagues of agricultural workers] along lines and methods used by Di Vittorio in the Apulia region [around Bari] in the early 1900s—he was a teen-ager, imagine! We did start neighborhood councils, but Flor-*

*ence improved on the idea.\* We've taken concepts of city planning
from the United States, from England, from Scandinavia."*

*We were speaking in Italian interspersed with English phrases.
As a historian of economic thought, he had learned the language to
study Adam Smith, Ricardo, Marshall, Keynes, and so on.*

*"It is true," said Zangheri, "that Bologna is a small city, with a
strong artisanate and petty bourgeoisie, and has always had a strong
civic sense.*[32] *The city and the region have a great progressive
tradition—after all, we have the oldest university in Europe, founded
in the eleventh century. Bologna has always been renowned for
learning, 'venerable and scholarly,' as Goethe said.*† *We had the first
Socialist deputy in 1892,*[33] *a follower of both Bakunin and Marx—
already," he smiled, "a unitary approach. Bologna had a Socialist
mayor in 1914, a Communist mayor in 1920. This city was the heart of
the resistance to Mussolini in the twenties and again in the forties. We
had fifty thousand partisans from Emilia and six thousand were
killed. Our first postwar mayor, Giuseppe Dozza, was a great partisan leader. So we started out with some advantages. But the point is
that we Communists have increased our vote steadily in each election. We got over 50 percent of the vote, the Socialists another 10
percent, so we have 36 seats out of 60 on the city council. In contrast,
the DC, which had run Turin and Florence for twenty-five years, was
thrown out in 1975. Quite simply, the people like what we are doing."*

What Bologna is doing is taking care of its citizens. The city initiated
free bus transportation during rush hours, increasing passenger traffic
50 percent in five years, reducing the use of autos and so diminishing
traffic congestion.‡ (One DC councilman complained, "Buses are
driving automobiles off the streets.") Seventy-seven percent of all
children between three and six were in kindergarten in 1975, and the
figure was close to 90 percent in 1978.[34] About half of all infants under
age three are in *nidi di asilo.*\*\* Retarded and handicapped children

---

\*   In Bologna the council members were appointed by the parties in proportion to the votes
received in each neighborhood. Florence took over the idea, but had the members elected directly
by the people, the candidates running without party identification. Florence also led the fight to get a
national law mandating councils for all cities.

†   A contemporary proverb says: *Bologna dotta, grassa e rossa.* "Bologna is learned, fat, and
red." It is *grassa* because of its fine cuisine.

‡   The city has estimated that for every million dollars it spent on buses, it was saving society $40
million in expenses for autos, gas, time lost, accidents, and so forth. In 1977, starved of funds,
Bologna instituted fares, but with the regional reform, Zangheri is hoping for better financing and
hopes to re-establish the no-fare policy.

\*\*   A charming name for nursery schools, "nests of refuge." Now, by a national law of 1977, they
are managed by the parents though financed by the municipality. Another example of participatory
democracy.

have been integrated into the school system, and the ghettolike special schools have been closed. Old people are sent on vacations to the seashore or the mountains and, since funds are limited, priorities are established by the neighborhood council, which knows the people.

Zoning laws are strict; speculation in real estate has been curbed. Practically no buildings are torn down; they are restored, and while restoration goes on the families live in special "parking homes" in the neighborhood so they do not lose their environment.[35] Stores are licensed so that every neighborhood has adequate commercial facilities, in contrast to Naples, where one neighborhood of seventy thousand does not have a single store. Consumers' co-operatives have been organized and tied into producers' co-operatives in the province, so that the cost of food in Bologna is 3 to 5 percent less than in other major cities.[36]

In every sector the statistics are impressive. While the population increased about a third between 1951–53 and 1971–73, the number of rooms doubled, schoolrooms tripled, recreational facilities—soccer fields, swimming pools, basketball courts, etc.—were increased tenfold.[37] The area for gardens and parks is nine square yards per capita (double that of Rome or Milan, and quadruple that of Naples).*[38] In the health sector, the number of hospital beds has doubled in twenty years (12 per thousand, compared to the national average of 7 per thousand).[39] Mobile medical units, including a psychiatric unit, go from neighborhood to neighborhood, practicing preventive medicine, providing tests, X rays, inoculations, etc., with emphasis on care for pregnant women and small children. Despite the progress, many facilities are still inadequate, and plans have been drawn up for the coming years. Bologna has plans for everything: housing, education, health, traffic, parks, commerce, old-age assistance.

For thirty years *Bologna rossa* has been a bone in the throat of the DC government in Rome, a constant reproach to DC administrations in other cities. They have countered with obstruction, sabotage, and financial shortchanging of spiteful proportions. For example, there is throughout Italy an after-school program to prepare slow learners for exams.† In 1972, Rome assigned 25 teachers to the program in Bologna whereas Milan received 2,000! (Milan had three times the population). In 1974 the quota was cut to 14 teachers.[40] The

---

*    This figure is miserly by modern standards. Stockholm has 80 square yards per inhabitant, London has 30, New York City, 18. Bologna plans to achieve 39.

†    Four hundred thousand Italian children flunk their June exams every year and take them again in October. In preparation they go to private "cram schools" at an annual cost of 45 billion lire. That amount of money added to public school funds would eliminate most of the failures, which are due more to inadequate teaching than to "slow learning."

central government owes Bologna accumulated arrears of 131 billion lire—one quarter of the city's indebtedness.*[41]

Despite all the problems, the city's achievements speak for themselves. Zangheri ascribed the success of his administration to the PCI's unitary line in politics and its commitment to participatory democracy. For Zangheri, the neighborhood councils are the most important development in Italy, on a par with the factory workers' councils and the autonomy of the regions. Begun in 1964, the councils have the support of all parties (only seven of the eighteen council presidents are Communists), and year by year they have assumed more responsibilities: they allocate funds for welfare, renovation of buildings, supervision of schools; they establish priorities for vacations and nursery schools and so on. Problems which cluttered the mayor's desk are now solved by the councils. Bologna's population is probably the most politically developed in the world.[43]

The people's participation in politics is direct and palpable. Foreign correspondents have noted how groups of people gather impromptu for an argument or discussion.[44] On Sundays, the main squares are filled with people talking. These are not radicals or crackpots on soapboxes, but average citizens. A couple of friends, or strangers, start talking, passers-by stop to listen, join in, and soon a dozen or so people are involved. A family with children, out for a stroll, may pause, catch the drift of the argument, and go on, husband and wife continuing the discussion.

I spent an entire afternoon on the main square fronting the Church of St. Petronius, and while the arguments were animated, sometimes very sharp, there was an accepted give and take that was very engaging. There was no problem of "law and order," and the minuscule sprinkling of policemen, young men with longish hair, stopped here and there to participate in genuine friendliness. This was a common, and striking, phenomenon. The previous day, I had come across a demonstration of several hundred young workers before the administrative offices of the "150 Hours." This institution is a result of a law providing full pay to workers for up to 150 hours of night classes that will improve their skills on the job. It wasn't clear what they wanted, but they were blocking traffic. Half a dozen policemen, under a sergeant, were trying to clear a passage for cars. They were

---

\* The fiscal policies of the government toward the municipalities are a nightmare of disorder. The national budget allocates the over-all funds, which are then broken down for the various towns. The budget is often late; payrolls must be met on time, so the towns *borrow* against their expected allocation: i.e., they borrow money which is theirs! They can borrow from the treasury at 7 or 8 percent, but the treasury will not lend more than, say, 50 percent of the previous year's allocation. So the municipalities borrow from *private* banks at interest rates as high as 20 percent. There are eight thousand muncipalities in Italy, and their total deficit runs between three and four billion dollars a year. This deficit could be drastically reduced, and perhaps eliminated, by a more coherent public finance policy.[42]

friendly, gently persuasive. "Please, comrades, move in closer. You are making it rough for us." A speaker, on a chair by the building, interjected: "Yes, comrades, close in." A couple of voices protested: "No, no, widen up, stretch out. Block the traffic and they'll pay attention upstairs."

The firebrands got nowhere. The demonstrators closed in toward the building, their mood clearly one of co-operation with the police, not out of fear but common sense. Several demonstrators on the periphery smiled and exchanged wisecracks with the policemen.

*I told Zangheri of the incident, and he nodded contentedly: "We have a splendid police force, professional, well educated. The men are all high-school graduates or better [40 percent of all policemen in Italy have finished only grammar school].*[45] *Our citizens respect them; and the police feel part of the community. When there are strikes or demonstrations, the police say to our organizers: 'What can we do to help?' We show our appreciation and they respond."*

*When I spoke of the atmosphere on the square, Zangheri's manner changed. During our talk he had been courteous and responsive, but rather detached. Now he spoke eagerly. "You are seeing the process of democracy at work. It—" he searched for a word, leaning forward slightly. "It is . . . a* capillary *process permeating our whole city. And the heart—the ventricles—of that process are the neighborhood councils. I'll never forget that day in 1964 when we held the first meeting of all the councilmen and women in the hall next door—280 of them. We then had fourteen councils."*

*His face was alight, his hand cradled the air as he sought the right words: "Senti, guarda. Listen, look. One speaks of grassroots, but it is a poor metaphor. These councils are more like ground cover, you know, ivy creepers that blanket an area, the tendrils crisscrossing every which way. You pick one up and a whole patch quivers.*

*"Each council has twenty members and a portion of them changes from election to election. In every neighborhood there are perhaps a hundred people who have been members of the council. Add to that the unionists who live in the area and have been members of factory councils; and the residents who are city employees— teachers, bus dispatchers, health and housing inspectors, and so on; add shopkeepers, small businessmen, ex-army noncoms, and you get five or six hundred people who have had organizing experience. When you consider that each of them works with four, five, ten people, you are talking of three or four thousand people in a neighborhood of about fifteen thousand adults."*

*He held up his hand, as if I were the one being carried away. "Of course, we must not exaggerate. Everyone doesn't eat, drink, and talk politics. Still, we must not minimize their concern. They do vote—in astounding numbers. You know that over 90 percent of eligible Italians vote in elections. In Bologna this figure has reached as high as 95 percent—it's incredible. When you consider that because of illness and other reasons, some people can't get to the polls, it means that, practically speaking, every person in Bologna votes."* He gave me an ironic smile. *"Will Americans believe that figure? I read that only half of eligible Americans vote."*[46]

I said that sounded a little low to me, but I did not want to get sidetracked from Bologna. I asked him about the city's relations with the Church.

*"Not exactly cordial, but friendly. We had friction in the days of Cardinal Lercaro, but Pope John changed his attitudes. Besides, more Catholics in Bologna vote Communist than Christian Democratic, and the Church is well aware of this fact.*[47]

I told Zangheri that many people on the left in Italy and abroad regarded efficient Socialist city management as an aid to capitalism, what Marx called *"sewer socialism." Many cities in Europe have had Social-Democratic administrations. Reforms do not change the system; the New Deal made many reforms, yet capitalism emerged stronger than ever.*[48]

*"I know,"* said Zangheri, speaking with the authority of one who was a member of the Central Committee of the PCI. *"I've read the arguments, the doubts, the criticisms. Frankly, I think most critics are prisoners of a rigid frame of mind.*

*"Reforms work both ways. In the New Deal, the reforms were used to strengthen the system, to preserve the basic* status quo. *If the DC reforms itself and eliminates corruption, it makes itself stronger. If it reforms tax collection, that makes the state stronger. Reforms are the* end *of a process.*

*"For us Communists, reforms are the* beginning *of a process. In the course of the struggle for reforms, we train people to organize and to educate themselves so we can go beyond the* status quo. *Reforms of corruption, taxation, and so on provide social capital, make us less dependent on the capitalist system. The Communists are teaching democracy by practicing it. The Italian people are learning to lose their fear of authority, their internalized submissiveness—learning to stand up for themselves. If a city clerk in Bologna is officious, people complain; they call a policeman because they know the policeman is* their *policeman.*

*"The question at bottom is one of power. What differentiates the Italian Communists from the Social Democrats is not gradualism or reforms; it is the will to fight for socialism, the will to use power. We are getting power in the regions and the towns, and we are using it. Our people, not only our members, but huge sections of the popula-*

*tion, are learning to use power. This is what participatory democracy is all about.*

*"We have many problems. The country is in a perilous economic state. The unemployment among the young feeds despair and, ultimately, terrorism. Even if we had full power, it would be very rough going. Sharing power with a reluctant DC makes the going that much rougher. Perhaps it will not work—but we are trying."*

*As we parted he gave me a copy of a book titled* Il Sindaco di Bologna *(The mayor of Bologna). I asked him if he had ever regretted giving up his academic career. With a slow smile, he said: "All writers ask me that question. You'll find the answer in the book."*

Sitting in my hotel room later that night, I found this testament of Renato Zangheri, mayor of *Bologna rossa*: "I have lived through an extraordinary experience. . . . A city is a microcosm which reflects the great problems of the country, but above all it is a structure man has built for living. Often, however, the city lashes back against its creators, emits evil vapors, makes life more burdensome. To give a city back to its people is an impassioned struggle, particularly when it means giving it back to those who need it most and are most often excluded—the old people and the children. In Bologna, I think the old and the young live a little better. . . . I think the people count a little more. A mayor's job is difficult; often one borders on despair. I work very hard, stretching the working day to its utmost, and my private life is not unaffected. But I get back more than I give: I receive affection and understanding and thereby sustenance. In a society miserly with love, I have received more than my normal due."[49]

# CHAPTER 9

# How to Steal a Country

In 1976, after the revelations of the bribing and subversion of Italian governing parties by the CIA, Lockheed, and Exxon, a pacifist group within the Unitarian Church of Canada published a pamphlet entitled *How to Buy a Country*.[1] But for buyers to buy, there must be sellers who sell: Who owns a country? Abraham Lincoln said that a "country and its institutions belong to the people who inhabit it." Since the CIA, Lockheed, and Exxon had bribed, not the Italian people, but only individual politicians and officials, it follows that politicians must have appropriated the country. *How to Buy a Country* presupposes a text, "How to Steal a Country."

The "how" can be expressed in one word: corruption. William Gladstone said that the Bourbons in Naples had erected injustice into a system of government; over a thirty-year period the Christian Democrats have erected corruption into a system of society. The price paid has been the laceration of a country; for the DC the price has been a steady deterioration of its vote and, until 1979, a steady increase in the Communist vote. One may say that while the PCI was showing the nation that it was *fit* to govern, the DC was demonstrating that it was *unfit* to govern.

Corruption in Italy is not a matter of scattered bribes; it is so interwoven into the fabric of society, so capillary, that no aspect of it, including the economy, is unaffected. Corruption is an epidemic that almost defies description. The authors of a recent book, *L'anonima DC* (DC, Inc.), Orazio Barrese and Massimo Caprara, state that it would take an encyclopedia simply to enumerate the *known* scandals. Some are humble, as in the affair of the postage stamps; some are dazzling, as in the Lockheed bribery of a prime minister, a minister of defense, and a chief of staff of the air force—all in one operation.*

Consider the scandal of the postage stamps. In 1961 President Giovanni Gronchi visited Peru, and to mark the occasion three air mail stamps bearing a map of South America were issued. The map turned out to be 150 years out of date—as the Peruvian ambassador pointed out—and the postage stamps were ordered withdrawn. Somehow the order was not made public for three days. In that time insiders made tidy sums buying the "rose-colored Gronchis," which cost 205 lire each and were soon worth 250,000 lire as philatetic rarities.[2]

Not so pretty was the sale of a "surplus" destroyer to the firm Parodi Fabris for 100,000 lire; the firm resold it for 65,000,000 lire.[3] And there was the government's "present" to Achille Lauro of four Liberty ships in "recompense" for his shipping losses during World War II—a war he had backed and promoted on the fascist side. Lauro, an armament manufacturer, had been a pillar of the Mussolini regime and, as such, was interned in a prison camp by the Allied military government. As soon as the war was over, and the Italians regained control, he was released and returned to his political base in Naples. There he swung the right-wing deputies of the "Qualunquist movement"† to the support of De Gasperi. The "recompense" followed soon thereafter.[4]

This kind of sporadic, *ad hoc* corruption takes place in every country. It may be socially facilitated, but not socially organized. While reprehensible, it does not harm the country in the way that structured Italian corruption does. At the lowest level of that corruption is nepotism, favoritism, and patronage. The civil service is a joke; exams are often fixed. To get a position requires a connection. Patronage is common in politics everywhere, but in most western countries the beneficiary is expected to perform his job. Not so in Italy, where, in extreme cases, government employees will not even show up to work.

On a par with nepotism is clientism: the state giving favors, not for money but for votes or political help. It is not quite bribery, but it is getting something for nothing at the public expense. Usually these favors are administrative, e.g., granting a building permit in a prohibited zone or putting spurious invalids on the welfare rolls. Bruno Trentin, a CGIL leader, tells of villages where men drawing payments for blindness were driving taxis or playing on the local soccer teams.

A distinguished example of administrative favors was exposed

---

* The prime minister, code-named "Antelope Cobbler," was reputed to be either Mariano Rumor or Giovanni Leone.

† After the war, a reactionary, demagogic party, *L'Uomo Qualunque* (Everyman's party), had a brief vogue. Its voters were soon absorbed into the DC and the MSI.

by *L'Espresso* when it revealed that three high papal dignitaries had been granted exemptions from special taxes on personal assets.[5] The three high dignitaries were Prince Giulio Pacelli, a nephew of Pope Pius XII, Count Stanislao Pecci, and the Marquis Filippo Serlupi Crescenzi. These three were holding diplomatic posts at the Vatican as ambassadors to the Holy See from Costa Rica, Malta, and San Marino. On the basis of these posts the Vatican, since 1947, had requested the tax exemptions applicable to foreign diplomats, but a series of finance ministers had refused them, since the three were, in fact, Italian citizens. However, in 1958, the minister of finance decided to grant the exemptions. No one thought that Andreotti was bribed—but equally no one thought the minister was suddenly generous. Some political quid pro quo was involved.[6]

Such favors are often small, but when millions of people are involved, the totals can be staggering. For example, the law provides small subsidies to peasants to enable them stay on the land. Professor Luigi Spaventa, a leading economist, told me that while the census shows 5 million farmers, subsidies go to 6 million.[7] The subsidies perform a political rather than an economic function. Each subsidy is tiny, a few dollars a week, useless to production, but it helps assuage the misery of the poor. It also assures a cluster of votes for *Democrazia Cristiana*.

There are two vast areas of clientism and wasteful expenditures: the *enti pubblici* (public agencies) and the nationalized industries. Public agencies do not mean the post office, the army, etc. The *enti* are agencies for welfare, social security, workmen's compensation, veteran benefits, orphans, health, farmers' assistance, and so on. According to Franco Cazzola, there were forty-nine such agencies in 1977, and they had spent in thirty years 204 trillion lire at 1974 prices (roughly $300 billion).[8] Emiliani estimates that in 1977 some 2,000 billion lire was spent on "institutionalized" (out of the home) welfare and 8,000 billion on health—half for hospitals.[9] In all, the *enti* are administering or spending annually some 20,000 billion lire, a stupendous sum and a cornucopia for clientism.* Christian Democrats monopolize the jobs. The study by Cazzola shows that of every 100 identified individuals in the highest administrative bodies, 60 were Christian Democrats, 6 Communists, and 12 Socialists.†[10]

Fourteen ministries (out of twenty) supervise the *enti* operating through a network of over 40,000 agencies and offices, most of which

---

* This is 20 percent of the Italian gross national product; 20 percent of the American GNP would be $250 billion.

† Compare these percentages to the 1976 voting strength: DC, 38.8 percent; PCI, 34.5 percent; PSI, 9.7 percent. The left, with 44 percent of the votes, had 18 percent of the jobs. The Socialists had the major portion of those jobs because they had made some headway during their participation in the center-left government of the sixties.

are wholly or partially useless; they channel and supervise funds but do little actual work. For example, Terranova points out that in all of Italy, there are 401,392 beds in various institutions—orphanages, old-age homes, poorhouses, reformatories, etc. Of these, public agencies run only 34,958. The rest are in private or religious hands paid for by the government at so much per bed.*[11]

With such self-evident scope for abuse, there have been constant scandals. For example, during the 1960s the chief physician of the Forlanini Hospital of Milan, one Nicolo Aliotta, had set up a private society to take care of turbercular children. Aliotta was paid 2000 lire a day for each child assigned to him; he then "sublet" the care of the child to an order of monks (Trinitarians) for 800 lire. He was reported by the monks when he had refused to raise the compensation to 1100 lire per child.†[13]

The inmates of government-run institutions fare little better than those in private ones. Each of the eight thousand municipalities has an agency for public assistance, ECA (Ente Comunale di Assistenza). ECA spent 38 billion lire in 1970, of which 11 billion were used up in overhead. The dole per needy person came to 45 lire a day, then about 7 cents. EONALI (Ente Nazionale per l'Assistenza agli Orfani dei Lavoratori Italiani), an agency for orphans, spends 8000 lire a day per child whereas if the child is placed within a family, the cost is 2000 lire. By restricting its services to perhaps half of the actual orphans, EONALI built up a financial empire with assets of 103 billion lire and an operational "surplus" of 18 billion. With these assets it operated like a private corporation, lending money, speculating in real estate, depositing in favored banks, at low interest rates (7 percent), funds that the banks lent to customers (including municipalities) at 20 percent. The opportunities for corruption are considerable and are seldom disdained. For years the State Auditing Board had been drawing attention to the shocking activities of EONALI. but nothing was ever done.[14] At present the agency is slated for elimination, its functions to be transferred to the regions; but so far it has resisted liquidation.

Concomitant with nepotism and clientism at all levels is outright bribery—the bustarelle, as the Italians say.‡ These range from sub-stantial bribes to tax assessors to the huge payoff made by Lockheed

---

* The location of the institutions is itself a scandal. Only one quarter of the beds are in the south, whence come perhaps half of the people helped. This means that tens of thousands of children and old people are taken away from their communities and sent north without any hope of visits from friends or relatives.[12]

† The agency assigning children and paying for them was the Istituo Nazionale di Previdenze Sociale (National Welfare Institute, INPS). Not surprisingly, Dr. Aliotta's father was a member of the administrative council of INPS.

‡ Busta is "envelope," and the diminutive means "little" with a nuance of jocularity. Bustarelle could be translated as "cheerful little envelopes."

and Exxon to cabinet ministers and air force generals. We are not speaking of sporadic bribes but of organized bribery over a long period of time—in the Exxon case, at least nine years, from 1963 to 1972.[15]

Bribes and kickbacks are interwoven into the fabric of nepotism and clientism of *Democrazia Cristiana*. Prosecutors never seem to find the guilty persons despite palpable evidence of crime. In Naples, for example, it was discovered that the zoning map of the city had been forged. The copy on file in Rome headquarters showed certain areas colored dark green, which meant building was forbidden because of soil conditions, lack of sewers, etc. In the Naples map the green had been colored yellow—the code for unrestricted building. As a result, in 1967, there were 3 landslides, 25 houses totally demolished, 11 chasms, 8 sinkings, 3911 building and street inpairments. In 1968, 32 buildings collapsed and there were 12 landslides; in 1969, 25 houses and 3 landslides. The casualty toll over the three years was 9 dead and 37 severely injured. With grim effrontery, a provincial bulletin edited by Antonio Gava, son of DC Senator Silvio Gava, reported: "A dreadful color blindness has caused some administrators to see yellow for green."[16]

In Palmero, where the Mafia is deeply intertwined with the DC, a total of 4305 building licenses were issued over a period of five years, 1959–63. Of these, 80 percent were issued to five people who were fronts for the Mafia.[17] In Agrigento, a city built on porous ground, a law sets building heights at 25 meters (82 feet) but exemptions were granted by the regional official to build buildings as high as 54 meters. The weight of the tall building provoked a terrible landslide on July 19, 1966, with great destruction and casualities. An investigation by Dr. Raimondo Mignosi found a series of criminal irregularities in permits and inspections, and he forwarded them to the judicial authorities. No one was ever sent to jail, but Dr. Mignosi found his career at an end.[18]

Bribery has been institutionalized within government agencies, with the money going in part to the administrators and in part to the DC. The extent is enormous and well known, but again, as with building permits, difficult to prove. Occasionally, a scandal is proven, as in the case of the bananas. AMB *(Azienda Banane),* a government agency under the ministry of foreign commerce, received a regular kickback of ten lire a kilo of bananas from the tax levied on licensed importers. Since imports were around 125 million kilos a year, this meant a kickback of 1.25 billion lire a year. A famous writer, Ernesto Rossi, wrote that "AMB was found to be the most generous source of funds for the DC." The bribery was finally exposed by the secretary of the Banana Wholesalers Association, who, having been implicated, was fearful of becoming the fall guy.[19] The low man in the hierarchy of thieves took the blame and was sentenced to three years.

He was Franco Avveduti, once secretary to the minister for foreign commerce, Giuseppe Trabucchi, and then promoted by Trabucchi to the presidency of AMB.[20]

Everyone in Rome knew that the real guilt rested with the minister, Senator Trabucchi. Trabucchi continued as minister (and unofficial fund raiser) until he was indicted in 1965 in another importing fraud, this time involving Mexican tobacco.[21] A DC controlled parliamentary commission found Trabucchi not guilty by such a close margin that the verdict was not legally valid; the Chamber and the Senate in joint session had to decide whether the senator's parliamentary immunity should be lifted.

The DC closed ranks in the debate. The secretary of the DC and later premier, Mariano Rumor, ostentatiously seated himself beside Trabucchi throughout the days of the debate. Trabucchi stated that he "did go, and was forced to go, not against but beyond the law," because the applicable legislation was "antiquated and incoherent." A DC deputy, Renato Dell'Andro, said that the minister "had no intention, and did not, harm anyone." A young DC deputy for Sardinia, Francesco Cossiga, a professor of constitutional law, made his reputation as the leader of the defense.* His thesis, for which he would surely have flunked his students, was "that only the minister has the right to decide if an administrative act conforms to the law."[22]

On the twentieth of July 1965, the vote was taken: 461 to 440 in favor of indicting Trabucchi. But the law requires an absolute majority (at this time 476) to indict a member of Parliament, so Trabucchi was home free. The debate was noteworthy for the intervention of Premier Aldo Moro, who said flatly and arrogantly that no one could ever indict the DC.

An ineluctable consequence of the corruption has been the growth and audacity of organized crime. One instance of criminal daring has become a classic. There was at one time a sudden influx of cheap gasoline onto the black market, so huge a supply that the authorities assumed it was coming in by tankers. But how could such tankers be hidden? How could such a supply be maintained? Finally, a brilliant captain of the Finance Guards decided that not tankers, but a refinery was the source. He verified that there were strict controls at the gates, so how did gasoline get out? He got a job inside the refinery and within weeks discovered the secret: the fire-fighting sprinkler system had been used! The huge pipes bringing in water had been drained and filled with gasoline and the flow reversed. A mile or so beyond the gates, tanker trucks pulled in at a big valve to get filled up. It was a mammoth operation, involving dozens of workers and managerial connivance at several levels.[23]

* Cossiga was minister of the interior in the Andreotti cabinet and prime minister in 1979–80. His star rose after his defense of Trabucchi; he became undersecretary of the defense ministry.

The connection between organized crime and politics is not unknown in American cities. But in southern Italy, organized crime has been institutionalized for centuries in the Neapolitan *camorra* and the Sicilian Mafia.

The *camorra's* origins are obscure. It seems to have been organized within Neapolitan jails a couple of hundred years ago. By the middle of the nineteenth century, the organization was protected by the Bourbon rulers, who were using it as a secret police against the liberals working for Italian unification. In 1862, according to Professor P. A. Allum, "the Piedmontese government undertook the first of a series of campaigns against it. It did not succeed in eliminating it because the *camorra* took the obvious step in self-preservation of 'going into politics'. . . . Since 1945 a series of gangs and gangsters have been operating rackets. . . . The tie-up with politics is simple: the racketeer supplies the politicians with the vote in return for protection of his own activities."*[24] The various political bosses of Naples, principally the Lauro and Gava families, have either been members of *Democrazia Cristiana* or its right-wing allies.

The Mafia is more than a racket; it is a way of life. Originally Sicilian, centered in Palermo, it expanded in the postwar period to all major cities—Rome, Turin, Milan—as five million southerners went north to work. However, its main stronghold is still Sicily, where it has intertwined itself into DC politics as it had previously done with the fascist regime.

*The Mafia, also known as "the Honorable Society," is a venerable institution, probably dating back a thousand years. The word is neither Italian nor Latin. It has been suggested that Mafia is derived from the name of the Arab tribe,* Maafir, *which ruled Palermo prior to the Norman Conquest in* A.D. *1060.† On this hypothesis, it was a self-defense organization of surviving Arabs against the Norman conquerors. It then derived continuity as a defense arm of the population.*[25]

*Whatever the myth, the reality is that, since feudal times, the Mafia has been intertwined with the power structure: great landed proprietors, merchants, the royal bureaucracy. It is a secret society, based on family and clan and on blood feuds, and it is thoroughly sexist. Its cult is one of violence, machismo, and power: "It is better*

---

\*  Professor P. A. Allum of the University of Reading, England, is the author of the definitive study, *Politics and Society in Post-War Naples.*

†  The *American Heritage Dictionary* suggests that the word meant boldness and was derived from the Arabic *mahyah,* "boasting." Nichols, although leaning to the *Ma afir* interpretation reports that the word is still used by old-timers in Palermo to describe beauty and pride, as in calling a girl *"na carusa mafiusa."*

*to rule than to fuck" is a Mafia proverb. Patrick Meney, Rome correspondent of Agence France Presse points out that the word* omertà, *always associated with the Mafia, originally meant 'man,' and 'of man'; that is, be strong, be powerful, have your say. Never betray; never inform. By extension,* omertà *has come to mean the law of silence.''* [26]

*With the unification of Italy, a tacit alliance was created between northern industrialists and feudal southerners. The Mafia entered politics on a wholesale basis, fighting centralization, controlling local governments, provincial administrators, and national politicians such as southern deputies and ministers. With fascism, the same pattern obtained. Mussolini sent a prefect, Cesare Mori, to smash the Mafia. Mori, nicknamed "the Iron Prefect," began arresting the small fry and worked his way up to the top men tied in with fascist ministers, including Antonio Di Giorgio, the Palermitan minister of war. At this point, Mussolini stopped the investigation and kicked Mori upstairs to the Senate.\**

*With the invasion of Sicily during World War II, the Mafia smoothly shifted its allegiance. Aided by the American Army and the Office of Strategic Services, which used the Mafia as an intelligence gatherer and organizer, the organization grew stronger.* [27] *After the war, it flirted with various political movements, including separatism, but settled down with the DC after the elections of 1948, and has maintained its influence in that party. The apex of the Mafia's political structure is Giovanni Di Gioia, vice-secretary of the DC when Fanfani was secretary, a deputy since 1958, and a minister in three cabinets. He was minister of the merchant marine in the Andreotti cabinet until forced to resign because of the scandal of "the ships of gold"—three ships bought in Japan by a private company and leased to the government at double their value. In December of 1976 Gioia was found guilty by a Turin court of consorting with the Mafia.* [28]

*The Mafia has exercised its control by terror and intimidation. To say that the people protect the Mafia as their own is nonsense; the people are cowed and fearful because they do not feel protected by the state, but see the state and the DC as tacit accomplices of the Mafia. Its defeat cannot come only from the police authorities, even if honest. It has to come, and it is coming, from the mobilization of popular forces.*

Aside from the Mafia, which is *sui generis*, the corruption outlined so far is not unknown in other countries; Italy simply has more of it. But

---

\* A movie on Mori, *Il Prefetto di ferro*, which ran in the major Italian cities in the fall of 1977, puts to rest the myth that Mussolini clipped the wings of the Mafia. The film was based on a book by historian Arrigo Petracco, who said that when he began the research, he believed in the Mussolinian myth.

beginning in the sixties, a vast new area was opened up whose potential for corruption was greater than all the rest combined, namely, the nationalized industries. Today they cover over 50 percent of the economy, including 90 percent of shipbuilding, 75 percent of steel, 80 percent of chemicals, 45 percent of machine production, 30 percent of textiles, and nearly the whole of banking. "Nationalization," which covers both state ownership and state participation, is more extensive in Italy than in any other western country.[29]

The vast extent of nationalization results from two factors. The first is the fascist heritage. In its drive for autarchy, the fascist regime initiated many industries and took over those that verged on bankruptcy. The second reason was the deliberate policy of De Gasperi, who said in 1948 that "banks, publishing houses, large industries, and agricultural estates are still in the hands of men who are basically anticlerical."[30] If they shifted parties, the DC might be isolated. To obviate that danger, De Gasperi projected a public sector of the economy. In 1953, ENI *(Ente Nazionale degli Idrocarboni,* National Hydrocarbons Institute) was created; it controlled petroleum and natural gas. This was the first in a series of agencies that proliferated throughout the sixties.[31]

The potential for corruption was fully consummated, both in providing high-paying jobs for political barons and in the wheeling and dealing with private industry, all to the greater glory of *Democrazia Cristiana.* Funds for the party became plentiful, and an enormous clientism was created that generated votes as effortlessly as the sun evaporates the waters of the earth. The distribution of plums verged on the farcical. Take, for example, ESPI, *(Ente Siciliano per la Promozione Individuale,* Aid to Small Businesses in Sicily). The agency has a roster of 108 persons, and more generals than troops:

| | |
|---|---|
| 1 Director General | 42 Generals |
| 1 Vice-Director General | 34 Functionaries |
| 3 Central Directors | <u>32</u> Employees |
| 12 Chiefs of Services | 108 |
| 13 Assistant Chiefs of Services | |
| 9 Office Managers | |
| <u>3</u> Assistant Office Managers | |
| 42 Generals | |

An investigation of the agency by the Republic's district attorney for Palermo revealed that the annual pay, benefits, bonuses, and other "perks" of the top five jobs cost the agency *630 million lire each;* at the time, the takehome pay of a deputy in Parliament was 12 million lire a year. Altogether, with benefits, pensions, the use of limousines, etc., the cost to society of one deputy was around 30 million lire—one twentieth of the cost of an ESPI manager.[32] This explains why the lucrative posts rotate. In six years (1967–73) there were six ESPI director-generals, all Christian Democrats.* Three held other government offices; one, Onofrio Niceta, general accountant for the region, almost never appeared in his ESPI office; another, Marcello Rodino, spent two days a week at ESPI.

ESPI made investments or loans in dozens of shaky firms. In the six years after its founding in 1967, between overhead and bad loans, the agency showed a loss of 106 billion lire—or more than the total capital allocated to it by Parliament—probably setting an international record for the squandering of public funds.[34]

ESPI is a tiny agency. A middle-sized agency, EGAM (*Ente per la Gestione Mineraria,* Mineral Resources) controlled firms having 32,000 employees. It was liquidated in 1977 at a total loss of *3,000 billion lire,* or "five times the amount that Italy was begging from the International Monetary Fund." The quote is from the newspaper *La Repubblica.*[35]

When we come to the giants of nationalization, like ENI, the country is faced by veritable sovereignties having their own inner dynamics and strategies—feudal baronies set up, manned, and protected by Christian Democratic ministers, premiers, and presidents impervious to public control—somewhat analogous to the FBI and the CIA of our recent past. Enrico Mattei, the first president of ENI, set prices, cheated the state, bought newspapers, and was instrumental in the election of Gronchi as president of the Republic.† Writes his biographer, Giorgio Galli: "Mattei accumulated and dispersed, without public control, enormous superprofits derived from a monopoly position. . . . he had a very clear idea of power. . . . In this way he poisoned the body politic."[36]

The Establishment in Italy was well aware of Mattei's role and influence. One of his closest friends, Raffaele Mattioli, president of the Commercial Bank of Italy and a prestigious insider, said of Mattei after his death: "He taught his successors how to buy the Republic."[37]

Mattei was only the most colorful of the great barons managing as their fiefs an array of agencies whose acronyms dismay the foreigner—such as ENEL (*Ente Nazionale di Energia Elettrica,* National Institute for Electrical Energy) or *Finsider* (the national

---

* Six years seems to be standard. According to Franco Cazzola, 61.4 percent of higher personnel last less than six years.[33]

† Mattei also fought the American-controlled oil cartel, the so-called Seven Sisters, and made his own deals with producers, paying them higher royalties. When he was killed in an air crash, many people suspected sabotage.

steel industry). Posts in nationalized entities and in private industry are openly available to government officials, deputies, senators.\* The record is probably held by Senator Teresio Guglielmone (DC) of Turin. In 1950 the Communists were seeking a law of "incompatibility" (or, in American terms, "conflict of interests") to block such corruption, and they focused on Guglielmone, who answered them in a tone half resentful, half piteous: "If you had a family as big as mine, you would not insist so much on incompatibility."†[38]

Guglielmone, it turns out, was president of three major banks in Turin, two manufacturing companies, a shipping company, a publishing company, a liquid-gas equipment and distribution company, a chain of retail stores and a personal loans company. He was also director of three major credit institutes and of the Turin telephone company, and, he owned shares in three newspapers. He was also the honorary president of the society of Roman newspapers.[40]

Nearly all of these posts were well paid; all had patronage potential. The number and range of his activities mark Guglielmone as either a business genius, or a shrewd exploiter of his political positions: he was a member of the national executive of the DC and president of its commission for finance and economics.

The Italians have a name for the totality of this corruption: *il sottogoverno*. Literally, it means "the undergovernment," but it may be better expressed as the "underworld of government." Except for the Communists, every political party and every institution in Italy has been enmeshed in the *sottogoverno*. This includes the Vatican, whose status as a sovereign power has facilitated illegal flight of capital and illegal speculation in foreign currency. The *sottogoverno* entails a constant obstruction of justice by officials, high and low. From cover-ups of money scandals to cover-ups of political scandals is an easy step, often on the same staircase. Italian politics is a never-ending Watergate.

One of the biggest questions in Italy today is this: When the Communists share power with the Christian Democrats, will the PCI be able to resist the temptations of the golden calf. The Socialists, who participated in governments from 1963 to 1970, were unable to resist. According to Peter Nichols, the *Times* correspondent, many high Socialist personalities, aside from a few incorruptibles such as Nenni, "demanded and got a slice of this *sottogoverno*. Soon after, a leader of the DC left, who had favored the entry of Socialists into the

---

\* A powerful, bitter film, *Todo modo* (In every way), was made in Italy in 1976 by Elio Petri. It exposed the corruption of the DC, using the detective-story genre: the plot hinged on the acronyms of nationalized industries. The film was banned in Italy.

† A law of incompatibility was passed by Parliament on February 15, 1953, prohibiting members from holding offices in public or private corporations. The policing is to be done by members filling out declarations. *Twenty years later*, less than half of the deputies had even troubled to make out declarations.[39]

government, was heard to bemoan their attitude. 'We Christian Democrats may be characterized as corrupt, if you wish; but we distribute jobs and favors for votes. The Socialists enjoy the favors and jobs themselves and don't even bother with votes.' Clearly there is a useful corruption and a corruption that is pure and simple."[41]

Many DC spokesmen, such as Colletta in Bologna, believe that once Communists are in the government, they, too, will succumb to corruption. They argue that the DC didn't invent the *sottogoverno*; it has always existed in many regions of Italy As individuals, Italians are no more dishonest than other peoples in their personal relations, but have no sense of civic honesty. Having lived under foreign rule for many centuries, they have developed a tradition of mistrust of governments; tax evasion, for example, is an achievement, not a shame.[42] Fascism exploited these traditions, made nepotism and clientism a commonplace and raised governmental corruption to new levels. The occupation of the Allied troops, following the Italian defeat, added their corrupting influences, not only in making deals with the Mafia and old fascist elements but also because Allied money, food, and supplies fed gigantic black markets. The DC inherited a disintegrated society, a society turned inward to the family with people fighting for daily survival and acquiescing to the mores of the jungle.

There is validity to this argument. But the gravamen against *Democrazia Cristiana* is that instead of fighting this tradition of corruption, its political leaders embraced it. In the Constituent Assembly of 1947, monarchist and right-wing elements seized on this corruption to attack and destabilize the government. A Sicilian deputy, Finocchiaro Aprile, a separatist leader who was seeking to water down the proposed Constitution, brought substantiated charges against many of the DC leaders. He said to Gronchi (later a President of the Republic): "When you were undersecretary of state for Mussolini, you were a ragamuffin. Today you have millions."[43]

*The issue of corruption is still used by neofascists at every level of life, as I had occasion to note on a visit to the old apartment building in Largo Leopardi where I was born. In the courtyard, three workers were finishing their lunch. A huge scaffolding had just been set up for them to paint the building. A wizened, toothless man of sixty was seated on a step munching a sandwich; the two other workers, in their forties, were having a last sip from a bottle of wine.*

*I told them who I was and how I used to live there. They asked questions about America; I asked questions about Italy. I found out they were making 300,000 lire a month for a six-day week, or about*

*$80 a week. I thought it was not very much and asked if they were unionized.*

*"Unions, bah!" said one of them, a burly, friendly giant. "They are the worst. Take your money, run your life, tell you what hours to work—they are wrecking the country."*

*"You must vote for Andreotti," I joked.*

*The giant spat. "Him? That crook? Not even if I was blind."*

*"If you don't vote DC, who do you vote for?"*

*He drew himself up and gave me a fascist salute. I was taken aback, then grabbed him by his vest in mock ferocity (he made two of me) and shook him. "How dare you give me that salute. I told you my father had to run away into exile. Mussolini wrecked this country with a stupid war, and you haven't learned anything."*

*The man laughed, a little shamefacedly, his companions laughing at him, particularly the old man. Shuffling his feet, he looked down, embarrassed, then looked at me stubbornly: "All right, all right, but say what you will, Mussolini was not a crook. When he died, Donna Rachele [his wife] had to get a pension from the government to live on. When Andreotti dies, you'll find out he's got millions."*

*Three weeks later, on a train, a university student, who clearly had some sneaking sympathy for the Red Brigades, used almost the same words in comparing Mussolini to Leone, the then President of the Republic, who was to resign over the Lockheed scandal.*

The ultimate price paid by Italian society for the *sottogoverno* has been foreign interference. American corporations and government agencies—Exxon, Lockheed, the CIA— have had a strong influence on Italian politics and economics. Between 1963 and 1972 Vincenzo Cazzaniga, Exxon's representative in Italy, distributed $46 million of Exxon's money, in return for which the oil corporation got an estimated $600 million in deferred taxes, reduction of tax rates on refineries, increased prices to ENI and ENEL, extra quotas for the importation of oil, and so forth.[44] (Cazzaniga served a brief prison sentence for his role in the affair.)

Lockheed's bribes in Italy have not been computed, but it is known that $200 million were spent in various countries. The CIA contributed close to $100 million over a twenty-year period, the bulk of it to *Democrazia Cristiana*.[45] These funds were distributed covertly—targeted to specific individuals and specific purposes at specific times. Vast sums have been given overtly, beginning with a $100 million loan in January 1947 which gave De Gasperi the leverage to expel the Communists from the government.[46] Thirty years later, the International Monetary Fund granted a loan of $1.5 billion, with a tacit understanding that no substantial changes occur in the Andreotti government.[47]

The vast extent of corruption in Italy is a byword to students of the subject. The foremost American expert on the oil industry said that Italy "illustrates not only Lord Acton's celebrated dictum but its converse: Corruption is power and absolute corruption is absolute power."[48] A large part of the Communist appeal to voters comes from their having "clean hands." No other institution in Italy can say the same, including the Vatican, which has been involved in many scandals and has not been above receiving undercover money from abroad. For example, the splitting of the CGIL in 1948 and the formation of the Catholic unions in which the Vatican was a prime mover, was partially financed by the AFL and the ILGWU, with the probable connivance of the CIA.[49]

The Church has been contaminated at every level. Nepotism, for example, applies in a literal sense to Pope Pius XII (Eugenio Pacelli), whose three nephews, Prince Giulio, Prince Carlo, and Prince Marcantonio Pacelli, have cushy jobs: Giulio is ambassador of Costa Rica to the Vatican and administrative counselor to the Banco di Roma (the "bank that smells of incense," as the Italians say); Carlo is general counsel of Vatican City and legal representative of the patrimony of the Holy See, *Propaganda Fide* (the congregation of Catholic education), and a half dozen other papal agencies; Marcantonio is president of *Linee Aere Italiane* and of Molini Biondi.[50] All three princes have been involved in scandals touching Vatican agencies, particularly the Pontifical Aid Agency.

In 1944, Pope Pius XII set up the Pontifical Aid Agency (POA), to secure scarce food for the Vatican and its institutions. The agency, growing stronger over the years, extended its aid to refugees and to exiles, to abandoned children, associations of "unions" of fishermen, shepherds, agricultural laborers, trade schools, and so forth. It now has 30,000 employees and 200,000 volunteers. The agency received food and money, particularly from the United States, for distribution to the needy. Almost from its inception it became involved in scandals. For example, several million kilos of flour were sent by the United States to the POA for feeding the needy, with strict provision against its sale or barter. Nonetheless, the flour was sold on the open market by the Molini Biondi company.

The U.S. embassy, which had winked at several such scandals, found this too much. On September 20, 1958, it made formal demand at the foreign ministry for "explanations." None were forthcoming, except that, three days later, *L'Osservatore romano* intervened, not to answer the charges, but to say the pope knew nothing about the matter. The reason for the solicitude of the paper was that the president of Molini Biondi was Prince Marcantonio Pacelli, and a member of the administrative council of POA was Prince Carlo Pacelli.[51]

Undeterred, POA continued. In 1970 another scandal surfaced: POA was manipulating the Common Market to buy sugar and butter at the low prices established for the third world. The staples were first sent to Vienna to obscure their destination, then brought into Vatican City (a sovereign state) untaxed, and finally sold on the Italian market at six times the cost.[52]

In 1978, the Banco di Roma (of which Prince Giulio Pacelli was an administrative counselor), was enmeshed in a scandal involving the flight of capital from Italy. The fiscal promoter was the banker Michele ("Mike") Sindona, who had enjoyed the complete confidence of the Vatican. The supervisor of Vatican finances, Monsignor Paul Marcinkus, had used Sindona for currency speculations.* A series of scandals broke, implicating several banks; and Sindona fled to the United States, where he is fighting extradition to face Italian indictments!†

Another papal relative in the administrative council of the Banco di Roma was Ludovico Montini, brother of Pope Paul VI. Ludovico was also a DC deputy, but incompatibility didn't trouble him—he was also president of the Administration of International Aid (AAI); on the administrative council of the Bank of St. Paul in Brescia, as well as the Italian Institute of Credit, General Company for Public Works, and the Amati Telectric-Mechanical Company.[54]

The Church and the DC are close, so that scandals are apt to overlap. When the Bank of Sicily went bankrupt in 1967 with a loss of 45 billion lire, the auditors found that *Democrazia Cristiana* had unsecured loans for 625 million lire. The Church was heavily involved in the direction of the bank, including its financial adviser, the Marquis Giovambattista Sacchetti, who was president of the Bank of the Holy Ghost, and directors Monsignor Asta and Monsignor Travia of the diplomatic corps of the Vatican. There were also unsecured loans to leading DC politicians and to the parents of Ernesto Cardinal Ruffini of Palermo.[55]

Particularly susceptible to corruption are the religious agencies for welfare and aid to orphans. Their funds come from many sources and are difficult to supervise; they also deal with corrupt state agencies. They are often unwitting or tacit participants in fraud, as in the case of the Trinitarian Fathers "subletting" tubercular children

---

\* Marcinkus seems to have survived his connection with Sindona. He acted as advance man for Wojtyla and then as his bodyguard during the papal visit to the U.S. in 1979.

† Sindona went from the frying pan into the fire. Once in the U.S., he was indicted for fraud in the failure of the Franklin Bank, which he controlled. Just before his trial, set for September 1979, he disappeared. He reappeared seventy-five days later, claiming he had been kidnapped. At his trial in March 1980 the prosecutor showed that Sindona had traveled to Italy and back on a false passport, presumably to confer with the Mafia. He was found guilty, March 27, 1980.[53]

from Dr. Aliotta. But in many cases, the agencies are themselves responsible.

Peter Nichols, who bears no trace of anticlericalism, is scathing on the subject: "Most of the scandals about mistreatment of children involved institutes run by monks, nuns, or people close to the hierarchy who pretended piety while making profits. The worst cases were found in Prato, Cagliari, and Rome. They were examples of open cruelty, systemized and associated with a certain financial acumen. From charity one can always make a good deal of money, obtaining public funds for child maintenance while saving on food and services, with the complicity, or the absence, of controls."[56]

Child abuse has been thoroughly documented; the examples are chilling. For example, at Grottaferrata, following a detailed denunciation, the magistrate authorized a police raid on the Institute of Santa Rita, managed by Sister Colomba. The police report states: "Opening the door of the dormitory, we found a horrendous scene. In a room full of unbearable stench, on eight beds, were fifteen children, their legs tied by rags, their arms raised back to the iron headboard where they were chained and padlocked. The poor children were thus immobilized. Locked up alone and without any help, they had developed contusions and swellings due to the chains and ties that impeded blood circulation."[57]

At the trial of Sister Colomba, it came out that she had been paid 2500 lire per child per day. The actual cost to her was 300 lire per child. In addition, there were donations from abroad. In January 1967, these came to 627,000 lire. In the same month she spent 82,000 lire on food for twenty-five children. Sister Colomba had run the Institute of Santa Rita for eighteen years, in the course of which thirteen children had died. The bishop of Frascati, Monsignor Luigi Liverzani, who had vouched for and defended her, was implicated, and penal proceedings were instituted against him; they were soon dropped. Sister Colomba was found guilty, but received executive clemency.[58]

Scandals such as these have weakened the Church in its struggle against Law 382, and the Church is now on the defensive because the decree of execution puts teeth into Law 382. At stake are such "religious" institutions as orphanages; homes for the elderly, for the mentally ill, for the poor; maternity clinics, kindergartens, day-care centers, and other charities. They number about 40,000 and serve 7 million people. a formidable social power for patronage, indoctrination, and fund raising.

The interpretation of Law 382 is probably the most important issue facing the Italian hierarchy. It is indispensable to an understanding of the exchange of letters between Luigi Bettazzi, bishop of

Ivrea, and Enrico Berlinguer, general secretary of the PCI. Dr.
Germano Marri, in Perugia, explained the point to me.


*Marri had asked me if I had read the exchange of letters. I had. So
Marri explained: "The key point is buried toward the end, where the
bishop asks the PCI not to hold religious institutions in 'hostage.'
Berlinguer assured him that the party had no such intention; all
institutions of the state would be under the people's democratic
control and therefore Catholic influence could flourish within the
institutions. The pluralism of interested parties is guaranteed by
democracy in the institutions, but the Church wants exclusive control: it is allergic to internal democracy."*
    *"Like the party," I interjected.*
    *"Touché," said Marri lightly. "But, in fact, nowhere near. Our
democratic centralism at least has the forms of democracy, and it's
getting more democratic all the time. But the Church is inherently
authoritarian. We have no pope; they do! Anyway, the argument
now, as presented by Bettazzi and Berlinguer, comes down to
grammatical conflict of two prepositions: whether there should be, as
the Church wants, pluralism* of *institutions, or pluralism* within
*institutions."*
    *"A conflict of two prepositions," I joked. "A typical Italian way
to confuse foreigners."*
    *Marri smiled. "Of course, neither Bettazzi nor Berlinguer be-
lieves that they are solving the conflict. They are airing it, making it
public property, so to speak, and forcing a clarification of each
position. Bettazzi says: you have the power; use it wisely and gently.
The regions now have the legal right to interpret Law 382—and the
Church has to deal with us. It gives us leverage with the hard-liners on
other issues, and it opens the door to further discussions. I'll give you
a good example.*
    *Marri got up and went to his desk. He came back with a copy of*
Cronache umbre, *the party's regional review for February 1976—a
136-page booklet in standard review format of six by nine inches.
"There was a strong attack on the party by Bishop Cesare Pagani of
Gubbio. We reprinted it and ran articles on his pastoral letter by
Catholics with differeing viewpoints. Editorially, we answered him by
quoting from Cardinal Pellegrino's pastoral letter,* Camminare insieme. *This issue of the review was sold out."*
    *As he handed it to me, he went on. "You'll see he emphasizes
that the Church has the duty to help the poor, the orphans, the sick
and the disabled, and that it does so at a minimum cost to the public.
Now, most of that is hot air. The Church's charities get state*

*subsidies and often part of that money finds its way into the DC election funds. The worst example is OMNI,\* which controls all maternity agencies, many of them managed by religious orders. In 1969 and 1970 there was a series of scandals. In Rome, ex-mayor Amerigo Petrucci of the DC, who was in charge of OMNI for the region, was indicted for diverting funds.[59] He was acquitted, but everyone knew he was guilty. The price of corruption is paid by the people. Our infant mortality rate of 32 deaths per thousand is one of the highest in Europe; in the south it is 48 per thousand and in Naples, in 1970, it reached 64 per thousand![60]*

*"But in the long run, it is not the Church scandals which are important, but the separation of Church and state, which Article 7 of the Constitution mandates.† The Church wants to keep its network of agencies because of power—patronage, community influence, and social control. We want what you in America have always had: to make religion a private, not a state affair."*

In the long run the separation of Church and state will come not only by revision of the concordat but by popular consensus. People do not care who runs the social services so long as they are administered well. In Bologna, the Church has practically given up on welfare work; the city coverage was more thorough and better run. The Church itself is divided on the importance of its religious institutions, the conciliar people like Bettazzi being more concerned with spiritual and moral values. It is the integralists, the hard-liners, who want to keep the Catholic social services. To do so, they will have to compromise with the Communists.

Similarly, the *sottogoverno* has made the DC vulnerable as people see the fruits of thirty years of DC rule. In 1975, a Socialist deputy, Antonio Giolitti, gave a generally accepted verdict: "The intertwining of politics and the economy, between mores and scandals, between industrial policies and *sottogoverno*—in short, the rise of a new feudalism—is the true Italian problem. The problem is the intertwining of the DC and the barons of nationalization."[61]

The Italian economy is hemorrhaging; tens of thousands of billions of lire are being wasted "by chaos, corruption, thievery, outrages of all kinds—the blackmail and violence of power."[62] The

---

\* OMNI stands for *Opera Nazionale di Maternita ed Infanzia*, or National Agency for Maternity and Infancy. It controls maternity clinics, pediatrics centers, etc.

† Marri was not quite accurate. Article 7 is deliberately ambiguous. It reads, "The state and the Catholic Church are each independent and sovereign in their respective spheres. Their relations are governed by the Lateran Treaties. Any modification of the treaties, bilaterally accepted, will not require constitutional amendments." The first sentence is in conflict with the second, because the Lateran Treaties, in effect, made the Church a state religion.

words are those of Guido Carli, former governor of the Bank of Italy, a man who knows where all the bodies are buried, and who is himself enmeshed, however reluctantly, in this inextricable complex which the DC has built and can no longer control.

The corruption and waste of the *sottogoverno* strikes at the jugular of the Italian economy: lack of capital. The waste is twofold; on the one hand, it fritters away capital; on the other, it makes inefficient use of existing capital. No one knows the cost of the *sottogoverno*, but it is undoubtedly several times the billion-dollar loan granted by the International Monetary Fund. As we have seen, EGAM alone ran up deficits of 4 billion.[63] The flight of capital from Italy is enormously greater than the loan; estimates run between $35 and $50 billion. Tax evasion runs about the same.

These facts and figures are well known to Italian economists, legislators, and opinion makers, but there is a tendency to fatalism—the *sottogoverno* has always existed, is now and forever shall be—Italians are corrupt. The Communists passionately reject the cliché as an unwarranted slander of the people. They point to Bologna; they point to the unions, not only the Communist-led CGIL, but the Catholic CISL and the Socialist UIL, which in the past ten years have sloughed off leaders who were corrupted by employers during the collaboration period of the fifties. They point to the many non-Communist independents elected to Parliament in 1976 on the Communist ticket; 20 percent of Communist-listed senators are independents; 7 percent of the deputies. They point out that Italian voters have thrown out corrupt governments in Naples, Turin, Rome, Venice, and dozens of towns.[64] One of the weightiest testimonials to confidence in PCI morals came in November 1979 from the mayor of Rome, Giulio Carlo Argan, who had been a professor of the history of art at the University of Rome. Argan had been a man in the socialist area, and when the left won Rome in 1976 the PCI accepted him as mayor though the PCI had three quarters of the seats. When Argan resigned because of ill health in 1979 and withdrew completely from politics, he also applied for membership in the Communist party because, he said, "in Italy, without the Communists, democracy cannot be saved. . . . I have come to assess the high moral ascendancy of the Communist party."[65]

The *sottogoverno* can be defeated. Aside from the increase in class consciousness of the population, there are movements for reform within the DC and the Church, often led by anti-Communists who realize that corruption pushes voters toward the PCI. For example, after the Friuli earthquakes, the anti-Communist *Communione e Liberazione* (Communion and Liberation) organized fund collections and relief teams that were honest, selfless, and efficient.

The PCI welcomed the competition for which it had established the parameters:anti*sottogoverno*, anticorruption. This is what is meant by cultural hegemony.

To the many skeptics who argue that corruption is so pervasive and traditional that its elimination is utopian, the Communists reply that an informed people can do anything, that, in fact, only the people can carry out certain tasks. For example, the PCI has embarked on a struggle that the government has avoided: the Communists have taken on the Mafia.

*Inside a courtroom in Reggio Calabria, sitting on the press bench with Ugo Napoli, secretary of the regional CGIL on one side, and Attilio, secretary of the bricklayers' union on the other, I watched an epoch-making trial. Two Mafiosi were being brought to book for beating up Attilio, and the CGIL was demanding the right to interplead with Attilio as the injured party. If that right was won, every organizer and every union man fighting the Mafia would henceforth have the full power of the union behind him as a legal right. Newsmen and television cameras from the national network were present, underlining the importance of the case.*

*The small courtroom had a high ceiling and perfect acoustics. The walls were weather-beaten, the plaster falling off in patches, the paint faded and peeling. A dilapidated building in a dilapidated town. Behind the press a high wooden railing held back a crowd of standing spectators. In front of us there was a long table for the attorneys. Against the left wall, a raised desk for the prosecutor; on the right, chairs for the accused. In the center, three raised desks for the judges, the middle one considerably higher than the other two. Off to one side, a small raised desk for the court clerk.*

*High above the judges, a huge carved crucifix hung on the wall; beneath it, the inscription* EQUAL JUSTICE UNDER LAW. *It reminded me of the inscription on the pediment of the Supreme Court building in Washington, D.C., and I thought wryly that Moscow courts probably exhibit similar sentiments: the same tribute that power pays to virtue the world over.*

*The three justices in black gowns were a study in typecasting. The chief judge looked like an El Greco—tall, thin, with a high-domed forehead and a severe, ascetic face. The judge on his right was a bluff, hearty type with a toper's red cheeks and a gray crew cut—an unusual hair style in Italy. The judge to the left was a small plump fellow, with wisps of hair, a pince-nez, a prissy mouth—a fussy abbot out of Chaucer. I had been told that one was progressive, the other reactionary, and the chief judge an unknown quantity. I surmised to Napoli that the rotund, pouter pigeon was the reactionary; the rubicund hearty fellow, the progressive. He whispered back that it was the other way around.*

*The lawyers facing the judges were practically symbols of the struggle at issue. There were three of them for the accused Mafiosi, middle-aged, well dressed, well fed, with the practiced oratory of provincial politicians, as indeed they were. Two lawyers represented the union, a man and a woman—in itself a novelty. The man, in a well-worn gray suit, was the recently elected Communist deputy from the area (the party, like the Mafia, had brought forth its heaviest artillery). While deferential to the court, he spoke sharply and incisively. The woman, in her thirties, was more neatly dressed. She, too, was self-assured and professional.*

*The defendants, handcuffed and chained, were brought in by four policemen. The prosecutor, in black gown, began reading the charges as established at the preliminary hearing. The accused Mafiosi had jumped Attilio inside a big construction yard, and had begun to beat him with lengths of two-by-fours. When Attilio fought back, one of the attackers had drawn a revolver and held him at gun-point, while the other continued the beating. The prosecutor cited the criminal statutes involved and quoted various phrases by the attackers: "This will teach you to mess with the Mafia"; 'You think you're cock-of-the-walk, but you're a lousy informer"; "We catch you here again, we'll cut your balls off." The beating—and the threats—had been witnessed by the foreman in charge of the yard, who had testified that he knew the attackers well, that they were well-known Mafiosi. "If it pleases your Honors," the prosecutor concluded, "there is no question but that the attack was premediated. It was conceived as antiunion intimidation by the Mafia. The language of the accused testifies to this fact. The accused are tools of a broader antiunion conspiracy. Your Honors, I submit that the Mafia is on trial."*

*Napoli stirred happily, "Good man," he whispered, "even if he is a Demochristian. Of course, the police are veering left, and the union is beginning to carry weight." He grinned. "Those bastards are in trouble."*

*I looked at the Mafiosi, two young men, one tall, one short, both solidly built and wearing neat blue suits: two smalltime hoods oozing confidence. Presently, the reason became clear; the chief witness to the attack, the foreman in charge of the yard, had retracted his testimony. He was now escorted in by a sergeant and sat in a chair before the court.*

*What followed was fascinating. The chief judge spoke in chatty, friendly tones, now and again with a hint of steel. The witness was defiant, argumentative, and kept interrupting the judge. He was not disrespectful, but neither was he intimidated by authority. "You're putting words in my mouth,'' he would say, and the judge would gesture acquiescence: "Then tell us in your own words,'' Point by point, the judge took the foreman over his original deposition: "You now say you don't know these men, and yet you described them accurately.'' The foreman: "That's because the police described them.'' "But there are witnesses who have seen you drinking with them—several witnesses.'' "Maybe I did a few times.'' "More than fifty?'' "Oh, no.'' "Less than forty?'' "I don't remember.'' "But more than ten?'' A sullen yes. The judge would turn to the clerk: "The question asked was, 'Did you know the accused before the attack?' The answer is 'yes.' '' The clerk, a fat youth in his early twenties, wrote industriously, if slowly.*

*After two grueling hours, the judge had re-established all the facts of the original deposition. Throughout, no one intervened, not the prosecutor, not the lawyers. At the end, the foreman was led away by a police sergeant, held in protective custody as a material witness.*

*"The next matter,'' said the judge, "is the petition of the CGIL to be admitted to the proceedings on a par with the victim in the redress of grievances. I have read the briefs on both sides. Would you gentlemen care to comment?''*

*One of the Mafiosi's lawyers got up and spoke for ten minutes on one point: the attack was a prank, a youthful letting-off of steam. Deplorable, of course, the defendants should be punished, but why this great to-do about nothing? He sat down and one of his colleagues got up. He spoke for fifteen minutes in a tone of deep outrage: the trial was a shabby piece of melodrama cooked up by the union and the complaisant police. Everybody knew the local police were organizing and currying favors with the unions. It was a puppet show, with the strings being pulled by the Communists. The Mafia had been dragged in to make headlines—as an excuse for a gladiatorial show.*

*The third colleague got up. He could not agree more with his distinguished colleague. Look at this display of force: four policemen to guard two kids. Four grown men with the flaps of their revolvers unbuttoned as if there were going to be a commando raid. What utter nonsense. Two young punks attack a busybody they dislike. What has the union got to do with it? Nothing. What has the Mafia got to do with it? Nothing. Why should the Mafia care about unions? Would the Mafia be so stupid as to trust two dumb vitelloni?\* Besides, what is "the Mafia''? A word to frighten children. And so on.*

*The woman lawyer got up and spoke for three minutes. This was no prank. A revolver had been used. The attack had been premeditated.*

*The Communist deputy then spoke for five minutes. The victim*

---

\*   *Vitelloni,* "bull calves''; in American idiom, "young studs.''

*had been attacked because he was a union organizer—a fact admitted by the attackers. The right to unionize was written into the Constitution, and the union, therefore, had a right to participate in proceedings that affected its interests. He could quote precedents: in the case of a health officer in . . . The judge interrupted him. "I have read your brief," he said, "and the precedents do not apply in this case." Sitting beside me, Napoli groaned. The deputy bowed and concluded his argument: Naturally the case should be judged on its merits, but the union was clearly involved, and its interests should be protected.*

*The court declared a recess in order to deliberate the issue. Our group, including Nando, the assistant police commissioner, went to a neighboring cafe for a quick bite (calzone, beer or cappuccino). "It is ironic about the Mafia," said the police official. "Until recently, they flaunted their power, publicized their punishments. But the Mafia bosses sense a new mood among the people—a shift away from fear. They are keeping a low profile. Probably they did not order this particular beating. But they had passed the word to discourage unionization and these two eager beavers figured on praise if they went for a big union official. The stupid jackasses."*

*"Maybe they'll knock them off," said Napoli.*

*Nando shook his head. "No. The Mafia chiefs want no more headlines. They see the interest aroused, the television coverage. They are going to lie low."*

*Two hours later, the court reconvened. The chief justice read a long, carefully worded statement, sprinkled with learned quotations, full of "on the one hand" and "on the other hand," emphasizing the constitutional rights of individuals to unimpeded association, asserting that the case had peculiar characteristics, which meant that the decision was not establishing a precedent. Until the very end we did not know which way the verdict would go, and then—Tombola! Bingo!—the union was admitted! The television cameras whirred, the newsmen scribbled, our people glowed.*

*There was not one word in the statement about the Mafia, and I suddenly realized that the union lawyers had not mentioned it either. The stress had been on constitutional rights, which is what the court had played up. Yet everyone knew that the Mafia had suffered a clear defeat at the hands of the union—a red union. Television and newsmen were sending that message throughout the nation.*

*Later that afternoon, I was at the home of the correspondent of L'Unità, Enzo Lacaria. As he was tapping out his dispatch, he said to me: "Senti, Carlo, it may not seem much to you, but what happened today is tremendous. The fear is lifting. The prosecutor was not afraid, the judges were not afraid, even the foreman, in a way, was not afraid. He was fearful enough to retract, but still he talked to the judge. Ten years ago, he would have been mute. Now he* fears the law *more than the Mafia.*

*"Once the people see that the Mafia can't deliver the goods and that the union can, those brigands are on the way out. Not today, not tomorrow, not in a year, or two years . . . but before I die, the Mafia will have become a historical curiosity."\* He was a happy man as he finished his dispatch. "All this, my friend, is possible because of the political framework, the political climate, which the party has built. That's hegemony!"*

Next morning, I left Reggio Calabria and crossed the Strait of Messina, guarded by Scylla and Charybdis of the Odyssey. Unlike Ulysses and his unidirected sails, my hydrofoil spurned wind and wave on a diagonal course to Messina, the hills of Sicily stretching out in the hazy distance. I thought of Lacaria's words about the political framework built over thirty years, and they brought to mind the meeting at the Fiat-Mirafiori. The unions, old Zuccotti had said, had been able to maintain their real wages and resist the pressures of the employers in a time of depression and unemployment, an unprecedented achievement in Europe. The basic reason, said Zuccotti, was the political framework. The trial was another example of how deep social changes could take place because of that framework.

In Reggio Calabria, a corner of the backward south, where 40 percent of the people were still illiterate, the party was making its contribution. What was the nature of this party? There was the deputy, working free for the union, turning back to the party a portion of his parliamentary salary; the woman lawyer, still an anomaly in the profession, moving among men as an equal; the aging and hardworking Lacaria. There was Nando, the assistant police commissioner (not a member of the party, but well on the way). There was Napoli, the unionist, street-wise and ebullient. Above all, there was Attilio, the bricklayer, who had taken his beating and preferred charges against the Mafiosi.

Of all the people I met that day, Attilio was inescapably symbolic of the new Italy, of the men and women who are taking charge of their country, wresting power from a corrupt, outworn class. Yet judging by appearances, there could not have been a more improbable symbol than this man with the doltish raw-red face and lusterless eyes, a few short hairs bristling from a mottled dome. Physically big and brawny, over six feet tall, he wore a thin overcoat down to his ankles, so that he looked like a howitzer shell of large caliber, a tube of flesh with a

---

\*　The PCI has maintained its pressure for anti-Mafia measures and organization. For example, it held a major anti-Mafia congress in Palermo, Sicily, November 23–24, 1979.[66]

pointed head sunk into the shoulders.* When he was introduced to me that morning as "our comrade, Attilio," my first mental reaction was "Attila the Hun." As I tried to penetrate his inarticulateness, I began to think of him as Markham's "Man with the Hoe," "brother to the ape."

The hydrofoil skimmed the blue strait, the town of Messina growing ever larger. But Attilio filled my mind. I had spent considerable time with him. Attilio had followed me around, a step behind, like a feudal retainer. When asked a question, he replied laconically, groping for words, and I was not surprised to learn he had only finished second grade before going to work in the fields. I *was* surprised to learn he was the leader of the bricklayers' union. How was he able to lead, I wondered, when he had such difficulty expressing himself?

When I asked about the beating, he suddenly found his tongue. It became clear that his inarticulateness had been caused by shyness concerning personal matters. Now he said, "At first I thought it was a *ragazzata* [a kid's prank], these two coming at me with sticks, and I said, 'Hey, cut it out,' but when they started to call me a *sbirro,* curse the union, and mention the Mafia, I realized they were Mafiosi and that they meant business. So I smacked one of them hard, grabbed his two-by-four, and started to beat him up. This son-of-a-bitch takes out a gun, and I thought, he's just crazy enough to use it, so I stopped fighting, just protecting my head with my arms and ducking the blows. It hurt plenty, but it wasn't too damaging, and I finally got away. The foreman was watching and laughing. I thought to myself, *Ridi, stronzo* [laugh, turd], he who laughs last laughs best. They think they are dealing with a *cafone* [redneck]; they don't know what a union means, the dumb shits. Anyway, I got Napoli out of bed, and we went to Nando then and there. Next day the two Mafiosi were locked up, never knew what hit them. Nando pulled the foreman in, scared the hell out of him, and got his deposition. One, two, three, *piazza pulita* [the square was swept clean]."

He must have been ready to kill them. How did he feel now?

"Well, I was pretty mad then, but now . . . well, it's life. Anger serves no purpose." He then proceeded to give me the most extraordinary Gramscian lecture. "*Guarda,* they are ignorant sons of an oppressed class. We have to teach them where their true interests are, put our values into their heads. That's cultural hegemony. Anger doesn't teach. You get sore at a man, he gets sore at you. You yell, he yells. It's a dialectical process: hostility breeds hostility. Sooner or later, you still have to talk, to reason. That's historical perspective." He went on in this vein, his language a racy mixture of sophisticated

---

* He reminded me of Herblock's cartoon character of the atom bomb.

words and earthy phrases—dialectical, capillary, hegemony; shit, hard-on, *chiavare su moglie, una crusca all'asino, stuzzica fuori la merda.*\* When discussing politics, his use of words was proper and coherent. Arguing the necessity of *il compromesso storico*, he was totally unself-conscious and confident—of himself, his union, his party. He kept saying: "we, the party of the working class."

Attilio's confidence is matched only by that of the Church, and, once more, the encounter made me reflect on the two opposing institutions. The Church had gestated within the Roman Empire for three hundred years, a tremendous liberating revolution. Having come to power, it became corrupt, arrogant, ruthless, finally guilty of terrible crimes, including the extermination of whole populations—the Albigenses in France, the Crusades in the Near East. It had had the Inquisition, the Borgia popes, the burning of heretics. Protestantism had checked its hubris, but the great renewal had not come until Vatican II.

Communism gestated within Europe for less than a century. In 1917 it had given birth to a great liberating revolution. As the party consolidated its power under Stalin, it became uncritical, arrogant, and tainted by crimes as offensive as those of the Church. Eurocommunism was the new protestant revolt, and the Attilios were its core.

The comparison may seem far-fetched. Despite its many faults, the Church has been a civilizing influence. Prelates such as Pellegrino and Roncalli are luminous personalities, and to compare Attilio to them seems presumptuous. And yet . . . consider: those outstanding men had been culled by the Church as children at nine, ten, eleven years of age, placed in seminaries, surrounded by love and culture, their physical needs provided for.†

The Communists take the poor, the wretched, the illiterate, and turn them into educated purposive individuals. Attilio was exceptional in his tenacity; he was unexceptional in his origins. Moreover, as Gramsci pointed out, the Communist works without the sustenance, and the spur, of a heavenly reward.[67]

I asked Attilio how long he had been a Communist. "Only six years," he said. "I hadn't got to know them before." When I suggested he go to the party school, he smiled. "I've been asked," he said, "but I'm not smart . . . have trouble reading." I was both

---

\* *Chiavare.* . . : turn the key in your wife; i.e., have sexual intercourse. *Crusca.* . . : a crust to the donkey; i.e., a sop to workers. *Stuzzica.* . . : tickle out the excreta; i.e., remove obstacles. Hungry children of the poor would eat bark and stuff themselves with cactus fruit, which is practically all seeds embedded in a little pulp. Constipation would follow as the excreta impacted, and the mother would take a twig and gently "tickle out" the excrement of the bent-over child.

† When I was nine and just out of elementary school, my father took me for a walk around the Colosseum, a stone's throw from my school. He told me that Father Natale, my principal, had offered me admission to the seminary—a career in the Church. I said "No!" with some vehemence, for I had always been ambivalent about the dogma: it asserted atheists were evil, but I knew my father was an atheist—and he wasn't evil.

touched and impatient. "Nonsense. You are smart and party people value your experience. I can tell," I said. "It's their judgement after all." He agreed. "But it's not so simple," he explained. "I've got a wife and three children. My brother is working in Germany, and I've got to watch over his family too. My brother-in-law is dead. So that's another family. Three women and a houseful of children. It's not easy. Still, who knows? My brother is coming back."

Attilio the Hun: Attilio the bricklayer; Attilio the Communist.

The hydrofoil slowed, settled into the water, nosed in to the landing. There was a long walk ahead to the railroad station and the train to Palermo.

# CHAPTER 10

# Salvaging Agriculture

THE MOST MORDANT CRITICISM of Eurocommunism has been offered by Marxist economists. These critics point out that since Eurocommunist governments have to function within a market economy, they would be at the mercy of Big Brother. There is validity to this criticism, and in theory the problem is insoluble. But in practice there is room for maneuver. The capitalists are neither as omnipotent nor as recalcitrant as the theories predicate.

In the case of Italy there is one important sector where the interests of the PCI and Italian corporations converge: agriculture. Food, particularly meat, is a large component of Italian imports,* a major factor in trade deficits, inflation, and the weakening of the lira, yet the Italian people are not as well fed as the French. A rise in the productivity of agriculture is essential to a healthier economy, and it is of concern to all classes.

In the past century Italian agriculture has been the victim of feudal practices. To this day, southern Italy contains one half of the agricultural labor force yet has only one third of the nation's population.[2]

In the past the remnants of feudalism, exemplified by huge estates, on the one hand, and oppressive sharecropping, on the other, had resulted in stagnant productivity. Big landowners sent their capital abroad or to northern industries, while sharecroppers had little incentive to use innovations, so that the increase in productivity between 1919 and 1939 (9 percent) was much less than the increase in

---

* In 1977 food imports were $11 billion, 30 percent of total imports.[1]

population.[3] The land could not feed the people, and the solution was emigration. Between 1890 and 1930 12 million people emigrated—one half to remain permanently.*[5]

In some ways, the fascist regime was helpful, pursuing a vigorous reclamation policy (draining swamps, building dams and dikes, etc.) which in twenty years increased the amount of fertile land by 2 million acres. This land was made available to the peasantry so that, by 1936, 70 percent of the people had some land as either part-time or full-time farmers.[6] But other fascist policies were counterproductive. In a drive for autarchic self-sufficiency there was an emphasis on wheat and cereals even where the land was not suited to growing them, as on hillside grazing lands.† There was price manipulation to finance armaments, exploitation by middlemen and processors, a lack of capital. Above all, the coercive power of the state prevented protests and reforms. Productivity went up a mere 1.3 percent in twenty years—the lowest on record![8]

Agriculturists remained in the most abject poverty and there was *no increase whatever* in per capita consumption of the entire population during those twenty years![9] The overwhelming majority of people ate meat only at Christmas, Easter, birthdays, weddings, and similar special occasions. Dairy products were restricted.‡ Both in the north, in the Veneto, and in the south, *polenta* (corn meal pudding) was the staple; its deficiency in niacin and animal protein induced pellagra, the debilitating disease of malnutrition.

World War II devastated the already weak agriculture, particularly in the destruction of livestock. There was *a decrease of 80 percent* in the total number of animals—cattle, pigs, sheep, goats, horses.[10] After the war was over, starvation was only staved off by the vigorous relief program of the United Nations Relief and Rehabilitation Administration (UNRRA), which poured $2 billion worth of all kinds of supplies into Italy.[11]

UNRRA was supposed to trigger a process of rehabilitation, but the Cold War began, reforms were vitiated, and the south, in effect, became more and more an internal colony of the industrial north. Only since 1975, under Communist pressure, have serious programs endeavored to solve the so-called southern question. Naples is the center of agricultural research and economics, so I spent a few days there on the way south to Calabria and Sicily.

---

\*   Of the six million permanent emigrants, four million went to the United States.[4]

†   Erosion of topsoil as grass is plowed under leads to denudation of hillsides, loss of water retention, and devastating floods. The same consequences follow from unrestrained logging—three-fourths of a million acres of woodland were destroyed between 1925 and 1950. Ever-recurring floods have caused enormous damages, as high as $10 billion in one year.[7]

‡   As a child in Rome, I got a half pint of milk for breakfast; cream and butter were rarely seen. And ours was not a poor household.

*Naples, ancient capital of the Bourbons, is a ticking time bomb in the social structure of the south. There are three hundred thousand unemployed, one half of the unemployed in the south, the majority young and desperate. If the nihilistic ideology of the Red Brigades gets the upper hand, the city will explode. "It could happen any day, any hour," was the constant refrain of everyone I talked to, whether Liberal, Socialist, Christian Democrat, or Communist.*

*Naples had long been a stronghold of reaction and corruption, but after the cholera epidemic scare of 1973, the people began to veer left, supported the divorce law in 1974, and voted into power a Communist-Socialist administration a year later. The left inherited a municipal government in chaos, and a laborious process of reconstruction began. The unemployed increased their pressure.*

*On the afternoon I arrived from Rome, the unemployed had taken over the railway station, spilling over the tracks, preventing trains from arriving or departing. There was a deafening clamor in the vast station as huge groups of young men and women shouted, sang, milled about, argued with their leaders—mostly Communists—who cajoled and entreated them: "Comrades, you've made your point!" "Comrades, let the trains pass!" "The demonstration is a great success; please disperse. They can hear you all the way to Rome!" The police ringed the station, held in check by a Communist police commissioner, his men uneasy but not hostile. A city official on a stepladder was trying to make himself heard: "Comrades, friends, citizens, please have patience. Give us time—a little more time. City affairs are in a crazy mess. . . ." He was having little effect as I got into a bus near the huge statue of Garibaldi.*

*Naples has probably greater extremes of wealth and poverty than any other European city, polarized between the north and the south sides. The city is stretched out, hugging the coastline of its famed bay, with the headlands of Posilipo on the north and the suburb of Portici on the south. By accident, I visited the two extremes on the same day, during a morning meeting with Father Carlo Greco, S.J., in a retreat near Posilipo and a late lunch date at the University of Naples in Portici.*

*The city bus climbed upward on the broad boulevard carved into the hillside, the bay on the left, serried ranks of luxury apartments on the right—cool, chic, aloof. The Catholic retreat was a refurbished nobleman's palace—cool, elegant, affluent. The priest, a slender man in his thirties, was wearing dark pants and a gray turtleneck: he looked like Albert Camus. Father Greco was one of a group of young theologians throughout Italy who were working to nudge the Church along conciliar paths, an informal network that Father Bartolomeo Sorge of* La Civiltà cattolica *nurtured and guided. He talked freely and at length.*

*After the interview, I went to keep my lunch date at Portici. The bus careered down the boulevard and traversed the city, plunging into the southern quarters. The atmosphere changed abruptly: squalid tenements, congested streets, narrow alleys. The bus negotiated corners with only inches to spare. Dark artisan shops— welders, tinsmiths, woodworkers, television and radio repair shops—tiny food stores, here and there a child or an old woman on the sidewalk with a box displaying a pitiful bit of merchandise: a few loose cigarettes sold singly, a bowl of olives, a dozen little fishes, a scattering of onions and potatoes. Even the shafts of sunlight could not redeem the relentless poverty of the quarter. Here the un- employed lived; here the anger shown at the railroad station was fueled, stoked, compressed.*

*The stark juxtaposition of the two neighborhoods forced on me an insistent and unsought symbolism of a country teetering on disaster, the more somber because of the soft, warm skies and the idyllic bay. As the bus squeaked by the jalopies parked in the narrow streets, I thought of Father Greco, of his intent lineaments and pioneering theology: the Jesuit as a socialist citizen!*

Father Greco's theology was not really revolutionary: he would never make a guerrilla priest. But he was firmly grounded in the views of the anti-imperialist conciliar Church, the defender of the poor and op- pressed. He had written extensively on the small, but not negligible, movement known as Catholics for Socialism and urged me to discuss the Communist-Catholic dialogue with conservative prelates. Greco had smiled sadly: "The hierarchy changes slowly . . . but it does change."

This change, he explained, is helped by a significant shift in class origins. In the past, the bulk of the clergy had come from the peasantry; the working class and the commercial classes made poor recruiting grounds. But there had always been a minority from the upper classes—the younger sons—who made a career in the Church and ended up as the majority of bishops and cardinals. Today, however, these younger sons went into business or the professions, and the peasant priests were filling the void—in sociological jargon, they were "upwardly mobile." These priests were devout, but at the same time very conscious of poverty and oppression as stressed by the conciliar Church. The next pope, said the Jesuit, would probably be a conservative, but in the long run, given the shift and the weight of the third world, the views of Vatican II would dominate.*

We went on to talk about conditions in the country. On

---

* Father Greco must have been inspired: he was right on the mark.

economics, Father Greco was diffident: "I am not an economist, but it seems to me that the key problem in the economy is one of morality. I am not speaking as a priest but as a citizen. From what I observe, people are dispirited and demoralized. They feel helpless, exploited, and do as little work as possible."

Although he disclaimed professional expertise, he was in fact extremely knowledgeable about agriculture. In a few broad strokes he sketched out for me the heart of the southern question. At the end of the war radical change seemed imminent. The feudal landowners were fascist to a man, and many had run away. Peasant submission had been shaken by the war, the power structure was in disarray, with Communists in the government and in charge of the ministry of agriculture. Unwittingly, the American Army blocked change. It had recruited hundreds of Italo-Americans for intelligence purposes to facilitate the invasion, and among them were many Mafiosi. As the combat troops swept ahead, the Mafiosi remained behind, some with important jobs in military government. Father Greco didn't think the Americans had done this on purpose; they had been ignorant.

Not wholly ignorant, I said. I had been at Allied headquarters in Caserta at the end of the war, and our officers knew that many of the Italo-Americans had been a part of organized crime in the States. But the Mafiosi were useful. Bilingual, with family and village connections, they knew everything, knew everybody, could get things done. Further, the Mafiosi were ultrapatriots and free-enterprisers.

So far, Father Greco and I were in agreement. We differed a little on the innocence of American officers. I thought a few of them had made a deliberate choice; Father Greco disagreed. In his view there had been an imperceptible and inevitable restoration—the underlings replacing the better-known fascists. A prefect would be jailed and his former secretary became a police chief. A mayor would disappear and his cousin would be installed. The landlords came back, protected by the U.S. Army: why not, it was their land, wasn't it?

As the peasants tried to seize the land and form collectives, Mafia-organized vigilantes beat up the militants and killed their leaders.[12] As the violence spread, the military government came down heavily on the side of law and order. In Rome a compromise was reached: the government would institute a land reform, but armed seizure was out. The reform would take place from the top, not from below. The government took title to the lands of the more notorious fascist officials and to uncultivated lands. It also bought what it could. A massive distribution began, supplemented by a law making funds available to poor peasants at nominal interest rates. Four million acres were distributed to eight hundred thousand individuals, an average of five acres per holding.[13] Hundreds of thousands of holdings were, of course, well below the average; they were minimal "handkerchief" plots, insufficient to feed a family.

The Communists were thrown out of the government in 1947. Antonio Segni became minister of agriculture, and in 1949 he appointed Paolo Bonomi, an old-line collaborator with fascism, to take charge in the south. Bonomi proceeded to create a vast, enormously corrupt, patronage system, known as the Bonomiana. He reestablished the peasant councils of the fascist regime, the Federconsorzi, which distributed the UNRRA aid. The Federconsorzi bought the produce, set prices, sold it to favorite wholesalers and food-processing companies with built-in kickbacks. Banks set up to grant agricultural credits were manned by Bonomi's men; loans were made through friendships and payoffs. Fiat monopolized tractor production and sales; the tractors were often too costly and too big to be effective. The large manufacturer of petroleum products, Montecantini, monopolized fertilizers, again at prices which forced the peasant into further debt. Poor peasants were kept quiet and persuaded to vote Christian Democrat through the granting of small subsidies. Subsidies, high costs, corrupt loans, frittered away capital, and the taxpayers footed the bill, The Bonomiana developed into a system that guaranteed minimum production—and maximum votes.[14] Said Father Greco:"The Bonomiana is an Augean stable. It will take truly herculean labors to clean it up, and the first condition is an honest government."

At Portici the city bus dropped me in a little square fronting the old Bourbon palace where the Center for Southern Agrarian Economics is housed. It is a dilapitated but still substantial building, with impressive archways, wide stone staircases, and huge windows and doors. The walls were flaking and covered with political graffiti. Past an old sentry box in the courtyard, I went up to a first-floor portico overlooking the old royal gardens. The paths, lines with weathered marble busts, were overgrown with weeds. What appeared to be experimental plots were badly tilled; a furrowed field in the middle distance was littered with rusty bits of machinery. A desolate, poverty-striken scene—a reminder that many programs had died a-borning.

I sought out my host, Professor Enrico Pugliese, an expert on southern agriculture. Born in Calabria in 1942, he was graduated from Portici in 1965, and later studied at the University of California and Columbia University. He has published many important books on southern agriculture.

*I found Pugliese in a huge, sunlit room, with two wooden desks, a large table, and a welter of files, bookcases, cupboards. He was working at the table, immersed in a sprawl of books, monographs, and mimeographed papers, arguing with an assistant, who was introduced to me as Comrade Elena. They were both in their thirties and very attractive: he with a shock of unruly black hair and a relaxed manner, she with a tight bun and a tart tongue. Both were members of the* Manifesto *group, though Pugliese was closer to the PCI and Elena more to the left. For lunch they took me to an inexpensive cellar tavern where the wine was excellent, the fish soup delicious. Pugliese gave me a thumbnail survey that was very similar to Father Greco's.*

"The American Army didn't mean to protect fascists; it didn't know."

*Elena interrupted. "Of course it did—you call yourself a Marxist? But I don't blame the Americans. I blame the party that came in and said: 'Halt!' "*

"No," *said Pugliese, shaking his head.*

"Yes," *said Elena.* "The PCI blocked the revolt. You know it's true. Who was minister of agriculture? A Communist!"*

*Pugliese smiled at me. "She goes on like this all the time. She hates the party."*

"I do not. I was in for fifteen years. What I hate is Berlinguer."

"Ma che vuoi? I don't like him either." *He turned to me.* "What Elena says is true. The party did intervene to stop the violence. Collectives were attacked, people killed. The violence was escalating and it meant a serious confrontation with the Allies. The party didn't want that: the compromise was agrarian reform from the top."

"Gullo did it," *insisted Elena.*

"Of course it was Gullo. But his intention was to follow up the land division with co-operation—the peasants getting together with help in seeds, machinery."

"In other words," *said Elena,* "to re-establish capitalism."

"Not at all," *Pugliese protested.* "A strong co-operative movement can undermine capitalism. Look what the town of Bologna is doing in the surrounding countryside."

"Tokenism," *said Elena.*

"Come on, Elena. Right now there are almost thirty thousand co-operatives in Italy. They produce $8 billion, about five percent of the GNP. Three fifths are Communist-led, and there are hundreds more every month. Their political influence is tremendous, and they can multiply."* [15]

"What about capital?" *I asked.*

"What's wasted and stolen in the Bonomiana is more than enough," *said Pugliese.* "There are six million useless subsidies to peasants—a million of them nonexistent. At $500 a head, that's*

---

* Fausto Gullo (1887–1974) was a PCI member and minister of agriculture in 1946–47.

*$3 billion. But things are changing; loans are more stringent and monitored . . ."*

*"Yes" Elena said bitterly. "Loans to the rich landowners."*

*"True," said Pugliese, "but not the whole truth. The present law ties loans to acreage; obviously the big farms benefit. But, small farmers can form a co-op and get loans based on their total acreage. That's in the law, too. It gives us a big lever. Moreover, with the regions and the cities coming under left control and with Law 382 giving them the power to create agricultural programs, the sky's the limit. One half of all the left-wing co-ops are in Emilia-Romagna, the region around Bologna."*

*"Meanwhile," said Elena, "the rich get richer."*

*"Meanwhile," said Pugliese, "production goes up."*

*"You sound just like the party," said Elena. "You don't belong in the Manifesto."*

*Pugliese grinned. "Yes, I do. Berlinguer's too soft. But the party is right. We do need production, especially in meat; it's our biggest import item. It's amazing what can be done with brains, hard work, and modern techniques. There's a livestock co-op in the middle of Sicily—I'll send you there, Carlo—they've performed miracles. You know it's true, Elena. You've been there."*

*We returned to the palace and were greeted in the corridor by an elderly man. Elena went ahead while Pugliese paused to introduce me. "This is Professor Augusto Graziani," said Pugliese fondly. "My old professor and the best economist in Italy." Professor Graziani was small and thin, and wore a quizzical expression.*

*When I asked Graziani if he thought there was any hope for the Italian economy, he answered quietly: "None at all." "Even with the historic compromise?" He shook his head: "It is too late." "What will happen?" I asked. "I don't know," he replied. "Riots, killing, anarchy. I don't know." His expression was tranquil: he meant every word, and he had made his peace with the coming catastrophe. Pugliese sensed my uneasiness and clapped me on the shoulder. "Professor Graziani has seen a lot of life—he's nearing eighty—and he inclines to pessimism."*

*"Unusual for a Marxist," I said, and Graziani smiled gently.*

*"True," said Pugliese. "Trouble is, he has not often been wrong."*

For days, Graziani's words were to haunt me. Gloomy predictions were commonplace in Italy, but they generally came from those on the far fringes, both left and right. Red Brigades argued that capitalist society was putrified beyond redemption: it had to be annihilated. The neofascists held that the Communists had already taken over, and were diabolically disintegrating the society. But the pessimism of such people could be discounted.*

Clearly, Italy was in a serious crisis; everyone was conscious of it. Giorgio Napolitano, one of the PCI's top men, had said to me: "I don't know if this society can be saved. Even if we had full power, it would be a formidable task. *And we will not* have full power. Yet there is no alternative but to try." Graziani's words, in the context of his calm self-confidence and expertise, had given resonance to Napolitano's warning.

Intrigued by Graziani, I questioned Pugliese back in his office. Elena wasn't there, and I sat at her desk. Was Graziani in favor of armed revolt? Was he sympathetic to the Red Brigades? Not at all, said Pugliese, he despises them as fanatic fools. Graziani simply thinks that the economy is so disorganized, the corruption so pervasive, and the sense of helplessness so widespread that nothing will make any difference. "We of the *Manifesto* group, for example, don't disagree with the strategy of the party; we disagree on the tactics. Graziani thinks the strategy itself is irrelevant."

"And the alternative?"

"In his mind, there is none," said Pugliese. "Graziani thinks that the disintegration is irreversible."

"You obviously disagree."

Pugliese would not be drawn out. "Maybe I just *want* to believe," he said. "I want to live. I am young and he is old, twice my age."

"I'm nearly as old as he is," I said, "and I agree with you."

"Oh, *you!*" Pugliese laughed. "You are an American. All Americans are born optimistic." He made it sound like a disease. "Listen, you talk about data. Graziani and I agree on the data. We even agree on which programs would work. In my view, the economic problems of Italy *can* be solved."

Pugliese took meat production as an example. Italy pays $2 billion a year for imported meat and another quarter billion for corn and oats for domestic livestock. That's 20 percent of imports.[16] According to Pugliese, some economists have argued that meat and the unions were responsible for inflation. I thought he was joking, but it seems that Guido Carli, the former head of the Bank of Italy and a brilliant economist, had made just such an argument. It went like this: In the late sixties unions won wage increases and escalator clauses; that is, when the cost of living index went up, wages automatically went up by the same percentage. That's premise number one.

Premise number two. With higher wages, workers began to eat better. Whereas they used to eat meat once a month, now they ate it

---

* My old schoolmate Manlio talked gloomily of "execution squads at every corner" and a "new era of Genghis Khan."

once a week—in some parts, even every day.* Meat being scarce, prices rose, and since food is a major part of the cost of living index, the index went up. Index up, wages up; wages up, more meat eaten—more meat, higher prices, index up, wages up, and so on in a vicious inflationary cycle.[18]

I thought it was a big theory to rest on such a rickety basis, and Pugliese said that it was purely a propaganda ploy. Actually, the price of clothing and housing went up about the same as food; many items—electricity, health, and transportation—went up considerably more. "Still," said Pugliese, "there is a point to be made. If we produced all our meat, the economy would benefit greatly. And we can do it."

With pencil and paper, and referring to the statistical tables, Pugliese laid it all out. The key was the amalgamation of tiny farms into co-operatives of 100 to 200 acres.† He estimated that thirty thousand co-ops capitalized at $100,000 each would eliminate the need for foreign meat, corn, and oats. The capital needed, 14 billion, would be available from the present subsidies given to farmers.[19]

"Fourteen billions sounds like a lot of money," said Pugliese, "but when you think that tax evasion runs to maybe $20 billion a year, you can see that we can find the capital. All we have to do," he said mockingly, "is to stop tax evasion, stop subsistence subsidies, get farmers to join co-ops, and put in honest bureaucrats to run the programs. One can't blame Graziani; he doesn't think it remotely possible."

"And you do?"

"I? I don't know, but I think there's a chance. Tremendous struggles of course, but. . .what else can we do?" He looked at me with a bitter smile. "You want to know what Graziani really thinks? He thinks the moral fiber of the nation has been destroyed, that everyone is looking for the fix, for the easy way, the eat-and-don't-work way. He thinks that even if you were to change politics and social institutions, it would be too late. Twenty years of fascism and thirty years of DC have conditioned people to selfishness and greed—their own version of *la dolce vita*—even if it's just hanging around on a street corner."

He paused, his eyes hooded. "And what do I think? The weight of the evidence is on Graziani's side; our moral fiber has been severely damaged, our self-confidence eroded. Graziani thinks the

---

\* Nevertheless, Italians still fall below most European standards. In 1969 per capita consumption of animal protein was 38 grams per day compared to 64 grams in France. By 1975 the gap had narrowed, but the Italian ration was still only 48 grams. And, of course, unevenly distributed. There's an old saying that a man from Bologna eats in a day what a Roman eats in a week and a Genoese in a month.[17]

† There are one million farms under five acres each; they would be combined into 100,000 to 120,000 co-operatives. One third are suitable for growing fodder and raising livestock.

damage is irreparable. I don't. I think there can be a great moral renewal, a fervor to rebuild the country if people see that their work matters. I think the Communists can do it, can create that fervor. They are the strongest defenders of the people and of the country—recognized as such even by their enemies. This is a tremendous achievement. For the first time since the French Revolution the left stands as the defender of the nation."

I told Pugliese of my conversation with Father Greco, of how he, too, talked of the necessity of a moral renewal. It seemed to me significant that the Communist and the Jesuit sought the same goal, although Father Greco believed that the renewal could best come from religion. Pugliese nodded. "I know. Greco is entitled to his opinion. We welcome the competition in motivating people, but believe me, our results compared to theirs are as a hundred to one."

"The more you talk, the more hopeful you sound," I said, and Pugliese laughed. "Self-hypnosis. . .and yet. . . . Hardly a day passes that some event doesn't make my day. Take that co-op in Lazio near Rome, started yesterday. Twenty-three people, some of them teachers and lawyers, took over a tract of uncultivated land and started working it.[20] Imagine, lawyers! It's like the kibbutzim in Israel—true they had a greater motivation, but also a harder task, to make the desert flower. We have to get something of their dedication and I think we can. One thing is clear: if the Communists can't do it, nobody can!"

"You are always speaking favorably of the PCI," I said. "Why aren't you in the party?"

"Oh, that. . .that's nothing. We are all Communists in the *Manifesto* group, and in a showdown we'll be with the party. We're not antiparty. It has done great things. . .but we think it is too accommodating toward the DC. I think that's the wrong line in the south, where the DC is powerful, based on clientism. We have to attack it; that's what Elena is asking for. If the PCI play footsie in Parliament, people will think the PCI has sold out and will be disillusioned."

This had been Amadeo's complaint with the party, and here was an echo from outside the party. There was obviously a great deal to the criticism. The *Manifesto* people whom I met were able, serious people with no malice toward the PCI, but rather concerned by its vulnerability to disillusionment.* It was difficult for me to make an assessment, but I felt the party's line was correct and that it hadn't percolated deep enough throughout the left.

---

* Nearly two years later, the June 1979 elections showed a substantial drop in the PCI vote in the south, and I remembered Pugliese's forebodings. I couldn't see him, for I had to go north to Ivrea after the election; but I saw an article he wrote in *Il Manifesto*, restating his thesis and ending: "It is to be hoped that the setback to the PCI will make it re-examine its line, as well as its style of work."[21]

I thought of the question of Parliament as discussed by Peter Nichols in *The Italian Decision* and by Pietro Ingrao in *Masse e potere* (Power and the masses), the first a liberal Englishman, the second the president of the Chamber and on the left of the PCI.* Nichols pointed out that the Italian Parliament from its inception in 1870 had never had the governing power of the English Parliament or the American Congress. "It had been simply a debating arena echoing decisions taken elsewhere." He quotes a DC deputy, Piero Bassetti, on the shift that has taken place in Italy, a shift spearheaded by the PCI: "Until today, it was the government that made the laws and the decrees; Parliament, at the most, introduced a few amendments. Now, Parliament will make the laws and the government will introduce some technical amendments. The situation has been reversed."[23]

Actually, Bassetti was too sanguine. Again and again the government has sabotaged laws passed by Parliament, yet it is true that the Parliament has been growing stronger and Ingrao has been successful in increasing its power. Among its other innovations is a wider use of investigative committees. It is in Parliament that the parties deal with each other, and the institution plays a key role in PCI strategy. Says Ingrao: "If we examine the meaning of the strategy of the 'historic compromise,' we find at bottom the affirmation that to deal with the historic problems of Italian society any *one party is not sufficient.* The strategy of the PCI asserts that *not even all the parties are sufficient;* and this is proven by the growth of a unitary labor movement free from the parties which gives voice even to the nonunionists; by growth of a network of democratic organisms at the grassroots. . . ." (Ingrao's italics.)[24]

I didn't think that either Pugliese or Amadeo fully understood the place of Parliament within PCI strategy, whereas Zuccotti did. Zuccotti had also put his finger on another issue that Pugliese stressed: the degree of accommodation to the DC. To some extent, Moro, Andreotti, and Zaccagnini had been politely blackmailing the PCI, just as De Gasperi had blackmailed Togliatti over the Lateran Treaties. Push us too hard, they said, and the alliance will break up. Yet I did not feel it was true that the party was soft, but rather that it preferred the use of brains to brawn, a well-executed flanking maneuver to a frontal attack. Success is what counts. I found leftists within the PCI perfectly happy to use their heads.

For example, while I was in Reggio Calabria, Napoli arranged for the organizer of the unemployed councils in the area to come in to talk to me. He came down from the mountains, fifty miles away, and met me at the courthouse while the judges were recessing in the Mafia case

---

* He resigned in 1979 and his place was taken by Nilde Jotti, the first woman president of the Chamber.[22]

(described in Chapter 9). Comrade Settimo turned out to be a young firebrand of twenty-three with a college degree in physics and a passion for the *Little Red Book* of Mao Tse-tung.

His mind was well organized: he made what amounted to a two-hour report on his activities without using any notes, but with a liberal sprinkling of Mao's aphorisms. He had led many seizures of uncultivated land, but, he added, he always tried to give his actions a "tincture of legality." He had also circumvented the DC's proclivity for *passivi*.* As I already knew from Germano Marri, municipalities had to present plans to get their allocations of money. Since many did not have administrators or technicians capable of planning, the *passivi* would stay in the bank. Settimo had organized squads of unemployed technical men—engineers, architects, accountants, etc.—who would work for a municipality for free, draw up plans, and get paid when the money came in. Settimo was being paid by the party in Reggio Calabria, and he assured me that there had been no restraint on his actions or his initiatives. He was clearly a militant Communist and clearly supported by the party. He had learned to take advantage of the laws, laws passed in a Parliament heavily influenced by Socialists and Communists. It seemed to me at the time, and it seems to me now, even after the setback of the 1979 elections, that the "historic compromise" is a viable strategy but that its application requires consummate organizing skill. When the skill is there, the results can be breathtaking, as I saw at the co-operative in Sicily.

*A month after talking to Pugliese I stood on a hilltop near the center of Sicily, looking down on the farm buildings of a Communist co-operative. Standing beside me was Salvatore Fratelio, who had picked me up at the station of Cammarata-San Giovanni Gemini.† He had stopped the two-door Fiat in the middle of the graveled road, and tortuously extracted his six-foot bulk from the tiny seat. "Best spot here to see it all," he said, leading me to the lip of the hill. We were in gently rolling country, with the co-op below us, but our side of the hill was steep, so that the co-op was quite close; we could see the chickens and dogs. A big yellow tractor was digging a large hole, the driver getting occasional directions from a man standing to the side. They spotted us and waved; Salvatore waved back.*

* The PCI has made a frontal attack on the *passivi;* it is pushing to get the funds out of La Cassa del Mezzogiorno into the hands of the regions for them to distribute. Translated literally, the name means Bank of the South, but a better translation would be Bank for Southern Development. It is, of course, a government agency.[25]

† The names represent two villages, one of eight thousand, the other eleven thousand, mostly peasants with a sprinkling of workers in small factories: a brickyard, a tanning plant, a manufactory of aluminum windows, which was the largest employer, with thirty-seven workers.

*"They are digging the foundations for our new houses," he said with great pleasure, then went on with the intermittent argument we were having. He wanted me to stay overnight and meet his brother.*

*"Believe me," I said, "I'd like nothing better. But I can't: the only train back is the one this afternoon. I have to be at the university in the morning, then fly to Rome for the metal workers' demonstration. I can't miss that!"*

*"No, of course not. It's going to be big, historic!"*

*This argument had actually begun in Palermo the previous evening between Salvatore's brother and Comrade Pino, the executive secretary of* Alleanza contadina *(Peasants' alliance), who had been alerted by Pugliese. Pino, a lanky youth of twenty-six in a white turtleneck, had telephoned in my presence, and I could hear remonstrations from the other end.*

*"No, he can't," said Pino firmly. "Tomorrow morning is the only time he has. Listen, this isn't just another American professor, this is a comrade. He has been in jail in America—three years! What? Of course, he's a Marxist.* Cristo in croce, *he translated Gramsci!* Va bene . . . benissimo!" *He hung up and winked at me triumphantly. "That fixed him. He's got to go for permits and bank loans to Agrigento and can't change the appointments. You take a train early in the morning, six o'clock, and his brother Salvatore will meet you at 8:30. There's a train back at one." He waved my thanks away. "Any time,* amico. Ciao."

*"Our houses," Salvatore said again, savoring the phrase. "We are going to build five, three now and two next year. We've got five families and five single men, all living in that big house there," he pointed. "Crowded as mice; two rooms to a family, one big kitchen. We'll keep the house for the single men. The new houses will be for one family, American style! Bathrooms with bathtubs and showers, running water, We'll even put in the pipes for hot water, and someday we'll have central heating . . . American style."*

*He pointed to a huge barn. "For forage. We grow our fodders: hay mixed with high protein crops,* lecce *and Roman beans." He blew a kiss with his fingertips. "Fabulous. Very rich in nutrients." The speech flowed easily, technical words dropping in place. "How much schooling did you have?" I asked. "Grammar school. We were very poor. My brother made it to high school, two years only, but he reads everything. The vet is educated too. We all read some, though it's hard; in a place like this the work never stops. But our kids . . . they're flying. One is already a doctor, not mine, another family here. He's in a hospital in Rome. Said he didn't want to practice on fellow Sicilians, but he's coming back here when he's well trained and get married here: says northern girls are too cold. I've got two nephews at the university, and my daughter just started this year. She's studying archeology. My daughter studying archeology!"*

*His finger pointed out a row of four long, low structures of cinder blocks, nestling into the brown earth. "Our sheds," he said proudly. "See the first, it's bigger than the others. Holds one hundred fifty cattle. The other three take a hundred each. We've got room for 450 cattle or the equivalent in pigs—take the stanchions out, put in pens. Right now we are low on everything; only 150 head of cattle and only a dozen hogs. There was a pig epidemic last year, and while we didn't lose any, the strain we had was too susceptible. So we butchered our hogs and we're developing a more resistant strain. We had to slaughter a lot of cattle, too, because there wasn't enough fodder; a bad year, a long drought."*

*"How about buying fodder?"*

*"It doesn't pay. Prices were way up because of the drought and that meant more imports. The country's trying to cut down on imports . . . I mean, we have a political responsibility." He said this last without self-consciousness, as if it were the most natural thing in the world. I thought to myself that this grammar-school man would put many of our college graduates to shame. Later, as we went through the stalls, we paused before a magnificent bull: "Bought in France, by me and my brother. A million lire!" I asked him if he liked his life in the co-op. He smiled shyly, "It's like a dream come true. Ever since I was little, I loved to touch cows, smell them, be with them. As I got older, I dreamed of having a cattle farm, a dozen head or so. Then the party gave a push—and look!"*

*"The party and your brother," I said.*

*"My brother is the party. The party made my brother. We are all Communists in the co-op, except the vet, he's a Socialist, but we are Communists of the heart, you know, class-struggle Communists, poor against rich, against the padrone! But my brother, he's a head-and-heart Communist, a historic Communist. You understand what I mean? He's a change-the-world Communist! I am a change-Sicily Communist."*

*As we wandered around the various buildings, the story of the co-operative emerged. It had been started in 1969 under the leadership of Salvatore's brother (whose name I never learned), the eldest of four Fratelio brothers, all of whom had gotten a little land during the reform—four to five acres each. By hard work the four had enlarged their holdings to forty-seven acres, plus some forty-odd acres on long-term leases. The impetus for the co-op had been political: the Twelfth Congress of the PCI, in February 1969, had set the highest priority on agricultural work. The Fratelio brothers felt they had to do something dramatic, because in Cammarata the party was fairly small. So they conceived the idea of starting a co-*

*operative. A house and twenty acres adjacent to their own land was available. They talked to their neighbors about buying the house and pooling their lands and leases.*

*"We made no political conditions," said Salvatore, "only that people get along like one big family . . . no stuff like workdays or time sheets. Everybody works, and if someone is sick, the rest take up the slack. Just like Marx said: From each according to his ability; to each according to his needs. And, by God, that's just what we've done."*

*With four brothers as the nucleus, the co-op ended up with twelve members, all Communists but one, the veterinarian.\* Among them, five had families and seven were single, including the two younger Fratelio brothers. In the intervening years there had been two marriages, so now there were seven families and five single men. Two of the families lived in town, running the co-op butcher shop: "We make more profit on retail sales," said Salvatore. All receipts from the shop went to the co-op, which provided food and rent. The veterinarian was available to other farmers, and his fees also went into the co-op treasury. The co-op rented out its machinery—tractor, ten-ton truck, harvester-thresher (American-made), all with a driver whose wages also went into the co-op.*

*"We produce 90 percent of our fodder and practically all our food: cheese, meat, wine, vegetables. We buy coffee, sugar, and flour for baking. The co-op pays all health bills, all child education expenses. At the end of the year, after expenses, interest, and reserves are taken care of, we divide the money equally among the adults, men and women alike, and everyone uses the money as he sees fit: clothes, radios, books, recreation, savings, and so on. It has worked well; we've had some arguments, but nothing to tear us apart."*

*"The first couple of years were hard," Salvatore went on. "The* padroni *and the bureaucrats were against us, sabotaging, and we had to fight for our rights. The man in charge at the* Cassa del Mezzogiorno *acted as if it was his money he was lending, a clerical bigot who hated us with all his heart. Miserable soul! But as the Communist vote increased, we began to have some power, and my brother had him transferred.† Now things are going well. With the new land, based on acreage, we're rolling. We can get all the financing we want. In fact, we are arguing right now about what to do."*

*Salvatore paused, somewhat embarrassed. "I'd like to tell you about it," he said, and his embarrassment grew. "I mean, it would be a help to us . . . you're from the outside, and a Marxist and all. . . ."*

---

\*  The co-op owned 116 acres and leased about 100, for a total of a little more than 200 acres. By judicious leasing, buying, and trading, the acreage was a compact whole. This size farm had been postulated by Pugliese in his calculations.

†  A little judicious hegemony.

*"Sure," I said, puzzled by his attitude. "I wish you would tell me."*

*"Well, if our stalls were full, we could double production with only a small increase in costs. We got the barns, the machinery, the routine. We could lease land and we could hire workers. But once we hire, we become capitalists. Right? I mean hiring is exploitation."*

*"Naturally." I said. "What else?"*

*"We could get two or three new members, from our neighbors. With what they own and lease we'd have the three hundred extra acres we need, and the manpower. We could get them tomorrow, like that."* He snapped his fingers. *"We can take our pick. Everybody wants to join us because we're so successful. But these are the people we asked nine years ago who said no. They didn't come in when the going was rough, so why should we let them in now? I say to hell with them."* His voice had risen and he was as vehement as his good nature would allow. *"The others disagree, including my brother. What do you think?"*

*I sensed the reason for his discomfort, and tried to avoid the issue. "Is there any other way?"*

Salvatore shuffled his feet, glanced at me furtively. *"I had an idea. We could pick up three unemployed young men, intelligent, hard-working, dedicated Communists, and make them full members."*

*"Madonna, just like that! No land, no money, nothing?"*

*"Just like that."*

*"Well,"* I mused, *"that's certainly a Christian thing to do."*

*"Not Christian,"* said Salvatore sharply. *"Communist!"*

*"What does your brother say?"*

*"He says at this stage it's not politically correct."*

*Now I saw why he had acted so embarrassed. On this issue he was in a minority of one, and he was looking for support. Here, by the coincidence of his brother's absence, he had at his disposal this Marxist from overseas, this translator of Gramsci, no less, who would see how sound was his proposal, how class conscious, how Marxist! My approval might turn the tide. I felt a little silly, and more than a little touched.*

*"Salvatore,"* I said gently, *"*caro compagno, *your feelings do you honor. But consider. You are asking me for an opinion, for a judgment, me who am a stranger. Who am I to be set against your brother?"*

*He gave me a shamefaced smile, lifted an eyebrow, and gave an almost imperceptible shrug—a big hulking man who had stepped out of line. I loved him like a brother.*

*"No, no* Salvato*'! I don't mean this as criticism. If you want my uninformed opinion, I think you should take your neighbors in. Of*

*course, people want to join a success. Why should you penalize them
for lacking the faith, the perspective that you had nine years ago?"*

*"They are all bigots, the worst of* Democristiani," *muttered
Salvatore.*

*"But those are just the people the party wants to influence; you
are supposed to win over the Christian Democrats. That's the line,
the name of the game—how to make the DC drink." I told him of
Zuccotti's formulation. "Here you have an example, an extraordinary
example of how steady, persistent work pays off. In this backward
area you've got 20 percent of the vote, two Communist councilmen
and a friendly DC mayor. That's a great achievement, it really is.
You've trusted the party line, you've trusted your brother's political
sense—why not go with him again?"*

*"You're right, I guess. He's right, I guess." But I could see it
came hard, giving up his wee utopia. "Listen,* caro compagno," *I
said. "Get your neighbors in, prosper, help other people start collectives. In five years, ten years, you can turn Sicily upside down—from
the most conservative region to the most progressive."*

*Salvatore took a deep breath and exhaled sharply as if I had
touched a spring within him. "Come," he said abruptly and plunged
downhill through unplowed fields, then up an opposing slope to a rise.
His legs were longer and stronger than mine, and I trailed. When I
caught up to him, he was standing like a modern Balboa, pointing
ahead. There, in the middle distance, a deep triangular hollow
marked the conjunction of three long slopes, the thighs and belly of an
earth-goddess.*

*"That hollow," said Salvatore, "can be a small lake, and I have
a dream."*

That dream of Salvatore's, which he described in detail, was a magic
antidote to Graziani's pessimism, just as the co-op was a vindication
of Pugliese's programs. Salvatore's dream was to see the lake come
into being and used to irrigate five thousand acres, increasing the
herds and multiplying production ten- or twentyfold. At the same
time, the co-op would be turned into a combination research and
production unit. According to Salvatore, most experimental stations
suffer from being separate from production, and a close tie would
benefit both sides, creating something different, unique, and path-
breaking.

Feasibility studies had been made in the past, and the lake was
judged a sensible project; the subsoil was right, the watertable high,
the rainfall adequate, and earthen dams feasible. But there had never
been a follow-up; private capital was not interested, and the government had no agencies to run such an enterprise. The co-op was a

perfect organizational tool, but, said Salvatore unhappily, it would take a Communist Sicily to achieve his dream. "I'll never see it," he said.

I demurred. It seemed to me that Law 382, giving agricultural control to the regions, was the answer. A regional government, even if Christian Democrat, could be influenced by the party. If the co-op got some new members, helped to start new co-ops, and developed a loose political alliance, it was not unreasonable to realize his dream in five to ten years. As I argued, Salvatore kept nodding. "Yes, it's true," he said finally. "With the DC moving, it's not an impossibility. In ten years." He gave me a wide grin. "I must seem to you a little backward, eh?"

I couldn't help laughing. "Believe me, Salvatore, in the United States you would be considered very advanced. Very advanced indeed." I thought of Attilio in Calabria, and now Salvatore in Sicily, shy, modest men of little schooling, yet with a solid grasp on their problems. Their very language, a racy mixture of earthy phrases and political formulations, was a language of compelling authority: they knew whereof they spoke.

The visit to Camarata was a definite turning point in my thinking about the Italian economy, which had been far too colored by conventional economic considerations: lack of resources, low productivity in agriculture, the vulnerability of exports, the noncompetitive status in many areas of the Common Market. The fact was that the Mezzogiorno could be turned from the weakest link in the Italian economy to its strongest support.* The organization of co-ops is not a major *economic* task; it is a *social and political* task. It may be flatly stated that *to revitalize Italian agriculture, the social and political components are more important than the economic ones.*

The problem is one of priorities. Agriculture provides more jobs per unit of investment than does industry. It is estimated that, in Italy, it takes $50,000 in capital to provide one job in a major industry; the same amount of money would capitalize a co-op involving ten adults.[26]

The political mechanism already exists in the region's power over agriculture as mandated in Law 382. There is hardly a region in Italy that cannot initiate remunerative schemes in a short time. Nichols, for example, cites the region of Lucania, which has an abundant rainfall that feeds five rivers. Their waters are wasted in the seas—nearly three million cubic yards a year—instead of being put to work for irrigation.[27]

---

* We have focused on southern Italy since it is the area most in thrall to economic stagnation, just as we have focused on the meat-producing sector as the draining of foreign exchange. But the problem of agriculture is also acute in the north of Italy and in other agricultural sectors, north and south, such as cereals, citrus fruits, wine-making. Allowing for these differences, the general problems are similar.

It isn't only a question of money; there is a tough problem in changing popular attitudes. Physical labor is scorned, and farm labor is considered the lowest of the low. In the rural areas, the more intelligent and ambitious males migrate to the industrial towns; young women prefer to marry factory workers. Though the city ghettos are unspeakable, the city *is* exciting. The village has to change, with schools upgraded, and cinemas, libraries, sports and cultural centers established. The rewards of country life, with modern amenities, have to be stressed and publicized. The prestige and dignity of farm work has to become a national concern, as was done with the kibbutzim in Israel.

There are hundreds of thousands of young men and women who are sick of unemployment and ready to build new lives. There are tens of thousands of Attilios and Salvatores who can provide the cadres for thousands of co-ops. The co-op movement is already a big success in Emilia. It is taking root in many regions, and it is accelerating in the south.[28] Moreover, the co-ops are emphasizing relations with socialist countries in Eastern Europe and with the third world, increasing trade and creating new markets for Italian exports.[29] It is the job of the Communist party to create a triumphalist atmosphere, to fight for the money and the tools to do the job, to stimulate the will and desires of the rising generations. Slow to start, a thoroughgoing agricultural reform will feed on itself; once it gains momentum, Salvatore may even surprise Graziani.

# CHAPTER 11

# Salvaging the Economy

THE MOST WIDESPREAD MISCONCEPTION abroad concerning Italian Eurocommunism is that the PCI and the large corporations, such as Fiat, are in tacit, if not overt, agreement to collaborate. This misconception is fed by the low-key tone of their polemics. This tone, while genuine, is deceptive: there is a war to the knife between Communists and big capitalists, and everyone in Italy knows it. As one well-informed journalist said to me, "Agnelli and Berlinguer twist each other's *coglioni;** their public smiles are grimaces of mingled pain and sadistic pleasure."

Giovanni ("Gianni") Agnelli is Italy's most powerful person. He is a Renaissance prince, a bundle of superlatives: handsome, intelligent, charming, wealthy, a connoiseur of art, women, and fast cars. As a businessman he is the fantasy incarnate of the modern capitalist: shrewd, restless, adventurous, decisive—and with massive financial resources.[1] Italian prime ministers may come and go, but in the stratosphere of international capitalist conclaves, Agnelli is a permanent presence: *the* voice of Italy.† Postwar, Agnelli's multinational Fiat shaped and dominated Italy's export-oriented economy to such an extent that economists speak of it as the "Fiat model."

The second most powerful man in Italy is acknowledged to be Enrico Berlinguer, general secretary of the PCI, a man as charismatic

---

\* *Coglioni* is slang for "testicles."

† The two most influential groups of the capitalist world are the Trilateral Commission and the Bilderberg Conference. David Rockefeller plays the key role in both, aided by people like Zbigniew Brzezinski and Henry Kissinger. President Carter was nourished by the Trilateral Commission. Agnelli is a permanent member of both groups. He also serves on the International Advisory Committee of Rockefeller's Chase Manhattan Bank.[2]

in his way as is Agnelli.* But whereas Agnelli is an exuberant extrovert, flamboyant, and public, Berlinguer is reserved, private, and introspective. Agnelli looks like a movie star—Rossano Brazzi perhaps; Berlinguer looks like a tormented writer and has been compared to Albert Camus. Each is extremely attractive to women, but while Agnelli revels in the role, Berlinguer is a family man, devoted to his wife and four children. The first is the mythic individualistic hero, a fine-honed product of a competitive society; the second is the anti-hero, subsumed in the collective, an *apparatchnick* shaped by the party.[4]

Berlinguer showed early promise. Jailed by Mussolini in 1943 for organizing a Marxist study group, he came to the attention of Togliatti in 1944 and rose rapidly in the party. "He came into the leadership at a very tender age," Giancarlo Pajetta says of Berlinguer.[5] In 1945, at age twenty-three, he was elected to the Central Committee. At twenty-seven he was general secretary of the Communist Youth Organization and at twenty-eight president of the World Federation of Democratic Youth. At thirty-one he was in the party's secretariat and the director of Frattochie, where future leaders studied and were trained. There Berlinguer got to know the coming organizers.

A final contrast between the two men goes back to the war and the resistance. The Agnelli family prospered under fascism; Giovanni fought on the Russian front and under Rommel in Africa. The Berlinguers were antifascist; Enrico was in jail.

The contrasts between Agnelli and Berlinguer are endless, yet there are also affinities. They are almost the same age (born 1921 and 1922); both are upper-class, the first through wealth, the second through aristocratic inheritance (Berlinguer's grandfather was a Sardinian marquis); both come from dour, hard-working regions, Piedmont and Sardinia, noted for tough-minded realism. Above all, both are intensely patriotic, intellectual, and serious. "Agnelli is an Italian through and through," a high Communist leader told me; of Berlinguer Agnelli has said, "He is the one other serious Italian."[6]

Just as Pope John XXIII and Togliatti symbolized the relationship between the Church and the Communist party, so Berlinguer and Agnelli symbolize the relationship between the party and Big Business. In both instances, natural enemies have been forced by circumstances to come to terms with one another. With the economy near collapse, Agnelli, Berlinguer, and their advisers† are fully con-

---

* This was the ranking of a poll in the spring of 1978. Aldo Moro was ranked third.[3]

† Guido Carli, former governor of the Bank of Italy and at present head of the *Confindustria*, and Ugo La Malfa, (who died in 1979) former minister of the treasury and head of the Republican party, are two men who have shared Agnelli's general economic outlook. In Berlinguer's case, there is a more collegial approach to economics. Giorgio Napolitano is very close to Berlinguer and is the party's principal economic spokesman, with inputs from economists such as Luigi Spaventa and Luciano Barca.

scious that unless drastic remedies are undertaken, a catastrophe is imminent. The continuing strength of the Red Brigades and the restiveness of the unemployed are clear warnings.

The word "catastrophe" is used in all sobriety. The crisis in Italy is such that unrestrained class warfare might well end "in the common ruin of the contending classes," to use the famous expression of the *Communist Manifesto:* it is the gravity of the crisis and the strength of the working class—the unions and the left parties—that forces the ruling groups to envision concessions and compromises. Agnelli told an American journalist in June 1978: "I don't think one can run Italy against the Communist party and the trade unions. . . . They are too powerful, and the country has been too badly run by the actual leading class."[7]

This awareness on the part of Agnelli that Italy cannot be governed against the Communists has been interpreted abroad as an indication that Agnelli welcomes Communist entry into the cabinet. Even John Kenneth Galbraith, the Harvard economist, who is a friend of Agnelli's, has failed to catch the nuances in Agnelli's position and reports that "now that the Italian Communists have come to accept the system, [Agnelli] says they should not be excluded from the government."[8] But Agnelli only says that because he doesn't see how they can be excluded; he fights them at every turn. As he says: "I fight them because I do not want them to become too strong."[9] He is fully aware that there is a price for Communist co-operation, and that price is control of the society. In June 1975, when the Communists made huge gains in the municipal elections, Agnelli said unequivocally: "We are faced with the attempt of new social forces to assert their hegemony. The stakes are high for all concerned."[10]

In plain language: workers are trying to take over, and we capitalists are in big trouble. Carli hates the PCI, but he is also realistic. In an interview with *Panorama* at the end of 1979 he said that the PCI had to participate in the government.[11]

The crisis of the Italian economy is insoluble in terms of the old capitalist remedies: cutting wages, unemployment, inflation. To understand why this is so, one must examine the reasons for the utter prostration of the economy, reasons that are accepted by both capital and labor. In fact, a refreshing aspect of Italian polemics is the comparative lack of hypocrisy on all sides: Guido Carli and Gianni Agnelli for the Establishment; Luciano Lama, Bruno Trentin, and Giorgio Benvenuto for the unions; Pietro Ingrao and Giorgio Napolitano for the Communists, are in accord on wide areas of economic analysis.[12]

For example, they all agree that the world-wide rolling recession of the last ten years, which has devastated the Italian economy, was caused primarily by the Vietnam War and President Lyndon B. Johnson's fiscal policy of "guns and butter." Further, the export-oriented economy of Italy has been particularly susceptible to that recession; as the saying goes, when the United States sneezes, Europe gets a cold—and Italy catches pneumonia.[13]

Both sides also agree that the weaknesses of the economy are a result of the distortions introduced during the thirty years of Christian Democratic rule. The world-wide recession exposed those weaknesses, which were accentuated by two factors: a corrupt nationalization and a sharp rise in real wages. At this point the two sides part company, each stressing one factor and minimizing the other.

The best presentation of the Establishment's point of view was made by Guido Carli in a book published in 1977, *Intervista sul capitalismo italiano* (Interview on Italian capitalism).* Guido Carli was for many years the head of the Bank of Italy, which was the nerve center of the economy. Professor Paul A. Samuelson of Harvard has commented sardonically: "In most countries, central banks have to work hard to preserve their independence from the government; in Italy, it is the government that must fight to achieve its independence from the central bank."[15]

The witticism contains much truth. Carli dominated the cabinet on economic matters, intimidated ministers, controlled the strategies of development. He became governor of the bank in 1960, in the boom period when the gross national product increased an average of 6.6 percent a year, reaching a high of 8.1 percent in 1961.† Then everyone marveled at the Italian "economic miracle." In 1975, when he resigned, the country was mired in depression. Carli knows first-hand what happened in those fifteen years. He remains a strategist for the Establishment.

In his book, Carli deals at length with the boom-to-bust history of his tenure. He argues that, taking the international situation as given, the boom was the product of entrepreneurial vigor, while the recession was a result of the strangling of free enterprise by nationalization and the unions. In Carli's view, the proximate cause of stagnation has been union pressure on wages rather than corrupt nationalization, because the unions have interfered with the capitalist mechanism of adjustment.[17]

He asserts that whereas in Europe and the United States, real wages went up slowly, in Italy the unions forced up wages precipitously. In America, for example, real wages went up 11 percent

---

* Publishers in Italy have developed a genre of small books, interviews of experts by experts, on the important issues of the day. Carli was interviewed by Eugenio Scalfari, a renowned editor and journalist.[14]

† This growth rate has been surpassed in the postwar period only by Germany and Japan.[16]

between 1969 and 1973; in Italy, they went up 47 percent.[18] Escalator clauses have protected Italian workers from inflation;* unions have a strong say in hours and conditions of work (for example, Fiat workers won't allow overtime): further, it is impossible to fire a union man. All these factors have increased costs and lowered profits.

Low profits mean low investments, for two reasons. They make for low savings and a consequent shortage of capital; they provide little incentive to invest whatever capital is accumulated. The over-all result is stagnation, inflation, unemployment. Q.E.D., says Carli.[19]

The unions and the Communists concede some merit to Carli's argument. Professor Asor Rosa, writing in *L'Unità*, says: "The crisis is due to a totality of elements which prevent the system from regaining its equilibrium. . . .Many of those elements have been created by us: our unions, our Communist party, our student and workers' struggles."[20]

Asor Rosa deepens his analysis of the crisis and faces the issue squarely in a book, *Le Due società* (The two societies), which is subtitled "An Hypothesis on the Crisis":

Very well then. . .yes! At the core of the Italian crisis there are *also* the struggles of the working class, of the trade unions, of the organized workers' movement and of the Communist party. And what do you prove with this? That we have brought down an archaic system and created the premises to transcend it. . . .the crisis is a product of a series of battles which affirm the capacity to govern of a subordinate class, and, at the same time, the failure of the ability to govern on the part of a dominant class. This is a *political* result, even before it is an economic result.[21]

The Communist party has officially agreed. Giorgio Napolitano, a member of the seven-man directorate of the party, wrote in *Foreign Affairs:* "It is true that the intense wage push and the massive increase in public spending that took place after 1968. . .were factors in creating the present crisis in Italy. . . .Wages have gone up sharply, even if they still are, on an average, lower than in Western European countries. . .profit margins, and hence the amount available for self-financing, have been severely squeezed."[22]

But he utterly rejects Carli's argument that workers' demands have been the chief cause of the Italian crisis; on the contrary, the culprits have been the Christian Democrats (and their business allies). They are responsible for the enormous corruption in the nationalized industries and the mismanagement of the economy during an uninter-

---

* In fact, Carli argues that the escalator clauses have accentuated inflation due to the disproportionate weight of food in the cost-of-living index; this is the "meat-eating" argument discussed in Chapter 10.

rupted tenure of thirty years. Napolitano proceeds to a telling indictment:

> In the years when profit margins and self-financing prevailed in industry, when there were larger resources available for investments and considerable state aid for private investment, did not the spontaneous choices of industry, especially of large-scale industry, still leave the problems of the south and of unemployment unresolved? Did not these spontaneous choices actually destroy resources and seriously weaken Italy's balance of payments? Was it not true that in the south priority was given to capital-intensive operations, while agriculture and food-producing industries were seriously neglected? That there was a continuous diversion of capital into speculative and luxury building, to the point that today large cities, such as Rome, have thousands of empty apartments that cannot be sold or rented? That the productive capacity of the petrochemical and synthetic fibers industries were expanded beyond all reasonable marketing estimates? And we could go on adding to this list of industrial mismanagement.[23]

Not only Communists, but liberals and progressives, take this view, and they are not slow to put the Establishment on the defensive. Eugenio Scalfari, for example, in the interview with Carli, challenged him directly: "I'll tell you quite frankly that your arguments are one-sided. Your thesis that the major responsibility for the crisis is due to the excessive demands of workers strikes me as very superficial, especially coming from someone like yourself who aided from within the gradual corruption of the system."[24]

Carli rejoined that he was speaking of the *proximate* cause. The corruption had been there all along, said he, although he agreed that it had increased with nationalization. The nationalized industries had become baronial fiefs—"confraternities of power," said Carli, which had "plundered the economy." As for his role, everyone knew he had been part of the Establishment—the *palazzo**—and he had contributed to the errors of the past. It was clear now that there had not been sufficient social investment during the boom period, that schools, hospitals, housing, transportation, had been neglected.[25]

The substantial areas of agreement among economists is in large part due to the comparative simple structure of the Italian economy in which mistakes are obvious and the responsibility of the DC indisputable.

Italy emerged from World War I a predominantly agricultural country. Despite the efforts to industrialize under fascism, it entered

---

* *Palazzo,* "palace," is a slang term for the power structure.

World War II with its agricultural sector slightly larger than its industrial sector. Wartime destruction accentuated the disparity, and by 1945 agriculture was about three times as large as industry.[26] A united effort of the whole population* repaired the worst damages of the war. By 1948 agriculture had tripled, industry had multiplied eight times, and services six times. Industry gained the most but, as of 1951, agriculture still accounted for 25 percent of the economy and 45 percent of the labor force.[28]

The stage was set for the "economic miracle." The Communists had been thrown out of the government; the unions were split and emasculated. The Marshall Plan was pumping in dollars, and the Common Market was on the horizon. Between 1951 and 1963 the gross national product doubled and industry zoomed, as a low-cost labor force was recruited from the land. Three and a half million people were moved out of agriculture and jammed into urban slums lacking such essentials as living space, schools, health facilities and transport.† Industry was focused on exports, with emphasis on durable consumer goods, autos, refrigerators, washing machines, etc. Fiat led the way, developing an internal market as thousands of kilometers of superhighways were built. Wrote the English *Economist:* "Kicking and howling, Italy was dragged into the twentieth century, changing from a peasant to an industrial cast."[30] Unfortunately, as Professor Spaventa made clear to me, the transition was anything but complete.

*Luigi Spaventa is professor of economics at the University of Rome and was elected a deputy on the Communist ticket, although he is neither a Marxist nor a Communist, because he considered the PCI the only "serious" group in the country. Coming from an old academic and political family in southern Italy, he is typical of a substantial number of noted personalities who have been elected as independents on the Communist ticket.*

*We met in the vast marble lobby of the Chamber of Deputies with clusters of chairs and small tables anchored to black leather sofas spaced along the walls for discreet conversations. He is a slim, self-possessed man in his forties, speaking excellent English—either cause or effect of marriage to an Englishwoman. As one of the chief economic advisers to the PCI, he remarked that while the top men,*

---

* Capital and labor co-operated; Communists and Socialists were in the government. Employers, many of them fascists, were keeping a low profile. The present general secretary of the CGIL, Luciano Lama, who was then twenty-three years old, reminisces that he had negotiated his first contract nine days after the liberation, and had found the employers very, very reasonable. "Of course," he added, "it was a peculiar climate: we were armed."[27]

† The trend continued at a slower pace between 1963 and 1970, when another 1.5 million people left agriculture.[29]

*such as Napolitano are knowledgeable about economics, this is not true of the middle echelons of the party or the trade unions.*

*"This creates problems: the comrades think that will and organization can overcome objective limits, and while they have a point, those limits do exist and can only be pushed back so far." He smiled, "The comrades say this is a 'bourgeois' outlook; my answer is, I am a bourgeois."*

*Spaventa was astringent in thought and concise in speech, rare virtues among Italians. He gave me a mini-bibliography of a dozen books, including Carli's, as required reading for an understanding of the Italian economy.*[31] *When we began to discuss the knotty question of whether it is possible to make a transition to socialism within a capitalist structure, he laughed. Half joking, completely serious, he said: "Everyone is talking about the transition from capitalism to socialism; the problem in Italy is to make the transition from feudalism to capitalism." (Carli made a similar point in his interview, saying that Italy is "in a situation which I may be allowed to define as schizoid, because we are: one, a country which is economically industrial; but, two, with huge peasant islands; and three, with a public administration and political institutions which in large part are tethered to the laws of 1865.")*\*[32]

*For Spaventa, as for Carli, Italy's present plight stems from the failure of entrepreneurial nerve by the Italian bourgeoisie; that failure opened the door to the expansion of nationalization, and given the corruption in the political structure, the newly nationalized industries became "feudal fiefs" mired in clientism. A spectacular example of this process was the nationalization in 1963 of the electric utilities, which had been notoriously inefficient. The nationalization was pushed by the Socialist party, which had made it a condition of participation in the center-left government. In the process, one of the problems was how to compensate the stockholders. The Socialists wanted to pay them directly, a specific sum for each share of stock. Carli, speaking for the Establishment, insisted that the money be paid in bulk to the expropriated companies as capital assets. He was afraid that the capital involved would be dissipated if handed out to thousands of individual stockholders.*† *Spaventa told me: "You'll find the whole story in great detail in* Razza padrona *and the* Intervista sul capitalismo italiano, *both on the reading list I've given you."*[34]

---

\*   The Carli analysis leads to the conclusion that Italy's problems are those of a backward country which needs only to push harder along the capitalist road to modernization. Communist theoreticians disagree. Pietro Ingrao, for example, then the president of the Chamber of Deputies, has argued in *Masse e potere* that it was the capitalist model of development which brought Italy to the brink of catastrophe.[33]

†   Guido Bodrato told me he had proposed a third alternative: pay individual stockholders in government bonds.

*"The point I wish to make here,"* Spaventa said, *"is not that the nationalized energy industry has become even more inefficient because of corruption,\* but that the businessmen at the head of the expropriated companies were totally lacking in enterprise. They wasted the stockholders' money. The sums involved were enormous—over 1,500 billion lire (almost $2 billion), and only about half found its way into productive, long-term investments. The other half was frittered away on stupid speculations, not to mention some self-serving schemes. This is the crux of the matter. By and large, the business community is not fit to govern."*

The harsh judgment of Luigi Spaventa, Communist deputy, is reaffirmed by Carli, the mentor of Big Business. He told Scalfari: "I had hoped that this money would open a new phase of free enterprise. I was wrong. The directors of those [expropriated] companies proved unequal to their historic task. Their failure is one of the most serious setbacks to free enterprise in Italy. We are now paying for the consequences, and we will pay for a long time."[35]

But the mistake was also Carli's. One of the ironies in Italy, is that Carli, the most lucid defender of free enterprise, is also the man, who *malgré lui,* triggered its greatest failure.

The inefficiency and corruption of the nationalized industries was to grow immeasurably as the boom petered out after 1963. Serious stresses in the economy had already developed. The public sector, except for highways, had been neglected, so that the infrastructure—railways, post office, telephone, bus lines, housing, schools, etc.—was too rickety to support the industrial expansion.

The expansion itself developed in a dangerously lopsided manner. Industry split into two diverging branches. The more technologically advanced sectors, which were export-oriented, increased in productivity and lowered prices.† The older sectors of the economy, starved of capital, became less efficient, and they compensated for this by raising prices.‡ The average consumer was paying *more* for *essential* goods, and *less* for *nonessentials.* For example, in the decade of the boom, from 1953 to 1963, the prices of vegetables went up 60 percent while the prices of automobiles went down ten percent.[36]

Simultaneously, wages remained practically stationary (increasing less than one percent a year over the decade), while produc-

---

\*   Under Enrico Mattei, there was efficiency—and a high level of corruption. His successors increased the corruption and destroyed the efficiency.

†   Most export-oriented sectors were tied directly or indirectly to the auto industry—steel, petroleum, machinery.

‡   Textiles, footwear, leather goods, furniture, foodstuffs.

tion and profits increased enormously.[37] By 1962 workers' dissatisfaction broke out in a rash of spontaneous strikes—181 million work hours were lost. Wages went up 18 percent in one year.[38]

At this juncture the ruling class made its greatest error. Instead of adapting and giving a little (profits were huge), they arrogantly cracked down, thus guaranteeing a later explosion. Their immediate response to worker militancy was a classic capitalist maneuver: inflation* followed by deflation. The Bank of Italy clamped down on credit.[40] Carli, who had been in charge at the time, explained to Scalfari that "a restrictive credit and monetary policy mitigates the union pressure—" when Scalfari interrupted him: "You mean it strengthens employers' resistance?"

CARLI: You use brutal words, but the answer is yes.

SCALFARI: This is a precious confirmation that monetary and credit policies are not "neutral" toward the social and political situation.

CARLI: You needed me to tell you that? Even children know it.

SCALFARI: Modern young people do know it, but many economists, bankers, and businessmen continue to deny it.[41]

The employers' counterattack was at first successful; the unions suffered a severe setback. In 1964–65 real wages fell nearly 5 percent while unemployment increased the same percentage. Productivity per workers went up 14.5 percent and profit margins rose. Gross national product increased almost at the pace of the boom years.†[42] Wages remained depressed while the speedup, accidents, and parcelization of work increased. At the same time, social services and living conditions deteriorated further.

The result was the explosion of 1969, far surpassing that of 1962. This was a period of profound mass radicalization accompanying the tremendous strike wave. Moreover, these strikes were not spontaneous, as in 1962, but highly organized on a national scale. Over 300 million work hours were lost,[44] almost double the previous high in 1962. The unions were in full control: wage increases averaged 24 percent.[45] In the ensuing five years the power of the unions (strikes and strike threats) resulted in additional wage increases—the highest in the capitalistic world: 27 percent in Italy compared to 5 percent in the U.S., 14 percent in Germany, 15 percent in Japan.[46]

By 1975 the power of industrialized workers had become formidable. Their strength lay in the unitary movement of the three great federations into one umbrella organization, the Federation of Trade

---

\* Prices increased 7.5 percent in 1962-63.[39]

† In the period 1966–69, GNP rose at the rate of 6.1 percent annually.[43]

Unions, bolstered by the spreading democratic councils of action in the factories.* Union power spilled into the political arena; it was a major component in the resounding left victory of the referendum on divorce of 1974.

In Italy today the trade unions have achieved substantial economic power. They have significant control over conditions of work, including overtime, and increasing control over labor mobility, recruitment, and training. Escalator clauses tie automatic wage increases to the cost-of-living index and nullify the classic weapon of wage-cutting: inflation. The power of the union rests on the twin pillars of unity of the three federations and the favorable political climate of Communist and Socialist strength.†

Most important, there has been an irreversible growth of class consciousness and independent thinking within the unions. While guided by the strategies of the parties—Communist and Socialist—they shape their own tactics. The unions have a rule of "incompatibility," which means that no union official can be a party official or participate in the policy-making process of the parties. This rule facilitated the coming-together of the three federations into one united body. This independence makes for greater flexibility in working-class tactics as the unions intervene directly on the political scene. An outstanding example of union power, independence and political savvy was the huge demonstration of December 1977. Over a quarter million metal workers of the three federations went to Rome with only one purpose: to change the government and bring the Communists into the cabinet. Within a month, the government fell and a new government was negotiated.

The sophistication of the Italian working class is a crucial ingredient in salvaging the economy without falling into the trap of salvaging capitalism. The classic prescription of capitalism in a crisis is austerity: cut wages and consumption, cut social and public service—health, schools, welfare—and shift the burden of recession onto the shoulders of the mass of the people. This is the prescription of the International Monetary Fund, dominated by the United States. These were the conditions of its loan to Italy.

The unions reply that capitalist austerity is a one-way street: sacrifices for workers, business as usual for the bourgeoisie. The unions are not against sacrifices—for everybody. They are willing to sacrifice wage increases in exchange for a powerful say in the economy. They support the strategy of the Communist party to weld together a coalition of farmers, storekeepers, artisans, and small

---

* Councils of action are not trade-union bodies, but bodies of *all* the workers, whether unionized or not. There is no closed shop in Italy.

† The two points Zuccotti emphasized. See Chapter 7.

businessmen to wrest control of the economy from Big Business, using wage increases as a tradeoff.

Says Napolitano: "The need to fight inflation, and to devote a larger share of the resources to investment, also implies that the cost of labor must be contained. This should not be regarded as the only problem of Italian economic development, but it is a significant aspect of the effort to secure needed investments, to enlarge the productive base, to develop the south, and to increase employment. *The trade unions have openly recognized this.*" (Italics added.)[47] He epitomized this position for the *Manchester Guardian:* "We are for zero wage increases in real terms to increase employment and investment."[48]

The unions, while restive, have not been unwilling to trade wage increases for control over the economy. In an important interview in February 1978, Luciano Lama, general secretary of the CGIL, said that excessive wage increases had contributed to unemployment and that too rigid job protection was harming industrial recovery.* Lama's position created friction with the leadership of the CISL, and led some foreign observers to conclude that the Communist leadership of the CGIL was going contrary to workers' interests and selling out to the capitalists. But Lama's interview had a snapper: the unions must assume complete control over the labor market and over investments. This was merely a restatement of what had been said by his deputy, Bruno Trentin (former head of the metal workers in the CGIL), who pointed out that the unions' proposals

> must inevitably lead to a qualitative modification of the system. Not to a more rational capitalism, but to a transitional economic system. When the collective manages . . . through mass action, new forms of workers' control, new relationships among the traditional representative institutions, and new forms of rank-and-file democracy . . . to determine a new allocation of investments, a policy of reconversion of the sort supported by the trade-union movement today, then one cannot speak merely of restructuring or capitalist rationalization. I think, and Italian capitalism is well aware of this, that it is the power of capital to command a profit that will then be challenged.[50]

The capitalists are well aware of the long-term implications. Carli's immediate response to Lama's remarks was that "they imply

---

* Lama's interview was given to *La Repubblica,* January 24, 1978. The key passage was: "The capitalists maintain that profits is an independent variable. The workers and their unions, in recent years, have retorted that wages are an independent variable and so is the work force. Well, we must be intellectually honest, and declare that this is nonsense, because in an open economy, all variables are dependent on each other."[49]

eventual expansion in the area of union power in running companies."[51] By coincidence, *Le Monde* had just published an interview with Agnelli in which he mused that perhaps the time was coming when capitalists like himself would become employees of the unions.[52]

Of course, this was simply a wisecrack* and Agnelli is not prepared to concede defeat. But he understands, as does Carli, that the control of the economy is the issue, "the stakes are high."

Because capitalism is called the profit system, and because corporate decisions are made on the *expectation* of profit, it is often forgotten that the *point of decision* for business is investment. That is the control point for the economy. There is a very good reason why Communists talk about "allocation of investments," whereas Carli talks about unions "running companies"; the reason is that both are addressing the small businessman, who is not concerned about investments,† but who *is* concerned about running his own company. The unions, the Communists, and the Socialists do not want to run the companies; in fact, the Italian unions refuse to take responsibility for managerial decisions and think that, in a capitalist system, workers' self-management is an illusion.[54] They say: Let the entrepreneur make his decisions; we are concerned with working conditions.

While Carli tries to scare the small businessman and turn him against the Communists,‡ the Communists say to the small businessman, "We are not against profits. Run your business well, efficiently, and you can keep your reward.** But the government must determine the broad lines of economic development for the best welfare of the nation, rather than any one of the big corporations."

To make investments, of course, one must have capital. Here the left-wing skeptics of Eurocommunism make their most telling criticism. Owners of capital will not invest if they do not have a free choice. They will not invest in public housing (offering a return of 3 percent) when they can invest in condominiums on the Sardinian Emerald Coast (offering a return of 30 percent). The capitalists will go on strike, keep their money liquid, or send it abroad, and the economy will be strangled.

The need for capital is axiomatic in any industrial society, whether capitalist or socialist. Under capitalism, capital formation takes place through profits. The Communists agree that more capital

---

\* The opposite comment of Aurelio Peccei (a consultant to multinational corporations) was also a wisecrack: "We are lucky to have that kind of a Communist party." This has been used to show that Big Business is pleased with the PCI.[53]

† Most small businessmen have few reinvestment problems as they do not generate sufficient reserves. Their problem is credit, which Communists assert they will help through the state.

‡ Carli is trying to reform the *Confindustria*, which has been dominated by Big Business, to give a greater voice to small business.[55]

\*\* Subject, of course, to standard, and established, taxation.

should be formed. Furthermore, all economists, of whatever persuasion, in Italy and abroad, agree that the lack of capital is a major, if not
*the* major problem of the Italian economy.

The Communist answer is that enough capital can be generated
within the economy and *prevented* from being sent abroad.[56] It has
been the *capitalist state* which has allowed the flight of capital.
Beginning in 1963, with the nationalization of the electrical industry,
the well-to-do in Italy systematically sent their money abroad, the
transfers protected in part by a dubious legality, including so-called
"banking secrecy"—or the refusal of banks to reveal to the treasury
the foreign accounts of their clients. It is estimated that between $30
and $50 *billion* have been sent abroad. Since 1975, under Communist
pressure, exchange controls have been instituted, showing that
political decisions are at the core of capital retention.[57]

Even more important than the flight of capital has been the waste
due to corruption and clientism, particularly in the nationalized
industries, as we have seen in Chapter 9. Untold billions have been
frittered away; one agency alone, EGAM, wasted five times the
amount of the loan Italy sought from the International Monetary
Fund.

But the greatest drain of capital—capital that could be at the
disposal of the government—lies in income tax invasion, both personal and corporate. This has been estimated to amount to $15 to $20
billion a year, a sum which could *triple industrial investment!*\* The
tax evasion ranges from celebrities such as Sophia Loren (one billion
lire) to a bricklayer in Bolzano (Otto Mair, 20 million lire). Corporations are among the big tax evaders: Goodyear di Latina, 379 million
lire; Siderlamina, 172 million lire; Fonte della Mangiatorella, 130
million lire, etc. The effrontery of the evasion is almost beyond belief.
Thirty-three percent of all lawyers, 19 percent of all doctors, and 18
percent of all manufacturers declared a net income of two million lire
in 1978 (a little over two thousand dollars)—which is about what a
peddler of postcards makes. A random sampling of five hundred
returns showed that the overwhelming majority had defrauded the
government by as much as 97 percent.[59]

Tax evasion is a hemorrhaging of resources which only an honest
government can cure. Even moderate enforcement brings dramatic
results. For example, between 1973 and 1976, when the government
slightly tightened up collections, personal income tax returns doubled
while corporate tax returns increased sixfold. At the same time, the
gross national product increased less than 45 percent—in other
words, increased tax collections were the result, not of people and

---

\*   Industrial fixed investment from 1960 to 1975 averaged $6 billion a year. In 1975 it reached 9
billion.[58]

corporations making more money, but of less tax evasion.[60] While the widespread use of cash, rather than checks, makes evasion easier, the fact remains that corruption is responsible for the lax enforcement of the tax laws.

The economic crisis is directly related to gross inefficiency and corruption. As we have seen in the previous chapter, politics was more important than economics in overcoming Italy's agricultural shortcomings. This is not true to the same extent in industry. A government with Communists in the cabinet would probably have to contend with economic pressures from the United States. Still, there are countervailing pressures. For example, it is interesting to listen to Agnelli in this context: "In Italy, I fight the Communist party. When I talk to foreigners, I try to give them credit. We must try to beat them [the Communists] electorally . . . but when I talk abroad, I try to give them the most possible credit because I think they are better than foreigners think they are."[61]

Agnelli, looking ahead, is angling for forbearance from the United States. If the Communists go into the government, it is because they cannot be kept out. He doesn't want this to result in punitive economic measures from the rest of the capitalist world— measures which would hurt Fiat as well as the country, exacerbate the anger and mistrust of the workers, and strengthen the forces of violent revolt.*

Germany, which has hitherto followed the U.S. lead, is getting restive and is interested in neutralizing Europe vis-à-vis both the two superpowers and finds a reliable ally in the PCI. Moreover, the working class of Italy and the trade unions are powerful and class-conscious. The peculiar nature of the crisis also works to the advantage of strong unions, as is made clear by a very elegant analysis of Giovanni Arrighi.[62] It is not at all ordained that the Eurocommunist concept of a "transition economy" shall be doomed to failure. By good luck, I had a chance to talk about the economy with a top industrial manager who had had dealings with Agnelli and was thoroughly familiar with the history and problems of Italian industry. The interview, which took place in a northern city, was arranged by the Catholic regional secretary of CISL.

*We met in a hotel lobby. He was in his middle fifties, dressed in English tweeds, with a square face, blue eyes, and a crew cut, rare in Italy. Rather dour and blunt-spoken, he was in charge of a large industrial complex (perhaps twenty thousand workers) of a major corporation).*

---

\* Agnelli is also gambling that with the Communists in the government the state might be modernized (reduction of tax evasion, corruption, nepotism, etc.) and that the economy, *still a market economy*, will withstand and absorb the "socialist elements" which would be introduced. He believes capitalism has great recuperative powers. In any case, he sees no alternative.

*I asked his opinion on the reasons for the economic crisis in Italy. He replied instantly that the chief reason was the world-wide recession. "We are at the mercy of world prices; we have to import food and raw materials; we export finished goods. If prices for imports go up, as with the oil prices, we are caught." Did he think the wage increases were crucial? They contributed, certainly, but he thought the damage lay further back. He then preceeded to give me an analysis which echoed Carli, Spaventa, Father Greco, Claudio, and Pugliese. "Italian businessmen are to blame," he said, adding the common cliché; "Like the Bourbons, they forgot nothing, and learned nothing. After the war, I was just at the foot of the management ladder—I was put in charge of a division. Right away, I had problems with my superiors."*

*He sipped his coffee and continued. "Workers were supposed to be fined for different infractions—coming in late, cursing the foreman, etc. I didn't hand out fines——I have never fined a worker in my life and my shops are as efficient as anyone's–and I was called down by my superiors. 'Why no fines?' I said I hadn't found them necessary, and besides, I didn't think it right that workers should be fined while the white-collar employees were not. 'They don't need to be fined,' I was told, 'they are better educated.' I said that maybe we should educate the workers as well. I did not say that they were talking nonsense. I came from a worker's family and my father could reason with the best of them, and so could most workers I know. Just prejudice. And greedy—my God, they were greedy, in the midst of a great economic boom when they could afford so much. Well, they sowed the wind in the fifties and now they are reaping the whirlwind. I have no sympathy for them."*

*"There is a current of thought in America," I told him, "that thinks the Communist party and the CGIL have sold out to Big Business, that they and Agnelli are in tacit agreement to force austerity on the workers. What do you think?"*

*The manager snorted. "Ma quante sciocchezze! What nonsense! The Fiat has been one of the worst in squeezing workers; the company has never given more than it had to. Agnelli took over in 1966 and went right along with the company tradition, until the unions got strong and forced him to make concessions. Which, by the way, he can well afford to do. He did do it with grace. . .and a clear sense of public relations. But he fights the Communists at every turn; fights them and fears them.\* With reason, for the Communists are getting stronger all the time. They mean business, their administrations are honest, and more and more people trust them."*

---

\* The shrewd insight of this manager was vindicated in 1979 when Agnelli moved on the offensive against the unions under cover of combatting terrorism.

*"Do you vote Communist?" I asked.*

*"No, Communism is too utopian—you can't change human nature—I vote DC. But I stand with Zaccagnini, Moro, Bodrato. . .the group that wants to work with Communists."*

*I sought his opinion on the economy, and his answer surprised me. He thought the Italian economy far stronger that its present crisis indicated. "In 1977," he said, "we produced as much steel as England. This is quite an achievement for a country which has practically no coal or iron ore. Still, the economy needs fresh impetus—more diversification, for one thing. We must improve our technology—our research effort is too low—we spend about one percent of our national product on research, while Germany spends 2 percent and the United States 2.5 percent. We need more use of solar energy in agriculture—expand our greenhouses. Increase nuclear energy and so on."*

*The manager grew animated as he warmed to his subject. "We have great potential in Europe. We can be competitive—look at Olivetti, look at Fiat. Hell, we sell 49 percent of all refrigerators in the Common Market. In the last ten years, our increase in productivity in manufacturing has been double that of the United States or Great Britain—very close to that of Germany and France.*[63] *We have an enormous potential in the third world. Where we are efficient, we make headway. For example, sales of machine tools abroad went up 25 percent in 1977. Why? Because the machines were produced in medium-sized industries that are well managed and efficient. Our worst industries are the nationalized ones because of corruption and nepotism. We need a modern, honest, forward-looking state."*

*"What about the south?"*

*"Agriculture has been a stepchild; it needs attention. But even there, industry is responsible for its backwardness. In the sixties, the government made loans at low interest rates to stimulate investments. The result was huge complexes—we call them "cathedrals in the desert"—very capital-intensive, so that they have had little impact on unemployment. But the sin was in not building an infrastructure—no network of smaller plants, repair shops, and so on, to use the petroleum products and steel produced. The big barons, with their corruption and patronage, distorted the development of the south.*

*"Are you saying that politics is more important than economics in stimulating the Italian economy?"*

*"I hadn't thought of it that way, but in a way, yes. The population is demoralized; it needs to see changes taking place, have assurance that corruption, patronage, tax evasion are being attacked."*

*"You see the Communists as a strength, then?"*

*"Absolutely. They are honest and they are serious. You can't take that away from them."*

I was struck by his emphasis on Italy's competitive ability within European industry when its firms were well managed, and recently I ran into a striking confirmation of this fact in the report of the Genoa fair on naval technology, which closed on June 1, 1980. Over sixty nations attended, and large contracts were signed with Iraq, Australia, and Brazil. The industry is *fourth* in size in the world market (after the US, the USSR, and France) with estimated sales of $7 billion a year for 1981.*

Italy has an enormous potential for recuperation and growth in industry, agriculture, and services, but economic considerations are inextricably interwoven with the political ones. In a recent book, *In mezzo al guado* (In the middle of the ford), Giorgio Napolitano has a long introduction, written after the June 1979 elections, in which he surveys the line of the party and shows the coherence of that line through his speeches and articles of the previous five years. The coherence is based on that interweaving of economic and political factors which I have been trying to present realistically.

After we parted, I asked my union friend if the manager was typical. No, he said, he wasn't typical, but neither was he unique. There was a definite group within the managerial class which thought as this man did, and was deeply concerned with the crisis and impressed by the probity of the Communists. These managers were a minority, perhaps 10 or 15 percent, but they were influential beyond their numbers within *Democrazia Cristiana.* "They are our allies," said my friend with a smile. "I mean we Catholic unionists. Because of them, we get a lot of support from the progressive Catholic hierarchy. This current is the strength of Moro and Zaccagnini. "He paused, "you know of course, that Moro will be the next president."

"So I've heard. Everyone seems to think that's very good."

"It is. Italy needs a period of tranquillity, of different factions working together. Moro is ideal. He's respected by the Communists, trusted by all parties, and he has a good grip on the DC. I don't know what we'd do without him."

Within four months, Moro was assassinated: Clearly, politics was more important than economics.

---

* Warships and attendant systems—electronic interception, communications, naval airplanes and helicopters, gun controls—call for a high technology and a skilled working force. To stake out such a successful position in the world market, the quality of the Italian naval industry must be exceptionally high. (See *Il Progresso Italo-Americano,* June 2, 1980.)

# CHAPTER 12

# Contrapuntal Politics, 1978–1980

BY ALL THE BEST-LAID PLANS, Italian politics in the year 1978 should have unreeled as a good-natured soap opera with mild elements of suspense: When would Communists enter the cabinet? Would the skittish DC horse, so often brought to water, finally consent to drink?

But history is tricky. Placid 1978 turned out to be a catclysmic year for Italy: one assassination of the powerful president of the DC, one resignation for corruption by the President of the Republic, two dead popes within two months, and two unprecedented demonstrations of the metal workers intervening directly in the political process. The tremors of this series of shocks to the body politic are still being felt.

The two union demonstrations were huge—around 300,000 persons at each*—which, by comparison, would be like 1.5 million steel and auto workers descending on Washington. The demonstrations bracketed the crisis period chronologically (the first took place in December 1977 and the second in June 1979) and symbolically, for it is the organized working class that is the major protagonist of contemporary Italian politics. The PCI is only effective to the extent that it can articulate the feelings of that class, and only as powerful as its connection to the workers.

*I sat on a bus on the way to the first (1977) demonstration, going a long roundabout route because the center of the city had been*

---

* Estimates for the first demonstration range from 250,000 by the police to 350,000 by the organizers of the demonstration. By general agreement, the second demonstration was considerably larger, perhaps 10 to 20 percent more.

254

*blocked off to facilitate the rivers of humans expected. Dozens of special trains, hundreds of chartered buses, thousands of auto cara-vans had been pouring into the city throughout the night of December 1. From assembly points at the various terminals, three major parades wound through the city, ending on the twin plazas around the Cathedral of St. John. From every part of the city minor parades flowed into the major ones. From my seat I saw a stream of young people crossing the street and bringing my bus to a halt. I thought they were high schools students until I saw the red banners of the unemployed councils.*

*The demonstration was both a climax and a point of departure. Since the election of June 1976, the DC had needed the support of the PCI to be able to govern, and had gained that support by concessions such as passage of Law 382. For the right wing of the DC, each concession was supposed to be the last; but for the PCI each concession was a steppingstone to the next, a process leading ulti-mately to PCI entry into the cabinet. It was a minuet that was well understood by everyone in Italy, and it was orchestrated by Aldo Moro, five times prime minister, chairman, and elder statesman of the Democrazia Cristiana. Moro had been a hard-liner in the past, and his distaste for Communism was deep and open, but he had understood the implications of the DC defeat in the 1974 referendum and the subsequent elections. He made a virtue of necessity and worked out the various agreements. The last, in the summer of 1977, was the so-called pact of the six parties,\* where a specific set of reforms had been spelled out.[1] These reforms had not been carried out, and the demonstration was called by the metal workers as a major protest.*

*When I reached the cathedral, the sun was out, a winter sun in a clear sky, pallid but welcome. As far as the eye could see, a restless expanse of faces looked back, undulating in huge concentric circles around the speakers' platforms. There were few children, this was not a family outing. The crowd was genial but purposive. The slogans on the red streamers were all political:* DOWN WITH THE GOVERNMENT OF CRISIS; DOWN WITH UNEMPLOYMENT; DEFEAT TERRORISM; WORKING CLASS TO GOVERNMENT; WE GOVERN OR STRIKE. *This last was not an idle threat. The metal workers of the three confederations had agreed on a general strike to be supported by the entire labor movement.*

*The enormous success of the demonstration guaranteed the end of the government. Ugo La Malfa, leader of the PRI, led a move of the minor parties, backed by the PSI and, reluctantly, by the PCI, to withdraw support of the Andreotti cabinet. The government fell in*

\* DC, PCI, PSI, PLI, PRI, PSDI. See page 121.

*January, but Prime Minister Andreotti was charged by President Sergio Leone to form a new cabinet.*

La Malfa demanded that the Communists enter the government, a demand supported by the Socialists, and, orally, by the Communists. In fact, the Communists thought the demand premature, for two major reasons: the first was the strong anti-Communist resistance within the Church hierarchy and the middle echelons of the DC, which would sabotage reforms. The second reason was that Communist cadres were stretched thin by the electoral gains of 1975 and 1976, which had required thousands of them to fill elective and administrative posts. The breathing space of a year or so would give confidence and experience to the new Communist administrations, provide training time for several thousand additional workers, and erode substantially the resistance within the DC and the Church.

Yet the Communists were not free agents. The militancy of the working class, as shown on December 2, forced them to take the hard-line of demanding cabinet posts. However, everyone knew they would settle for less. During January and February the triumvirate of Aldo Moro, Benigno Zaccagnini, and Giulio Andreotti worked out a satisfactory compromise. Communist technicians would participate in planning and programming and, in Parliament, the Communist party and other parties would move from abstention to voting with the government. In effect, the Communists would now be officially consulted and drawn into policy decisions, directly and openly, as part of a legislative coalition. The compromise was promptly dubbed *la maggioranza* by the newspapers, meaning that the DC and PCI had gotten together. Yet not wholly; yet not quite—a typical Moro solution. It was the package of a master diplomat, the artisan of the ambiguous phrase that soothed and smoothed. On the relation between the DC and the PCI, Moro had coined the phrase, "converging parallels." Euclid might spin in his grave, but people sensed what he meant: never the twain shall meet, but they've got to work together.

The scenario for 1978–79 had taken firm shape. First, in March 1978, the Communists would be part of the government on the legislative side; then, after the middle ranks of the DC had digested this step, the Communists would enter the cabinet in early 1979. The DC horse would finally drink; *il compromesso storico* would become a reality. The scenario, written by Aldo Moro, was self-fulfilling, for the scenarist was also the executive producer: Moro held the DC under firm control. As its national chairman he also had two disciples in the key roles of general secretary (Zaccagnini) and prime minister (Andreotti). In December 1978 Moro would become president of the Republic (already agreed to by the six parties), Zaccagnini would move up to national chairman, Andreotti would remain as prime minister, and a firm Moro supporter would become general secretary. The strong triumvirate would become an irresistible quadrumvirate; and given the tacit support of Paul VI (already assured), the scenario couldn't miss. The entry of the Communists into the cabinet seemed certain.

The compromise hinged on Moro. His was the prestige that held in line the middle ranks of the DC, because they knew he was going to be president and could be trusted to block any Communist takeover. If he were making compromises, it was for patriotic rather than self-serving reasons. He, the anti-Communist, was opening the door to the final step because he was aware that the national welfare required the "historic compromise." Moro was the only leader who could keep the *Democrazia Cristiana* unified and still bring in the Communists, the only man who could make the DC horse drink. He was unique in his role, that of a stabilizing influence on a shaky nation.

That role made Moro the natural target of the destabilizers. On March 16, 1978, the very day the new government of *la maggioranza* was to be installed, the Red Brigades kidnapped Aldo Moro, killing his five bodyguards in the process. The operation, flawless in execution, marked the apogee of terrorism in Italy.

*The Red Brigades are the largest and best organized of some hundred-odd terrorist groups in Italy.*[2] *This terrorism is a part of a wider phenomenon of European terrorism, which came into being at the end of the sixties,* \* *and which many observers link to the American war in Vietnam. A German teacher in Berlin told Andrew Kopkind: "Vietnam was the start of it all for us, as it was for the Americans. Remember that we are still an occupied country. We saw ourselves then as an outpost of the same empire [the U.S.] that was acquiring more territory in Asia."*[3] *European disapproval of the Vietnam War was massive: the French called it "external fascism."*

*The American influence has been attested by a wide variety of personalities. Horst Mahler, an early ideologue of the German terrorists, says, "The first stage of our 'illegal' activities was helping American deserters go to France, to Italy, to Sweden. We developed contacts all over Europe for the first time."*[4] *Alberto Ronchey, the liberal journalist of* Corriere della sera *gives as his opinion that terrorism in Italy is the result of "mixing the egalitarian myths of the East with American permissiveness: the two influences combined into an explosive mixture."*[5] *Adalberto Minucci, editor of* Rinascita, *the PCI theoretical journal, sees a deeper American influence: the*

---

\* This "new" terrorism is distinguished from the "old" terrorism of Algerians, Irish, Basques, Palestinians, which is motivated by nationalist drives.

*American model of a welfare state conjoined with a rapid indus-
trialization that was breaking up the traditional culture. In his view, a
kind of neurotic society emerged which particularly affected the
middle classes.*[6] *Morris West, the well-known Catholic novelist who
resides in Italy, tangentially supports Minucci on the nature of the
society: "Unless you live there, it is impossible to believe how crazy
the country can be, how precarious are the foundations upon which it
rests."*[7]

*Whatever theory of causation is accepted, everyone agrees that
the corruption, venality, nepotism, clientism, and the appalling
bureaucracy make fertile ground for terrorism and anarchy. West
goes on: "The result? A total breakdown of public confidence, a great
universal cynicism, a fall back to the most primitive tribal violence. . . . It is in this climate of cynicism and disillusion that the
doctrine of 'spontaneous anarchy' finds ready adherents. The only
remedy for the ills of the body politic is drastic surgery. . . . For the
young workless and the students, angry and frustrated in universities
grossly overcrowded and understaffed, it is a seductive gospel. For
them the future is a wasteland."*[8]

*The nihilism of the Red Brigades is unrelieved. Not only the
state, but every aspect of the existing society must be destroyed, root
and branch. The road is through civil war, as outlined in a sixty-page
manual seized in March 1978, and the chief enemy is the Italian
Communist party, defined as a lackey of the bourgeoisie and a jackal
preying on the proletariat.*[9] *From captured documents, it is evident
that Berlinguer, rather than Moro, was to be the number one target,
but he was too well guarded, and Moro was substituted. The enmity
toward the party is reaffirmed in another seized document of thirty-two
pages, dated September 1978, which lays down the strategy of
escalation in the post-Moro period.*[10]

The Moro kidnapping showed the strength of the Red Brigades; his
execution showed their ultimate weakness. The strength lay in their
discipline, organizational ability, and the efficiency of their security
measures. For fifty-four days a tremendous manhunt was carried out
involving 16,000 *carabinieri*, 18,000 police, 4,000 frontier guards,
hundreds of army units. Six million seven hundred thousand people
were checked, 3.3 million cars and trucks examined at 62,000
roadblocks; 35,000 houses were searched, 5,900 boats were in-
spected. There were 1,200 group arrests. Many petty criminals were
caught, and the crime rate dropped precipitously. The crime business
turned so bad that it was rumored the Mafia was going to murder the
terrorists in jail if Moro was not freed.[11] But of Moro not a clue was
found. Over the weeks, while the search was on, Moro sent a number

of letters to leaders of the DC and personal friends suggesting ways he could be traded for captured Red Brigade leaders. The government remained firm, and on May 9, Moro's body, stuffed in a car trunk, was left in the heart of Rome, midway between the headquarters of the DC and the PCI.

It became clear that there was some protective indifference, if not connivance, within the population and within the bureaucracy. It has been estimated that there are no more that five hundred "Regulars"—committed terrorists—distributed in a few major cities, with perhaps a thousand "Irregulars" in a secondary reserve. But perhaps as many as thirty thousand people are helping them on a tacit, no-questions-asked basis and also providing a recruiting base. Not one informed.

The terrorist groupings had begun to evolve in 1970. The leaders at that time were Catholic and Marxist fanatics. The founder of the Red Brigades, Renato Curcio, was a staunch Catholic. One of his professors, Franco Ferrarotti, a leading sociologist, said: "Renato and many of his supporters come from old-fashioned, conservative Catholic families. They are basically religious people who come to politics and violence with all the conviction of zealots."[12] Many had been Communists, and as the PCI grew, so did their expectations of drastic change. But *il compromesso storico* is a long-range strategy, and the impatient were disillusioned and left the party or were expelled for ultraleft views and actions. In the early seventies there were fires and bombings, and by 1974 the violence had turned to kidnappings and "knee-capping" (shooting in the legs). The violence steadily escalated. The number of attacks by the Red Brigades jumped from 48 in 1974 to 1,198 in 1976 and 2,365 in 1978—a 5000 percent increase in five years.[13]

But as the killings and woundings increased, popular opinion turned from indifference to disgust. By the end of 1977, the killing of Carlo Casalegno had begun to split the ultraleft; the murder of Moro—and his bodyguards—heavily tipped the scales. The Red Brigades found themselves completely isolated. They had hoped to free the imprisoned terrorists in exchange for Moro's life, but the government adamantly refused to negotiate. The decision was officially supported by the six parties, especially by the PCI, which forestalled any wavering by announcing it would withdraw its support if the cabinet gave in. The major goal of the Red Brigades had been to achieve a *de facto* status as combatants, to be considered "prisoners of war" if caught. Frustrated, they executed Moro, but the execution split them internally, and some terrorists began to leak information to the police.[14] Throughout 1978 and 1979 there were dramatic arrests, particularly that of two terrorists, Adriana Miranda and Valerio Morucci, captured in an apartment of Giuliana Conforto, a lyceum teacher of physics. In a closet was found an arsenal including a submachine gun, a Skorpion, which was later proven to have been the weapon used in Moro's murder.[15]

Giuliana Conforto claimed she didn't know the two as terrorists; she had let them stay as an act of friendship to her friend Franco Piperno. The four of them had been members of an ultraleftist group, *Potere Operaio* (Worker Power), of which Piperno had been one of the leaders, along with Oreste Scalzone and Toni Negri. Negri, born in Padua in 1933, was a child prodigy. At thirty-four he became a professor at Padua University, the intellectual leader of the extreme left, and there conducted seminars on political warfare. As a reputable newsman put it: "At the university, Negri's institute was a bunker of the *autonomi*: only those who had the secret sign could enter."[16]

*Autonomi* are members of *Autonomia Operaia* (Worker Autonomy) a name designed to stress its independence from the "establishment" trade unions, CGIL, CISL, UIL and their top federation. The *autonomi* established considerable influence within the working class, though they were primarily unemployed youths or students. They are totally committed to violence, including killing, but not in the clandestine fashion of the Red Brigades. Rather, *autonomi* seek confrontations with police or trade-union meetings, using revolvers and Molotov cocktails to disrupt and do damage. Classically, they form small squads which come to a meeting unarmed, then a woman comrade brings and distributes pistols. They shoot, give the pistols to another squad, and so on.[17]

In September 1977 the *autonomi* staged a national congress in Bologna, and caught the city administration by surprise when the demonstration turned into a rampage through the center of the city, breaking store windows, beating up individuals, and terrorizing the population. In November 1977 they attempted to repeat the outrage, but this time the city, the party, and the unions were ready for them. Five thousand policemen and fifty thousand workers penned the demonstrators in an area of a few blocks and held them there until they could be slowly dispersed. The *autonomi* have gradually lost whatever sympathy they had within the working class. *Lotta Continua* finally broke with them and condemned them.[18] At the Rome demonstration of December 1977 they were told they could march as a group, provided they were first searched by trade union marshals and were escorted by them. When the *autonomi* refused, and gathered for the march on a campus of the university, they were surrounded by police and held there until the demonstration was over. In the huge demonstration of June 1979 they didn't even attempt to participate, but carried out a few hit-and-run raids on the periphery of the parades.

*Autonomia Operaia* was a successor organization to *Potere Operaio*, which was dissolved in 1973 at a meeting in Rosolina. According to the public prosecutor, Pietro Calogero, the dissolution was a sham. *Potere Operaio* actually divided itself into two arms: a clandestine arm, the Red Brigades, and a legal arm, the Autonomia, with a single directing center led by Toni Negri. Negri functioned in a dual role: an open theoretician of the Autonomia and a secret member or head of the strategy body, the Red Brigades.[19]

Negri was arrested on April 7, 1979, and his arrest brought a wave of world-wide protest from intellectuals, including Raymond Aron and Eugène Ionesco from France, Nobel Prize winner George Wald, Paul Sweezy, and James O'Connor from the United States.[20] Negri's defense has been that he has attacked the Red Brigades constantly and that he is being persecuted because he is violently opposed to the Communist party.* He has accused his prosecutor, Calogero, of being a pawn for the PCI, and in a letter to *L'Espresso*, he said he had no intentions of "being handcuffed by the ideology of Eurocommunism and its agents."[22]

At first Negri's accusation carried weight.[23] But as time passed, his protestations appeared more dubious. Captured Red Brigades documents were found to have been typed on Negri's typewriter.[24] Most serious, an American expert, Professor Oscar Tosi, decided that a key telephone call from the Red Brigades to the Moro family during the kidnapping was almost certainly made by Negri: "The voice of the unknown caller and that of Professor Negri are identical within a probability higher than 80 percent." Moreover, since four Italian experts concluded that the two voices were of the same quality and Negri's could not be excluded, Tosi went on to say that this added weight to his judgment and that "the margin of error in the probability [of 80 percent] was substantially reduced." Since then, several captured terrorists have decided to talk, and two of them, Carlo Fioroni and Carlo Casirati, have implicated Negri. Casirati is an ex-gangster whose motives are suspect, but Fioroni is a young intellectual who says he was shocked by the murder of Moro (he had been in jail for three years at the time), and decided to confess. Negri has denied their charges.[25]

Italian judicial procedures are involved and lengthy. Until the trial all the facts will not be known—if then. But there is little doubt that Negri and his friends have been fostering terrorism. A balanced and thoughtful review essay by Professor Thomas Sheehan in the *New York Review of Books* shows how Negri kept insisting on the necessity of violence and immediate armed struggle. "Perhaps, as his

* Both the Red Brigades and the *autonomi* see the PCI as their main enemy.[21]

lawyers claim, Negri has now abandoned that position. But the professor cannot put the blood back.''[26]

In the long run, the revulsion within the ultraleft may be decisive. The *Manifesto* group, which had always been ideologically opposed to terrorism, now denounced the Red Brigades as fascist. *Lotta Continua,* which in the past had equivocated, saying they were "mistaken comrades," had begun to split with the killing of Casalegno. His son, Andrea, once a member of *Lotta Continua,* had given a moving interview denouncing the murder as a sordid crime, without any justification. He and his father had disagreed politically, he said, but he was a good man, a conservative of integrity. He did not deserve bullets: that was not the way to resolve political differences. The interview was published in the newspaper *Lotta Continua,* provoking a sharp debate as some argued that innocents are bound to suffer in the class war.[27] After the murder of Moro, there was no attempt at justification. Some of the *autonomi* who had been very close to the underground also denounced the murder. A re-examination of the value of terrorism is taking place in Italy and in other countries, perhaps best summarized by Horst Mahler, one of its early ideologues.

Mahler, arrested in 1970, had had time to read, think, and observe. A few weeks after Moro's kidnapping he was interviewed in jail by an American newsman. He said:

Armed terrorism cannot protect its revolutionary promises or guarantee an improvement in people's lives as the guerrillas could do in China, Cuba, or Vietnam. In Italy, for instance, the Red Brigades cannot protect the workers from the repression they are provoking. . . . They are not revolutionaries but pawns in the hands of the most reactionary forces.

. . . It *is* possible to use the state for the common good, for common interests . . . That means we have to find a way to do it all better than "they" are doing it, that we are ready to make demands, that we can supply an alternative, that we can build a better society.[28]

The Red Brigades are far from finished; the corruption in the society, the unemployment of the youth, and the frustration of the students guarantee a fertile soil until people can see that the government is seriously attacking those problems. The provocation is ample: one half of Italy's unemployed are under thirty, and half of those are college graduates. "Why bother to graduate?" said one student. "Better hang around with your friends in the university." In 1977, of 700,000 students only 10 percent, 71,000, took the trouble to graduate.[29]

But the attraction of terrorism is waning: it doesn't deliver the goods, and the wanton assassination of Moro was sobering.* The Red Brigades failed in their primary goal to be recognized as a "belligerent" group by trading, as it were, "prisoners of war." But their secondary strategy was to undermine the "historic compromise." In this they were temporarily successful. Moro's murder threw a big monkey wrench into the political machinery of the country. The assassination removed that delicate fulcrum within *Democrazia Cristiana* which had opened the way to the "historic compromise." Almost immediately after his death, the scenario that Moro had so patiently woven began to unravel. The anti-Communist wing was strengthened and their strength further increased by the results of the partial municipal elections five days after Moro's death.

On May 14, some 10 percent of the electorate voted in local elections, with surprising results. Compared to 1976, the Communists dropped 9 points, the Christian Democrats and the Socialists gained nearly 4 points apiece and the neofascists dropped 2.5 points.[30] Everyone felt that the Moro assassination had redounded to the benefit of the DC and to the detriment of the PCI. Throughout the agonizing fifty-four days, the center and right press had hammered at the theme that the terrorists were the product of Communism. As a colonel of *carabinieri* in Turin put it: "The Communist party is the mother of terrorism. For thirty years it preached an indefinite kind of war of the classes. Now they say that class war is unnecessary for state power. But their children do not believe them."[31]

The colonel was not accurate: Sociologists and political observers studied the terrorists and concluded that among them were as many children from Catholic and affluent families as there were children of Communist and working-class families. But in the popular mind, as reflected in the colonel's views, Catholicism and wealth were not associated with violence; Communism was.

The murder of Moro and the elections convulsed the internal power structure of the DC. There were now, in effect, two vacancies: chairman of the DC and, soon, the presidency. Whatever the distribution of the four posts (say, Andreotti for president and Zaccagnini for chairman) it would be impossible to get left-wingers in the other two posts. At best, two centrists might be acceptable, but the Moro line would change. Flaminio Piccoli, head of the DC group in Parliament, immediately asserted his claims to leadership and a new line by giving a long interview to *L'Epoca*.[32] In his view, the electoral

---

* This does not mean the Red Brigades are finished. They set off a bomb in an electric substation serving the building where the DC Congress was being held (February 17, 1980), and just before the Congress assassinated a leading DC figure, Professor Vittorio Bachelet, vice-president of *"la magistratura,"* the body of Italian judges (*Il Progresso Italo-Americano*, February 19, 1980).

success of the Socialists objectively detached them from the Communists. The DC should join the PSI "in an effort at collaboration which would emphasize what they had in common"—a diplomatic way of asserting an anti-Communist line. Piccoli had correctly judged the relationship of forces: by the end of June Zaccagnini had to court him and offer him the job of national chairman.

Bettino Craxi was not slow in responding to Piccoli's invitation. Craxi was now in firm control of the Socialist party, having forced out his last opponent, Paolo Vittorelli, editor of the Socialist organ *Avanti!* because Vittorelli disagreed with the Craxi line on the Moro tragedy. Craxi's policy had been one of duplicity, breathtaking in its effrontery: On the one hand, as general secretary of the PSI, he had supported the government's policy of no bargaining with the Red Brigades; on the other hand, ostensibly as an individual, he publicly called for saving Moro by a trade. Soon after the assassination he began a campaign of innuendo against other political leaders. He told Mitterand, head of the French Socialists, who repeated the accusation, "Someone wanted blood," and "Were he [Moro] to come back, he would be one too many."*33

With the same consummate duplicity, he continued to be part of *la maggioranza,* while at the same time intriguing with the conservative forces within the DC and other parties to restore a center-left government, that is, a government of Socialists and Christian Democrats such as had existed in the sixties. But whereas the previous center-left government had been a coalition with the left wing of the DC (organized by Moro), now the coalition would be with the right of the DC—Amintore Fanfani, Antonio Bisaglia, Massimo de Carolis. "There is not an enemy of Zaccagnini . . . who has not been in touch with the leaders of the PSI," wrote Carlo Rosella in *Panorama,* adding that "It has already been called 'Operation Amarcord.' Its objective is to restore the collaboration of the DC with Socialist and lay parties. Its principal protagonist is Bettino Craxi . . . with a vast line-up, from conservative DC forces, with Fanfani at the head, to technocrats around Umberto Agnelli [brother of Giovanni]. . . . The project, officially denied by the PSI, has found acceptance at the American Embassy, has the sympathy of the German Social Democrats and is warmly approved by newspapers of Rizzoli as well as the *Giornale nuovo* of Indro Montanelli."34

The right lauded Craxi. "I have known Craxi a long time," said the neofascist Raffaele Delfino. "He's a good man, a very good man." Montanelli, a major voice on the right, wrote: "The PSI is blood of our blood." Leaders of the DC right wing, such as Rossi,

---

* While in captivity, Moro wrote fifty-three letters, some made public, some kept private, which attacked many individuals as wishing him dead. The letters, written by him, were clearly forced (various drafts for him to copy were later found). Craxi echoed many of the slanders.

Carenini, Mazzotta, openly supported the Craxian plan, and Rosella quotes Mazzota as planning to create within the DC "a centrist grouping aimed at a political understanding with the PSI." Craxi felt it necessary to issue a disclaimer: "With the PSI becoming stronger, we go left not right."[35]

One of the aims of Socialist maneuvering was the election of a Socialist as president. Craxi reasoned that he could get right-wing support in the DC for an anti-Communist Socialist and that Zaccagnini would have to go along. Delfino told *Panorama* that he and other right-wing politicians inside and outside the DC had already promised Craxi to support such a candidacy. By the middle of June 1978 Craxi had been working for nearly three months on his scheme, and it looked very promising. He had six more months of politicking before the presidential election in December of 1978. With Piccoli as probable chairman of the DC, the election of an anti-Communist president would finish the historic compromise. Following upon the debacle of the French Union of the Left, the defeat of the Italian Communist party would set back Eurocommunism for many years, if not decades.

But the jubilation of the right and of the United States turned out to be premature. The Communist party was not completely helpless. On the morning of June 15, 1978, the PCI informed Prime Minister Andreotti that unless President Giovanni Leone resigned immediately, the PCI would withdraw its support of the government and the government would fall. It was a totally unexpected move; yet, with hindsight, it appeared inevitable. Leone was extremely vulnerable, and the DC couldn't defend him. Scandal after scandal had broken around him, his friends, and his relatives, including the charge that he was involved in the Lockheed scandal.[36]

A book by a well-known journalist, Camilla Cederna, *Giovanni Leone: La carriera di un presidente,* (The career of a president), contained a devastating exposé of Leone's alleged malfeasances in office, exploitation of his position for gain, corruption, venality—the epitome, as it were, of DC corruption. The book had sold 130,000 copies in two months, an enormous circulation for Italy. Then, late in May, the magazine *L'Espresso* charged, with documentation, that Leone had cheated on his tax returns, particularly in regard to the property tax on his palatial million-dollar home known as *Le Rughe* (The Wrinkles). Rome happily dubbed the affair "Wrinklegate."[37]

On the evening of the fifteenth, Leone resigned. He appeared on national television, in the midst of a World Soccer telecast, protesting his innocence—he had been an "honest man" as president, he said*—and announced his resignation. Craxi was caught by surprise.

---

* People thought of Nixon's remark, "Your President is not a crook."

The Communists had not even informed him of their plan. As *Panorama* pointed out, the action cost Craxi "180 days of subtle weaving of intrigues." But Craxi was not finished. Immediately, the right-wing DC deputy, Carenini, speaking for a large group, said: "We will vote for whatever candidate is proposed by Craxi." *Panorama* presciently commented: "The only card of the Communists is to bring about the election of a Socialist candidate who is not loyal to the secretary."[38]

An electoral assembly of 1010 people chooses the Italian president. These include all the deputies and senators, plus delegates from the twenty regions. Voting began on June 29 and went on intermittently for eleven days, with hard bargaining behind the scenes. At the end, Craxi emerged with a pyrrhic victory: he got a Socialist president—*who was completely against Craxi's policy*. Zaccagnini and Andreotti had prevailed in the councils of the DC (Piccoli had backed them in exchange for the post of chairman of the DC) and the new president was a man well known for his support of the Moro-Berlinguer line.

The elected president, Sandro Pertini, was an eighty-two-year-old hero of the resistance, one of the makers of the Italian Constitution, a former president of the Chamber of Deputies, a lifelong Socialist who had often fought Togliatti without ever being anti-Communist. Said one of the leaders of the PCI, Giorgio Amendola (who had been the PCI candidate for president): "With Pertini, I do nothing but fight. . .but always affectionately. . . ."[39] Communist historian Paolo Spriano wrote that "Pertini is a disconcerting Socialist. I hope he will be a disconcerting president. In fact, I am sure he will be."[40]

President Pertini was elected by a record vote of 832 out of 955 electors present—only the ultraright voting against him. His election was popular throughout Italy: some said he was the lay Pope John. He immediately set an example of probity that was not lost on the population. On a private trip to Turin to visit his parents' grave he rejected the air force plane at his disposal and bought a ticket on Alitalia. On arriving at the airport, he insisted on paying instantly for the flowers that a prefect had brought for the grave.[41]

*Sandro Pertini's wife, Carla, set another example. She rejected the role of First Lady, refused to enter the presidential palace, preside at teas, accept the customary presidency of the Red Cross (with an office and two secretaries). She continued her work as a psychologist at the drug-abuse center of Gemelli Polyclinic. "I don't ask Sandro to hold the hands of my patients," she said, "and I don't see why I should hold those of his problems." The president quietly chuckled: "I have always fought for freedom, and I cannot deny it to my wife."*

*Carla Pertini was fifty-seven at the time of her husband's elec-tion. She had been in the resistance (where she met Sandro), she was an activist in the Socialist party, and had worked as one of the editors of* Noi donne, *the organ of the Union of Italian Women (UDI). She was one of the leaders of UDI who had pressed for autonomy. At age fifty-one, she had gone back to school, undertaken postgraduate work in adolescent psychology, and dedicated herself to fighting drugs. A self-reliant, outgoing personality, she doesn't fear being photographed with a long drink in her hand. She laughs at the angry comments of the right attacking her as "the first lady in jeans," and "the feminist* presidentessa," *but writers and teachers applauded her refusal to accept what* Noi donne *had called* il mestiere di donna valigia *("the job of woman-suitcase"). The writer Parise spoke for all: "Here is a true feminism. After the Italy of family and privileges, we finally show an Italy which values persons for their work and not for their position."* *42

The combination of honesty and hard work of the Pertini family has set a badly needed example for all Italians. But the impact of the new president went deeper. Although the presidency is chiefly a ceremo-nial office, it does have three important prerogatives. The president is chief of the armed forces, he issues the call for general elections,† and he picks the prime minister—more precisely, he asks a political leader to form a government acceptable to Parliament. While this power is meaningless when a party has a clear majority in Parliament, the power becomes important when no party has a majority and coalition politics come into play.

No DC president would ever appoint a left prime minister; he would rather call for an "anticipated" election. But Pertini would not hesitate to pick a left prime minister, and, in fact, he was soon to do so. For the first time in postwar history, there was an alternative to DC rule.‡

If the left formed its own government, it would give a rude shock to DC politicians accustomed to "owning" their jobs as fiefs. Each ministry has some two hundred to three hundred high-level jobs, well

* The reference to family and privileges is to the previous president, Leone, whose children and relatives were heavily involved in scandals. The joke in Rome was that the new president should be a widower with no children. The Pertinis have no children, and as far as Carla's involvement in the government goes, Pertini is as good as a widower.

† Elections take place automatically every five years unless a government cannot be formed, in which case the president then calls for "anticipated" elections. He cannot do this, however, in the last six months of his tenure. Leone was forced out eleven days before that period began.

‡ The Communists did not want a left government with a precarious majority. Overcoming the crisis would demand sacrifices from many strata and only a broad government could diminish the inevitable shocks and tensions. However, if the DC refused such a broad government, a left government had become a possibility.

paying, prestigious, and of considerable influence on policies and patronage. The DC would be loath to give them all up: perhaps a half loaf would be better than none. The pressure for a coalition government now went beyond its importance to the welfare of the country: it included the welfare of the political leaders of *Democrazia Cristiana*.

By the end of July 1978, therefore, it seemed as if the Moro-Berlinguer policy was back on track, despite Moro's assassination and Craxi's unavowed defection. Then, on August 6, Pope Paul VI died. Paul had accepted Moro's policy, but it was an open question whether his successor would continue in his path. By the end of the month (August 26) there was a new pope, John Paul I, and the answer was clear from his background and sponsorship: a resounding no!

The election was a tremendous setback for the Moro-Berlinguer strategy. The influence of the Vatican within *Democrazia Cristiana* was decisive. The Communists could counteract Vatican influence among the people, as in fact they had been doing for a long time, but they were nearly helpless within the DC. The right wing would become more powerful and aggressive, wavering elements would undermine the center, the left strength would be eroded as opportunists jumped on the bandwagon of anticommunism. For the third time in six months, the PCI's political line received a grievous wound, which, barring a miracle, would take a long time to heal.

But providence intervened: Thirty-three days after his election John Paul I died. In a surprising *volte-face,* on October 16, an identical conclave elected a cardinal who was practically the opposite of his predecessor. The new pope, John Paul II, is anti-Communist as a matter of course; but he is also a realist. In his very first speech, he said that the Church should steer clear of purely political matters.*

The concept of the historic compromise seemed to be back, but there had been too much erosion within the DC. The right wing was dominant, and Andreotti trimmed his sails accordingly. He began to take important decisions without consultation. He appointed General Alberto Dalla Chiesa to head a special antiterrorist unit. Dalla Chiesa was an arch-conservative, the unit of dubious constitutionality, and the appointment was called a "minor coup d'etat" by the press.[43] Andreotti made several high appointments to nationalized industries, again without consultation.[44] The Communists began to issue warnings (Napolitano in September, Amendola in October), but Andreotti was clearly bent on a provocative course.[45] Then, in December, the DC tried to water down the six-party agreements on agriculture; and, finally, on December 12, Andreotti reneged on a promise to Socialists and Communists to wait six months before entering the European

---

* Pope John Paul II kept his hands off the 1979 elections.

Monetary System:* He signed the treaty with parliamentary authorization.[46]

On January 31, 1979, the PCI withdrew its support, and the government of Giulio Andreotti was out of office. Andreotti tried to form a new government but could not overcome internal DC opposition to the PCI's entry into the cabinet. The PCI would settle for nothing less. Then Pertini asked Ugo La Malfa, leader of the small but influential Republican party.

La Malfa had two alternatives. One was to form a government with five parties, including the Communists and excluding the Christian Democrats. Such a government would guarantee the united opposition of the DC and would be very precarious—his majority would be so slim that a few defections would destroy it. The second alternative was to exclude both the Communists and the Christian Democrats, with the Communists agreeing to support the government in exchange for secondary government positions—undersecretaries to the ministries and so on. Such a government might get a substantial number of votes from left DC deputies and would enable La Malfa to begin the arduous task of cleaning up corruption, eliminating clientism, reducing tax evasion, and so forth.

The key to both alternatives was the agreement of the Socialist party; the Communists were known to favor the second alternative. But Craxi refused to go along.[47] Judging that his party would gain at the expense of both the Communists and the DC, he wanted a national election. On March 2, 1979, after a long discussion with Craxi, La Malfa quit and President Pertini was back at square one. He called for national elections on June 3, 1979.

The campaign was noteworthy for the concerted attack on the Communist party throughout the entire political spectrum, from the extreme right to the extreme left. In some cases, the attack was very subtle. For example, the left-of-center *L'Espresso* published in May, just before the election, a fifteen-page essay on Karl Popper, the German philospher, saying he was practically unknown in Italy because he was a critic of Marxism. The implication was that the PCI's cultural hegemony had censored Popper, and *L'Espresso* was remedying the situation by letting people know the truth.[48] In the same month, the left-of-center *Panorama*, normally critical of the DC, had a long interview with Zaccagnini, giving prominence to his views that after the election the DC and the PSI would form a government. The title was "Hurrah for *demoCraxiana*."[49]

---

* This was a new system, sponsored primarily by Germany, tying in the currencies of the Common Market. Economists such as Luigi Spaventa felt that Italy's adhesion would be disastrous, since the lira was weak. The British had decided to wait six months, and Andreotti promised to do likewise. His unilateral act destroyed any credibility he had; obviously, he did it on purpose.

The attacks on the Communists reinforced each other, and the seeming isolation of the party found its reflection in the polls, which predicted increases in the DC and the PSI votes ranging from 3 to 5 points and a drop in the PCI vote of over 4 points. One of the surprises in the vote was the expectation that the small Radical party would increase its vote by more than 4 points.[50] The Radical party, led by Marco Pannella, was a catchall party of single-issue voters— feminists, environmentalists, soft-drug users, hippies, etc.—and of people disillusioned with the major parties. They tended to be young, and in 1976 they had elected four deputies who acted obstreperously in Parliament, blocking bills, acting rowdy, etc.

I had gone to Italy for the elections, and the morning after, I sent to *The Nation* the following dispatch, which arrived too late for publication:

*Rome, June 4, 1979*
*All the action was in Piazza Navona last night where the Radical party had its election rally. As the night wore on and the returns came in, the crowd of young people grew denser and more abandoned. The polls were proven partly right; the radicals gained and the PCI lost, but neither the DC nor PSI did well.*

*The huge piazza, which the ancient Romans flooded to hold mock naval battles, was like a scene out of a Fellini movie. A warm night, a half-moon peeking over the dome of the Church of Saint Agnes, and, hiding the central fountain, an immense white rectangle, 30 x 70 feet, to show the election returns. On the rectangle, the names of the parties and their showing in 1976.*

*In front of the rectangle was a platform for rock musicians, speakers, and a clutch of young men and women manning the elections returns from the two tall stepladders. On the side, tall tubular scaffolds held lights and TV cameras.*

*The several thousands of young people who jammed the square were cheerful and noisy, but hardly boisterous or rowdy. There wasn't a policeman in sight, and the crowd was remarkably well behaved. By two o'clock, the bulk of the returns were in, and the final results in the morning confirmed the shape of the elections. The Radical party had gone from 1.1 percent of the votes in 1976 to 3.4 percent, gaining fourteen seats in Parliament to add to the four it already had. No other party gained as much. Although the percentage of the vote was small, it was of great significance when tied to other factors, namely a 3 percent drop in total votes compared to 1976 and an unprecedented number of blank ballots—people who expressed their distaste for all parties by handing in a blank ballot. The Radicals had campaigned on a rejection of all parties—a kind of left-wing know-nothingism which clearly struck a responsive chord in the youth of the nation.*

*Yet the claims of several newspapers that Italy had swung to the right cannot be sustained. Although the Communist party was the greatest loser, dropping from 34.4 percent to 30.4 percent, the right-wing parties did not get their votes. The Christian Democrats lost one seat and dropped 0.4 percent, the neofascists dropped from 6.1 percent to 5.3 percent, their votes picked up by the Liberals (really a conservative party) which went from 1.3 percent to 1.9 percent. The Center gained a little, with the Republicans and Social Democrats going from 6.5 to 6.8 percent of the vote.*

*The Socialists held firm, from 9.6 to 9.8 percent and the ultraleft gained a point and a half. In effect the Communist loss went to the Radicals and the ultraleft parties. The indications are clear that the youth is not going to the right but is disgusted with the major parties.*

*The result is a stalemate, very similar to the previous configuration of forces. In a sense, the real losers are the Christian Democrats. They had hoped to cash in on the assassination of Moro and the hatred of terrorism, gain several points, and be able to govern with right-wing allies. Now they have only the alternative of making a center-left government in coalition with the Socialists or patching up a government of national unity by making compromises with the Communist party.*

*An important element of the election was the scrupulous neutrality of the Vatican. In addition, U.S. officials kept quiet. In conclusion it may be said that while Eurocommunism has been battered, it is still very much alive.*

My insight that the DC was the real loser of the election was shared by only one Italian commentator, Giorgio Galli, and this was nearly two months later: "The determinant fact of the elections is the failure of the DC to obtain a majority mandate . . . . the DC has remained fixed between the 38 and 39 percent of the vote which has characterized it since 1963."[51]

Practically all Italian and foreign commentators in the days following the elections were too euphoric at the PCI's loss to think the matter through. Headlines proclaimed the death of *il compromesso storico. Time* magazine exulted: "A stunning defeat," "Hammer and sickle at half-mast," "Eurocommunism in defeat." But as the weeks went by, reality prevailed. The PCI's loss was significant but not crucial: the stalemate between PCI and DC still existed. Although courted, Craxi did not dare join the DC, the Communists passed into opposition, and a patched-up government under Francesco Cossiga was suffered to limp along, since no party wanted a new election. The pre-eminent fact was that the PCI votes had stayed left—in the Radical party and the ultraleft. Moreover, the high abstentions were a warning to the major parties.

In the long run, the loss was salutary for the PCI. It gave weight to the concern of people like Amadeo in Turin, Elena in Naples, Luciana Castellina in Rome. The party had to give more attention to the unemployed; it had to step up its work among the youth; it had to increase education of southerners in the northern plants. At the same time, there were certain plusses: the Vatican had been neutral, the women had held firm, the veteran unionists had been as reliable as ever. Moreover, where the party had worked well, the results were rewarding. The classic case, used by Berlinguer, was the town of Gallipoli in Apulia, where a series of struggles led by the party radicalized the population so that the vote went from 32 percent in 1974 to 40 percent in 1979.*

The following week saw the elections for the first European Parliament. The PCI held its ground, and in some cases, such as Sardinia, advanced two points. The DC lost a point and a half,† the PSI gained a point. The most significant result, however, was not in Italy, but in Germany, where the ruling Social Democratic party (SDP) got only 41 percent of the vote while the German Christian Democrats (CDU) got practically 50 percent.[53] The German DC is much more reactionary than the Italian DC, and the weight in Europe was decidedly to the right: 255 to 155. The European Community is a major issue dividing Eurocommunism: the Italian party seeing an ally in SDP, the French party seeing an enemy. The weakness of the SDP vis-à-vis the German DC has opened up perspectives of collaboration between the PCI and the SDP.

The DC, after its first jubilation over the PCI loss, realized that it had suffered a substantial setback. Many centrists, such as its president, Flaminio Piccoli, saw that a stalemate existed. To underline the dilemma of the DC, the working class staged an enormous political demonstration. It had not been planned as such, although the background was not devoid of politics. In expectation of a major political defeat, and a resurgence of the DC to govern without restraints, many of the largest corporations had been deliberately dragging their feet on negotiating new contracts. The exasperated unions, well before the elections, had called for a general strike for June 19, a strike designed to deal with economic issues.

The results of the election turned the strike into a demonstration of political resistance. The strike was extremely successful and all

---

* The trend has continued. In the partial municipal elections of October 14, 1979, which included Gallipoli, the PCI got 46 percent of the vote.[52]

† Of great pleasure to the left was the defeat of Mario Scelba of the DC, the hated former minister of the interior and organizer of the *Celere*.

major cities had huge demonstrations. The largest was reserved for Rome, on June 22, 1979.

*Once again, a year and a half later, I found myself on a bus going to the Cathedral of San Giovanni and its twin piazzas. Once again I walked and mingled with the crowd and couldn't help comparing the atmosphere and situation with the demonstration of December 1977. So much had happened in the intervening twenty months—deaths and assassinations and a deepening world recession. Yet this crowd was much more cheerful and outgoing than the previous one, which had been grimmer and more determined. Perhaps it was the summer-time that did it . . . . perhaps the tens of thousands of women and children interspersed in the crowd\*—a huge, sprawling, never-ending mass of people, estimated at close to four hundred thousand persons.*

*It was a carnival atmosphere, with thousands of drums made of five-gallon cans, hundreds of banners and streamers, and one four-foot bell mounted on wheels that tolled a deep, throaty bong! bong! There were clowns and a couple of amateur acrobats. There were food stands, soft drinks, and beer. There were pennons with the unions initials and so many with hammer and sickle that it looked like the revolution had won.*

*It was so unexpected, this joy and abandon, this sense of confidence and power, that the one ever-present slogan struck me not as defiant but as matter-of-fact assertive:* PADRONI: IL 3 GIUGNO NON CI TORNA INDIETRO! *(Bosses: The 3rd of June doesn't take us backwards!) Leaders of the three federations spoke, and Luciano Lama, of the CGIL, voiced the common feeling:* "Fate bene i vostri conti signori; questa è la classe operaia con cui avete a fare." *A free translation is:* "Watch your step, masters; you're dealing with the entire working class." *What was so astounding for an American was to see how instinctively the unions, which were mingled Catholic, Socialist, Communists, and what not, identified themselves with the PCI; how they took it for granted that a loss of votes by the PCI might tempt employers to adventurist attacks on their workers.*

The lesson was not lost on the DC. As the months went by, even right-wing leaders of the DC began to seek PCI support of a govern-ment of *la maggioranza*, but that game was over. The PCI was busy setting its house in order. In the second half of 1979 there were many discussions within the party. They climaxed in a meeting of the

\* One reason was lack of fear of *autonomi* attacks both because of the security by the trade unions marshals and because of the discrediting of the *autonomi*.

Central Committee on November 14–16, 1979. The highest body of the PCI reaffirmed the strategy of *il compromesso storico* and considered the results of the June elections as an electoral setback rather than a political defeat. An ample debate set the two major lines of struggle in the coming months: an aggressive policy of aiding the unemployed, the pensioners, and the poorer sectors of the population and a vigorous fight for peace and disarmament around the issue of new U.S. missiles in Europe. The goal of the struggles is to renew and govern the country through the mobilization of the people.[54]

Several conferences were projected from the Central Committee meeting—one for Fiat workers, to be held in Turin in January 1980; one against the Mafia in Palermo, in late November 1979; one on the southern question, to be held in Bari in early December 1979. The Bari conference was particularly noteworthy for the attendance of Berlinguer, who emphasized the necessity of forcing the government to spend sums already appropriated by Parliament for various projects for the South. He also made a major appeal for unity of Catholics, Socialists, and Communists on the deployment of American missiles in Europe.[55]

The PCI position on the missiles is very clear: there should be negotiations with the USSR before any decision is made. It is a position which has great resonance in Italy, where one third of the missiles are to be deployed. In Sardinia already, all parties have gone on record against the missiles.[56] The PCI position also has a strong appeal to Catholic organizations, such as ACLI and *Mani Tese* (Outstretched Hands). Even bitterly anti-Communist groups, such as *Azione Cattolica* and *Comunione e Liberazione* took positions parallel to the PCI. It was known that Pope John Paul II was in favor of prior negotiations, and the Church mobilized in many areas for demonstrative "vigils for peace."[57]

However, on December 6, 1979, Prime Minister Cossiga forced through Parliament a motion approving the missiles, although nearly half the deputies were against it. Once again, as in the Italian adherence to SME (European Monetary System) a year before, the DC administration had disregarded the widespread opposition in the country. Cossiga squeezed through only by the support of the Craxian wing of the Socialist party, which was itself a minority within the PSI on this issue.[58] The Italian decision was of great importance to the American strategy, which succeeded in getting an endorsement of its proposals at the NATO meeting in Brussels, December 12, 1979, despite the strong reservations of the Dutch and the Belgians: "The decision was endorsed only after sharp argument and dilution of the prepared communique."[59] Obviously, had the Italians voted agains͏ᵗ the Americans, there would have been a further dilution of the proposals. However, the question of the deployment of the missiles remains alive and will profoundly affect Italian politics in the next four years (the time needed for the deployment).

All in all, as January 1, 1980, ushered in a new decade, it seemed as if Eurocommunism in general and the PCI in particular had received such serious wounds that a long recuperation would be required. *The Economist* of London, perhaps the ablest conservative journal in the English-speaking world, rang out the decade in its issue of December 29, 1979, with a contemptuous dismissal: Eurocommunists were opting for multiparty pluralism but "few people believe them."

Yet within a month the situation had dramatically altered, and the PCI was closer to power than it had ever been. The catalyst was the Soviet invasion of Afghanistan, which triggered a sharp cooling of detente and a warming-up of a neo-Cold War. The consequences in Italian politics were unexpected, and to a high degree ironical.

It had been received wisdom, to which the PCI had subscribed, that a renewed Cold War would freeze the PCI's prospects and destroy Eurocommunism. Indeed, as Marchais and the PCF supported the Soviet invasion, *The Economist* gloated over the demise of Eurocommunism. In the issue of January 12, 1980, the table of contents said: "GOING . . . GOING . . . Eurocommunists on the Way Out (p. 51)." On page 51 a major article led off the section on Europe with the title, "The Case of the Vanishing Eurocommunists," with the opening sentence: "An Afghan sword has hacked Eurocommunism in two."[60] But the dramatic glee was premature. The political consequences in Italy were exactly the reverse of those expected. Both Carrillo and Berlinguer denounced the invasion. *L'Unità,* in a front-page editorial, thundered that the invasion violated "some of the best traditions of the workers' movements; the defense and respect of national independence and sovereignty, the inexportability of revolutions, the stubborn search for peaceful and political solutions instead of military ones. . . . [The invasion brings] new elements of tension and alarm into a world situation which is already explosive enough."[61]

The editorial also attacked previous American policies for creating the climate of confrontation, and in a subsequent detailed analysis Berlinguer listed those policies: the Congressional attacks on Salt II, the exclusion of the USSR from Middle East solutions, the creation of an American fleet in the Indian Ocean, the placing of new missiles in Europe, the thesis of Brzezinski that to stimulate the armaments race was a way to squeeze the socialist world economically.[62] Nevertheless, said Berlinguer, the US policies did not excuse the Soviet invasion. Berlinguer made it clear that the PCI line was not one of neutrality or equidistance from the two superpowers, a line of "not taking sides"; on the contrary, the PCI line was an active one of supporting European interests, in the first place the interests of peace. He scorned the idea that the PCI's condemnation of the Soviet invasion was a ploy to enter the government.

Except for a few diehards, most commentators took Berlinguer at his word, and his speech made a profound impression, not because the PCI line was new, but because the PCI's position on an issue of such importance to the USSR convinced centrists of the autonomy of the PCI in foreign affairs. Berlinguer's insistence on the defense of European interests touched deep chords among his countrymen. While there is great affection in Italy for "the American way of life," there is no great admiration of American foreign policy. It is seen as bumbling, naive, knee-jerking in its responses; the left sees it as brutal, the right as "soft" and muddled. The concept of an autonomous Europe has great attraction.

Even before Berlinguer's speech, the PCI position on the Soviet invasion had given Prime Minister Cossiga a powerful talking point when he visited Washington, D.C., in late January. According to Eugenio Scalfari, editor of *La Repubblica,* Cossiga made it clear to President Carter that Italy could not be governed without the PCI.[63]

Behind Cossiga's initiative was the pressure of Italian events. The DC had tried hard to involve the Socialists in a new center-left government. Craxi was willing, but the price was his becoming prime minister. While the DC vacillated, that option was closed within the PSI by Craxi's support of the American missile proposals.[64] The other major event was the failure of the Fiat antiworker offensive and the PCI's counterattack both on the terrorist issue in Turin and on the economic problems of Fiat (discussed in Chapter 7).

Suddenly, despite Afghanistan, it seemed possible that the PCI might enter the government, depending on the results of the DC Congress in Rome, February 16, 1980. There was a moment of euphoria when right-wing DC leaders said they had dropped, in principle, their veto on PCI participation. "The startling announcement," said a liberal commentator, "may result in a serious dicussion on the birth of a government of national unity."[65] Others saw the move as a disarming feint, and so it was.

At the Congress, the right coalesced uneasily with part of the center. The left and center-left coalition of Zaccagnini, Andreotti, and Cossiga had 42 percent of the delegates plus the overwhelming support of the galleries, though visitors' tickets had been distributed proportionately to members of the various currents of the DC. The percentage among the delegates (mostly functionaries) was therefore very close to that among the membership shown in the Doxa poll.[66] The right and center-right coalition got 57 percent, but it was a tenuous union of disparate elements that could not even agree on a joint resolution, but agreed to pass each other's resolutions (three of them) with a single identical preamble.[67] The preamble categorically opposed any collaboration with the PCI at government level. Commented Fausto De Luca in an article, "Moro è rimasto senza eredi [Moro is without heirs]": ". . . anti-*morotei* DC has gone back to its original calling, which is anticommunism, and has recomposed a majority including even men of the extreme right such as De Carolis. . . ."[68]

The so-called *preambolisti* dominated the new National Executive which in March elected the vacillating Flaminio Piccoli as DC secretary, thus crowning his maneuvering after Moro's assassination. The Communist line had suffered a sharp setback, with two important caveats. One, to capture some centrists, the extreme right had to drop "in principle" its veto on the PCI. Two, the conflict within the DC was so virulent that the specter of a split arose. DC minister of defense Adolfo Sarti said: "In these days, for the first time, I have seen the germs of a schism within the DC. It is a sinister omen which I try to forget."[69] Right-wing intransigeance had solidified an opposition of 42 percent, clarifying many issues. In the past, many DC politicians had looked on PCI collaboration as a way of holding on to jobs and patronage. Now they realized that what was at stake was the future of the country. As Zaccagnini said bitterly to the jubilant right-wing delegates: "You people are going to paralyze democracy."[70]

On March 19 the PSI withdrew its support of the government and Cossiga resigned.[71] The *preambolisti* expected to form the government, but President Pertini neatly blocked them by asking Cossiga (of the 42 percent minority) to try again. Cossiga approached the Socialists and the Republicans, who agreed.[72] The *preambolisti* were trapped; they could not easily disown a major DC figure—Piccoli wouldn't go along—and the new government was formed, promptly dubbed Cossiga *bis* by the Romans. The inability of the right wing to prevent Cossiga *bis* turned their success at the Congress into something of a pyrrhic victory. Pietro Longo, secretary of the excluded Social Democrats (PSDI), underlined the ambiguity of Cassiga *bis*. "It is," he said, "A bridge-government to the historic compromise."[73]

There may have been ambiguity in Cossiga; there was none among the *preambolisti*. Donat Cattin began an iron-fisted campaign for the June local elections with a ferocious attack on the PCI on the issue of terrorism. The PCI, he said, was responsible because of its revolutionary ideology—the terrorist leaders were its children. This was pure demagogy, since many leaders, like Renato Curcio, founder of the Red Brigades, were Catholic fanatics and since the PCI had thrown all its weight into the fight against terrorism. Moreover, it was irresponsible since it ruptured national unity on the issue. It was, however, a powerful weapon, unwittingly aided by the Vatican.* The polls predicted an increase in the DC vote, a sharp drop for the PCI, and losses of major cities such as Naples and Turin governed by the left.[74]

The elections were to take place June 8 and 9. Some two weeks before hand, a bombshell exploded: The son of Donat Cattin, Marco, was identified as a terrorist and a fugitive. Further, his father had helped him escape abroad after a warning from Cossiga. While all Italians, including Communists, excused the paternal act, few excused Cossiga or Donat Cattin's lies about his involvement.[75] The June elections took place in this context, and the results were hardly pleasing to the DC. While it gained a point and a half over the 1975 local elections, and the PCI lost two points, the Socialists gained one point, and the left coalition lost none of the major cities (in Turin the PCI gained 2 points and the PSI 4; in Bologna the increases were 1 and 2 points respectively).

More important, given the fact that the DC had made anti-communism *the* issue of the campaign, nearly all the commentators argued that the significant comparison was with June 1979. Here the DC had lost ground, 1.3 points. The PCI had held, with increases in the north and a drop in the south, for a total drop of 0.3, roughly holding their own. The PSI had made the greatest gains, 2.8 points.[76] Craxi had emerged triumphant, and it was freely predicted he would purge his left opponents at an extraordinary party Congress in 1981.[77]

The most ominous sign was the growth of abstentions and blank ballots from 11 percent in 1975 to 13.4 percent in 1979 to 17.5 percent in 1980. In a country where voting had reached as high as 95 percent, this was a sign of deep disaffection with the political system. Furthermore, the losses of the DC went to the extreme right—the neofascist MSI and the rightest PLI. Should the trend continue, the creeping paralysis of the democratic process, already underlined by Zaccagnini, bodes ill for the future of Italy.[78]

Overall, a stalemate continued. The PCI—and Eurocommunism—were not flourishing in mid-1980, but they were hardly moribund. What was significant is that, given the swing to the right in Europe, and given the traumatic vicissitudes of 1978–1980, the PCI and its ideas were holding their own. Eurocommunism was here to stay.

* See page 92 above. The word "unwittingly" not an obeissance to the Vatican, but the recognition of a coincidence. The Vatican strategy (and the editorial in *La Civiltà cattolica*) had been precipitated by the sociological discussions on terrorism and decided upon well in advance of Donat Cattin's campaign.

# PART THREE

# Perspectives
# of Eurocommunism

# CHAPTER 13

# Theories and Realities

LENIN'S MAXIM, "There can be no revolutionary movement without a revolutionary theory," has done considerable harm to human progress. Meant as a corrective to a vulgar pragmatism, it has overemphasized the role of theory, fostered doctrinal hairsplitting, and, twisted by Stalin, legitimized a sterile catechism. Theory is invaluable, a compass in the exploration of the unknown, a major tool for new discoveries. This is readily apparent in the physical sciences, but it holds true in all fields of knowledge: Aristotle, Adam Smith, and Marx are as important as Archimedes, Copernicus, and Darwin. But the Marxist founders, while insisting on the unity of theory and practice, also asserted the primacy of practice. It seems sound Marxism to temper Lenin with Goethe: "Gray is all theory, but green is the tree of life."

Marxism has not been the least effective of social theories, witness the momentous revolutions it has inspired and guided in our century. Yet it hardly guarantees omniscience. Marxists of the caliber of Lenin and Trotsky thought the fledgling Soviet regime could not long survive the unremitting hostility of the capitalist world, but it did. Capitalist complicity gave the fascists a free hand in Spain. This policy culminated in the dismemberment of Czechoslovakia at Munich in 1938, opening Hitler's road to the East. What Marxist (or other) historian could have predicted then that within three years the greatest colonial empire and the most powerful capitalist nation would unite with the only socialist power to bring down Hitler and his allies? Who would have thought that the imperialist horse would be forced to drink the waters of socialist survival?

Who could have predicted the vertiginous dismantling of the colonial world? On Christmas Day in the year of Munich, this writer was the dinner guest of Jawarhalal Nehru in Allahabad. We spoke at length of the struggle for Indian independence. No one could have persuaded us that evening that India would be free within a decade, and neither of us, as Marxists, would have accepted the idea that her freedom could be achieved without a bloody Anglo-Indian clash. History is tricky, and the perspectives of Eurocommunism are offered with a great deal of trepidation.

The emergence of Eurocommunism as a major current of Marxist theory and practice has precipitated an impressive amount of discussion throughout the world. In the decade of the seventies a small library of books, monographs, and articles was written, testimony to its vitality and importance. Criticisms from the right have often been self-serving, considering the new current a Machiavellian ploy by Moscow to lull the West into inactivity. These critics tend to be the same people who for years considered the Sino-Soviet conflict a put-up job to disarm the West. For them, Eurocommunism is a Trojan Horse.

In Italy, more sophisticated conservatives, such as Professors Augusto Del Noce and Adriano Blausola, challenge not the sincerity, but the analysis, of the PCI. They argue that once in the government, the austerity of the Eurocommunists will alienate large strata of the population and they will be driven to coercive measures. At this juncture, right-wing critics are in ironic consonance with left-wing critics, such as the editors of *Monthly Review* or Ernest Mandel, whose book *From Stalinism to Eurocommunism* is such a sustained and cogent attack on Eurocommunism as to pre-empt the field for some time. A summary is given by Mandel in the Winter 1979 issue of *Marxist Perspectives*, and this writer reviewed the book in the October 1979 issue of *Monthly Review*.

Mandel's arguments, by their sobriety and scholarship, provide an excellent framework for the theoretical perspectives of Eurocommunism. They are at once political, economic, and military, although Mandel treats the military aspects too lightly. Only the last page and a half is devoted to this problem, less than one percent of his 220 pages. His italicized contention is that it would be *"politically impossible"* for the United States to intervene militarily if there were a real revolution in Italy. But his premises are flawed; he projects "a repetition of a Vietnam-style adventure" (p. 219), whereas a more fruitful analogy is to the Spanish Civil War. In a destabilized Italy, wracked by terrorism, strikes, and violence, a coup by the military is not a paranoid fear of the PCI. The Italian Communists are confident that an aroused population would defeat the neofascists, just as the Spanish Republic would have defeated Franco but for outside intervention. This began with Mussolini's airlift of the Moroccan troops, then Hitler's Condor Legion, the 150,000 Black Shirt troops and the embargo of arms to the Republic by the capitalist powers. How can one be sure that the United States would find it "politically impossible" to intervene surreptitiously and by proxy, or even directly? Would the Soviet Union meekly stand by? Would there not be a danger of a thermonuclear confrontation? Even if the chances were not high, should responsible revolutionaries disregard the risk? Mandel pooh-poohs the danger of war, but his views are perilously close to Mao's assessment of the U.S. as a paper tiger. Right or wrong, no policy should be based on their assumptions. Although revolutionary caution inherently gives the U.S. a margin of international "blackmail," that margin can be reduced by skillful tactics.

On politics, Mandel charges that Eurocommunists deny the *class* nature of the state (p. 167); that the top bureaucrats "constitute the famous 'state machine' which . . . the working class must smash" (p. 155); asserts the "tendential, and in the long run, irreconcilable conflict between the representative institutions of *indirect democracy* [e.g., Parliament] and the manifestations and institutions of *direct democracy*." (p. 163) He dismisses cultural hegemony as a myth: "To believe that an educational system in a bourgeois state can be dominated by Marxism is to credit fairy tales." (p. 204)

His dismissal of cultural hegemony is a clear example of the divergence between Mandel's theories and the realities of the world around him. In Italy today there are only two dominant philosophies, the Marxist and the Catholic. Marxist ideology suffuses the society; Marxist writings permeate it. The majority of active students are Marxists, whether PCI or PSI members or sympathizers, or to the left of the party. So, too, with a substantial number of the teachers at all levels, including two of my relatives in Rome—one in an elementary school, the other in a secondary school. They are devout Catholics and vote DC, but both work with PCI members, respect them, and listen to them. One out of three people votes PCI; together with other left groups the proportion is almost one out of two. Frattochie does not teach the Bible, but every Catholic university and college has courses on Marxism.

The rest of Mandel's political arguments are also vulnerable. The dichotomy he presents between indirect and direct democracy is untenable in a Marxist analysis. Marx, Engels, Lenin, all stressed repeatedly that both roads should be used according to circumstances. Rosa Luxemburg wrote at length on the importance of bolstering parliamentary activities with extraparliamentary measures, and vice-versa, which is precisely what Eurocommunists do. There is a flowering of direct democracy in Italy. The factory councils and the neighborhood councils are open to everyone, irrespective of affiliations to unions or parties. They are "soviets" in the strictest sense of the word. As Luciano Gruppi and Pietro Ingrao have pointed out, Parliament itself can play a progressive role against the executive. Mandel qualifies his position by saying that the two are irreconcilable "in the long run," but this is a rhetorical cop-out. We are dealing with current issues, and as the Keynesian cliché has it, in the long run we are all dead.

Mandel's restriction of the "state machine" to the top hierarchs is curious analysis for a Marxist. A bureaucracy, like the army or the Catholic Church, is a whole entity in the body politic. It is true that the top hierarchs ordinarily make policy and control the whole, but this condition disintegrates with the growth of class consciousness. This is one aspect of "revolutionary situations"; this is what revolutions are all about. When the mass of the underlings, or a substantial portion, is class conscious and organized, the top echelons are isolated—they hang in space. This erosion is taking place in Italy, and Mandel's premise that Eurocommunists deny the *class* basis of society is contradicted by the PCI's daily actions.

Eurocommunists have stated repeatedly that no one can wish away the class struggle. They are acutely conscious of classes and have been the most meticulous students of what constitutes a class and its subdivisions. This research is basic to their political strategy, which seeks alliances with other groups. If they don't know who is who from a class standpoint, how can they work politically? Mandel may not like what Eurocommunists do, but one must grant that they know what they are doing.

On economics, Mandel is on stronger ground, but his arguments are still impaired by his polemical approach. He argues that so long as capitalist relations of production exist, every Eurocommunist reform—nationalization, taxation, control of investments, and prevention of the flight of capital—can only strengthen the existing capitalist structure. This is true only *if the capitalists are in control.* A reform such as nationalization is a two-edged sword; it can be used against capitalists as well as against workers. It depends on who benefits from the nationalized industry. You can nationalize coal or steel as the Labour government did in England, sell the product cheap to the auto manufacturers, and let the taxpayers foot the deficits. That's what the DC has done in Italy for thirty years.

In the modern world, there is an increasing necessity for the state to intervene in the economy. The interface between politics and economics becomes ever more shadowy; who controls the state is as important as who controls the economy. Here Mandel begs the question, writing: "The function of the bourgeois state . . . is to guarantee capitalist property, the valorization of capital, and the production of surplus-value." (p. 161) Who can disagree? But if the state is no longer fully controlled by capitalists, if there is in it a hard working-class component—a kind of dual power—then, *irrespective of relations of production,* in the short run, the state *can* control the economy and modify that economy. In the long run, politics and economics must come together, but the long run is made up of short runs.

Mandel is particularly scathing on the PCI program of "salvaging the economy" of Italy. Since the PCI agrees that the Italian economy must function within an international capitalist market (pp. 135–137), then it follows that salvaging the economy means salvaging capitalism (p. 145). The first part of this argument is his most telling theoretical argument. Moreover, there is no evidence to dispute it, since no Eurocommunist economy is functioning as yet within the international order. But there are speculative considerations of some weight, and they will be examined later.

On the second part, however, there are hard facts that cast doubt on Mandel's assertion. If, for example, co-operatives such as the Fratelio co-op in Sicily spread to the extent that Italy no longer imports meat, this would be a tremendous step in salvaging the economy. One may well ask: If the hard currency saved is used to modernize the nationalized steel industry and the energy complex, would this strengthen capitalism in Italy? With the commanding heights of energy, food, and steel controlled by a government in which workers have real power (and in food, direct power), what would happen to the system? Who would call the tune: the Agnellis and other private employers, or the working class? Bruno Trentin thinks the working class; Mandel says this "perspective is a utopian dream. The least one can say is that the verdict of history pleads in favor of our thesis, and not in favor of that of Eurocommunism." (p. 172) But the past is prelude; as far as Eurocommunism is concerned, the jury is still out, deliberating. The verdict is not in.

The issue of "salvaging the economy" is another clear example of the divergence of Mandel's theory from reality. He argues that presenting a *class* interest as a *national* interest has nothing to do with Marxism:

The ideology of the "general interest," of the 'fate of the nation' which must be of primary concern (Berlinguer uses both phrases again and again in the speeches cited), is obviously incompatible with the worn out theory of the 19th century lion of the British Museum that there is an *irreconcilable* conflict of interest between capital and labor, between the bourgeoisie and the proletariat in each capitalist country. (p. 129)

Sarcasm aside, Mandel says this is the classic mystification of capitalists, to identify their good with the common good, and that Eurocommunists are using the same deceit to disorient workers: "a mixture of naiveté, cynicism and insolence." (p. 145) Undoubtedly, mystification has been the purpose in bourgeois usage of "the national interest." But when the working class and its allies—the overwhelming majority of the population—talk about a "national interest" which does indeed correspond to their *class* interests, that is no longer a trick but a truism.

Furthermore, this truism is *the most significant political fact* in Italy today. For the first time since the French Revolution, the left is recognized by a majority of the population as a defender of the nation *tout court*. This is an aspect of the cultural hegemony which Mandel equates with "fairy tales." Mandel surely knows what is happening in Italy today, but will not accept the revolutionary implications of the training of cadres, party members, and voters in self-government. The profound influence of this process on the mass of people, including the personnel of the coercive structures of the state, is disintegrating the domination of the higher echelons which Mandel mistakenly identifies as "the state machine."

In the final chapter, "The Strategy of Eurocommunism," Mandel goes for the jugular, that is, to "prove" that Eurocommunism is the same as the German revisionism of Karl Kautsky and Eduard Bernstein, which Lenin mercilessly exposed. For a Marxist theoretician there could be no more devastating, or conclusive, blow. The strategy of Eurocommunism, he says, is the same as the strategy of "attrition" advocated by Kautsky as opposed to the strategy of assault—what Ralph Miliband calls the "insurrectionary politics" of Lenin. This is the same distinction Gramsci made between the "war of position" and the "war of maneuver," and since he favored the first strategy the Eurocommunists claim him as a precursor. Not so, says Mandel, Gramsci was a Leninist; for him the war of position was only a *preparatory* step to insurrection.

Mandel imputes to Eurocommunists Kautsky's view "in which the power of the bourgeoisie is represented as a fortress, standing *outside* the social body." This image, says Mandel, is "profoundly erroneous and mechanistic" because capitalism is more than that; "Capitalism commands innumerable machine-gun nests stationed around its 'fortress,' within the very social body that is supposed to be besieging it. These defenses permit no lasting assemblies [of the workers] or sieges of long duration." (p. 191)

Any attempt to circumvent those defenses by attacking them one by one would be self-defeating because such an attack would evoke "precisely the inexorable, head-on test of strength the strategy was designed to avert in the first place." (p. 192)

This image of a besieged fortress was analyzed by Gilles Martinet in *La Conquête des pouvoirs,* a book which Mandel rejects, though he considers it "the most coherent and sophisticated presentation of the 'attrition strategy' yet produced." (p. 193n.) The book has been used by others, notably the editors of *Monthly Review,* to demonstrate why the attrition strategy will not work. Even if the fortress is breached here and there, the bourgeoisie always has time to recuperate and repair the breeches.

The metaphor has the weakness of all metaphors: they illuminate but settle nothing. But at this pedagogical level, the book can be used *against* Mandel's position. For the Italian Communists have been capturing machine-gun nests without, so far, provoking a head-on collision. Furthermore, and crucial, the Eurocommunist strategy is specifically designed to insure that the eventual breaches *cannot be repaired.* The PCI is undermining those conditions which allow the ruling class to recuperate: in Martinet's words, "force of habit, respect for established heirarchy, the influence of traditional ideas." As we have tried to show in Part 2, this erosion of old structures is an ongoing and subverting process in Italy.

Despite this writer's disagreements with Mandel's theories, his book has two unique merits. First, particularly with regard to Italy, it constitutes an early warning of the pitfalls, dangers, and dilemmas that lie ahead for the PCI—witness the electoral setback of June 1979. The second merit lies within the scope of international politics, where Mandel's polemical tone softens and his dogmatism wanes.

On a global scale, Mandel sees Eurocommunism as a dialectical process which is at once the fruition and the subversion of Stalinism: counterrevolutionary within the imperialist world, progressive in the socialist world. In a chapter, "The Three Faces of Eurocommunism," he examines this movement vis-à-vis the imperialist bourgeoisie, the Soviet bureaucracy and the West European working class. In its first aspect, "Eurocommunism represents a codification of . . . a policy of ever closer collaboration with their own bourgeoisie . . . .The counterrevolutionary role of the Communist party leadership had already been pre-figured in Republican Spain in 1936–38. . . .Under these conditions [of present prerevolutionary crisis] it marks a sharper and more open class betrayal than in the past." (pp. 42–45)

Under the second aspect, there is "the fear and hostility of the Kremlin. In East Europe and the USSR the statements of the Eurocommunists in favor of political pluralism and democratic freedoms are avidly received *not* because they strengthen capitalism . . . but because they are seen as an alternative to the present political rule. . . . Therein lies the great objective explosive potential of Eurocommunism from the standpoint of the Kremlin." (p. 48)

Under the third aspect, "the dynamics of Eurocommunism undoubtedly widen the *field of workers' democracy*. . . . In place of a series of solidified dogmas, we now increasingly find critical questions." (p. 54) This freedom of thought undermines neo-Stalinism in the West and is useful to revolutionaries in all countries because it clears the way: "Eurocommunist strategy is doomed to failure. . . .it is but a way station. For real Communists there is no other road than Leninism, the road of the Fourth International." (p. 56)

While disagreeing with the first aspect, I find the second and third compelling. However, the combination of all three poses a real dilemma for Mandel: If Eurocommunism is indeed a cover for class collaboration, why does the bourgeoisie in each country fight it so tenaciously? If it is no danger to capitalism in the West, and if it undermines the Kremlin's control of its own population and its satellites, why does the United States fight it so ferociously? Why do imperialists use Social Democracy everywhere to eviscerate Eurocommunism?

Mandel's answer is that the bourgeoisie does not fear Eurocommunist leadership or ideology; it fears the masses whose expectations are being raised by class struggle rhetoric. Frustrated, the masses will sweep aside the Eurocommunist pied pipers and turn to real revolutionary leadership—the Fourth International. The weakness of this explanation is that it assumes Eurocommunist leaders are not very bright—which clearly is not the case. Or that they don't know the consequences of their actions—again highly debatable. It is they, the Eurocommunist leaders and theoreticians, who are devising diversified and innovative approaches to the masses, raising the class consciousness of the workers, strengthening unions, encouraging feminist and ecological movements, fostering mass actions for the unemployed, the students, the pensioners, promoting soviets in factories and neighborhoods, as well as massive electoral politics in a way which would have delighted Rosa Luxemburg and Lenin.

Are the ruling groups similarly unintelligent? For they do not believe that Eurocommunism is like Social Democracy. They have allowed Social Democrats into government in England, France, and Italy with hardly a quiver of their purse strings. But they are adamant against Eurocommunism: they believe it "supports" capitalism in the way of a hangman's noose. Agnelli is fighting the PCI and the workers' movement with all the skill and power at his disposal, as proven by his recent offensive against Fiat workers and their unions. Agnelli states bluntly: "We are faced with the attempt of new social forces to assert their hegemony. The stakes are high for all concerned."

Henry Kissinger may be despicable, but he is not stupid. He sees the danger of Eurocommunism to the system which he holds dear, and which has given him power and riches. He went out of his way to do a TV program attacking Eurocommunism when the attack would hurt the PCI electorally. And if John Paul II, who is hardly pro-Communist, should turn out to be tolerant toward Eurocommunism, it is not because he thinks Eurocommunism will strengthen an unjust economic order that he despairs of, but because it shakes Soviet controls over East European countries, helps to liberalize them, and offers the hope of a more just economic order.

On Mandel's own showing, he should give Eurocommunism a chance. He admits it is widening the field of workers' democracy and undermining bureaucracies, east and west. So why not go one step further and take Agnelli and the PCI at face value? Why not take a Copernican view and see an obvious relationship of forces rather than an intricate Ptolemaic view of tortuous epicycles within epicycles?

Mandel's references to the Fourth International provide at least a partial answer. This writer sees Eurocommunism as the fruition of Marx, Lenin, and Gramsci; Mandel sees it as the end product of the Stalinist concept of "socialism in one country":

> Soviet "national messianism" [Trotsky's phrase]. . .was to lead to a proliferation of "national communisms." *In this sense, the threads of Eurocommunism were woven into the future of the world communist movement from the very moment the theory of "socialism in one country" was adopted.* Trotsky, with his prophetic genius, understood this and proclaimed it from the outset. . . (p. 16; Mandel's italics).

Mandel is a leading exponent of Trotskyism. It is no disrespect to Trotsky to say of him that he was as dogmatic as any Marxist of his generation. His framework has become a straitjacket which hampers Mandel's thought. Mandel, however, is gracious and generous to his opponents. Dealing with Rudolf Bahro, the East German dissenter who wrote *The Alternative,* he calls it "the most important theoretical work to come out of the countries that have abolished capitalism since Leon Trotsky's *The Revolution Betrayed.*" (p. 100) This is generous praise, especially since the book tends to support Eurocommunist concepts. Mandel adds a gentle rebuke in words that might apply to himself:

> Preconceived ideas, prejudices, and false consciousness have an implacable logic, even (or especially) for a major theoretician like Bahro. The demon of false systemization lurks quietly behind the angel of necessary systemization. (p. 117)

Irrespective of theoretical considerations, events in the decade of the eighties will go far to prove or disapprove the validity of Eurocommunism, and Italy will unquestionably be the major testing ground. Assuming, which seems probable, that the Communists will become part of the Italian government during this decade, the key questions are: Can that government survive, and can it implement the PCI programs?

Mandel's forebodings on economic matters are well grounded. The Italian economy is export-oriented, depending on raw materials from abroad. It is peculiarly vulnerable to a capitalist economic boycott, and this writer would certainly agree that if it were to take place, the Eurocommunist experiment would be strangled at birth. Such a boycott was organized by the United States against Cuba, but Soviet economic support ($1 million a day) enabled that country to weather the worst economic impact, and the capitalist boycott slowly unravelled—though the United States still maintains one. But the Italian economy is much larger than the Cuban, and it is doubtful that the Soviet Union, even if it wanted to, could afford the cost of wholly supporting it.

This writer does not believe that the United States can mount an effective boycott of a DC-PCI-PSI government in Italy. While critics such as Mandel stress that Italy is part of a world-wide capitalist economy, the situation is in reality more complex and differentiated. There is a *commercial* world-market economy, heavily influenced, *but not controlled*, by the capitalist world. The socialist world, the third world and the capitalist world all trade with each other, including transfers of capital. These terms of trade may be unequal but they are not always determined by the capitalist world. Oil is an obvious case in point. Socialist states have a great deal to say about the terms of their trade. Even where the capitalist world invests in socialist states, as when Agnelli built a Fiat factory in the USSR, their investments are subject to conditions established by mutual agreement. The commercial competition within the capitalist world gives an area of maneuver to a Eurocommunist economy. For example, a Japanese auto company, Nissan, has sought an agreement to combine with the Italian Alfa-Romeo, controlled by the government. Fiat has fought the agreement; the PCI has supported it.

When we move from commerce to production, the degree of economic autonomy is even sharper. The socialist countries control their own production as substantially as do the capitalist countries. Third world countries have less autonomy, but the trend is all toward more economic independence. The bulk of socialist countries favor Eurocommunism, and even if the Soviet Union was hostile, China, Yugoslavia, Romania, and probably Hungary would support a new Italian government both politically and economically. When I was in

Belgrade and Bucharest in the winter of 1977–78, I found that economic studies were being made based on such an eventuality. Support would also come from third world countries, as I found out in Malta.

*I went to Malta in December 1977 full of the nostalgic romanticism of my childhood nourished by tales of corsairs and the Knights of Malta. The island did not disappoint me: the huge fortifications of Valletta harbor rise up tier on tier, menacing and awesome. The amount of human toil they embody is staggering. Malta is a small island, about a third the area of New York City, with a population of three hundred thousand. From any point on the island, one can see the blue sea, shimmering to the horizon.*

*Malta is at the center of the Mediterranean, part way between Sicily and Tunisia, and the Mediterranean is the cradle of western civilization. With the possible exception of Rome, no place is so steeped in the history of western culture. Two books by Ernle Bradford,* The Great Siege *and* The Shield and the Sword, *provided much information about this strategic fortress once owned and manned by the Sovereign Military Order of the Hospital of St. John of Jerusalem, popularly known as the Knights of Malta. In 1565 Valletta was besieged by a formidable Turkish armada of Suleiman the Magnificent. His defeat by the knights contributed to the Turkish defeat six years later at the Battle of Lepanto (where Cervantes lost a hand), a turning point of European history, marking as it did the end of Moslem expansion toward Europe.*

*In modern times, Malta was a strong point of British imperialism. As late as World War II its stubborn valor kept open the supply lines for the victory of El Alamein, the conquest of North Africa, and the invasion of Italy. The advent of nuclear arms stripped Malta of its strategic importance, and in 1964 the British granted it independence, retaining a lease on its naval base. When the lease terminated in 1979, the last British warships went home. No longer a military prize, the tiny island with its mixed language of Latin and Arabic, plays a substantial political and economic role as a bridge between Europe and the third world. The* Corriere della sera, *June 5, 1980, had three articles on Italo-Maltese co-operation.*

*I had an appointment with Prime Minister Dom Mintoff, but the day I arrived a last-minute meeting with the British prime minister came through, and Mintoff left the island. I was received by Acting Prime Minister Joseph Cassar, the minister of justice. Cassar, the self-educated son of a poor carpenter from a tiny village, managed to enter law school and became a leading lawyer. "I made a lot of* money," he said with pride, "but I prefer politics and its low pay." The probity of the Labour party matches that of the PCI in Italy.

The government is housed in the Auberge de Castile, a majestic feudal palace built around a courtyard with trees and fountains. The spacious rooms reflect in their rich furnishings the opulence of the knights and the lavish taste of the later British proconsuls. Cassar turned out to be a man in his fifties, with furrowed brow and deep-set black eyes, quietly dressed, with friendly, courteous manners. His speech was spiced with a touch of formality. He offered me tea, coffee, or a soft drink, and when I declined, he said: "Well, I am a bit tired and I am going to have a whiskey-soda." "In that case," I said, "I will join you."

He sat at the head of a long table, with me on one side and an aide on the other, and we talked about Eurocommunism. He didn't like the word, with its stress on Europe; he thought it too confining, but he bowed to a settled usage. I told him of fears on the left that Eurocommunists would end up as Social Democrats. He snorted. "That is nonsense. Though we call ourselves the Labour party, we consider ourselves Eurocommunists. We know we are changing our economic system and moving towards socialism. We move slowly, to avoid any feeling of coercion, but we move and we try to bring along the entire population to appreciate co-operation, develop a social conscience, have respect for work. For example, we are revamping our higher education, so that students will work part of the time." I told him that an American college, Antioch, had been pursuing that approach for well over a century. He was immediately interested. "Please send me material on it," he said. "If we can refer to an American experience, it will spike the guns of our conservative opposition." I asked if the opposition was strong. "Sufficiently," he said, "particularly among the Catholic clergy. We've had to fight them frontally, and we have beaten them in election after election. Recently we have been trying to introduce a national health system, including abortion, and the priests began a serious attack, charging that this was the first step toward euthanasia. A lie, pure and simple. I made a strong speech in Parliament denouncing such shameless propaganda, and we told the archbishop privately that if he wanted a disruptive fight we would meet him head-on. He promptly sent out a letter calling the priests to order."

He went on to discuss Malta's foreign policy. Malta was a country with no territorial or hegemonic ambitions. Its cardinal goal was a lasting peace, an end to all military bases and fleets so as to isolate the Mediterrenean from the rivalry of the two superpowers. He quoted a Mintoff slogan about Malta: "From a fortress of war to a citadel of peace." Then he said, "We see ourselves, with our culture and our language, as a bridge between Europe and the third world.

*We try hard to stay out of inter-Arab conflicts—for example, we have
excellent relations with both Libya and Saudi Arabia. We stand aside
from the Arab-Israeli confrontation. We try constantly to exert a
calming, mediating influence. We are a small country, but we do have
influence. For example, Mintoff is the only Westerner whom Colonel
Muammar el-Qaddafi trusts. They are like brothers, and when Mintoff is with him, he stresses the Arabic component of our language
and culture. The West regards the Libyan leader as a religious
fanatic, but he is an able man, sincerely devoted to the welfare of his
people. Now none of us here is religious, but we cannot let that divide
us from Libya. We have many Libyan students in Malta; we have built
a drydock there and are training many technicians. Our technology is
less advanced than Italy's, for example, but very advanced for the
third world. We are conscious of the third world, its needs, its claims.
We are knowledgeable about their problems. For example, no one
thought to invite third world nations to the Helsinki Conference,
because it dealt with Europe. But we proposed they be invited as
observers, and our suggestion was adopted."*

*I have telescoped our conversation, somewhat, but these sen-
tences I set down verbatim: "We feel very close to the Italian
comrades. We believe their fundamental strategy of more and more
democracy is a correct one and will open the road to socialism. We
know it can be done." We talked of possible economic measures
against Italy if the PCI went into the government, particularly in
regard to oil. He made the point that Libya, Norway, and Mexico had
plenty of oil and would resist, in varying degrees, any attempt of the
United States to stop oil shipments. Malta, of course, would work
hard to rally third world support for Italy against American coercion.*

I stayed in Malta for several days, resting from four months of
incessant travel, wearying rounds of interviews, irregular meals, and
late hours. I strolled on the British-built esplanade reminiscent of
Brighton, climbed the ancient fortifications, visited the sumptuous
cathedral, and spent time in the armories and at the displays of the war
museums.

Interspersing short bus hops and long walks, I roamed over the
tiny island, including the minuscule neighboring island of Gozo, with
its neolithic megaliths. Everywhere there were rocks, in fences,
houses, barns, cisterns—the parched land made New England seem
tropical—and I felt both oppressed by the toil of centuries and
admiring of a people's tenacity and endurance. The sun was warming,
hardly ever hot, the people kindly. I saw no signs of great wealth,
found opposition to the government among tradesmen and small

entrereneurs, hardly any among workers. They were delightful, refreshing days.

As I walked around, often alone, my mind reverted to the men and women I had met all over Italy and in the various European capitals, lingering over the more significant encounters. Over the many weeks, I had been subjected to so many impressions, ideas, and experiences, expected and unexpected, coherent and contradictory, that the circuits of the mind had become overloaded. Now, recollected in tranquillity, they slowly began to coalesce in meaningful patterns of time and place, forming a richly textured canvas in the mind's eye.

There grew within me in those walks an insistent feeling of confidence in my judgment that Eurocommunism was a major development in the history of our times. Joseph Cassar had contributed a great deal to this sense of confidence. The views of an active political figure brought a measure of objectivity to my own conclusions. I felt less and less like an intellectual spinning theories, what Gramsci wryly called "putting diapers on the world." He had, as it were, put an imprimatur on an as yet unwritten book.

Over the next two years, as I worked and wrote about the past, I tried to keep abreast of the news and to think ahead about the countervailing forces that will be at work in the event the PCI enters the government within the next few years. That government might be a coalition government of six parties, or a left government of PCI, PSI, PRI, PR, and smaller groups. I would term such a government "Eurocommunist."

Evidence has been presented of the probable political and economic support given to a Eurocommunist government by socialist and third world countries. These countries will act individually and collectively through the United Nations, where they dominate the Assembly and have considerable clout in the Security Council.

In an article in the *New York Times Magazine* (December 16, 1979) Jane Rosen, United Nations correspondent of the British newspaper, *The Guardian,* describes in detail the power of the third world and deplores their hegemony, forgetting that for twenty years the United States controlled the U.N. More relevant to Eurocommunism is that the third world hungers for a new economic order which will diminish the gap between rich and poor nations. The socialist nations support such a new order.

This new economic order, of which Eurocommunism would be a component, has potential sources of support even within the capitalist world. The European Common market, dominated by Germany, is becoming restive about American economic hegemony. The European Monetary System, organized under German leadership, is directed against American financial power. Politically also, Europe would like to opt out of the rivalry of the great powers, and here, too, there are indications that German Social Democracy may be reconsidering its options under the stress of events. According to Andrew Young, writing for the *New York Times*: "There seems to be a conscious strategy . . . to develop new West German trade-and-aid patterns with the progressive democracies of the world." (*San Juan Star,* January 18, 1980)

In the elections for a European Parliament, June 10–11, 1979, the Common Market countries, except for Italy, swung to the right, with almost two thirds of the seats right of center. In Germany, the Christian Democrats, under Franz Josef Strauss, obtained a majority of the votes and if they increase their strength they will surely govern Germany, with the result that the U.S. may swing its support to them. The Italian Communists have made overtures to Helmut Schmidt and the Social Democrats, and these overtures have not been rejected. In Britain, the blindly pro-American right wing of the Labour party has suffered a stunning electoral defeat, and the left wing, sympathetic to Eurocommunism, has gained the ascendancy. Everything is in flux, and it is not written in the stars that Eurocommunism will lack support within the Common Market.

Nor is it inevitable that the Soviet Union, fearing success will strengthen dissenters in the socialist world and endanger the Soviet political structure, will undermine Eurocommunism. At the Congress of Dissent in Venice, the Czechs pointed out that Alexander Dubcek was doing nothing more than the Eurocommunist PCI was doing. But the Soviet Union will have to come to terms with internal liberalization. Its economy is suffering because it is still too rigidly controlled from the top. The Soviet growth potential can only be achieved through greater decentralization and further relaxation of authoritarian management. Such economic measures are bound to spill over into the political arena, and the combination may favor economic aid to an Italian economy based on the historic compromise.

I have left for last a most important factor in any future power equation, and that is the role of the Vatican. Chapter 4 noted the trend in the Church to disassociate itself from present-day capitalism. This does not mean that the Church will be favorable to existing socialism. But the Vatican is deeply committed to a more just economic order in the world, one which will make possible a halt in the wasteful and exorbitant arms race. John Paul II seems determined to ameliorate the economic conditions of the third world, and papal initiatives to this end are not unlikely. Much of the world is ready for them.

The most powerful opponent of Eurocommunism is the United States, and the Vatican is the only independent force in our country powerful enough to be heard and, to some extent, heeded. The Vatican doesn't have to be in favor of Eurocommunism; it doesn't have to approve of it or like it. It has simply to tolerate it.

On the planetary chessboard, with Church interests at stake in various socialist and third world nations, the Vatican may well feel that it would be imprudent to fight the PCI and plunge Italy into turmoil. It may even feel that a more just social order will make Italian society less vulnerable to terrorism, to the anger and frustration of the young. If so, and if the Vatican says "Hands Off!" to Washington, the papal injunction may tip the scales against economic coercion by the United States.

The world is in a state of unrest and revolutionary ferment; a new economic order is long overdue. Eurocommunism offers a hope of a peaceful transition away from present-day capitalism. Agnelli said that new social forces are pushing for hegemony and that the stakes are high. He was speaking of Italy, but his aphorism applies to the entire world.

It seems fitting to close with Gramsci. He wrote some forty years ago: "The crisis consists precisely in the fact that the old is dying and the new cannot be born; in this interregnum a great variety of morbid symptoms appear." But today the new *can* be born. Slowly, painfully, a more just economic order may evolve. In the process morbid symptoms proliferate and despair is nourished. In this dubious battle for survival, despair plays a crippling role and must be exorcised. This is the task, and this is the promise, of Eurocommunism.

# Notes

*Shortened references are used throughout these Notes. For complete details, see the Bibliography. Most references here are to foreign-language editions, though where available references to English-languages sources are often included. This is particularly true of Gramsci's writings.*

## Chapter 1: The End of Soviet Hegemony,
## pp. 3–22

1. Fitzroy Maclean, *The Heretic*, chapter 3. Tito had been in Yugoslav jails from 1927 to 1934 and thus was uninvolved in internal factional fights or in disputes with the Comintern.

2. Winston Churchill, *The Grand Alliance* (Boston: Houghton Mifflin, 1950), p. 192. For the effect on Moscow, p. 358.

3. Maclean, chapters 9 and 10. Gives details of German troops, casualties, and the Comintern cable.

4. Maclean, chapters 11 through 13. Maclean relies heavily on Yugoslav and English documentation in addition to his own extensive first-hand experience.

5. Khrushchev's secret report was released by the U.S. Department of State on June 4, 1956. It has been said that Togliatti was the one who passed the report to the CIA. See Corrado Inserti, "Rapporto Cruscev da Togliatti alla CIA," *L'Europeo*, August 4, 1978.

6. Maclean, chapter 6.

7. One example from Khrushchev's report: The eighth congress of the CPSU (1934) had 1966 delegates, all strong supporters of Stalin. Of these, 60 percent were workers, 80 percent had joined the party before 1921 and had fought in the civil war. More than half were arrested in the next four years. A Central Committee of 139 members was elected at this Congress. Within four years 98 of them (70 percent) had been arrested and shot.

8. Vittorio Vidali, *Diario del XX congresso*, p. 18. An English translation, to be published by Lawrence Hill and Co., is in preparation.

9. *Ibid.*, p. 86.

10. *Ibid.*, pp. 153, 161.

11. *Ibid.*, p. 160.

12. Harry Gelman, "The Sino-Soviet Conflict," p. 264 ff., from which the facts are summarized.

13. See, for example, Vidali, p. 173.

14. Gelman, p. 280.

15. Palmiro Togliatti, "Risposta a '9 domande sullo stalinismo.' "

16. Vidali, pp. 157–58.

17. This comment of Togliatti's has often been mentioned in journalistic accounts, but I have not been able to find a first-hand source. Vidali, who was at Togliatti's side during Mao's speech, wrote me that he had not heard the exclamation, but adds, "It is possible that Togliatti used that phrase after the session, and if he did not say it, he certainly thought it" (Letter to the author from Vittorio Vidali, Trieste, December 23, 1979). Giuseppe Boffa, former correspondent in Moscow of *L'Unità*, states that he never heard Togliatti use the phrase. Further, he discussed this point with Nilde Jotti, who told him "categorically" that Togliatti would never have used the phrase (Letter to the author from Giuseppe Boffa, February 20, 1980). Vidali, however, is more independent politically.

18. "Il testo integrale dell'ultimo scritto di Togliatti a Yalta," *Rinascita* 21, no. 35 (September 5, 1964): 1–4; Palmiro Togliatti, *Opere scelte*, p. 1170.

19. Fernando Claudin, *Eurocommunism and Socialism*, pp. 43–45.

20. *Ibid.*, p. 50; Max Gordon, ed., "Joint Declaration of the Communist Parties of France and Italy."

21. For further information on the Berlin Conference, see M. Cesarini Sforza and Enrico Nassi, *L'Eurocomunismo;* and Ignazio Delogu, ed., *La via europea al socialismo*. See also Bernardo Valli, ed., *Gli eurocomunisti*.

22. Vadim Zagladin, ed., *Europe and the Communists*, pp. 68–114. Resolutions, communiques, or official editorial comment of the parties attending the Berlin Conference are listed. By checking for certain code phrases, such as "Marxism-Leninism," "dictatorship of the proletariat," etc. (either presence or absence), one can see that of the 29 parties present, 17 backed Eurocommunist views.

23. Claudin, p. 54.

24. *Ibid.*, p. 55. Marchais did not stick to his guns. He supported the USSR on Afghanistan, and on April 28 the PCF hosted a conference in Paris of East-West Communist parties to fight the new NATO missiles. The Italian, Spanish, Yugoslav, and Romanian parties refused to attend, and the conference was something of a fizzle, with only second-ranking officials present from the other parties. (See *The Economist*, May 3, 1980.)

25. *Ibid.*, p. 54.

26. *Ibid.*, p. 56.

27. "Contrary to the Interests of Peace and Socialism in Europe," *New Times* (Moscow).

28. Enrico Berlinguer, "Il movimento socialista e il cammino del PCI: Il discorso di saluto di Berlinguer." See the English version: "The Socialist Movement and the PCI's March."

29. "Incontro tra Breznev e Berlinguer alla fine della seduta al Cremlino," *L'Unità*, November 4, 1977, pp. 1, 14.

30. Diane Johnstone, "Socialists Compel Communist Leader to Define Leninism," *In These Times*, March 3, 1978, pp. 9–10.

31. "Hua Moves On," *Time*, September 9, 1978, p. 25.

32. Henry Tanner, "Hua Arrives in Rome on Last Leg of Tour," *New York Times*, November 4, 1979, p. 1–3, for the meeting. On Berlinguer's visit to China, Jennie Summa of ANSA reported long stories in the Peking press on the PCI's history, and articles, with photos, on Berlinguer conferring with high Chinese leaders (*Il Progresso Italo-Americano*, April 14–16, 1980; see also Lina Tamburrino in *Rinascita*, April 25, 1980).

33. See Louis Althusser's important speech in the *Manifesto* Conference: "Due, tre parole (brutali) su Marx e Lenin." Mimeographed copies of most of the speeches, and summaries of the rest, are in the hands of the author.

A major issue at the Congress was whether the USSR could be considered socialist. While peripheral to this book, it is an extremely important issue, to which Immanuel Wallerstein has made a major contribution in his introduction to *Revolution in the Third World* by Gerard Chaliand. In it he makes the point that the transition to socialism should be seen not in terms of a single country, but as a transition from a world system of capitalism to a world system of socialism. For a discussion of this insight, see the review of Chaliand by Robert E. Wood, *Socialist Review*, no. 35 (May–June 1979), p. 168.

In the same issue Fernando Claudín has an essay, "Reflections on the Crisis of Marxism," p. 137, which is germane to the Venice Congress. Claudín deals with the great renewal of Marxism in the last decade, but warns lest the studies become merely academic and not be integrated into the class struggles of mass organizations.

## Chapter 2: "Eurocommunism, Democracy and the State, pp. 23–38

1. Ralph Miliband, *Marxism and Politics*, p. 78.
2. *Ibid.*, p. 40.
3. *Ibid.*, p. 79.
4. *Ibid.*, p. 80.
5. *Ibid.*, pp. 80–81. This quotation of Engels's is an example of the "battle of quotations" endemic to the left. See Max Gordon vs. Paul Sweezy (*Monthly Review*, June 1977) and Ernest Mandel vs. Santiago Carrillo in their books on Eurocommunism listed in the Bibliography.
6. *Ibid.*, p. 80.
7. V. I. Lenin, *Collected Works*, vol. 19, p. 91.
8. V. I. Lenin, *Selected Works*, pp. 264, 290.
9. Isaac Deutscher, *Stalin* (New York and London: Oxford University Press, 1949), p. 244n. "About half a million former Tsarist officials were employed by the Soviet Government shortly after the Civil War."
10. Charles Bettelheim, *Class Struggles in the USSR*, p. 166.
11. See Richard Hunt, *The Political Ideas of Marx and Engels*.
12. Miliband, pp. 90 ff.
13. *Ibid.*, p. 138n.
14. Antonio Gramsci, *L'Ordine nuovo, 1919–1920*, p. 13; *idem., Selections from Political Writings, 1910–1920*, p. 68.
15. Rosa Luxemburg, *Selected Political Writings*, p. 250.
16. Rosa Luxemburg, *Rosa Luxemburg Speaks*, p. 289. It should be noted that she was not against discipline and was ambiguous about the degree of centralism. See Miliband, p. 125.
17. *Ibid.*, p. 391. Rosa Luxemburg is not to be encapsulated in a few excerpts. She is presented here only to show the continuity within Marxist thought of the value of democracy. Her influence on Eurocommunism was not direct, but mediated by many writers, including Gramsci.
18. For a discussion of the theoretical issues around the concept of the dictatorship of the proletariat, both from the left and from the right, see the works by Balabar, Althusser, Mandel, and Del Noce listed in the Bibliography.
19. Miliband, p. 81.
20. William Safire in the *New York Times*, December 16, 1979. Safire rebukes Kissinger by showing that Mao had used the word a long time ago. The term's currency has come via Gramsci; the word, of course, derives from ancient Greek.
21. The term "hegemony" had been the subject of many discussions and interpretations. See Perry Anderson, "The Antinomies of Antonio Gramsci"; E. P. Thompson, *The Poverty of Theory*, pp. 72–77; John Cammett, *Antonio Gramsci and the Origins of Italian Communism*, pp. 204–5.
22. There are seven such PCI schools in Italy. See note 12a, Chapter 8.
23. Shortly after the school opened, Maruice Thorez, general secretary of the French Communist party, came for a visit and found it "too elegant" (Bocca, *Togliatti*, p. 402).
24. The relation between economics and politics was a major concern of Lenin and, via Gramsci, Togliatti. See Luciano Gruppi, *Togliatti e la via italiana al socialismo*.
25. Marxism is not a closed system, and its classics are not sacrosanct. Quotations illuminate, but settle little. As Miliband says, "There are many worse slogans than 'Everyone his own Marx,' for in the end there is no 'authoritative interpretation'—only personal judgment and evaluation" (*Marxism and Politics*, p. 5).
26. Gramsci was fond of quoting Engels's letter to Bloch: "People think they have mastered a theory and can apply it without more ado from the moment they have mastered its main principles . . ." (*Selections from the Prison Notebooks*, p. 472; cited hereafter as *Prison Notebooks*).
27. Miliband, pp. 162–63.
28. *Ibid.*, pp. 189–90.
29. See the review of Miliband's book by James Miller, "Marxism and Politics." His opening criticism seems to me to be somewhat carping—if not captious.
30. See, for example, the comment of historian E. P. Thompson on the Labour reforms immediately after the war: "Those reforms, if sustained and enlarged by an aggressive socialist strategy, might well have effected such a cancellation of the logic of capitalism that the system would have been brought to the point of crisis—a crisis not of despair or disintegration but a crisis in which the necessity for a peaceful revolutionary transition to an alternative socialist logic became daily more evident and possible" (*The Poverty of Theory*, p. 144).

31. Gramsci's tenacity was also operative against the censor and the warden in obtaining books, reviews, and newspapers. He built up a library of about a hundred volumes, including some twenty Marxist texts. For more details, see Attilio Baldan, "Gramsci As an Historian of the 1930s"; and Giuseppe Carbone, "I libri del carcere di Antonio Gramsci." (Mussolini's jailors were more lenient toward Gramsci than were U.S. prison authorities toward this author in the 1950s: I was allowed no book by Marx or Lenin, etc., and no progressive newspapers or magazines.)

32. Gramsci, *Prison Notebooks*, p. lxxxix. See Domenico Zucàro, ed., *Il processone: Gramsci e i dirigenti comunisti dinanzi al Tribunale speciale* (Rome: Editori Riuniti, 1961), p. 109, fn. 1, and p. 219, where the prosecutor referred to Gramsci as "the leading mind of the Communist party."

33. Gramsci, *Prison Notebooks*, 229–39; idem., *Quaderni del carcere*, pp. 122–23, 120–22, 1613–16, 865–67. These by now famous passages on "war of movement" and "war of position" were first written in several different notebooks, as the 1975 Gerratana edition of the *Quaderni* shows.

34. The concept of a war of position had been adumbrated by Kautsky in his "siege" analogy (see Mandel, *From Stalinism to Eurocommunism*, p. 191), which was brought forward again, and attacked, by Gilles Martinet in *Marxism of Our Time*. This attack was used by the editors of *Monthly Review* (November 1976) to argue against Eurocommunism and the strategy of the PCI. A rebuttal by this writer, "In Defense of the Italian CP," was published in *Monthly Review*, in June 1977.

35. Paolo Spriano, *Storia del Partito comunista italiano*, vol. 3, p. 156.

36. Gramsci's influence on the PCI is indisputable, but it is not linear. We have stressed the continuity between his work and the contemporary PCI, but there are also strong elements of discontinuity. For a long time Gramsci was mediated via Togliatti, and Togliatti himself changed a great deal. It is easy to quote Togliatti against himself: "From the development of productive forces there emerge new conditions for our struggles, but there does not emerge a tranquil road to that utopian peaceful transformation from capitalism to socialism of which no one has given, or will ever give, an example" (Report to the VIII Congress, PCI, in *Opere scelte*, p. 845).

The discontinuity in Togliatti's line has been amply discussed by his biographer, Giorgio Bocca, under the general rubric of *doppiezza* (see chapter 5, below). But though respectful, Bocca is also carping, accusing Togliatti of censorship in the first publication of Gramsci's notebooks. The definitive Einaudi edition of 1975 has shown the deletions to be minimal and merely prudent vis-à-vis Stalin.

By far the best discussion of Togliatti's line is in a symposium by the *Manifesto* group: Lucio Magri, "Relazione," *Da Togliatti alla nuovo sinistra*.

37. See Miliband on this subject, with extensive quotations from Mao, pp. 62–64.

38. Gramsci, *Quaderni del carcere*, p. 1263; idem., *Prison Notebooks*, pp. 343–44. I have preferred my own translation as more idiomatic for the United States. See my *Open Marxism of Antonio Gramsci*.

39. Gramsci, *Quaderni*, p. 1509; *Prison Notebooks*, p. 388.

40. Gramsci, *Quaderni*, p. 1493; *Prison Notebooks*, p. 404.

41. Gramsci, *Quaderni*, p. 1393; *Prison Notebooks*, p. 341.

42. The wide acceptance in Italy of PCI "seriousness" and "democratic commitment" has been noted repeatedly by foreign observers. I cite just two: Peter Nichols of the London *Times* has written that the Communists "are better prepared, more methodical and more available when needed. . . . They insist that students study and act responsibly." Further, the PCI "maintains its reputation for excellent administration" (*The Italian Decision*, p. 133).

Diane Johnstone, correspondent of *In These Times*, writes: "The view of the PCI as a principal mainstay of Italian constitutional democracy has been growing into a virtual consensus in Italy in recent years." She quotes the Catholic theologian Baget Bozzo, "The PCI today, more than any other social unit, defends in Italy . . . the democratic nature of the state" (October 11–17, 1978).

43. Antonio Gramsci, *L'Ordine nuovo, 1919–1920*, pp. 377–78; Miliband, p. 181.

# Chapter 3: Eurocommunists and Eurosocialists, pp. 39–61

1. There are many histories of the various internationals. I have used primarily Fernando Claudín, *The Communist Movement from Comintern to Cominform* as well as the *Encyclopedia Britannica*. By now, there is an extensive bibliography on the Third International. For the documents, see Jane Degras, ed., *The Communist International: Documents;* Helmut Gruber, ed.,

*International Communism in the Era of Lenin* and *Soviet Russia Masters the Comintern;* and now Aldo Agosti, *La Terza internazionale, storia documentaria.*

In addition to Claudín, other histories of the International are: Franz Borkenau, *European Communism* (New York: Harper, 1953); Hugh Seton-Watson, *From Lenin to Khrushchev: The History of World Communism* (New York: Praeger, 1960); and, especially important for Italy, Jules Humbert-Droz, *Memoires, 1921–1941.* For Italy and the Third International, see also Ernesto Ragionieri, *La Terza internazionale e il PCI* and *Lenin e l'Italia.*

2. The Second International expired during World War II and was resuscitated in Frankfurt in 1951, according to Carl Gershman, "The Socialists and the PLO," *Commentary* 68 (October 1979): 36–44.

3. Quoted in Ernest Mandel, *From Stalinism to Eurocommunism,* p. 9.

4. *Ibid.,* p. 9n.

5. Claudin, *The Communist Movement from Comintern to Cominform,* p. 53.

6. The split between the Bolsheviks and Mensheviks in the Russian Social Democratic Party centered on the nature of membership—the duties assumed, the degree of discipline, the nature of the organizational ties. The Bolsheviks prided themselves on their discipline, their activism, and their study of Marxism, the French Revolution, and the Paris Commune.

7. "Then and there the socialist leader [Ebert] and the second in command of the Germany army [Gröner] made a pact which, though it would not be publicly known for many years, was to determine the nation's fate. Ebert agreed to put down anarchy and bolshevism and maintain the army in all its traditions. Gröner thereupon pledged the support of the army in helping the new government establish itself and carry its aims. . . . Hindenberg and Gröner pressed Ebert to honor the pact between them" (William L. Shirer, *The Rise and Fall of the Third Reich,* [New York: Simon & Schuster, 1960], pp. 54–55).

8. Rosa Luxemburg, *Selected Political Writings,* p. 250; Claudín, *The Communist Movement from Comintern to Cominform,* p. 92. See also Louis Menashe, "Vladimir Ilyich Bakunin: An Essay on Lenin."

9. Claudín, *The Communist Movement from Comintern to Cominform,* p. 70.

10. *Ibid.,* p. 93.

11. The interdependency of the Communist parties and the Communist International in this period is well known. Few experienced this interdependency—or "internationalism," if you will—so intensely as the Italians, for their party suffered the earliest and longest period of complete clandestinity of any "section" of the Comintern. As Umberto Terracini put it in July 1925: "In its founding theses the Communist International presented itself to the working masses not indeed as a federation of parties but rather as one world party subdivided into a certain number of national sections. . . . Each section established its own programs and resolved the problems of its own activities by making use not only of the experience of its own membership but also that of the entire International" (Archivio del Partito comunista (APC). Fascicolo 303–3, foglio 53/Circolare no. 28 [Il luglio, 1925], f.to. Laguska [Umberto Terracini]). See also on this point M. L. Salvadori, *Gramsci e il problema storico della democrazia,* pp. 23–24.

12. Claudín, *The Communist Movement from Comintern to Cominform,* p. 106.

13. Frederick Schuman, *Europe on the Eve: The Crisis of Diplomacy, 1933–1939* (New York: Knopf, 1939), p. 461.

14. Vivian Gornick, *The Romance of American Communism,* p. 250.

15. Gramsci, *Quaderni del carcere,* p. 1750; *idem., Prison Notebooks,* p. 155. Gramsci pushed the concept of democratic centralism further than an internal party mechanism to the broad question of social discipline. Under the subtitle, "Organic Centralism and Democratic Centralism: Discipline," he wrote: "What do we mean by discipline, if this word signifies a continuing and permanent relation between governors and governed to realize a collective will? Certainly not as a passive and supine acceptance of orders . . . but as a conscious and lucid assimilation of the directive to be realized. . . . Discipline does not annul personality and liberty: the question of 'personality and liberty' is posed not by the fact of discipline but by 'the origin of the power that orders the discipline.' If this origin is 'democratic' . . . and not a 'diktat' [*un arbitrio*] . . . then the discipline is a necessary element of democratic order, of liberty" (*Quaderni del carcere,* pp, 1706–7).

16. Gramsci, *Quaderni del carcere,* p. 1635; *Prison Notebooks,* p. 189.

17. Adalberto Minucci, "La Fiat 'anticipa'? Ma non siamo negli anni '50," *L'Unità,* November 3, 1979; *Panorama,* November 5, 1979.

18. See Santiago Carrillo, *Eurocommunism and the State,* pp. 103–4; Napolitano, *The Italian Road to Socialism,* pp. 29–30.

19. *New York Times Magazine,* November 19, 1978, p. 158.

20. *Ibid.*, p. 162.

21. The Spanish Socialist Party Congress held in Madrid, May 16–20, 1978, repeatedly voted for more left positions than its leader, Felipe Gonzales, thought proper, so he resigned, and a caretaker group was appointed (*New York Times*, May 21 and 22, 1978). In December 1978 another Congress was held, and after some compromises Gonzales resumed the leadership (*Panorama*, November 5, 1979).

22. James M. Markham, "Spain's Left Is Jubilant over Election Victory in Cities," *New York Times*, April 5, 1979, p. A-6.

23. Studies of French voting which go back to 1871 show remarkable stability between the left and the right. On only two or three occasions has the electorate shifted its allegiance by as much as 8 percent (Godfrey Hodgson, "France Votes to Wait and See: The Communist Monkey Wrench," *The Nation* 226 [April 15, 1978]: 428–30).

24. Albert Soboul is professor of the history of the French Revolution at the Sorbonne. He made his reputation with the monumental study of the Parisian *sans-coulottes*.

25. Walter Schwartz, *Manchester Guardian Weekly*, December 18, 1977.

26. *Ibid.*

27. *Ibid.* Schwartz quotes Mitterand to show he deliberately broke off negotiations and sources close to Marchais to show that Marchais was taken by surprise.

28. Diana Johnstone, *In These Times*, March 22–28, 1978. Previously, André Fontaine had argued that as far back as 1974 the Soviet government had been favoring the French conservatives (*Manchester Guardian Weekly*, October 9, 1977).

29. "French Swing to Left Gives It 54.6% in Local Vote," *New York Times*, March 27, 1979.

30. Victor Zorza, "Why Nationalization Matters to the Communists," points out that the Common Program of 1972 called for a board of managements for nationalized industries to be appointed equally by consumers, unions, and the government. With the minister a Communist and the union Communist-led, control of the board was guaranteed.

31. The figures are taken from an article by Gilbert Mathieu, "Nationalization: How Far Should the Left Go?" Mathieu also presents arguments for and against Socialist and Communist positions.

32. Place Colonnel-Fabien was named after a hero of the resistance whose real name was Pierre Georges, born in Belleville. At seventeen, he fought in Spain in the International Brigades; at twenty-three, he was the first member of the resistance to shoot a German officer (in the Paris subway); at twenty-six, after the Liberation of Paris, he was killed in action on the Lorraine front.

33. For the stirrings and debates in both parties, see Diana Johnstone, *In These Times*, May 17–23, 1979. See also Jonathan Kandell, "France Gets a Rare Peek at Discontent in Communist Ranks," *New York Times*, April 5, 1978, p. A-2.

34. On the Communist party congress, see the letter of correspondent Peter Avis, *Manchester Guardian Weekly*, June 10, 1979. For a longer treatment, covering the eighteen months following the election debacle, see Jacques Rouse, "Marchais rameute," *L'Express*, September 15, 1979, pp. 42–43.

35. Giorgio Bocca, *Palmiro Togliatti*, p. 363.

36. The letters were written by Togliatti, Gramsci, Scoccimaro, Terracini, Tasca, and others, and were published in Palmiro Togliatti, *La formazione del gruppo dirigente del PCI nel 1923–1924*.

37. Oriana Fallaci, *Intervista con la storia*, pp. 313–14.

38. Peter Nichols, *Italia, Italia*, p. 140.

39. Pietro Ingrao, *Masse e potere*, p. 132.

40. Peter Nichols, *The Italian Decision*, p. 108; Celso Ghini, *L'Italia che cambia*, p. 526.

41. Giorgio Galli, *Opinioni sul PCI*, p. 114.

42. President Carter had reiterated U.S. opposition to the PCI in his meeting of January 24–26, 1980, with Prime Minister Francesco Cossiga (*Panorama*, February 14, 1980). For Helmut Kohl's speech, see *Il Progresso Italo-Americano*, February 17, 1980.

43. Lenardo Paggi, "L'europeismo della sinistra nell'Europa della crisi."

44. In an interview, "L'amichevole Cremlino," with *L'Espresso*, October 15, 1978, Berlinguer pointed out that at a meeting with the SDP in Strassbourg, the two parties had agreed to support each other in the European Community.

45. "Berlinguer and the French Left," *Manchester Guardian Weekly*, November 1, 1978.

## Chapter 4: "The Vatican and Eurocommunism,"
## pp. 62–92

1. G. Balistrieri, *Papa Giovanni* (Milan: Mazzotta, 1964), p. 12.

2. *Ibid.*, p. 24.

3. Sergio C. Lorit, *La vita raccontata di Papa Giovanni*, p. 39. In 1906 Angelo Roncalli discovered in Milan the documents of a sojourn in Bergamo by the saint and set out to edit them. Fifty-two years later, three months before he became Pope John XXIII, he finished the fifth and last volume of *The Acts of the Apostolic Visit to Bergamo of San Carlo Borromeo*.

4. Peter Nichols, *Italia, Italia*, p. 229. In 1966 the Italian clergy counted 47,000 members; in 1970 there were 43,000 and the population had increased. The decline is world-wide, from 1 priest per 1000 Catholics in 1963 to 1 priest per 1700 in 1979.

5. Alceste Santini, *Questione cattolica, questione comunista*, p. 26.

6. Karol Wojtyla was one of the youngest bishops attending Vatican II, and he participated vigorously. Monsignor Bartolomeo Sorge says he is the first pope to be "a son of the Council." See Aldo Biscardi and Luca Liquori, eds., *Il papa dal volto umano*, p. 39.

7. Balistrieri, p. 97. The liturgy perpetuated this slander: "Let us also pray for the perfidious Jews that God may cure the blindness of their hearts."

8. *Ibid.*, p. 85. In the *Syllabus of Errors* by Pius IX, Article 38 declares it "a grave error to say that the Roman popes, by their arbitrary conduct, had contributed to the division of the Church." Pope John's rectification: "The responsibility is in part theirs, but in great part ours also."

9. *Ibid.*, p. 36. Pius XII had said: "Parity of rights with men has induced [the woman] to abandon the home where she has reigned as queen . . . the essential complement of man."

10. *Ibid.*

11. UPI dispatch, *San Juan Star*, February 14, 1978.

12. Kenneth A. Briggs, "Women and Catholic Church," *New York Times*, November 16, 1979, p. A-13. The proposal was directed specifically at the liturgy where it says that Christ sacrificed Himself "for you and all men." The Aramaic, from which the translation was made, doesn't say "all men" but "all people." The proposal obtained a majority of votes, but failed to get the two thirds needed to carry.

13. Michele Pellegrino, "Pluralismo e cristiani di fronte al marxismo." The quotation from *Le Monde* was used by the editors of the review as an introduction to the article.

14. *Ibid.*

15. See, for example, the Convocation on *Pacem in Terris* held in New York City in March 1965 by the Center for the Study of Democratic Institutions. The convocation had greetings from Chief Justice Earl Warren, Vice-President Hubert Humphrey, Senator William Fulbright, Ambassador George Kennan, and so forth. New York: Pocket Books, 1965.

16. Balistrieri, p. 25.

17. Santini, p. 25.

18. Balistrieri, p. 30.

19. *Ibid.*, pp. 27–28.

20. Giorgio Bocca, *Palmiro Togliatti*, p. 192.

21. Peter Nichols, *The Italian Decision*, p. 100. A book by an ex-Communist leader, Renato Mieli, accused Togliatti of having participated in the trial of the Poles. An aide to Togliatti, Davide Lajolo, confronted Togliatti with this and later wrote that the party leader, pale and upset, had confirmed the accusation.

22. John Cammett, *Antonio Gramsci and the Origins of Italian Communism*, p. 131. Gramsci chided comrades who resisted organizing workers' councils in Bergamo for fear that the priests would take them over.

23. Lorit, pp. 30–35. Of course, nearly all other deputies were Catholic by religion, but not elected as such.

24. Here is a typical Bergamo quote (taken from Lorit) that sounds contemporary: "It is not enough to shout and preach against socialism; we must have the courage to confess our own social sins."

25. A famous pastoral letter of Cardinal Pellegrino (1972) was entitled *Camminare insieme*. It received the blessings of Pope Paul VI, who was "pleased" by it, adding typically, "I do not wish at this time to comment on it." The phrase has become a political code phrase for co-operation with the PCI. When Amintore Fanfani, right leader in the DC, wished to announce his shift to the dialogue in December 1977, he did so by relating how he and Pope John had been in a train and saw some people walking on a road. Said the pope to Fanfani: "You see them? To get anywhere we must *camminare insieme*." After the Moro assassination Fanfani swung back to the extreme right position. I used the phrase in the dedication of this work.

26. Bocca, *Palmiro Togliatti*, p. 2.

27. Carl Marzani, *The Open Marxism of Antonio Gramsci*, p. 8. Of course, Gramsci also pointed out the great differences between the two world views and wrote extensively on "the two cultures." On Gramsci's comparison of the two cultures—Catholicism and Marxism—especially in their differing attitudes toward education, see Hugues Portelli, *Gramsci e la questione religiosa*,

pp. 204–16.

Included in a recent anthology on the "historical compromise" are the following articles by the young Gramsci: "I cattolici italiani" (December 22, 1918); "Giolitti e i populari" (February 22, 1922); "Un compagno bolognese" (March 20, 1920); and "I popolari" (November 1, 1919). See Pietro Valenza, ed., *Il compromesso storico*, pp. 63–74. See also Gramsci, *Il Vaticano e l'Italian*, 2d ed.

28. Bocca, *op. cit.*, pp. 443–44.

29. Santini, p. 104. The article was published in *Lotta nostra*. The Valenza anthology includes Togliatti's most important contributions to the Catholic-Communist dialogue (pp. 57–134). Other works on the dialogue are *L'opera di De Gasperi* and *Comunisti, socialisti, cattolici*.

30. Palmiro Togliatti, *Opere scelte*, p. 442.

31. Santini, p. 113.

32. Bocca, *op. cit.*, p. 449.

33. The "trade" was clear. According to Togliatti, De Gasperi had made it clear to him that if the Concordat was voided, De Gasperi would seek another referendum to reverse the one that had rejected the monarchy. The Republic was at stake. The Concordat has been under revision ever since, with draft after draft drawn up and veering steadily toward a more lay position, particularly in reducing the status of the Church and in weakening its vetoes and other controls on public education. See *Il resto del Carlino*, November 5, 1977; *Paese sera*, December 12, 1978. On the fiftieth anniversary of the Concordat, *L'Unità* (February 11, 1980) had a long article by Carlo Cardia giving many details of the latest draft.

34. Togliatti, *Opere scelte*, p. 644.

35. *Ibid.*, p. 684; Santini, pp. 135–36.

36. Romano Paci, "I cristiani per il socialismo," in *I cristiani nella sinistra dalla resistenza ad oggi*, pp. 225–40.

37. Bocca, *op. cit.*, p. 663.

38. Alberto Cecchi, *Storia del PCI attraverso i congressi*, p. 247.

39. An interesting doctoral thesis on the Marxist view of religion, including an exegesis on this paragraph, was completed recently by Ireneo Bellotti of the University of Siena. Titled "Alcuni aspetti della nozione e funzione di 'religione' in F. Engels." The thesis was reviewed by a noted scholar on the Primitive Church, Professor Ambrogio Donini, a retired Communist senator and former Italian ambassador to Warsaw (*L'Europeo*, June 28, 1979).

40. Santini, p. 137.

41. These interpretations of *Pacem in Terris* were considered correct by the Vatican, according to Cardinal Roy. See the essay by Luigi Accatoli in *I cristiani nella sinistra dalla resistenza ad oggi*, p. 130.

42. Togliatti, *Opere scelte*, p. 1176.

43. Balistrieri, p. 105.

44. Bocca, *op. cit.*, p. 682. See also Franco Rodano, *Questione democristiana e compromesso storico*, for an appreciation of the two great architects, "the great elders" as he calls them (pp. 288 ff.).

45. Gary MacEoin, *The Inner Elite*, p. xxvii. This book gives a dossier on every cardinal who was alive in early 1978. It was commissioned by a group of concerned Catholic laypersons who wanted to be sure the conclave had full information on its participants.

46. Santini, p. 129.

47. *Ibid.*, p. 30.

48. *Ibid.*, p. 132.

49. Manlio Barberito and I were born two months apart in 1912. Our careers were curiously similar. We were both economists, and by the time he was thirty he was inspector general of universities for Mussolini and an undersecretary of agriculture. At thirty I went from teaching economics at New York University to the Office of Strategic Services (OSS). We met in Rome in early 1945. He was unrepentant. Mussolini had chosen the wrong side, but the United States was bound to go fascist.

I laughed at him, but three years later I was in jail and he was a high corporate executive. By 1960, when I saw him in Rome again, McCarthyism and the Cold War were on the wane, and Manlio told me he had become an "English-type liberal." By 1977 he was rejecting all politics, and by 1979 he was in despair. "It's all over, Carlo," he told me. "The Communists have the upper hand, the era of Genghis Khan is coming. There will be execution squads at every corner." He had retired into antiquarian studies of his beloved Rome.

The bonds of childhood and of affection hold us tight. He has been a great help to me in this book, serving as a litmus paper on politics. I had only to go counter to his predictions to be more often right than wrong.

50. MacEoin, p. xiii.

51. *I cristiani nella sinistra dalla resistenza ad oggi*, p. 136. An example of this hegemony is the fourth and final volume (1970) of *L'ateismo contemporaneo*, an encyclopedia of philosophy and theology. The authors, Guido Girardi of the Salesian order, and Vincenzo Miano of the Vatican staff, have impeccable credentials and the work has the ecclesiastical imprimatur. It defines "dialogue" as "a colloquium . . . involving individuals of differing viewpoints who nonetheless share many given values. A dialogue is so conducted as to lead to mutual understanding, rapprochement and enrichment of individuals and of ideas" (*Loc. cit.*, s.v. "dialogo").

52. Bettazzi, in conversation with the author.

53. Malachi B. Martin, "Papal End Game," *National Review* 30 (April 28, 1978): 532.

54. Santini, p. 83.

55. MacEoin, p. xiii.

56. The Sacred College had 130 cardinals but 15 were disqualified from voting because of their age, a rule laid down by Paul VI.

57. Gianfranco Morra, *Marxismo e religione*, p. 311.

58. Mauro Lancisi, "Il dito di Benelli," *Panorama*, October 10, 1978, pp. 46–47.

59. M[ario] T[edeschi], "Ritorno al prete," *Il Borghese*, September 3, 1979, p. 7.

60. *Le Monde* in *Manchester Guardian Weekly*, October 21, 1979.

61. M[ario] T[edeschi], "La fede di Papa Luciani: 15 anni e 33 giorni," *Il Borghese*, October 8, 1978.

62. "A 'Foreign' Pope," *Time*, October 30, 1978, p. 86.

63. M[ario] T[edeschi], "Che farà il nuovo Papa?" *Il Borghese*, October 22, 1978, p. 457.

64. Andrew M. Greeley, *The Making of the Popes, 1978*, p. 225.

65. *Ibid.*, pp. 242–44.

66. For my editorial, see "Aggiornamento," *The Nation*. For Father Greeley, see *The Making of the Popes*, p. 213: "If Benelli had not so vigorously and effectively engineered the election of Luciani, he might not have had such strong opposition."

67. See, for example, Marcella Leone's essay on the pope, "L'imperio karolingio," *Panorama*, October 29, 1979, pp. 235 ff.

68. Hans Küng, "Pope John Paul: His First Year."

69. The pope personally rebuked the Jesuits (*New York Times*, December 7, 1979). The Sacred Congregation for the Doctrine of the Faith (formerly known as the Holy Office, the Inquisition) condemned a book on sexuality edited by U.S. Father Anthony Kosnik (*New York Times*, December 9, 1979), called in for examination the Dutch Father Eduard Schillebeeckx (*New York Times*, December 14, 1979), and prohibited the Swiss Father Hans Küng from teaching Catholic theology (*New York Times*, December 19, 1979). The result has been a storm of protest, but Wojtyla clearly intends to hold firm.

Pope John Paul II is not shy about using his powers, and he is expected to strengthen Opus Dei as a counterweight to the Jesuit order. Opus Dei has been characterized as "The Holy Mafia" in a book of that title by Yvon Le Veillant. It is an elite organization of conservative professionals, businessmen, politicians, and media people with some 72,000 members dispersed in 87 countries with influence or control in 497 universities, 52 television stations, 694 publications, 32 newspaper information services, and 10 motion picture production or distribution companies. *Panorama* estimates that at least fifteen cardinals are its supporters, voted for John Paul II and are now pushing to remove the order from the jurisdiction of the hierarchy in the various countries and make it responsible only to the pope, thus matching the autonomy of the Jesuit order. All the regulations have been approved, despite the opposition of the liberal Eduardo Cardinal Pironio of Argentina, and the scheme awaits only the papal signature (Stefan De Andreis and Marcella Leone, "Opus Dei: la santa mafia di Wojtyla," *Panorama*, November 26, 1979, pp. 84–92).

70. According to *Il Messagero*, January 2, 1979, the pope "has been careful not to give pretexts for referendum battles," in contrast to Cardinal Benelli, who has been waging an unceasing campaign for a referendum on abortion.

71. See George Vecsey, "Prayer Vigils Focus on Decision Not to Allow Women to Help Distribute Communion," *New York Times*, October 1, 1979, p. A-9; *idem.*, "Quest for Equality in Chruch Dividing Catholic Women," *New York Times*, October 2, 1979, p. A-12; "The Pope in America," *Time*, October 13, 1979, pp. 14 ff.; *New York Times*, October 26, 1979.

72. Mario Tedeschi, "Giorni di fuoco," *Il Borghese*, October 28, 1978, p. 519.

73. *Il Messagero*, October 19, 1978.

74. Luigi Bettazzi, *Farsi uomo*, p. 87.

75. *Ibid.*, p. 92.

76. Santini, p. 172.

77. *Ibid.*, p. 173.

78. *Ibid.*, p. 170.

79. *Ibid.*, p. 37.

80. Santini told the author with a chuckle that the Curia has tried hard to revoke this papal dictum; but unfortunately for them, the pope's words were recorded by a reporter's tape recorder.

81. At Medellin, Colombia, in 1968, the Episcopal Conference of Latin American Bishops was dominated by radical theologians who formulated the so-called liberation theology and got it accepted. Ten years later, at Puebla, Mexico, at a similar conference, the conservatives were better organized and disowned the liberation theology, presumably with the support of the pope. Santini disagreed with this black-and-white approach, and his judgment was shared by a former Jesuit, Peter Hepplethwaite, lecturer at Wadham College, Oxford, and editor of the London-based Jesuit magazine, *The Month*. He writes: "The Pope was—depending on the paper you read—said to have attacked or defended liberation theology. . . . [in fact] John Paul II had recognized the validity of the aspirations of liberation theology while criticizing some of its methods. At the same time his energetic statements against the abuse of human rights would have brought no comfort to Generals Videla and Pinochet" ("How the Pope Will Change the World," *Esquire*, May 8, 1979, pp. 25–36).

82. I found the actual words later: "To construct a more just world means . . . that there will be no systems that permit the exploitation of man by man or by the State" (From a sermon in Santo Domingo, Mexico, January 15, 1979; reprinted in *News Magazine* for October 1979, an insert for the *New York Daily News*, during the pope's visit to America).

83. See the Reverend Sorge's report on Puebla, *La Civiltà cattolica*, April 7, 1979, which confirms that "evangelization" has become a code word for social activism.

84. *New York Times*, November 13, 1979.

84a. Alceste Santini in *L'Unità*, March 4, 1980.

84b. New York Times News Service report in the *San Juan Star*, March 5, 1980.

84c. Santini, *op. cit.*

85. *Manchester Guardian Weekly*, October 21, 1979.

86. *Commentary*, December 1979, pp. 56–61. Novak has to exercise a certain restraint in attacking the pope, so he uses a surrogate. One quarter of his six-thousand-word article is a ferocious attack on an American priest, Father Joseph Gremillion, who compiled a six-hundred-page book, *The Gospel of Peace and Justice* (Maryknoll, N.Y.: Orbis Books, 1975). In this book, says Novak, "the bias against democratic capitalism is thick and tangible; it is at times irrational." The book is made up only of official Church documents, so that, in fact, Novak is attacking Pope John XXIII, Pope Paul VI, Maurice Cardinal Roy, who headed a special commission on Peace and Justice, Bishop Luigi Bettazzi of *Pax Christi*, Bishop Thomas J. Gumbleton of Detroit, head of the U.S. section of *Pax Christi*, and any number of other prelates.

87. Peter Hepplethwaite also points out that Wojtyla is at home with Marxist concepts and often uses them ("How the Pope Will Change the World").

88. Alceste Santini, "Appello dei movimento cattolici: 'No ai missili, sì al negoziato,' " *L'Unità*, December 3, 1979.

89. I have called the pope "*il condottiere* in the Vatican" for his naked use of power, which he tranquilly justifies: "As Saint Thomas used to say, it takes power to realize the good" (*Panorama*, November 26, 1979). In regard to political neutrality, the pope issued no statement on the DC Congress of February 1980, and neither did any prelate, including the usually outspoken Cardinal Benelli (*La Repubblica*, February 12, 1980). On the papal commitment against war and for a new economic order, there are his speeches in Poland, at the United Nations, at Puebla, and his trips to Africa and the United States. In Paris he stressed both themes in four major addresses: to half a million people at Le Bourget Airport, to 100,000 youths at the stadium of Parc des Princes, to the UNESCO Executive Council, and to the French episcopate. For excerpts from these speeches and for his meeting with Giscard d'Estaing, see the *New York Times* and *Il Progresso Italo-Americano*, June 2 and 3, 1980. The papal shift in his speech on terrorism is given by Marcella Leone, *Panorama*, May 12, 1980.

# Chapter 5: "The Italian Contribution to Eurocommunism," pp. 93–115

1. Giorgio Bocca, *Palmiro Togliatti*, p. 509. The story of the attempted assassination and its aftermath comes mostly from Bocca's biography. A recent book merits attention: *L'attentato a Togliatti*, by Massimo Caprara, former secretary to Togliatti, reviewed in *Panorama*, July 11, 1978.

2. Bocca, p. 511. See also Mario Spallone, *Vent'anni con Togliatti*, p. 30. Spallone was Togliatti's personal doctor for twenty years.

3. *Ibid.*, p. 512.

4. *Ibid.*, p. 467.

5. The expulsion of the PCI from the government took place on June 1, 1947. The Marshall Plan was proposed on June 3 and rejected by Molotov on July 2. As late as July 7, Togliatti was ready to accept the plan, subject to certain guarantees. See *L'Unità*, July 7, 1947.

6. Bocca, p. 470. Togliatti told Kardelj in 1944 that an insurrection "would be adventuristic and the Italian working class could pay heavily for it." (Dusan Pilic and Gabriele Invernizzi, "Quando Tito diventò Tito," *L'Espresso*, March 2, 1980, pp. 54–63.)

7. *Ibid.*, p. 512.

8. *Ibid.*, pp. 510–15.

9. According to Bocca (p. 531), these were the figures for victims of the repression from June 1948 to June 1950: killed, 62 workers, of whom 48 were Communists; wounded, 3,126, of whom 2,367 were Communists; arrested, 92,169, of whom 73,870 were Communists.

10. NBC Special News, January 13, 1978. I was in Rome when Kissinger came for four days in December 1977, ostensibly to get material for his show on Eurocommunism. He talked to all the parties in Rome *except* the PCI, the subject of his research.

11. Bocca, p. 378.

12. See these recent books on the Italian Social Republic: Silvio Bertoldi, *Salò: Vita e morte della repubblica sociale italiana*, and Giorgio Bocca, *La repubblica di Mussolini*.

13. Bocca, *Palmiro Togliatti*, p. 373–74.

14. Control of investments, planning, and nationalization are not in themselves measures of socialism. They can all be to used to strengthen monopolistic capitalism, as was the case in Nazi Germany and Fascist Italy. To a lesser extent this has been true of postwar England, France, and Italy. The issue is one of power: For whose benefit are those measures taken?

15. An English version of the Constitution of the Italian Republic may be found in Norman Kogan, *The Government of Italy*, pp. 188–215. In addition to Kogan, another important commentary on the Italian system of government is P. A. Allum, *Italy—Republic Without Government?* See also the recent work by Paolo Barile and Carlo Macchitella, *I nodi della costituzione*. Umberto Terracini, a founding member of the PCI and holder of the record for most years spent as a political prisoner under fascism, was the president of the Constituent Assembly. See his "interview" of 1978: *Come nacque la costituzione*.

16. Alceste Santini, *Questione cattolica, questione comunista*, p. 134.

17. Bocca, pp. 472–73.

18. Luciano Gruppi, *Il compromesso storico*, pp. 18, 20.

18a. Edvard Kardelj, *Sećanja Edvarda Kardelja: Vorba za priznanje i nezavisnost nove Jugoslavije, 1944–1957* [Memoirs of Edvard Kardelj: The struggle for recognition and independence of the new Yugoslavis, 1944–1957].

18b. These excerpts from Kardelj's memoirs were published in Dusan Pilic and Gabriele Invernizzi, "Quando Tito divento Tito," *L'Espresso*, March 2, 1980, pp. 54–63.

19. For Bocca, Togliatti's *doppiezza* began at the Seventh Comintern Congress (1935) and continued throughout the resistance and postwar Italy. But Bocca does not fault Togliatti, whose line was "not a banal *doppiezza* or one due to base cunning, but imposed by the necessity to maintain simultaneously two political lines, the democratic one of the popular front and the revolutionary one of the Soviet myth." See particularly Bocca, pp. 381, 388, 404, 414ff.

20. Bocca, p. 511.

21. Enrico Berlinguer, *La questione comunista*, p. 637.

22. "Ecco la verità, tutta la verità," *Epoca*, September 1, 1979, pp. 23–25. The interview published in *Epoca* is not a retranslation from the German of *Stern*. It is the original Italian.

23. Enrico Berlinguer, "Ripensando a un editoriale di Togliatti del 1946: Il compromesso nella fase attuale."

24. For several articles of Gramsci's before his imprisonment which adumbrate this policy, see Gruppi, *Il compromesso storico*, pp. 33–46. The pertinent references in the prison notebooks are too numerous to list.

25. For example, Togliatti said of 1944: "The real content of the 'Salerno policy' was . . . the affirmation of a new national unity, in which the working class and its parties, collaborating with all democratic forces, assumed the role of protagonists" (Giuseppe Vacca, *Saggio su Togliatti*, p. 313).

26. Bocca, pp. 371–72. The high quality of *Rinascita* has been maintained, and it has been a major factor in furthering the cultural hegemony of the PCI.

27. In the steady increase from 1946 to 1976 there is an inner shift. From 1946 to 1963, the PCI vote increased 6 percentage points; from 1963 to 1976, 9 percentage points, or double the rate (0.35 per year vs. 0.70 per year). The drop in 1979 is analyzed in the text.

28. A Communist mayor has presided over a coalition of Communist and Socialist councilmen who have governed Bologna since 1947. In 1975 the PCI got an absolute majority, 31 seats out of 60, with the PSI getting 6 and the DC 14. However, the Socialist-Communist coalition has been maintained.

29. G. De Rosa, "Due mesi alla ricerca di un governo," *La Civiltà cattolica*, December 7, 1974, pp. 489–97.

30. Santini, *op. cit.*, p. 31.

31. Bartolomeo Sorge, "La 'scelta decisiva' dei gesuiti: portare le speranze degli uomini di oggi," *La Civiltà cattolica*, September 15, 1977, pp. 454–68. The passage quoted is from Sorge's report based on the decrees of the Jesuit Congress of 1975. The report was made to a conference in Padua, August 1977.

32. Although Pope John Paul II has reprimanded the Jesuit order for being too worldly, the position of Father Sorge as editor of *La Civiltà cattolica* seems secure—a significant index to papal thinking, since Sorge is a man of the dialogue.

33. Gianfranco Morra, *Marxismo e religione*, p. 14.

34. For a profile of Del Noce, see Stefano Malatesta, "Reazionario sarà Gramsci," *Panorama,* October 10, 1978, pp. 100–103, and Malatesta's interview with Lucio Colletti on Del Noce: "Del Noce non ha torto," *ibid.*, pp. 103–5.

35. Augusto Del Noce's book, *L'eurocomunismo e l'Italia*, is difficult to find in bookstores. Its publishing house is a made-up name, and the book was printed and distributed by the DC as campaign material.

36. See Natalia Ginzburg, *Family Sayings*, for background on the Olivetti family.

37. Morra, Appendix.

38. The Bettazzi-Berlinguer correspondence appears in Carl Marzani, ed., "The Church and the Party: Documents on the Catholic-Communist Dialogue in Italy," together with the commentary of *L'Osservatore romano* and an introduction by the editor. The Bettazzi-Berlinguer correspondence is also found in the Appendix of Bettazzi's book, *Al di là . . . al di dentro*, and in *Comunisti e mondo cattolico oggi* (Rome: Editori Riuniti, 1977).

39. Another significant incident drew heavy applause. Innocenti had poked fun at Serri's talk of repression by saying that it hadn't been hard enough, since there were so many Communists left. Coming from the DC, which had done the repressing, the joke showed bad taste, and the audience responded coldly, except for a claque of young toughs in a corner: they applauded vociferously. Serri, in his rebuttal, said he didn't mind Innocenti's jocular remark, but he did resent the applause of the toughs. He gave them a tongue-lashing, citing examples of victimization, and the audience, both left and right, applauded at length. See note 9 above for victimization.

40. A remarkable photo essay on the festival is found in *Modena '77: Una città, un festival.*

41. *La politica e l'organizzazione. . .*, p. 153.

42. Marzani, "The Church and the Party."

43. *La politica e l'organizzazione. . .*, pp. 150–51.

44. Bocca, pp. 435–36, 409–10, 269–71.

45. Peter Nichols, *The Italian Decision*, p. 7. For Gramsci, *Quaderni del carcere*, pp. 1201–2. "A permanent character of the Italian people [is] the naive and fanatic admiration for intelligence as such, for the intelligent man as such, which corresponds to the cultural nationalism of Italians, perhaps the only form of popular chauvinism in Italy." Gramsci goes on to say that the Neapolitans are the worst of such chauvinists.

46. Gramsci, *Quaderni del carcere*, pp. 1190–91.

# Chapter 6: "When the Women Counted,"
## pp. 119–37

1. The details of woman's oppression given here are not unique to Italy. They are duplicated *in toto* in many parts of the world, and, in part, in many countries of Europe and many states in the United States.

In Italy, too, indeed, more so than in most countries, the feminist movement grew very rapidly in the 1970s. Here are some recent publications dealing in various ways with *the role of women and feminism in the PCI:* Giulietta Ascoli, pp. 25–49 in *La parola elettorale* (Rome: Edizioni delle Donne, 1976); Franca Pieroni Bortolotti, *Feminismo e partiti politici in Italia, 1919–1926* (Rome:

Editori Riuniti, 1978); Guido Gerosa, *Le compagne* (Milan: Rizzoli, 1979); Laura Grasso, *Compagno padrone* (Rimini-Florence: Guaraldi Editore, 1978); Bianca Guidetti Serra, ed., *Compagne: Testimonianze di participazione politica femminile*, 2 vols. (Turin: Einaudi, 1977); Laura Lilli and Chiara Valentini, eds., *Care compagne: Il femminismo nel PCI e nelle organizzazioni di massa* (Rome: Editori Riuniti, 1979); Miriam Mafai, *L'apprendistato della politica: Le donne italiane nel dopoguerra* (Rome: Editori Riuniti, 1979); Daniela Pasti, *I comunisti e l'amore* (Milan: I Libri de L'Espresso, 1979); Carla Ravaioli, "La donna e le sinistre storiche in Italia," pp. 5–33 in Mechthild Merfeld, *L'emancipazione della donna. . . .* (Milan: Feltrinelli, 1974); Carla Ravaioli, *La questione femminile: Intervista col PCI* (Milan: Bompiani, 1976); Erica Scroppo, *Donna, privato e politico: Storie personali di 21 donne del PCI* (Milan: Mazzotta Editore, 1979); Adriana Seroni, *La questione femminile in Italia, 1970–1977* (Rome: Editori Riuniti, 1977); Nadia Spano and Fiamma Camarlinghi, *La questione femminile nella politica del PCI* (Rome: Edizioni Donne e Politica, 1972); and Aida Tiso, *I comunisti e la questione femminile* (Rome: Editori Riuniti, 1976).

See also the recent autobiographies of some older Communist women: Adele Faraggiana, *Garofani Rossi* (Rome: Editori Riuniti, 1978); Felicita Ferrero, *Un nocciolo di verità* (Milan: La Pietra, 1978); Cesira Fiori, *Una donna nelle carceri fascisti* (Rome: Editori Riuniti, 1965); Teresa Noce, *Rivoluzionaria professionale* (Milan: La Pietra, 1974); and Camilla Ravera, *Diario di trent'anni, 1913–1943* (Rome: Editori Riuniti, 1973).

2. Peter Nichols, *Italia, Italia*, p. 30.

3. *Ibid.*, p. 14.

4. Celso Ghini, *L'Italia che cambia*, p. 727. All references to voting records are taken from Ghini unless otherwise indicated. Ghini is the PCI specialist on electoral statistics. See also his general work on elections since 1946, *Il voto degli italiani, 1946–1974*, and his monograph on the regional elections of 1975, *Il terremoto del 15 giugno*.

5. Peter Nichols, *The Italian Decision*, p. 7.

6. Gore Vidal, "On the Assassin's Trail," pp. 17–23. Supposedly a review of Leonardo Sciascia's *Candido*, the article is as much an encomium to the Radical party as it is a deprecation of the PCI.

7. Nichols, *Italia, Italia*, p. 38.

8. Women's organizations and left parties are fighting to make rape a crime against the person. A television documentary in the spring of 1979, "Trial of a Rape," shook Italy by showing how judges in rape trials turn the violated woman into a defendant who provoked the attack. (A not uncommon twist in the United States and other countries.) The film is being used in mass meetings to change the law. I attended one such meeting in Rome in June 1979, which was amply reported. See *La Repubblica*, June 8, 1979; *L'Unità*, June 9, 1979.

9. Nichols, *Italia, Italia*, p. 231.

10. *Ibid.*, p. 232.

11. Enrico Berlinguer, *La questione comunista*, p. 687. Giorgio Almirante (b. Parma, 1914) has been a major leader of Italian neofascism *(Movimento Sociale Italiano)* since its founding in December 1946. Under fascism he wrote for the racist publication *La difesa della razza* and edited the newspaper *Tevere*. During the Italian Social Republic (1943–1945), he was cabinet secretary in the ministry of popular culture. For the story of Almirante and the MSI up to 1964, see Angelo Del Boca and Mario Giovana, *Fascism Today: A World Survey*, pp. 126–73.

12. Family conversations in Rome.

13. Ghini, *"L'Italia che cambia*, Plate 69.

14. Family conversations in Rome.

15. Peter Nichols, *The Italian Decision*, p. 14.

16. The most prevalent fraud was to switch the votes when they were forwarded to the Central Statistical Office. In the town of Argenta, province of Ferrara, the report sent in showed 446 yes votes and 36 no votes, which was the opposite of the tally. For this and other frauds, see Ghini, *L'Italia che cambia*, p. 475.

17. Ghini, *L'Italia che cambia*, p. 452. The actual figures were 59.3 percent for no, and the participation was 87.7 percent—an example of democracy in action that cannot be matched in the United States.

18. *Sesso amaro: Trentamila donne rispondono su maternità, sessualità, aborto* (Rome: Editori Riuniti, 1977).

19. Total of small groups, 1,250; participants, 11,500 women; regions involved, Lombardy, Liguria, Emilia, Tuscany, Marches, Umbria. Total of large meetings, 380; participants, 18,000; regions, Piedmont, Veneto, Lazio, Apulia, Calabria, Sicily. Total of interviews, 380, mostly in the region of Campania. It can be seen that small groups were more common in the north; large meetings more common in the south.

20. After three months a doctor's certificate is required; under sixteen years of age, parents'

permission. The law is progressive, but carrying it out is a never-ending struggle. A bitter joke has an official at a clinic saying to a woman: "Yes, yes, of course you can have a free abortion! But we are full up and there is a long waiting list. Please come back in a year."

The law also allows doctors to "opt out" of performing abortions as a matter of conscience, and some 80 percent did so, many because of social pressures. Still, in 1979, 200,000 legal abortions were done, one third of them in the south. (*Panorama*, May 12, 1980, p. 30.)

21. *Nuova società* 35 (June 15, 1974). This is a bi-weekly published by the PCI in Turin. Its editor, Diego Novelli, became Turin's mayor after the elections of 1975.

22. Nichols, *The Italian Decision*, p. 14.

23. Ghini, *L'Italia che cambia*, p. 481.

24. *Ibid.*, p. 479.

25. *Ibid.*, pp. 467–68. The vote could be pinpointed to nuns for two reasons: the voting districts were exceptionally small, and they mostly covered convents and institutions (clinics, orphanages, etc.) staffed by nuns.

26. *Ibid.*, p. 484.

27. *Ibid.*, pp. 493, 498. The two elections were in the region of Trentino-Alto Adige and the province of Avellino.

28. *Ibid.*, p. 549.

29. *Ibid.*, p. 727. The size of the DC vote had remained unchanged, masking the fact that its composition had changed. The DC had absorbed 5 percent of liberals (a conservative party, actually) and neofascists and lost 5 percent to the left, which now reached almost 50 percent.

30. Nichols, *The Italian Decision*, p. 14.

31. Alceste Santini, *Questione cattolica, questione comunista*, p. 90.

32. Marcella Leone, "L'imperio karolingio," *Panorama*, October 29, 1979, p. 247.

33. Santini, pp. 79–80. A few opinions by theologians: Patriarch Maximus IV, "The duty of the Church is to develop the moral sense of its children rather than envelop them in a net of prescriptions and commands." Father Simon, professor of morals, Faculty of Theology, Paris, "Matrimony must no longer be considered a destiny, but the story of a love which has to be lived in a social and temporal context." Peter d'Avack, "The traditional structure of matrimony and the family . . . is no longer adequate to . . . modern man." The conception of marriage as based solely on procreation is "not only anachronistic, but downright grotesque."

34. Leone, *op. cit.*, p. 235.

35. *Nuova società* 31 (April 15, 1974). All quotes are from that issue.

36. *Nuova società* 32 (May 1, 1974). In the town of Novara, an appeal for a no vote was signed by 22 priests; in Ivrea, a similar appeal was signed by 40 Catholic notables, including the DC mayor. In Saluzzo, "New Forces" (left-wing DC) called for a no vote. In Langhe, the group "Together" of the parish of Pollenzo declared in its bulletin: "We maintain it is politically just and proper to vote no." In Alba, dozens of Catholic notables signed a document inviting citizens to "reject with a no the attempt to impose on a pluralistic society the choice of a personal faith."

37. *I cristiani nella sinistra dalla resistenza ad oggi*, pp. 199, 228 ff.

38. Giuseppe Pasini, *Le ACLI dalle origini (1944–1948)*, p. 93.

39. *Ibid.*, p. 101.

40. *Il Popolo*, August 3, 1976.

41. Nichols, *The Italian Decision*, p. 12.

42. Berlinguer, *La questione comunista*, p. 746.

43. See Ghini, *Il voto degli italiani*, pp. 467–69. Indeed, Togliatti insisted on the independence of UDI from the party. See Palmiro Togliatti, *L'emancipazione femminile*, pp. 49–71.

44. Berlinguer, p. 739; Ghini, *Il voto degli italiani*, pp. 467–69.

45. The Salvemini Fund to publish young scholars is well worth American support. Contributions should be sent to Professor Sylos Labini, Sociology Department, University of Rome.

46. Carlo Rosselli had founded a socialist-oriented movement, *Giustizia e Libertà*, and a newspaper of that name was smuggled into Italy in ingenious ways—for example, reduced in size and printed on thin paper, it was sent in large tins of sardines. The movement had organized the Garibaldi Battalion of the International Brigades. Rosselli, an annoyance to Mussolini, was assassinated, along with his brother Nello, in France in late summer of 1937.

47. *Nuova società* 21 (November 15, 1973).

# Chapter 7: "The Hard Years at Fiat," pp. 138–63

1. *Corriere della sera*, November 17, 1977.

2. Luciano Lama, *Di Vittorio*, pp. 68–72. Giuseppe Di Vittorio (1892–1957) was secretary of the CGIL from its inception. He was born in Cerignola, Apulia, of illiterate *braccianti* (day farm laborers), went to work in the fields at age eight, organized the first socialist group in Cerignola at age fourteen, was elected a socialist deputy in 1921, and brought his left socialist group into the PCI in 1924. He was in Mussolini's jails during the war. Di Vittorio was an outgoing activist, extremely popular in the unions and in the party. Recent important contributions to the literature on this impressive man are: Anita Di Vittorio, *La mia vita con Di Vittorio* (Florence: Vallecchi, 1965); Luciana Lama, *La CGIL di Di Vittorio, 1944–1957: Scritti e interventi di G. Di V.;* Davide Lajolo, *Il volto umano di un rivoluzionario;* and especially Michele Pistillo, *Giuseppe Di Vittorio*.

3. Giuseppe Pasini, *Le ACLI delle origini*, pp. 137 ff.

4. Lama, *Di Vittorio*, p. 78. At first the Catholic union was called *Libera Confederazione Generale Italiana del Lavoro* (LCGIL), or "Free CGIL," and later changed to *Confederazione Italiana Sindacati Liberi* (CISL), or "Free Trade Unions," but then the last word was changed to *lavoratori*, so that the polemical word "free" was no longer in CISL when it became a part of the unitary federation of the three confederations.

5. Letter to the author from L. Bignami, chief of press and research for the CGIL.

6. *Ibid.* The *New York Times* (May 20, 1978) gives the following figures: CGIL, 4.3 million members; CISL, 2.8 million; UIL, 1.1 million.

7. Luciano Lama, *Il sindacato nella crisis italiana*, p. 37. The book reprints his article from *L'Unità*, July 23, 1972, announcing the formation of the federation.

8. Emilio Pugno and Sergio Garavini, *Gli anni duri alla Fiat*, Appendix, p. 320. Emilio Pugno was a worker at Fiat in the 1950s. He is now a PCI deputy.

9. *La Stampa*, November 19, 1977.

10. *Ibid.*

11. Pugno and Garavini, p. 74. This story was given to Pugno by Zuccotti, as were many other items in the books.

12. *Ibid.*, p. 17.

13. *Ibid.*, p. 8.

14. *Ibid.*, p. 250.

15. *Ibid.*, p. 230.

16. L. Bignami, letter to the author. See also Marisa Malfatti and Riccardo Tortora, *Il cammino dell'unità, 1943–1969*.

17. Luciano Lama, *Il sindacato nella crisi italiana*, p. 288. This volume reprints his article "Movimento operaio e diritti civili: Il divorzio non riguarda solo i borghesi," *Rinascita* 31, no. 14 (April 5, 1974): 14–15, giving the position of the CGIL, CISL, and UIL.

18. I checked this statement later and found it confirmed in Michele Salvati, *Il sistema economico italiano*, p. 93. Salvati got his figures from the National Institute *Economic Review*.

19. *Fare politica*—"to make politics, to be political"—is the essence of the PCI's antideterminist tradition. This accounts for Gramsci's first important article on the Russian Revolution, titled, significantly, "The Revolution Against 'Das Kapital,'" where he argues that *Capital* has been used to foster the deterministic idea that a western type of civilization must exist in Russia before the socialist revolution could occur. (See John Cammett, *Antonio Gramsci and the Origins of Italian Communism*, p. 61). In 1930, when lecturing his fellow prisoners, Gramsci asserted that the objective (i.e., economic) conditions for the proletarian revolution had existed in Europe for more than fifty years. The way out, he suggested, was for Communists to "to be more political, to know how to use the political element, to be less afraid of making politics." This is from a report of that year to the Party Center by one of Gramsci's fellow prisoners. See Athos Lisa, *Memorie: In carcere con Gramsci*.

20. Rent control laws in Italy are national, and known as *equo canone*, which translates as "equitable ordnances," meaning equitable to tenants and landlords alike. This attempt at squaring the circle has created a bureaucratic mess, as various courts have made various interpretations of its provisions.

21. Giorgio Napolitano, *The Italian Road to Socialism*, p. 54.

22. This was confirmed by President Germano Marri of the Umbrian regional *giunta*.

23. *L'Unità*, November 18, 1977.

24. Gramsci, *Quaderni del carcere*, p. 1591; *idem.*, *Prison Notebooks*, p. 161: "Hegemony undoubtedly presupposes that attention is paid to the interests and tendencies of the groups under the hegemony, that a certain equilibrium of compromises exists, that is, that the governing group makes economic sacrifices. . . ."

25. *Wall Street Journal*, September 13, 1978. Its correspondent, Felix Kessler, describes the growing repression. He quotes a Bundestag deputy, Dieter Luttman, who voted against the repressive laws, saying that the danger to democracy came not from terrorists but from the

democrats. Today in Germany people must be cleared of any taint of radicalism to get any government, academic, or professional job; any person near the scene of the crime can be searched and fingerprinted without being charged or arrested; a whole apartment building can be searched with *one* warrant.

26. This story of De Gasperi and Pius XII can also be found in Peter Nichols, *Italia, Italia*, p. 119.

27. Pugno and Garavini, pp. 172 ff. The transcripts of the conversations were published by Professor Gian Giacomo Migone in "Le origini dell'egemonia americana in Europa." Presumably, the transcripts came from Fiat files.

28. Diana Johnstone, *In These Times*, November 6, 1979.

29. *Ibid.*

30. *Ibid.*

31. See story in the *New York Times*, January 30, 1978.

32. Gerardo Chiaromonte, "Quali risposte alla Fiat? [What Answers to Fiat?]," *Rinascita* 36, no. 40 (October 19, 1979): pp. 1–2, and Adalberto Minucci, "La Fiat 'anticipa'? Ma non siamo negli anni '50," *L'Unità*, November 3, 1979.

33. "L'intervento di Berlinguer," *L'Unità*, November 5, 1979.

34. *La Repubblica*, November 18, 1979.

35. "Lama spiega il perchè dello sciopero," *L'Unità*, November 18, 1979.

36. See the editorial in *La Repubblica*, November 19, 1979; Franco Giustolisi, "Caso Fiat: Quelle di dentro e quelli di fuori," *L'Espresso*, November 25, 1979, pp. 31–32, and an editorial and story in *Euro*, November 1979. The slant is in favor of Fiat, especially the editorial in *Euro*, which lavishly praises Agnelli.

37. Guido Neppi Modona, "Terrorismo alla Fiat," *La Repubblica*, January 27, 1980.

38. Massimo Riva, "Berlinguer e l'avvocato," *La Repubblica*, January 27, 1980—the lawyer being Agnelli. Riva also points out that Volkswagen and Peugeot-Citroen welcome Fiat's problems and that Berlinguer and Agnelli can find common ground in resisting the damage done by Italian adherence to the European Monetary System.

## Chapter 8: "Why the DC Horse *Is* Drinking," pp. 164–88

1. In 1913, in the first election under so-called universal suffrage (but no women), Count Gentiloni, leader of the Catholic Electoral Union made an agreement with Prime Minister Giovanni Giolitti to support government candidates to check the socialists. See Antonio Gramsci, *Quaderni del carcere*, pp. 36–37; *idem.*, *Prison Notebooks*, pp. 93–94.

2. Teodoro Sala, "Un'offerta di collaborazione dell'Azione cattolica italiana al governo Badoglio (agosto 1943)," *Rivista di storia contemporanea* 4 (1972): 517–33.

3. Pietro Ingrao, *Masse e potere*, p. 56. My analysis of the DC owes a great deal to Ingrao.

4. Giorgio Bocca, *Palmiro Togliatti*, p. 447.

5. *Monthly Review* 19, no. 2 (June 1977): 21. This remark is in a "reply" by the editors to preceding articles by Carl Marzani and Max Gordon, "In Defense of the Italian CP," *ibid.*, pp. 1–8 and 8–15.

6. Guido Carli, *Intervista sul capitalismo italiano*, p. 75.

7. Gramsci, *Quaderni del carcere*, p. 1750; *idem.*, *Prison Notebooks*, p. 155. "The great industrialists utilise all existing parties turn by turn, but they do not have their own party. . . . Their interest is in a determinate balance of forces. . . ." Except, adds Gramsci, in times of great crisis.

8. Giorgio Galli, *Opinioni sul PCI*, p. 114; Peter Nichols, *The Italian Decision*, p. 135; Celso Ghini, *L'Italia che cambia*, p. 526. The gossip seemed well-founded, but the final decision was to stick with the DC. Gianni Agnelli's brother, Umberto, ran and was elected deputy on the DC ticket.

9. Angelo Costa (b. Genoa, 1901) was president of the *Confindustria* from 1945 to 1955. He was noted for his rigid defense of the industrialists' interests and his unwillingness to make any concessions to workers.

10. *Panorama*, October 29, 1978. See also Nichols, *The Italian Decision*, pp. 156–58. For a detailed view of De Carolis's position, see the long interview in Francesco Palladino, *Se il PCI va al governo* [If the PCI enters the government], pp. 105 ff.

11. After the 1976 election, the age limit was lowered to eighteen years, resulting in 3.5 million new voters. It was these youths whose expectations were most frustrated, and they moved left of the PCI. The vote in the Senate, which has a higher voting age, reflected this shift. There the PCI dropped only 2.5 percentage points, compared to a drop of 4 in the Chamber.

12. For data on the number of members and the social composition of the PCI, see *Dati sull'organizzazione del partito*, pp. 11, 15. For the years 1974–1978:

|  | Total Membership | Women Members |
|---|---|---|
| 1974 | 1,643,716 | 387,072 |
| 1975 | 1,715,203 | 405,424 |
| 1976 | 1,797,596 | 433,775 |
| 1977 | 1,797,489 | 437,308 |
| 1978 | 1,772,425 | 438,979 |

The social composition of members of the PCI in 1977 (p. 42), in percent:

| | | | |
|---|---|---|---|
| Workers | 40.08 | Clerks/Technicians | 6.92 |
| Agricultural wage laborers | 5.30 | Intellectuals/Liberal professions | 2.34 |
| Sharecroppers | 1.88 | Students | 2.09 |
| Farmers | 3.53 | Domestic Workers | 0.70 |
| Artisans | 5.34 | Housewives | 10.27 |
| Salesmen, etc. | 3.50 | Pensioners | 17.37 |
| Small businessmen | 0.28 | Various | 0.31 |

The PCI has conducted a sociological survey of its functionaries, a noteworthy step for a political party. More important, it published the results. They were summarized in "Portrait of a PCI Functionary," *L'Unità*, December 9, 1979: 65% were under forty (over half of them under thirty), and nearly half had joined in the decade of the seventies. One third were ex-workers or peasants, and over half had parents in these categories. More than half got paid less than a skilled worker, and 61% of married functionaries had a working consort. The survey won a lot of attention; three months later the DC did a similar study. See footnote, page 168.

12a. From 1975 to 1978 there were 16,415 students attending the seven party schools (three of them founded in 1977–78). Of these students, about 2,800 were women. In addition, between 1955 and 1977, 3,823 courses and seminars were held at the regional and provincial levels. The party schools produced 500,000 copies of thirty-nine publications and distributed them directly to the students. Eight of these publications (138,000 copies) dealt with the "thought and action of Gramsci and Togliatti." (See *Dati sull'organizzazione*, pp. 93–94.) For brief descriptions and addresses of these schools, see Supplement to the *Almanacco PCI* (Rome: Sezione Centrale di Stampa e Propaganda, 1979), p. 14.

13. *Avanti!*, September 20, 1977.

14. There are 1,362 PCI mayors out of 8,068 (16 percent, but in towns of over 5,000 the percentage goes up to 27 percent). Left *giunte* in towns of over 5,000 are 47 percent. (*Almanacco PCI '77*, p. 30).

15. Peter Nichols, *Italia, Italia*, p. 212.

16. On the Concordat, see note 33, Chapter 4. The conjunction of the revision of the concordat with the implementation of Law 382 has placed the Church on the defensive.

17. Gramsci, *Quaderni del carcere*, pp. 1383–84; *idem., Prison Notebooks*, pp. 331–33.

17a. For an interesting discussion of the history and present situation of the Umbrian Communists, see Raffaele Rossi, *Il PCI in una regione rossa*.

18. For many years the PCI has been very active in the area of publications. In 1953 the party established the Editori Riuniti, thereby replacing the old Edizioni di Cultura Sociale and the Edizioni Rinascita. Since then Editori Riuniti has published more than two thousand titles in more than eighteen million copies—very impressive numbers by Italian standards. See the recent *Catalogo generale degli Editori Riuniti, 1953–1979*.

Editori Riuniti is also directly responsible for the publication of eight periodicals: These are *Critica marxista* (founded 1963, political theory and philosophy); *Politica ed economica* (founded 1970, economics); *Riforma della scuola* (founded 1955, education); *Democrazia e diritto* (1960, law and society); *Studi storici* (1959, history); *Donna e politica* (1969, women's studies); *Nuova rivista internazionale* (1964, international politics); *Cinemasessanta* (1960, film studies). For an interesting article in English on Editori Riuniti, see Herbert Lottman, "Editori Riuniti. . ."

There are a great many other PCI publications which are not published by the Editori Riuniti. I mention only a few: *Il partito oggi* (1978, the monthly journal of the "cadres"); and many regional magazines, some on a very high level, such as *Società* (Bologna, 1977) and *Nuova società* (Turin, 1972). Then, too, there is the voluminous literature of the trade unions and the co-operatives, much of it "inspired" by Communists. Finally, we have *L'Unità*, the official daily newspaper of the PCI (founded 1924 by Antonio Gramsci), and *Rinascita*, the superb theoretical weekly of the party (founded 1944 by Palmiro Togliatti).

19. Giorgio Napolitano, one of the most influential leaders of the PCI, had given two interviews to British historian E. J. Hobsbawm (in 1975 and 1976). They were published in *The Italian Road to Socialism*.

20. Confirmed in Peter Nichols, *Italia, Italia*, p. 56.

21. See Chapter 5, note 14, for literature on the Italian Constitution.

22. The article was a rehash of the Gramscian theory of "substitution"; i.e., Marxism would take the place of religion in the "common sense" of the people as they developed their consciousness in struggles. The author concludes that the Church must renew itself and defend the downtrodden to block the Gramscian strategy. He hopes it is not too late—an unintended irony that is worth the whole article.

23. The article was by Professor G. Carancini of the law faculty of the University of Modena. According to him, regionalism had been made a goal of the *Partito Popolare* by Don Sturzo at its Third Congress. De Gasperi revived the goal in a clandestine pamphlet (July 1943), and the suggestion was formalized in the program of the DC published in 1944 in a book, *La parola dei democratici cristiani*.

24. Nichols, *Italia, Italia*, p. 236.

25. The text of Law 382, together with a long introduction, is in Augusto Barbera, *Governo locale e riforma dello stato*.

26. "Mountains of Civil Servants," *The Economist* 273 (December 22–28, 1979): 36. It gives the following figures for civil servants per 1,000 population: Italy, 12.8; Germany, 14.3; France, 14.6; England, 21.3.

27. Jane Kramer, "The San Vincenzo Cell," *The New Yorker*, September 24, 1979, p. 58. This article, though often cynical in tone, has much interesting information on the Umbrian Communists.

28. Vivian Gornick, *The Romance of American Communism*, p. 119.

29. Lucia Baroncini, *I comunisti umbri*, p. 362.

30. Gino Galli, "Umbria: Esperienza unitaria nella lotta per il piano."

31. All quotes are from the introduction to Max Jäggi, Roger Müller, and Sil Schmid, *Bologna rossa: I comunisti al governo di una città*.

32. Zangheri in conversation with Elizabeth Fox Genovese and Eugene Genovese.

33. Andrea Costa (1851–1910). His clamorous "conversion" from anarchism to Marxism in 1879 opened a new phase in the history of the Italian labor movement. Zangheri contributed the biography of Costa to *Il movimento operaio italiano: Dizionario biografico 1853–1943*, vol. 2, pp. 109–20.

34. Jäggi, Müller, and Schmid, p. 96.

35. *Ibid.*, p. 61.

36. *Ibid.*, p. 92.

37. Renato Zangheri, *Il sindaco di Bologna: Enzo Biagi intervista Renato Zangheri*, p. 140. This important book consists of a forty-page interview of Zangheri and about 140 pages of his writings on the politics and administration of Bologna.

38. *Ibid.*, p. 46.

39. *Ibid.*, p. 140.

40. Jäggi, Müller, and Schmid, p. 108.

41. Zangheri to author.

42. Jäggi, Müller, and Schmid, p. 23.

43. Doubtless this high political level of Red Bologna was a major reason for the 1977 challenge to the city on the part of some extremist groups and of certain French intellectuals. For a vigorous defense of the city, see Zangheri *Bologna '77: Intervista di Fabio Mussi*. For a vigorous attack on the city—as well as the whole PCI—see Maria A. Macciocchi, *Dopo Marx aprile*.

44. Andrew Kopkind, "Bologna: Socialism in One City."

45. Because of the terrorism, the questions of police reorganization, unionization, and "demilitarization" have become major issues in Italy, and the Communists are in the thick of these struggles. A major organizer of the police union is Franco Fedeli. See his *Sindacato polizia*. See also Alberto Bernardi, *Dalla parte della polizia: Smilitarizzazione e sindacato*. Recent historical surveys of the Italian police are: Romano Canosa, *La polizia in Italia dal 1945 a oggi*; Angelo D'Orsi, *Il potere repressivo: La polizia*; and Fabio Isman, *I forzati dell'ordine*. A sense of the political and social complexities in the lives of contemporary Italian policemen may be found in Giancarlo Lehner, *Dalla parte dei poliziotti*, and Sandro Medici, *Vite de poliziotti*.

46. *San Juan Star*, March 16, 1978. The Committee for the Study of American Elections, based in Washington, reported 54.4 percent of eligible voters participated in the 1976 presidential election, down from 63.4 percent in 1960. Carter was elected President by 27.2 percent of the electorate.

Some 30 million Americans are chronic nonvoters because (they say by a four to one margin) they are unhappy with government and political leadership.

47. Here are the results in percentages for the Commune of Bologna of the last two national elections (*Corriere della sera*, June 6, 1979):

| 1979 | | 1976 | |
|------|------|------|------|
| PCI | 45.15 | PCI | 46.7 |
| PSI | 7.81 | PSI | 8.0 |
| PSDI | 4.13 | PSDI | 4.2 |
| PRI | 4.56 | PRI | 4.5 |
| DC | 24.95 | DC | 27.3 |
| PLI | 2.68 | PLI | 1.7 |
| MSI | 3.68 | MSI | 4.4 |
| DN | 0.26 | DN | — |
| PDUP | 0.94 | DP | 1.2 |
| RAD | 4.76 | RAD | 1.8 |

At least one half of the 53 percent Communist and Socialist votes are Catholic. In addition, some, at least, of the 25 percent DC voters must be atheists, agnostics, or non-Catholics. As is noted elsewhere, the PCI in the 1979 elections lost 4 percent nationally but only 1.5 percent in Bologna. Nationally, the DC held its previous position, but in Bologna it lost nearly 2.5 percent. It seems clear that both the PCI and the DC in Bologna lost votes to the Radicals.

48. See, for example, the editors of *Monthly Review*, June 1977, p. 17.

49. Zangheri, *Il sindaco di Bologna*, p. 29–30.

## Chapter 9: "How to Steal a Country," pp. 189–215

1. Orazio Barrese and Massimo Caprara, *L'anonima DC*, p. 262.

2. *Ibid.*, p. 191. Those insiders lucky enough to mail letters (presumably to themselves) with the erroneous stamps on them ended up with an item worth 920,000 lire. See *Sassone: Catalogo dei francobolli italiani e dei paesi italiani* (1976), p. 168.

3. *Ibid.*, p. 190.

4. P. A. Allum, *Politics and Society in Post-War Naples*, p. 281; Barrese and Caprara, p. 32.

5. *L'Espresso*, March 30, 1958.

6. Barrese and Caprara, p. 129.

7. Spaventa spoke off the cuff and didn't define his categories. In 1976 the census of *contadini diretti* (excludes day laborers, sharecroppers, etc.) was 1,834,000. Enrico Pugliese, in *Agricoltura, Mezzogiorno e mercato del lavoro*, quotes INSTAT for 1969: 2,676,000 owners and co-owners and 1,316,000 dependent workers. Pietro Ingrao, in *Masse e potere* (p. 25), gives 2,350,000 as receiving social security and 2,238,000 as receiving pension. Illegal pensions are a huge drain. It is estimated that there are 21 million workers in Italy, and 12 million pensioners, many receiving two or three pensions, and many still working, undermining the pension administration, *Istituto nazionale della previdenza sociale* (INPS), whose deficit for 1980 is estimated at $25 billion. (Piero Fortuna, "Will we end up with no pensions?" *Epoca*, September 1, 1979.

8. Franco Cazzola, *Anatomia del potere DC*, p. 91, Table 7. This book, published in 1979, is a major study. I have also used Ferdinando Terranova, *Il potere assistenziale* (Welfare power), *Il libro bianco sull'assistenza in Italia* (The white book on welfare on Italy), and Vittorio Emiliani, *L'Italia mangiata* (Italy devoured). *Mangiare* means "to eat," but it is also slang for "taking bribes," so there is the double meaning of "Italy bribed."

9. Emiliani, p. 30, for welfare; p. 63, for health.

10. Cazzola, p. 114, Table 14. About a third could not be identified politically, so that the percentages in the table are DC, 38.5; PCI, 4.1; PSI, 8.4.

11. Emiliani, p. 32.

12. *Ibid.*, p. 33. The south actually has one third of the population, but the proportion of destitute people there is much greater than in the north.

13. Barrese and Caprara, p. 136.

14. Emiliani, p. 60.

15. Barrese and Caprara, pp. 254–56.

16. Allum, *Politics and Society in Post-War Naples*, p. 36*n*., for 1968 and 1969 statistics. Emiliani, p. 114, for 1967 statistics and for Gava quote.

17. Barrese and Caprara, p. 117. Of the permits obtained by the Mafia, 1,563, or about half, were issued to one man, a bricklayer named Giuseppe Milazzo.

18. *Ibid.*, p. 118.

19. *Ibid.*, p. 160.

20. *Ibid.*, p. 164.

21. *Ibid.*, p. 163.

22. *Ibid.*, p. 166.

23. Oriana Fallaci, *Intervista con la storia*, p. 296.

24. Allum, *Politics and Society in Post-War Naples*, p. 60.

25. Peter Nichols, *Italia, Italia*, p. 292.

26. Patrick Meney, *L'Italie de Berlinguer*, p. 83.

27. Nichols, *Italia, Italia*, p. 294.

28. *Panorama*, November 15, 1977.

29. Meney, p. 134.

30. Barrese and Caprara, p. 141.

31. *Ibid.*, p. 142.

32. *Ibid.*, p. 219.

33. Cazzola, p. 107, Table 11.

34. Barrese and Caprara, p. 220.

35. *Ibid.*, p. 235.

36. *Ibid.*, p. 190.

37. Eugenio Scalfari and Giuseppe Turani, *Razza padrone*, p. 48. ENI is still involved in scandals. The latest, of December 1979, involves tens of millions of dollars in kickbacks and bribes for intermediaries in the purchase of oil. Pending investigation by the Italian Parliament, Saudi Arabia cancelled its contracts. High government and political figures, as well as high management officials, are being investigated. (See Nazareno Pagani, "Un barile di dubbi," *Panorama*, December 10, 1979, pp. 46–55. DC Senator Cesare Merzagora is quoted as saying, "Are we going to continue with this system? Don't we realize we are digging our grave and justifying all reactions, including those which end in violence?")

38. Barrese and Caprara, p. 80.

39. *Ibid.*, p. 95.

40. *Ibid.*, p. 80. Specifically, Guglielmone was president of the bank Balbis and Guglielmone; president of the Loan and Savings Bank of Turin; president of the Lombardi and Mainardi Bank. He was president of Samis (pharmaceuticals); Turin-Savona (harbor works); *Popolo nuovo* (publishers); Coglie-Commercio and Liquigas (natural and liquid gas and equipment); Lloyd Mediterranean (shipping); the Florentine Loan Institute (loans on personal property); and Cogne (a retail chain). He was also a director of ICLE (Institute of Credit for Italians Working Abroad); STET (Turin's telephone company); Mutual Insurance of Turin; and Italian Institute for Africa.

41. Nichols, *Italia, Italia*, p. 114.

42. A not uncommon attitude in many countries, including the United States. The IRS estimates tax evasion at some $30 billion a year.

43. Barrese and Caprara, pp. 18–19.

44. *Ibid.*, p. 207. J. M. Blair, in his definitive book on oil, gives the details of the concessions (*The Control of Oil*, p. 96).

45. Pike Report: "The Report on the CIA That President Ford Doesn't Want You to Read," *Village Voice*, February 16, 1976.

46. Antonio Gambino, *Storia del dopoguerra*, pp. 263–66. The loan for $100 million was from the Export-Import Bank and was hedged with many restrictions.

47. It should be noted that IMF loans go only to member nations who have deposited their quotas, but while everyone contributes, the United States controls the loans.

48. Blair, p. 96.

49. Joseph La Palombara, *The Italian Labor Movement: Problems and Prospects*, p. 57; Sergio Turone, *Storia del sindacato in Italia, 1943–1969*, pp. 189–93.

50. Barrese and Caprara, p. 227, for Giulio; pp. 47 and 56 for Carlo; and pp. 49 and 94 for Marcantonio. *Linee aeree* are the internal airlines and Molini Biondi is a flour-milling firm.

51. Carlo Falconi, *Vie nuove*, October 4, 1958.

52. Barrese and Caprara, p. 50.

53. See *Il Progresso Italo-Americano*, March 2, 1980, for details about the false passport; the *New York Times*, March 28, 1980, for the verdict.

54. Barrese and Caprara, pp. 57, 84. Emiliani, pp. 70 ff., in a chapter titled, "The pope's brother builds barracks."
55. *Ibid.*, pp. 223–24.
56. Nichols, *Italia, Italia*, p. 224.
57. Barrese and Caprara, p. 134.
58. *Il Messagero*, December 29, 1971.
59. Barrese and Caprara, pp. 136–37; Nichols, *Italia, Italia*, p. 223.
60. Nichols, *Italia, Italia*, p. 223. These percentages exclude deaths during birth. In Naples, for example, out of 36,465 live births, 2,370 lived less than a year.
61. Barrese and Caprara, p. 235.
62. *Ibid.*, p. 237.
63. *Ibid.*, p. 235, for EGAM's deficits.
64. *Almanacco PCI '77*, p. 30.
65. Giulio Carlo Argan, "Ho conosciuto i comunisti, ora mi iscrivo."
66. Giorgio Frasca Polara, "Lotta contro la mafia: Per il PCI è impegno determinante di ogni intesa," *L'Unità*, November 25, 1979. Alessandro Natta and Achille Occhetto, two major PCI leaders, reiterated the party's determination to smash the Mafia and named the DC officials who were not doing their duty. The DC regional secretary attended the conference unofficially and begged in vain that the names not be given out.
67. Antonio Gramsci, *L'Ordine nuovo, 1919–1920*, pp. 156–57; Carl Marzani, *The Open Marxism of Antonio Gramsci*, p. 13: "Look at the Communist worker. Week after week, month after month, year after year, after eight dehumanizing hours at the machine, he goes on disinterestedly to give eight hours to his party, his union, his co-operative. In the history of mankind, he is a much greater man than the slave or artisan [the early Christian] who defied all dangers to go to a clandestine prayer meeting." Gramsci didn't think of the loneliness and sacrifices of the Communist's wife, who kept the family together.

## Chapter 10: "Salvaging Agriculture," pp. 216–35

1. See Gerardo Chiaromonte, *L'accordo programmatico*.
2. Enrico Pugliese and Giovanni Mottura, *Agricoltura, Mezzogiorno e mercato del lavoro*, p. 171, Table 2. The shift within the labor force over two decades has been enormous. Here are the figures in millions:

|  | 1951 | | 1971 | |
|---|---|---|---|---|
|  | Total Labor Force | Agricultural Labor Force | Total Labor Force | Agricultural Labor Force |
| South | 13.0 | 5.0 | 6.0 | 1.8 |
| North | 6.5 | 3.7 | 13.0 | 1.8 |
| Total | 19.5 | 8.7 | 19.0 | 3.6 |

Agriculture lost five million workers in all, but the south lost twice as many as the north. The distribution of the total labor force was reversed in the two parts of the country. The national labor force remained stationary, proof of emigration or unemployment or both.
3. *Almanacco PCI '77*, p. 129.
4. *U.S. Statistical Abstract*, 1949, p. 20.
5. *Encyclopedia Britannica*, vol. 15, p. 466. A study in 1924 showed that there were 40 million inhabitants of Italy and that another 10 million Italian-born were abroad—one in five of all native-born Italians (vol. 12, p. 762).
6. Pugliese and Mottura, p. 20, Table 1.
7. *Almanacco PCI '77*, p. 131.
8. Pugliese and Mottura, p. 25.
9. *Annuario*, p. 194, Table 86.
10. See Giacomo Acerbo, "L'agricoltura italiana dal 1861 ad oggi," in *L'economia italiana dal 1861 al 1961* (Milan: Giuffrè, 1961), p. 122; Giuseppe Mammarella, *Italy after Fascism*, p. 121; and Antonio Gambino, *Storia del dopoguerra dalla liberazione al potere DC*, p. 57.
11. Orazio Barrese and Massimo Caprara, *L'anonima DC*, p. 129.

12. For a good discussion of the neglected subject of the southern peasant movements or 1943–46 and the policy of the PCI, see Guido Quazza, *Resistenza e storia d'Italia* (Milan: Feltrinelli, 1976), pp. 389–99.

13. Pugliese and Mottura, pp. 27, note 46.

14. Barrese and Caprara, pp. 167–76.

15. Ann Crittenden, "Italy's Red-Led Co-ops Prosper," *New York Times*, June 18, 1978, p. III-1, confirms these figures, which include all co-ops, whether PCI, PSI, or DC led. The PCI has about 60 percent of the total, half of them in Emilia-Romagna.

16. ANSA report in *Il Progresso Italo-Americano*, August 23, 1978. There is no contradiction between the previous figures and these now given. In 1977 all imports were $12 billion, of which about 30 percent were food imports, around $3.5 billion. Meat was 75 percent of food imports, or about $2.5 billion, which is roughly 20 percent of all imports.

17. Joanne Barkan Proctor and Robert Proctor, "Capitalist Development, Class Struggle, and Crisis in Italy, 1945–1975," p. 24.

The question of consumption of foodstuffs in Italy is complex. On the one hand, there is no doubt that Italians are eating better than ever, and, in many parts of the country, on a fully "European" scale. For example, between 1951–55 and 1970–74, annual consumption of beef and veal per capita tripled, that of pork more than doubled, and that of fresh fruit almost doubled (see "Un secolo a tavola," in *L'Europeo*, January 18, 1979). This is a point often made by Giorgio Amendola (somewhat provocatively, as is his fashion!).

On the other hand, Amendola also points out that the increased consumption *"because of the absence of an agrarian reform and a modern agriculture* is one of the causes of the deficit in the balance of payments." (Amendola, *Gli anni della Repubblica*, p. xviii. [Italics added.] The introduction to this work has been translated and published in *The Italian Communists* 1 [January-March 1977], pp. 3–34.)

18. Carli made this argument in his annual report to the Bank of Italy in May 1964. Ingrao quotes the report in *Masse e potere*, pp. 14–15.

19. Evidence that the Italian labor movement in general and the PCI in particular are overcoming the "corporativism" (i.e., narrow sectoralism) endemic to many labor movements is provided by the fact that the FLM (Metal Workers' Union) devoted an entire double issue of its monthly journal to the problem of Italian agriculture. See *I consigli: Rivista mensile della FLM* 111–112 (February-March 1975).

20. New co-operatives are started almost every week. A British television report showed one from initiation to fruition: "Faces of Communism," Yorkshire Television broadcast over Channel 13, WNET in New York City, beginning July 9, 1978, and running four consecutive Sundays.

21. *Il Manifesto*, June 20, 1979.

22. Nilde Jotti was the second wife of Togliatti (common-law wife, because divorce was not permitted at that time). She was a member of the Central Committee for many years. The party wanted Ingrao to remain as president of the Chamber after the June 1979 election because DC politicians had become accustomed to him, liked him, and could accept him easily. Ingrao disagreed with the party, saying the position belonged to the PCI as such and not to him as an individual. He insisted on resigning and forcing a confrontation with the PCI. This would be an instance of "soft" versus "hard" positions within the PCI.

23. Peter Nichols, *The Italian Decision*, p. 164.

24. *Ibid.*, pp. 166–67.

25. *Panorama*, November 19, 1979. The idea is to get the bank out of the way and let the regions distribute and administer the funds.

26. The amount of capital needed to provide one job in an industry varies enormously. In a capital-intensive industry such as petrochemicals, it can run to six figures; fifty thousand dollars is a modest sum.

27. Nichols, *The Italian Decision*, p. 248.

28. Crittenden, "Italy's Red-Led Co-ops Prosper." An interesting, and related, job action was reported in "Quando il contratto serve a mettere a coltura 400 ettori di terra buona," *L'Unità*, March 13, 1979, p. 6. Agricultural workers struck a big farm in Rome province and demanded as part of the settlement that a thousand acres of uncultivated land on the farm be put into production.

29. Crittenden, *op. cit.* In this long report the *Times* paid attention to the development of co-operatives, which has a great potential for meeting future economic problems stemming from Eurocommunism. For example, the co-ops have been concentrating on construction contracts abroad. Instead of Italian workers going to work abroad as individuals, they go as teams of co-op members. The value of such contracts jumped from 96 billion lire in 1975 to 217 billion in 1977.

## Chapter 11: "Salvaging the Economy," pp. 236–53

1. Lally Weymouth, "On the Razor's Edge: Portrait of Agnelli," *Esquire*, June 20, 1975, pp. 25–30.
2. *Ibid.*, pp. 25, 29.
3. Michael Leeden, "Inside the Red Brigades," pp. 36–39. This ranking was given by readers of the magazine *Il Mondo*, who were asked to list the power brokers in Italy. Renato Curcio, founder of the Red Brigades, made number fifty on the list.
4. Vittorio Gorresio, *Berlinguer*, chapter 2.
5. *Ibid.*, p. 5, for the quote; pp. 167 ff. on the career.
6. Patrick Meney, *L'Italie de Berlinguer*, p. 21.
7. Weymouth, "On the Razor's Edge," p. 31.
8. *Ibid.*, p. 27.
9. *Ibid.*, p. 34.
10. Giorgio Napolitano, *The Italian Road to Socialism*, p. 54.
11. Massimo Riva, "Confindustria/Carli parla dei mali italiani: Qui ci vuole il PCI . . . ," *Panorama*, October 29, 1979, pp. 214–15.
12. See the Bibliography for books by various of these men.
13. Conversations between the author and Professors Spaventa and Sylos Labini.
14. Eugenio Scalfari, a Socialist deputy from 1968 to 1972, is currently the editor of the newspaper *La Repubblica*. He and Giuseppe Turani ran "The Financial Letter" of *l'Espresso*, which was a bible for Italian businessmen. The two also collaborated on *Razza padrona*, an exposé of DC patronage and corruption in nationalized industries.
15. Eugenio Scalfari and Giuseppe Turani, *Razza padrone*, p. 63.
16. Mariano D'Antonio, *Sviluppo e crisi del capitalismo italiano, 1951–1972*, p. 13; Peter Nichols, *Italia, Italia*, p. 167.
17. Guido Carli, *Intervista sul capitalismo italiano*, pp. 51–55.
18. Michele Salvati, *Il sistema economico italiano*, p. 97, Table 20.
19. Carli, pp. 80–83, for a generalized analysis. See also note 18 of chapter 10.
20. *L'Unità*, December 2, 1976.
21. Alberto Asor Rosa, *Le due società*, p. 47. Asor Rosa, professor of Italian literature at the University of Rome, is one of the leading Communist intellectuals.
22. Giorgio Napolitano, "The Italian Crisis: A Communist Perspective," pp. 790–99.
23. *Ibid.*, p. 795.
24. Carli, pp. 55–56.
25. *Ibid.*, pp. 11–13.
26. *Annuario*, p. 195, Table 87.
27. Luciano Lama, *Intervista sul sindacato*, p. 7.
28. *Annuario*, p. 211, Table 104.
29. *Loc. cit.* In all, a drop of 5 million in twenty years. The labor force remained stationary, thanks to emigration: 10 million Italians (one in five) were working abroad in 1977, sending home remittances and helping the economy while the well-to-do were sending their capital abroad. This contrast particularly incensed Monsignor Bettazzi.
30. Carli, p. 11.
31. Spaventa suggested Carli, Scalfari, Salvati, Amato, D'Antonio, Pugliese, Chiaromonte, and the *Proposte* of the PCI. (All are listed in the Bibliography.)
32. Carli, p. 49.
33. Pietro Ingrao, *Masse e potere*, pp. 13 ff.
34. See Scalfari and Turani, pp. 29 ff.
35. Carli, p. 86.
36. Joanne Barkan Proctor and Robert Proctor, "Capitalist Development, Class Struggle, and Crisis in Italy, 1945–1975," p. 23.
37. *Ibid.*, pp. 27, 29.
38. *Ibid.* From 1951 to 1958 GNP increased 5.3 percent annually, industrial production went up 95 percent, profits 86 percent, real wages 6 percent. In the next four years the GNP increased 6.6 percent, but wages remained stationary.
39. *Ibid.*, p. 28.
40. *Ibid.*, p. 28.
41. Carli, p. 56.

42. Proctor and Proctor, p. 28.
43. D'Antonio, p. 55, Table 1.
44. Proctor and Proctor, p. 29.
45. *Ibid.*, p. 30.
46. Salvati, p. 97. The comparison in the text is with 1962. In comparison with 1969 the disparity is not as great, but it is still substantial: Italy 47 percent, USA 11 percent, Germany 24 percent, and Japan 27 percent.
47. *Manchester Guardian Weekly*, January 23, 1978.
48. *Ibid.*
49. Diana Johnstone reporting from Rome, *In These Times*, March 8–14, 1978.
50. Quoted in Ernest Mandel, *From Stalinism to Eurocommunism*, pp. 139–40.
51. *In These Times*, March 8–14, 1978.
52. *Loc. cit.*
53. *New Statesman*, February 10, 1978.
54. See, for example, the article on "codetermination" in West Germany: "Worker-Directors Exportable?" *New York Times*, December 17, 1979.
55. Riva, *loc. cit.*
56. On the problem of the generation of capital, see Paul Baran's classic study, *The Political Economy of Growth*.
57. It is an interesting sidelight that exchange controls re-establish the confidence of investors, so that in the last three years there has been a modest but still substantial return of capital to Italy.
58. *Annuario*, p. 38, Table 24; p. 218, Table 108.
59. *Panorama*, July 4, 1978. More recent studies support our estimate of the magnitude of tax evasion. Professor Giuseppe Campa, chief advisor to the minister of finance, Franco Reviglio, estimated that in industry and commerce for 1977 there was a tax evasion of $6.1 billion in the value-added tax, or double what was declared (*L'Espresso*, March 3, 1980).
60. Interview with Filippo Pandolfi, minister of finance, in Ina Lee Selden, "Tax Reforms in Italy Double Revenues in 3 Years," *New York Times*, July 17, 1977, p. I-11.
61. Weymouth, "On the Razor's Edge," p. 34.
62. Giovanni Arrighi, "Towards a Theory of Capitalist Crisis," pp. 3–24. His argument is too complex to be reproduced here, but it is based on the realization of profits. The 1929 crash came because the rate of exploitation was too high (the working class having been beaten down) and the workers couldn't provide a high consumption; the present rolling depression because the rate of exploitation is too low (the unions are stronger) and the capital accumulation is not sufficiently rewarded. Arrighi has been professor at the University of Milan and at the State University of New York in Binghamton.
63. The figures on productivity are given in an editorial of the *Washington Post* (reprinted in *Manchester Guardian Weekly*, August 13, 1978), as follows: Britain and the United States at 27 percent, Italy at 60 percent, Germany and France at 70 percent.

## Chapter 12: "Contrapuntal Politics, 1978–1980," pp. 254–78

1. Gerardo Chiaromonte, *L'accordo programmatico*. The text of the agreement appears in the appendix, p. 51. In establishing the set of reforms, the political broker was Aldo Moro, whose consummate skill is described as diplomacy by his friends and hypocrisy by his enemies. The ultraleft argued that since the reforms would undermine the clientism of the DC, Moro was not sincere and was looking only to erode the PCI by involving it in parliamentary maneuvers and alienating its mass basis. The ultraright argued that he was selling out to the Communists in order to maintain his own power. That there was an element of *doppiezza* in Moro cannot be denied, yet it also seems the case that he put loyalty to the nation above loyalty to his class. See his long, off-the-record interview with Eugenio Scalfari in Scalfari's *Interviste ai potenti*, published after Moro's assassination. For a savage portrait of Moro, see the film *Todo modo*.
2. Curtis Bill Pepper, "Possessed," *New York Times Magazine*, February 18, 1979, p. 29. The author reports an estimated 21 right-wing groups and 116 left-wing groups with such names as "Armed Proletarian Nuclei," "First Line," "Red Flaying Squads," "Fighting Communist Units." The recurrent use of "Red," "Communist," and "Proletarian" confuses people, causing them to identify these groups with the PCI, and that, of course, hurts the party, particularly at the polls. It is also to be noted that neofascist groups and attacks have declined sharply as left-wing terrorism has increased, lending credence to the widespread belief that many right-wing groups

have simply joined or infiltrated left-wing organizations. However disparate their ideologies or goals, they all have one powerful common denominator: destabilization of the society.

In January 1980 Franco Originaro constructed a chart showing the evolution from 1970 on of the various "leftist" groups practicing armed struggle. Though partly based on the unproved allegations of Carlo Fioroni, it is nonetheless instructive. See the chart in *L'Espresso*, January 13, 1980.

3. Andrew Kopkind, "Euro-terror: Fear Eats the Soul."
4. *Ibid.*
5. Alberto Ronchey, *Corriere della sera*, December 10, 1977.
6. Adalberto Minucci, *Terrorismo e la crisi italiana: Intervista di Jochen Kreimer*, pp. 32–34.
7. Morris West, "Terror As an Historical Inheritance," *Esquire*, April 25, 1978, p. 77.
8. *Ibid.*, p. 78.
9. Michael Ledeen, "Inside the Red Brigades," pp. 36–39.
10. Roberto Chiodi, *L'Europeo*, November 3, 1978.
11. Oriana Fallaci, "After Moro," pp. 11.
12. "Inside the Red Brigades," *Newsweek*, May 15, 1978, pp. 43–49. The degree of involvement of Catholic fanatics has been documented in a 92-page study by the theological faculty of Padua University, released on February 28, 1980 and reported by Giuseppe Nicotri in "Padre, ho sparato. Quante volte, quante volte?" *L'Espresso*, March 2, 1980. The title is a parody of a confession: "Father, I've pulled the trigger." "How many times, [my son,] how many times?"
13. Pepper, "Possessed." In the eleven years of terrorism in Italy—"red" and "black"—200 have been killed and 500 wounded. See Valeria Gandus and Claudio Sabelli Fioretti, "Terrorismo: Un morto dopo l'altro," *Panorama*, January 21, 1980, p. 32. It is probably small consolation for Italians to learn that approximately 4.5 murders per day occur in New York City—by no means the most lethal of American cities. These are generally not "political" assassinations!
14. On the split within the Red Brigades, see Marco Ventura, "BR contro BR [Red Brigades versus Red Brigades]," *Panorama*, June 19, 1979, pp. 52–54.
15. The arsenal consisted of two submachine guns (including the Skorpion), five pistols, four detonators, two bullet-proof vests, and hundreds of rounds of ammunition.
16. *L'Espresso*, April 22, 1979.
17. Pino Buongiorno, "Autonomi: Covo d'isolate," *Panorama*, November 22, 1977, pp. 37–38.
18. *Ibid.*
19. *L'Espresso*, April 22, 1979.
20. Thomas Sheehan, "Italy: Behind the Ski Mask," p. 20.
21. Paul Hofmann, "Auto Dealers Are Hit by Bombings in Italy," *New York Times*, May 1, 1978, p. A-11.
22. *L'Espresso*, April 22, 1979.
23. *Ibid.*
24. *L'Espresso*, May 22, 1979.
25. For Tosi, see *L'Unità*, December 16, 1979. For Fioroni and Casirati, see *Panorama*, February 4, 1980. Negri, in an interview with *Panorama* (February 25) contested the accusations. He was helped by the arrest on February 20 of Patrizio Peci, head of the "Turin column," who confessed to participation in the Moro attack, led by Mario Moretti, a top Red Brigadeer. Peci said Moretti had made the call in question, and the charge of complicity against Negri was dropped, though he remained in jail for "armed insurrection." Peci's example was contagious; more people talked; and over 200 terrorists were caught in April and May (*New York Times*, April 15, 1980; *L'Espresso*, May 4, and 18, 1980). One of them, Roberto Sandalo, confirmed the suspicion that Marco Donat Cattin, son of the DC vice president, was a terrorist and accused the father, Carlo Donat Cattin, of helping his son escape after being warned by Francesco Cossiga, the present (June 1980) prime minister. Donat Cattin, the organizer of the reactionary coalition that won at the DC Congress (see page 277 on *preambolisti* and footnote 67), first said he hadn't had contact with his son for two years, but then recanted before a parliamentary inquiry and was forced to resign. The inquiry cleared the premier by a vote of 11 to 9 along party lines, but since 16 votes were need to quàsh, a parliamentary debate on the scandal became inevitable (*New York Times*, May 31 and June 1 and 3, 1980).
26. Thomas Sheehan, "Italy: Behind the Ski Mask." Sheehan is professor of philosophy at Loyola University, Chicago. Fluent in Italian, he was teaching in Rome in 1978. He updated his report in "Terror in Italy: An Exchange."
27. *Lotta Continua*, November 19, 1977. The interview with Andrea Casalegno was published on that date, and the letters of protest were published in ensuing days.
28. Kopkind, "Euro-terror."
29. "A Nation in Torment," *Time*, May 1, 1978, pp. 26–31.
30. Paul Hofmann, "Government Party in Italy Makes Gains in Local Elections," *New York Times*, May 16, 1978, A-1.

31. Kopkind, *op. cit.*

32. *Il Progresso Italo-Americano*, June 25, 1978, reprinted the Piccoli interview of a few days earlier.

33. *Il Messagero*, September 12, 1978. Mitterand had given the interview to *L'Europeo* in August. The newspaper reprinted excerpts, including the quote.

34. Carlo Rosella, "Buongiorno, Bettino," *Panorama*, August 1, 1978, pp. 30–32.

35. *Ibid.*

36. "An 'Honest Man' Resigns," *Time*, June 26, 1978, p. 38. Lockheed's bribes have already been mentioned. In order to sell fourteen transport planes, the company bribed a number of officials between 1965 and 1968, including the chief of staff of the air force, General Fanali, a defense minister, Tanassi, and a prime minister, code-named "Antelope Cobbler." There were three prime ministers in this period, Rumor, Leone, and Moro, but the last was above suspicion, so one of the other two was the guilty man. Both declared their innocence, but both were known to be venal and corrupt, and Leone was a close friend of the Lefebre brothers (Lockheed's bagmen), who had been found guilty together with Fanali and Tanassi. (They all got parole after a brief period.)

37. *Le Rughe* refers to the wrinkles in the terrain. The pun, of course, makes sense only in English, but for this purpose, all Romans seemed to recognize it. Subsequently, Cederna was charged with slander of the head of state by the public prosecutor, but the charges were later dropped (*Il Progresso Italo-Americano*, April 2, 1980).

38. *Panorama*, July 4, 1978.

39. Pasquale Nonno, ed., "Giorgio Amendola: Con Pertini no ho fatto che litigare," *Panorama*, July 18, 1978, p. 34. Amendola died June 5, 1980.

40. *Ibid.*

41. *Ibid.*

42. *Ibid.* All references to Clara Pertini are from a profile in this issue, including the joke in the footnote.

43. *L'Espresso*, August 20, 1978.

44. *Paese sera*, November 19, 1978.

45. Enrico Berlinguer, "L'amichevole Cremlino," p. 23.

46. *Il Manifesto* and *Il Messagero*, December 14, 1978.

47. *Il Messagero*, March 5, 1979.

48. Marcello Pera, "Karl Popper e il suo pensiero. . . ," *L'Espresso*, May 27, 1979, pp. 70–87.

49. Benigno Zaccagnini, *Panorama*, May 1, 1979.

50. Giampaolo Fabrio, "A giugno va a finire così," *Panorama*, May 8, 1979, pp. 40–42; Valeria Gandus, "Non mi piaci, ma ti voto," *Panorama*, May 15, 1979, pp. 52–56.

51. *Panorama*, July 23, 1979.

52. Enrico Berlinguer, "Una grande alleanza di lotta per un nuovo sviluppo del Sud," *L'Unità*, December 3, 1979. Berlinguer presented this information in his speech at the Southern Conference.

53. *La Repubblica* and *La Stampa*, June 12, 1979.

54. The conference was reported by *L'Unità*, November 16, 17, and 18, 1979. The paper published the major reports *in extenso*, including one on domestic affairs by Gerardo Chiaromonte, "Una azione politica e di massa sul terrero economica e sociale." It also published the long concluding speech of Berlinguer, "Per salvare l'Italia c'è una sola strada. . . ," and forty-odd contributions to the debate by Central Committee members. (The Central Committee has about 175 members.)

55. Berlinguer, "Una grande alleanza . . ."

56. "No dei partiti agli 'euromissili' in Sardegna," *L'Unità*, November 17, 1979, p. 20.

57. Alceste Santini, "Appello dei movimento cattolica: 'No ai missili, sì al negoziato,' " *L'Unità*, December 3, 1979.

58. *Paese sera*, December 7, 1979. The headline reads: "Cossiga Wins but the Socialists Are in Splinters." A long report by Sarno Tognotti gives the details of the fight within the PSI and shows that Craxi was in a minority.

59. Flora Lewis, "Nato Approves Plan to Install Missiles and Promote Talks," *New York Times*, December 13, 1979, p. A-1.

60. *The Economist*, January 12, 1980, p. 51.

61. *L'Unità*, January 27, 1980.

62. *Loc. cit.*

63. Eugenio Scalfari, *La Repubblica*, January 28, 1980, in an article titled "He Spoke Sardinian and Not in Doroteo." *Doroteo* is a political nickname for a DC centrist. Sardinians are stubborn and clannish, and although Cossiga's motivation was overwhelmingly political, it is not totally irrele-

vant that he and Berlinguer are cousins. President Carter was not impressed by either the motivation or the blood relationship and reiterated American opposition to the PCI.

64.  Even before the January 14 meeting, observers could see it would end in a stalemate, as arguments over the missiles had been tearing the PSI apart. See *The Economist*, January 12, 1980.

65.  Giorgio Rossi, "La DC sbanda a destra," *La Repubblica*, January 28, 1980.

66.  This 42 percent is of great importance, because the Doxa poll (see note at page 168) had shown that the middle echelons of the DC (whence came the delegates) were more anti-Communist than either the base or the leadership. As a result of the Congress, the base may shift even further left, and this could be of great significance in a potential schism.

67.  Centrists in the DC are called *morotei* because they followed the line of Aldo Moro—of collaboration with the PCI—although about half were against it. With Moro's death, the *morotei* split into a center-left headed by Zaccagnini, Andreotti, and Cossiga, and a center-right headed by Piccoli (about 24 percent of the delegates).

The coalition on the right was effected by Donat Cattin, Rumor, and Colombo, who held some 15 percent of the delegates. They brought together the reactionary Fanfani and Bisaglia, who held some 14 percent. Aside from anticommunism, differences among these groups are very sharp.

68.  Fausto De Luca, "Adesso Moro è rimasto senza eredi," *La Repubblica*, February 21, 1980. Massimo De Carolis was deeply implicated in the Sindona affair, having met with Sindona in Italy while the financier pretended to be kidnapped. See note, p. 203.

69.  Gaetano Scardocchia, in *Corriere della sera*, February 19, 1980.

70.  Piero Sansonetti, "Il monito di Zac," *L'Unità*, February 21, 1980.

71.  *New York Times*, March 20, 1980.

72.  UPI dispatch from Rome, in *San Juan Star*, April 4, 1980.

73.  *Il Tempo*, March 24, 1980. Longo spoke *before* the formation of the Cossiga government, when the three-party coalition was being shaped.

74.  On Donat Cattin and his campaign, see *Panorama*, May 12, 1980; on the polls, *L'Espresso*, May 4, 1980.

75.  On Donat Cattin's lies, see *New York Times*, May 31, 1980. Cossiga was cleared by a parliamentary inquiry by an 11 to 9 vote along party lines, but the margin was not sufficient to prevent an inquiry by the full parliament. See *L'Espresso*, June 8, 1980.

76.  The PSI obtained a large number of votes from the Radicals, whose party did not participate in the elections. The three major parties compare as follows (*Paese Sera*, June 10, 1980):

|     | 1980 | 1979 | 1975 |
| --- | --- | --- | --- |
| DC  | 36.8 | 38.1 | 35.3 |
| PCI | 31.5 | 31.8 | 33.4 |
| PSI | 12.7 | 9.9  | 12.0 |

77.  The predictions were made before the voting, on the assumption of a Craxi victory. See *L'Espresso*, June 1, 1980.

78.  For the statistics, *Il Progresso Italo-Americano*, June 10, 1980.

# Bibliography

Accornero, Aris. "Analisi e autoanalisi di 16,000 delegati." *Rinascita* 13 (March 30, 1979):17.

Agosti, Aldo, ed. *La Terza Internazionale, storia documentaria*. 3 vols. in 6 tomes. Rome: Editori Riuniti, 1974–79.

Albright, David. E. *Communism and Political Systems in Western Europe*. Boulder, Colo.: Westview Press, 1979. Chapters on the Communist parties of Italy, France, Spain, Portugal, Greece, Finland, Scandinavia, and Great Britain, and on Eurocommunism.

Allum, P. A. *Italy—Republic Without Government?* New York: Norton, 1973.

———. *Politics and Society in Post-War Naples*. London: Cambridge University Press, 1973.

*Almanacco PCI*. Rome: Sezione Centrale di Stampa e Propaganda, 1977 & 1979.

Althusser, Louis. "Communist Strategy in France." *New Left Review*, no. 104 (July-August 1977), pp. 3–22.

———. "Due, tre parole (brutali) su Marx e Lenin." *L'Espresso*, January 29, 1978, pp. 46–51.

———. *For Marx*. New York: Random House, Vintage Books, 1970.

———. "PCF: Out of the Fortress." *New Left Review*, no. 109 (May-June, 1978), pp. 19–45.

Amato, Giuliano. *Economia, politica, e istituzioni in Italia*. Bologna: Il Mulino, 1976.

Amendola, Giorgio. *Gli anni della Repubblica*. Rome: Editori Riuniti, 1976.

———. "The Italian Road to Socialism—An Interview." *New Left Review*, no. 106 (November-December 1977), pp. 39–50.

Anderson, Perry. "The Antinomies of Antonio Gramsci." *New Left Review*, no. 100 (November 1976-January 1977), pp. 5–78.

Andreucci, Franco, and Sylvers, Malcolm. "The Italian Communists Write Their History." *Science and Society* 40, no. 1 (Spring 1976): 28–56.

Antonetti, Luciano, and Volkov, Alexander, eds. "Communists in the Municipalities." *World Marxist Review* 20, no. 10 (October 1977): 69–95. Interviews with Armando Cossutta, Maurizio Valenzi, Diego Novelli et al.

Are, Giuseppe. "Italy's Communists: Foreign and Defense Policies." *Atlantic Community Quarterly* 14 (Winter 1976–77): 508–18.

Argan, Gian Carlo. "Ho conosciuto i comunisti, ora mi iscrivo." *L'Unità*, November 4, 1979.

Arrighi, Giovanni. "Towards a Theory of Capitalist Crisis." *New Left Review*, no. 111 (September-October 1978), pp. 3–24.

Ascoli, Giulietta. *La parola elettorale*. Rome: Edizioni delle Donne, 1976.

Asor Rosa, Alberto. *Le due società*. Turin: Einaudi, 1977.

"Autonomia: Post-Political Politics." *Semiotext(e)* 3, no. 3 (1980).

325

Baldan, Attilio. "Gramsci as an Historian of the 1930s." *Telos*, no. 31 (Spring 1977), pp. 100–111.
Baran, Paul. *The Political Economy of Growth*. New York: Monthly Review Press, 1957.
Barbera, Augusto. *Governo locale e riforma dello Stato*. Rome: Editori Riuniti, 1978. Contains the text of Law 282.
Barile, Paolo, and Macchitella, Carlo. *I nodi della costituzione*. Turin: Einaudi, 1979.
Barkan, Joanne. "The Italian Communists: Anatomy of a Party." *Radical America* 12, no. 5 (September-October 1978): 27–48.
———. "Italy: Working-Class Defeat or Program for a Transition." *Monthly Review* 29, no. 6 (November 1977): 26–38.
Baroncini, Lucia, ed. *I comunisti umbri*. Perugia: Edizioni di Cronache Umbre, 1977.
Barrese, Orazio, and Caprara, Massimo. *L'anonima DC*. Milan: Feltrinelli, 1977.
Bell, David. "French Communism." *New Statesman* 97 (May 25, 1979): 750–51.
Berlinguer, Enrico. "Address to the Twenty-fifth Congress of the CPSU." In *Building a New Society: The Twenty-fifth Congress of the Communist Party of the Soviet Union*, pp. 175–77. New York: NWR Publications, 1977.
———. "An Autonomous Policy of Disarmament, Peace and Cooperation for Western Europe." *The Italian Communists*, no. 1–2 (July-September 1977), pp. 3–20.
———. "Concluding Remarks to the Fifteenth National Congress of the PCI." *The Italian Communists*, no. 1–2 (January-June 1979), pp. 118–33.
———. "The DC's Anti-Communist Veto Is the Cause of the Breakup of the Majority." *The Italian Communists*, no. 4 (October-December 1978), pp. 76–88.
———. "For New Roads Towards Socialism in Italy and Europe." *The Italian Communists*, no. 2–3 (April-June 1976), pp. 54–65.
———. "An Emergency Government to Tackle a Crisis of Extreme Gravity." *The Italian Communists*, no. 1 (January-March 1978), pp. 45–85.
———. "The Goals for a More Incisive Government and Legislative Action." *The Italian Communists*, no. 3 (July-September 1978), pp. 3–37.
———. "The Innovating Force of the PCI's Policy for Unity and Vigor." *The Italian Communists*, no. 2 (April-June 1978), pp. 27–43.
———. "The International Policy of the Italian Communists." *The Italian Communists*, no. 6 (November-December 1976), pp. 40–45.
———. "One Year After June 20." *The Italian Communists*, no. 2 (April-June 1977), pp. 84–97.
———. "Opening New Roads to Democracy and Socialism." *The Italian Communists*, no. 3 (July-September 1978), pp. 64–89.
———. "Opening Report to the Fourteenth National Congress of the PCI." *The Italian Communists*, no. 2–3 (March-May 1975), pp. 5–82.
———. *La questione comunista*. 2 vols. Rome: Editori Riuniti, 1975.
———. "Report to the Fifteenth Congress of the PCI." *The Italian Communists*, no. 1–2 (January-June 1979), pp. 3–117.
———. "Ripensando a un editoriale di Togliatti del 1946: Il compromesso nella fase attuale." *Rinascita* 36, no. 32 (August 24, 1979): 1–3.
———. "A Serious Policy of Austerity as a Means to Transform the Country." *The Italian Communists*, no. 1 (January-March 1977), pp. 35–48.
———. "The Socialist Movement and the PCI's March." *The Italian Communists* 4 (October-December 1977): 120–22.
———. " '29 and '79." *New York Times*, October 29, 1979.
Bernardi, Alberto. *La riforma della polizia: Smilitarizzazione e sindacato*. Turin: Einaudi, 1979.
Bertoldi, Silvio. *Salò: Vita e morte della repubblica sociale italiana*. Milan: Rizzoli, 1976.
Bettazzi, Luigi. *Al di là . . . al di dentro*. Turin, Gribaldi, 1978.
———. *Farsi uomo*. Turin: Gribaldi, 1977.
Bettelheim, Charles. *Class Struggles in the USSR, First Period, 1917–23*. New York: Monthly Review Press, 1977.
Birnbaum, Norman. "Communists, Christian Democrats and Foggy Bottom: The Danger of Chaos in Italy." *The Nation* 226 (February 11, 1978): 140–44.

————. Laqueur, Walter, et al. "Euro-Communism Symposium." *Partisan Review* 46, no. 1 (1979): 9–42.

Biscardi, Aldo, and Liguori, Luca, eds. *Il Papa dal volto umano*. Milan: Rizzoli, 1979.

Blackmer, Donald L. M. *Unity in Diversity: Italian Communism and the Communist World*. Cambridge, Mass.: MIT Press, 1968.

————, and Kriegel, Anne. *The International Role of the Communist Parties of Italy and France*. Cambridge, Mass.: Harvard University Press, 1975.

————, and Tarrow, Sidney. *Communism in Italy and France*. Princeton, N.J.: Princeton University Press, 1975.

Blair, John. *The Control of Oil*. New York: Random House, 1978.

Block, Fred. "The Stalemate of European Capitalism: Eurocommunism and the Postwar Order." *Socialist Review*, no. 43 (January-February 1979), pp. 53–89.

Bocca, Giorgio. *La repubblica di Mussolini*. Bari: Laterza, 1977.

————. *Palmiro Togliatti*. Bari: Laterza, 1973.

Boggs, Carl. "Italian Communism in the Seventies." *Socialist Revolution*, no. 34 (July-August 1977), pp. 105–18. There are replies by Max Gordon, "Response to Boggs," *ibid.*, pp. 119–24; and by David Plotke, "Response to Boggs," *ibid.*, pp. 125–31.

Cammett, John. *Antonio Gramsci and the Origins of Italian Communism*. Stanford: Stanford University Press, 1967.

Canosa, Romano. *La polizia in Italia dal 1945 a oggi*. Bologna: Il Mulino, 1976.

Caprara, Massimo. *L'attentato a Togliatti*. Padua: Masilio Editore, 1978.

Carbone, Giuseppe. "I libri del carcere di Antonio Gramsci." *Movimento operaio* 4, no. 4 (July-August 1952): 1–53.

Carli, Guido. *Intervista sul capitalismo italiano*. With E. Scalfari. Bari: Laterza, 1977.

Carrillo, Santiago. *Dialogue on Spain*. London: Lawrence & Wishart, 1976.

————. *Eurocommunism and the State*. Westport, Conn.: Lawrence Hill, 1978.

————. "Genuine Democratisation of Society and Its Institutions." *Marxism Today* 21, no. 10 (October 1977): 306–13.

————. "Spain, Today and Tomorrow." With Régis Debray and Max Gallo. Introduction by Temma Kaplan. *Socialist Revolution*, no. 34 (July-August 1977), pp. 29–63.

Castoriadis, Cornelius. "The French Communist Party: A Critical Anatomy." *Dissent* 26 (Summer 1979): 315–25.

Castronuovo, Valerio, ed. *L'Italia contemporanea, 1945–1975*. Turin: Einaudi, 1976.

*Catalogo generale degli Editori Riuniti*. Rome: Editori Riuniti, 1979.

Cavalcanti, Pedro, and Piccone, Paul, eds. *History, Philosophy, Culture in the Young Gramsci*. St. Louis: Telos Press, 1975. Contains about forty articles which were not collected in Gramsci, *Selections from Political Writings, 1910–1920*.

Cazzola, Franco. *Anatomia del potere DC*. Bari: De Donato, 1979.

Cecchi, Alberto. *Storia del PCI attraverso i congressi*. Rome: Newton Compton, 1977.

Cerroni, Umberto. "Italian Communism's Historic Compromise." *Marxist Perspectives*, no. 1 (Spring 1978), pp. 126–44.

Chaliand, Gerard. *Revolution in the Third World*. New York: Penguin, 1978.

Charlton, Sue Ellen M. "Deradicalization and the French Communist Party." *Review of Politics* 41 (January 1979): 38–60.

Chevènement, Jean Pierre. "Socialism's Chances in Southern Europe." *Socialist Revolution*, no. 35 (September-October 1977), pp. 98–102.

Chiaradia, John, and Hofsten, Erland. "More on the New Reformism." *Monthly Review* 28, no. 6 (November 1976): 1–13.

Chiaromonte, Gerardo. *L'accordo programmatico*. Rome: Editori Riuniti, 1977.

Childs, David. "Eurocommunism: Origins and Problems." *Contemporary Review*, no. 232 (January 1978), pp. 1–6.

————. "Eurocommunism: Problems and Prospects." *Contemporary Review*, no. 232 (February 1978), pp. 66–71.

"The Report on the CIA That President Ford Doesn't Want You to Read." *Village Voice*, February 16, 1976. The Pike Report.

Claudín, Fernando. *The Communist Movement from Comintern to Cominform*. New York: Monthly Review Press, 1975.

————. *Eurocommunism and Socialism*. London: New Left Books, 1978: New York: Schocken Books, 1979.

"La conferenza di Berlino." *Nuova rivista internazionale*, no. 7–8 (July-August 1976), pp. 994–1059.

"Contrary to the Interests of Peace and Socialism in Europe." *New Times* (Moscow), no. 26 (1977), pp. 9–13. Attack on Carrillo.

Cowan, Suzanne. "On the Contradictions of the Italian Communist Party." *Socialist Revolution*, no. 33 (May-June 1977), pp. 93–98.

————. "The Unhappy Adventures of Alice in Blunderland: Counter-Culture, Revolt and Repression in the Heart of Italy's 'Red Belt.' " *Radical America* 11, no. 6; 12, no. 1 (November 1977-February 1978): 67–77.

*I cristiani nella sinistra dalla resistenza ad oggi*. Rome: Coines, 1976.

D'Antonio, Mariano. *Sviluppo e crisi del capitalismo italiano, 1951–1972*. Bari: De Donato, 1973.

*Dati sull'organizzazione del Partito*. [Rome]: Sezione Centrale di Organizzazione della Direzione del PCI, 1979.

Degras, Jane, ed. *The Communist International: Documents*. 3 vols. London: Oxford University Press, 1956–1971.

Del Boca, Angelo, and Giovana, Mario. *Fascism Today: A World Survey*. New York: Pantheon, 1969.

Del Noce, Augusto. *L'eurocomunismo e l'Italia*. [Rome]: Editrice Europa Informazioni, 1976.

Delogu, Ignazio, ed. *La via europea al socialismo*. Rome: Newton Compton, 1976.

Denitch, Bogdan. "Eurocommunism and 'The Russian Question.' " *Dissent* 26 (Summer 1979): 326–33.

Devlin, Keven. "The Challenge of Eurocommunism." *Problems of Communism* 26, no. 1 (January-February 1977): 1–20.

Diaz Lopez, Cesar Enrique. "The Eurocommunist Alternative in Spain." *Political Quarterly* 50 (July-September 1979): 349–58.

Di Nolfo, Ennio. "The United States and Italian Communism 1942–1946: World War II to the Cold War," *The Journal of Italian History* 1, no. 1 (Spring 1978): 74–94.

D'Orsi, Angelo. *Il potere repressivo, la polizia*. Milan: Feltrinelli, 1972.

Dougherty, James E., and Pfaltzgraff, Diane K. *Eurocommunism and the Atlantic Alliance*. Cambridge, Mass.: Institute for Foreign Policy Analysis, 1977.

Draghi, Stefano, et al. "Profilo del quadro comunista." *Rinascita* 14 (April 6, 1979): 18.

Duhamel, Olivier, and Weber, Henri. *Changer le PC?* Paris: Presse Universitaire de France, 1979.

Duroselle, Jean-Baptiste. "France and the West: Concerns and Hopes." *Review of Politics* 39 (October 1977): 451–72.

Ehrenreich, Barbara, and Plotke, David. "Notes on the World Left: A View from Cavtat." *Socialist Review*, no. 42 (November-December 1978), pp. 103–11.

Ellenstein, Jean. "Memo to France's Communists." *Atlas* 25 (July 1978): 25–26. From *Le Monde*, April 13–15, 1978.

————. *Le P.C.* Paris: Grasset, 1976.

Elliot, Philip, and Schlesinger, Philip. "On the Stratification of Political Knowledge: Studying Eurocommunism, an Unfolding Ideology." *Sociological Review* 27 (February 1979): 55–81. First rate.

Emiliani, Vittorio. *L'Italia mangiata*. Turin: Einaudi, 1977, "Eurocommunism: Does It Exist?" Symposium at Lisbon, May 26–27, 1978. *Atlantic Community Quarterly* 16 (Fall 1978): 259–98. Contains articles by Mario Soares, Pierre Hassner, Heinz Timmerman, Renato Mieli, Manlio Brosio, and Frank Roberts.

Evans, Robert H. *Coexistence: Communism and Its Practice in Bologna, 1945–1965*. Notre Dame, Ind.: University of Notre Dame Press, 1967.

Fabre, Jean; Hincker, François; and Sève, Lucien. *Les Communistes et l'Etat*. Paris: Editions Sociales, 1977.

Fallaci, Oriana. "After Moro." Edited by Philip Nobile. *New York Magazine*, May 22, 1978, p. 11.

——. *Intervista con la storia*. Milan: Rizzoli, 1974.

——. *Interview with History*. Translated by John Shepley. New York: Liveright, 1976.

Fedele, Marcello. *Classi e partiti negli anni '70*. Rome: Editori Riuniti, 1979. Statistical study of the party system in the 1970s, with special emphasis on the PCI.

Fedeli, Franco. *Sindacato polizia*. Milan: Sapere Edizioni, 1975.

Feenberg, Andrew. "From the May Events to Eurocommunism." *Socialist Review*, no. 37 (January-February 1978), pp. 73–108.

Fejtö, François. "A New Guru of the Paris Intellectuals: Gramsci in Paris." *Encounter* 50, no. 3 (March 1978): 37–40. Gramsci's influence in France since 1956.

Femia, Joseph V. "Gramsci, the *Via italiana*, and the Classical Marxist-Leninist Approach to Revolution." *Government and Opposition* 14 (Winter 1979): 66–95.

Fonvieille-Alquier, François. *L'Eurocommunisme*. Paris: Fayard, 1977.

Gallagher, Tom. "The Portuguese Communist Party and Eurocommunism." *Political Quarterly* 50 (April-June 1979): 205–18.

Galli, Gino. "Umbria: Esperienza unitaria nella lotta per il piano." *Rinascita* 20, no. 5 (February 2, 1963): 5–6.

Galli, Giorgio. *Opinioni sul PCI*. Milan: Editoriale Espresso, 1977.

Gambino, Antonio. *Storia del dopoguerra della liberazione al potere DC*. Bari: Laterza, 1975.

Gati, Charles. "The 'Europeanization' of Communism." *Foreign Affairs* 55 (April 1977): 539–53.

Gelman, Harry. "The Sino-Soviet Conflict." In *The China Reader*, 3 vols. Edited by Franz Schurmann and Orville Schell. New York: Random House, Vintage Books, 1967. Vol. 3, *Communist China*.

Gerosa, Guido. *Le compagne*. Milan: Rizzoli, 1979.

Ghini, Celso. *L'Italia che cambia*. Rome: Editori Riuniti, 1976.

——. *Il terremoto del 15 giugno*. Rome: Editori Riuniti, 1976.

——. *Il voto degli italiani, 1946–1974*. Rome: Editori Riuniti, 1975.

Goldsborough, James O. "Eurocommunism after Madrid." *Foreign Affairs* 55 (July 1977): 800–814.

Gordon, Max. "Italian Communism Today." *Marxist Perspectives*, no. 3 (Fall 1978), pp. 148–61.

——. "Joint Declaration of the Communist Parties of France and Italy." *Socialist Revolution*, no. 29 (July-September 1976), pp. 64–74.

——. "The Theoretical Outlook of the Italian Communists." *Socialist Revolution*, no. 33 (May-June 1977), pp. 29–58.

Gorresio, Vittorio. *Berlinguer*. Milan: Feltrinelli, 1976.

Gornick, Vivian. *The Romance of American Communism*. New York: Basic Books, 1977.

Gramsci, Antonio. *La costruzione del Partito comunista, 1923–1926*. Turin: Einaudi, 1971.

——. *Letter. dal carcere*. Edited by Sergio Caprioglio and Elsa Fubini. Turin: Einaudi, 1965. This edition supplants the original edition published in 1947 by Einaudi.

——. *Letters from Prison*. Selected, translated from the Italian, and introduced by Lynne Lawner. New York: Harper, 1973.

——. *The Modern Prince and Other Writings*. Translated and introduced by Louis Marks. New York: International Publishers, 1959.

——. *L'Ordine nuovo, 1919–1920*. Turin: Einaudi, 1954.

——. *Per la verità, scritti 1913–1926*. Rome: Riuniti, 1974.

——. *Quaderni del carcere*. 4 vols. Critical edition of the Istituto Gramsci, edited by Valentino Gerratana. Turin: Einaudi, 1975. This edition replaces the original edition published by Einaudi in six volumes between 1948 and 1951: Vol. 1, *Il materialismo storico e la filosofia di Benedetto*

*Croce;* Vol. 2, *Gli intelletuali e l'organizzaione della cultura;* Vol. 3, *Il risorgimento;* Vol. 4, *Note sul Macchiavelli, sulla politica, e sullo stato moderno;* Vol. 5, *Letteratura e vita nazionale;* Vol. 6, *Passato e presente.*

————. *Scritti giovanili, 1914–1918.* Turin: Einaudi, 1948.

————. *Scritti, 1915–1921.* Edited by Sergio Caprioglio. Milan: Moizzi, 1976.

————. *Selections from Political Writings, 1910–1920.* With additional texts by Bordiga and Tosca. Selected and edited by Quintin Hoare. Translated by John Mathews. New York: International Publishers, 1978. See also Cavalcante and Piccone.

————. *Selections from Political Writings, 1921–1926,* With additional texts by other Italian Communist leaders. Translated and edited by Quintin Hoare. New York: International Publishers, 1978.

————. *Selections from the Prison Notebooks.* Edited and translated by Quintin Hoare and Geoffrey N. Smith. New York: International Publishers, 1971.

————. *Socialismo e fascismo, 1921–1922.* Turin: Einaudi, 1966.

————. *Sotto la mole, 1916–1920.* Turin: Einaudi, 1960.

————. *Il Vaticano e l'Italia,* 2d ed. Rome: Riuniti, 1967.

Gray, L. E. "A New Look at the Italian Communist Party." *Midwest Quarterly* 18 (April 1977): 298–317.

Graziano, Luigi, and Tarrow, Sidney, eds. *La crisi italiana.* Turin: Einaudi, 1979, vol. 1, *Formazione del regime repubblicano e società civile;* vol. 2, *Sistema politico e istituzioni.*

Greeley, Andrew M. *The Making of the Popes, 1978.* Kansas City: Andrews and McMeel, 1979.

Gruber, Helmut, ed. *International Communism in the Era of Lenin.* New York: Fawcett, 1967.

————. *Soviet Russia Masters the Comintern: International Communism in the Era of Stalin's Ascendency.* Garden City, N.Y.: Doubleday, Anchor Books, 1974.

Gruppi, Luciano. *Il compromesso storico.* Rome: Editori Riuniti, 1977.

Gunder Frank, André. "Eurocommunism: Left and Right Variants." *New Left Review,* no. 108 (March-April 1978), pp. 88–92. Review of Claudín, *Eurocommunism and Socialism.*

Hammond, John L. "Eurocommunist Theory and Socialist Transformation." *Socialist Review,* no. 42 (November-December 1978), pp. 117–31. See also Larry Miller, "Spanish Eurocommunism: A Reply to Hammond. *Ibid.,* pp. 132–41; and Hammond's "Reply to Miller," *Ibid.,* pp. 142–44.

Harris, André, and de Sédouy, Alain, *Voyage à l'interieur du Parti communiste.* Paris: Editions du Seuil, 1974.

Hellman, Stephen. "The Italian CP: Stumbling on the Threshold?" *Problems of Communism* 27, no. 6 (November-December 1978): 31–48.

Hincker, François. "The Perspective of the French Communist Party." *Marxist Perspectives,* no. 2 (Summer 1978), pp. 124–37.

Howe, Irving, et al. "Eurocommunism: Reality, Myth, Hope, or Delusion?" *Dissent* 25 (Winter 1978): 26–42.

Humbert-Droz, Jules. *Memoires, 1921–1941,* vols. 2 and 3. Neuchatel: La Baconnière, 1971–72.

Hunt, Richard N. *The Political Ideas of Marx and Engels.* Pittsburgh: University of Pittsburgh Press, 1974.

Ingrao, Pietro. *Masse e potere.* Rome: Editori Riuniti, 1977.

Irving, R. E. M. "The European Policy of the French and Italian Communists." *International Affairs* 53 (July 1977): 405–21.

Isman, Fabio. *I forzati dell'ordine.* Venice: Marsilio, 1977.

Jäggi, Max; Müller, Roger; and Schmid, Sil. *Bologna rossa: I comunisti al governo di una città.* Milan: Feltrinelli, 1977.

Jenson, Jane, and Ross, George. "Strategies in Conflict: The Twenty-third Congress of the French Communist Party." *Socialist Review,* no. 47 (September-October 1979), pp. 71–99.

John XXIII. *Pacem in Terris.* New York: Pocket Books, 1965.

Johnson, Douglas. "Hard-line Communism in France's Grass-roots." *New Statesman* 95 (May 12,

1978): 635–36. Good article, despite title, on relations of French Communist and Socialist parties.

———. "Philosophy and the Crisis of French Communism." *New Statesman* 96 (July 7, 1978): 14.

Johnstone, Diana. Articles on the French and Italian Left in *In These Times* (Chicago, weekly since 1976).

Johnstone, Monty. "Socialism and the Democratic Exercise of Political Power." *Socialist Revolution*, no. 35 (September-October 1977), pp. 103–8. The author, a member of the Central Committee of the Communist party of Great Britain, expresses a number of views that are Eurocommunist in inspiration.

Kanapa, Jean. "A 'New Policy' of the French Communists?" *Foreign Affairs* 55 (January 1977): 280–94.

Kardelj, Edvard. *Sećanja Edvarda Kardelja: Vorba za priznanje i nezavisnost nove Jugoslavije, 1944–1957* [Memoirs of Edvard Kardelj: The struggle of recognition and independence of the new Yugoslavia, 1944–1957]. Ljubljana: Državna Založba, and Belgrade: Radnička Stampa, 1980.

Kogan, Norman. *The Government of Italy*. New York: T. Y. Crowell, 1962.

Kolakowski, Leszek. "The Euro-Communist Schism." *Encounter* 49, no. 2 (February 1977): 14–19.

Kopkind, Andrew. "Bologna: Socialism in One City." *Working Papers* 4, no. 2 (Summer 1976): 32–40.

———. "Euro-terror Eats the Soul." *New Times* (New York), June 12, 1978, p. 28.

Kriegel, Annie. *Eurocommunism: A New Kind of Communism?* Stanford, Calif.: Hoover Institution Press, 1978.

———. "The French CP Regroups." *New Republic* 179 (September 16, 1978): 9–10.

Küng, Hans. "Pope John Paul: His First Year." *New York Times*, October 19, 1979, p. A-35.

Kurzweil, Edith. "Louis Althusser: Between Philosophy and Politics." *Marxist Perspectives*, no. 6 (Summer 1979), pp. 8–23.

Lajolo, Davide. *Il volto umano di un rivoluzionario*. Florence: Vallecchi, 1979.

Lama, Luciano. *La CGIL di Di Vittorio, 1944–1957: Scritti e interventi di Giuseppe Di Vittorio*. Bari: De Donato, 1977.

———. *Di Vittorio*. Rome: Editrice Sindacale Italiana, 1972.

———. *Intervista sul sindacato a cura di Massimo Riva*. Bari: Laterza, 1976.

———. *Il sindacato nella crisi italiana*. Rome: Editori Riuniti, 1977.

La Malfa, Ugo. "Communism and Democracy in Italy." *Foreign Affairs* 56 (April 1978): 476-88.

Lange, Peter, ed. "Communist Party—Communism." In *Studies on Italy, 1943–1975*, pp. 18–22. Turin: Fondazione Giovanni Agnelli, 1977. A bibliography of earlier studies in English of the PCI after World War II.

———, and Vannicelli, Maurizio. "Carter in the Italian Maze." *Foreign Policy*, no. 33 (Winter 1978–79), pp. 161–73.

La Palombara, Joseph. *The Italian Labor Movement: Problems and Prospects*. Ithaca, N.Y.: Cornell University Press, 1957.

Lecoeur, Auguste. *Le PCF: Continuité dans le changement*. Paris: Robert Laffont, 1977.

Ledeen, Michael. "Aldo Moro's Legacy." *New Republic* 178 (May 13, 1978): 24–25.

———. "Inside the Red Brigades." *New York Magazine*, May 1, 1978, pp. 36–39.

———. "Italian Communism at Home and Abroad: The Soviet Connection." *Commentary* 62, no. 5 (November 1976): 51–54.

———. "The 'News' about Eurocommunism." *Commentary* 64, no. 4 (October 1977): 53–57.

———, and Sterling, Claire. "Italy's Russian Sugar Daddies." *New Republic* 174 (April 3, 1976): 16–21.

Leduc, Victor. "The French Communist Party Between Stalinism and Eurocommunism." *Political Quarterly* 49 (October-December 1978): 400–410.

Lehner, Giancarlo. *Dalla parte dei poliziotti*. Milan: Mazzotta Editore, 1978.

Lenin, V. I. *Collected Works*. Moscow: Progress Publishers, 1960–70.
————. *Selected Works*, 3 vols. New York: International Publishers, 1967.
*Lenin e l'Italia*. Moscow: Edizioni "Progress," 1971.
Levi, Arrigo. "Italy's New Communism." *Foreign Policy*, no. 26 (Spring 1977), pp. 28–42.
Lilli, Laura, and Valentini, Chiara. *Care compagne: Il femminismo nel PCI e nelle organizzazioni di massa*. Rome: Editori Riuniti, 1979.
Lisa, Athos. *Memorie: In carcere con Gramsci*. Milan: Feltrinelli, 1973.
Loewenthal, Richard. "Moscow and the 'Eurocommunists.' " *Problems of Communism* 27, no. 4 (July-August 1978): 38–49.
Lorit, Sergio C. *La vita raccontata di Papa Giovanni*. Rome: Città Nuova Editrice, 1965.
Lottman, Herbert. "Editori Riuniti: An 'Only in Italy' Communist Publisher." *Publishers Weekly* 214 (May 22, 1978), pp. 152–53.
Luxemburg. Rosa. *Rosa Luxemburg Speaks*. Edited by Mary-Alice Waters. New York: Pathfinder Press, 1970.
————. *Selected Political Writings*. Edited by Richard Looker. London: Jonathan Cape, 1972.
Macciocchi, Maria A. *Dopo Marx aprile*. [Milan]: I Libri de L'Espresso, 1978.
MacEoin Gary. *The Inner Elite*. Kansas City: Sheed, Andrews and McMeel, 1978.
McGregor, James P. "1976 European Communist Parties Conference." *Studies in Comparative Communism* 11 (Winter 1978): 339–60.
McInnes, Neil. *Euro-Communism*. Beverly Hills and London: Sage Publications, 1976.
Maclean, Fitzroy. *The Heretic*. New York: Harper, 1957.
Macridis, R. C. "Eurocommunism." *Yale Review* 67 (Spring 1978): 321–37.
Magri, Lucio. "Italy, Social Democracy, and Revolution in the West." Interview with Joanne Barkan. *Socialist Revolution*, no. 36 (November-December 1977), pp. 94–142.
————. "Relazione." In *Da Togliatti alla nuova sinistra*, pp. 26–62. Rome: Alfani Editore, 1976.
Malfatti, Marisa, and Tortora, Riccardo. *Il cammino dell'unità, 1943–1969*. Bari: De Donato, 1976.
Mammarella, Giuseppe. *Italy After Fascism*. Montreal: Mario Casalini, 1964.
Mandel, Ernest. "A Critique of Eurocommunism." *Marxist Perspectives*, no. 8 (Winter 1979–80), pp. 114–42.
————. *From Stalinism to Eurocommunism*. London: New Left Books, 1978.
"Il Manifesto." *Politics and Society* 1, no. 4 (August 1971): 407–77. The 1970 political platform of *Il Manifesto* and articles by Birnbaum, Adams, and Denitch.
Mannheimer, Renato; Rodriguez, Mario; and Sebastiani, Chiara. *Gli operai comunisti*. Rome: Editori Riuniti, 1979. Study of Communist workers of December 1977.
Maravall, J. M. "Spain: Eurocommunism and Socialism." *Political Studies* 27 (June 1979): 218–35.
Marchais, Georges. *Pour une avancée démocratique: Rapport au XXIIIe Congrès du PCF*. Paris: PCF, 1979.
Martinet, Gilles. *Marxism of Our Time*. New York: Monthly Review Press, 1973.
Marx, Karl. *Political Writings*. London: Pelican Books, 1973.
————, and Engels, Friedrich. *Selected Works*. Moscow: Progress Publishers, 1950.
Marzani, Carl. "Aggiornamento." *The Nation* 227 (October 28, 1978).
————, ed. "The Church and the Party: Documents on the Catholic-Communist Dialogue in Italy." *Marxist Perspectives*, no. 7 (Fall 1979), pp. 90–117.
————. "In Defense of the Italian CP." *Monthly Review* 29, no. 2 (June 1977): 1–8.
————. "A Marxist Variant?" *Monthly Review* 30, no. 5 (October 1979): 55–64. Reviews of Carrillo, Mandel, and Miliband.
————. *The Open Marxism of Antonio Gramsci*. New York: Cameron Associates, 1957.
————. *We Can Be Friends*. Foreword by W. E. B. DuBois. New York: Topical Book Publishers, 1952. Reprinted with a new introduction by Barton J. Bernstein. New York: Garland Publishing, Inc., 1971. The Garland Library of War and Peace.
Mathieu, Gilbert. "Nationalization: How Far Should the Left Go?" *Manchester Guardian Weekly*, July 17, 1977.
Medici, Sandro. *Vite di poliziotti*. Turin: Einaudi, 1979.
Menashe, Louis. "Vladimir Ilych Bakunin: An Essay on Lenin." *Socialist Revolution*, no. 12 (November-December 1973), pp. 9–54.

Meney, Patrick. *L'Italie de Berlinguer*. Paris: J. C. Clattès, 1976.

Migone, Gian Giacomo. "Le origini dell'egemonia americana in Europa." *Rivista di storia contemporanea* 2 (April 1964): 433–59.

Milanese, G. "Religious Identity and Political Commitment in the 'Christians for Socialism' Movement in Italy." *Social Compass* (Louvain, Belgium) 23 (1976): 241–57.

Milani, Lino. "Le cifre del PCI tra i due congressi." *Rinascita* 13 (March 30, 1979): 17–18.

Miliband, Ralph. *Marxism and Politics*. Oxford: Oxford University Press, 1977.

Miller, James. "Marxism and Politics." *Telos*, no. 36 (Summer 1978), pp. 183–91.

Minucci, Adalberto. *Terrorismo e la crisi italiana: Intervista di Jochen Kreimer*. Rome: Editori Riuniti, 1978.

*Modena '77: Una città, un festival*. Rome: Sezione Centrale di Stampa e Propaganda, [1978].

Morra, Gianfranco. *Marxismo e religione*. Milan: Rusconi, 1977.

Mortimer, Edward; Story, Jonathan; and Della Torre, Filo. "Whatever Happened to 'Eurocommunism'?" *International Affairs* 55 (October 1979): 574–85.

Moss, Robert. "The Specter of Eurocommunism." *Policy Review* 1 (Summer 1977), 7–26.

Mouffe, Chantal, ed. *Gramsci and Marxist Theory*. London and Boston: Routledge, 1979. Essays by Norberto Bobbio, Jacques Texier, Nicola Badaloni, Leonardo Paggi, Mouffe, Christine Buci-Glucksmann, Massimo Salvadori, Biagio De Giovanni.

*Il movimento operaio italiano: Dizionario biografico, 1853–1943*. 6 vols. Rome: Editori Riuniti, 1975–79. Authoritative biographies and bibliographies of the older generations of the PCI and of the Italian left in general.

Mujal-Leon, Eusebio. "The PCE in Spanish Politics." *Problems of Communism* 27, no. 4 (July-August): 15–37.

Napolitano, Giorgio. "The Italian Crisis: A Communist Perspective." *Foreign Affairs* 56 (July 1978): 790–99.

———. *In mezzo al guado*. Rome: Editori Riunti, 1979.

———. *The Italian Road to Socialism*. With Eric Hobsbawm. Translated by John Cammett and Victoria De Grazia. Westport, Conn.: Lawrence Hill, 1977.

Nazzaro, Pellegrino. "Italy: A New Adventure." *Current History* 73, no. 432 (November 1977): 160–64.

"The New Leading Organs of the PCI." *The Italian Communists*, no. 1–2 (January-June 1979), pp. 136–39. The members of the Central Committee, Central Control Commission, Central College of Auditors, Executive Committee *(Direzione)*, and Secretariat as of mid-1979.

Nichols, Peter. *Italia, Italia*. Boston: Little Brown, 1974.

———. *The Italian Decision.*, 1977.

Noce, Teresa. *Rivoluzionaria professionale*. Milan: La Pietra, 1974.

Novak, Michael. "The Politics of John Paul II." *Commentary* 68, no. 6 (December 1979): 56–61.

Nugent, Neill, and Lowe, David. "The French Communist Party: The Road to Democratic Government?" *Political Quarterly* 48 (July-September 1977): 270–87.

Ophuls, Maurice. "Eurocommunism and the Voice of God: Dr. Kissinger's New Clothes." *The Nation* 226 (February 4, 1978): 102–5.

Paggi, Leonardo. "L'europeismo della sinistra nell'Europa della crisi." *Rinascita* 36, no. 23 (June 15, 1979): 3–4.

Palladino, Francesco, ed. *Se il PCI va al governo*. Milan: Sterling & Kupfer, 1978.

Pasini, Giuseppe. *Le ACLI delle origini*. Rome: Coines, 1974.

Pasquino, Gianfranco. "Before and After the Italian National Elections of 1976." *Government and Opposition* 12 (Winter 1977): 60–87.

Pellegrino, Michele. *Camminare insieme*. Turin: Elle di CI, 1976.

———. "Pluralismo e cristiani di fronte al marxismo." *Rivista diocesana torinese*, September 9, 1975.

Pistillo, Michele. *Giuseppe Di Vittorio*. 3 vols. Rome: Editori Riuniti, 1973–77.

Platt, Alan A., and Leonardi, Robert. "American Foreign Policy and the Postwar Italian Left." *Political Science Quarterly* 93 (Summer 1978): 197–215.

Plotke, David. "Italian Communism and the American Left." *Socialist Revolution,* no. 31 (January-February 1977), pp. 7–23.

*La politica e l'organizzazione dei comunisti italiani: Le tesi e lo statuto approvati dal XV Congresso nazionale del PCI.* Rome: Editori Riuniti, 1979. The "Draft Theses" for this Congress are now available in English. See "Draft Theses for the Fifteenth National Congress of the PCI," *The Italian Communists,* special issue, 1978.

Portelli, Hugues. *Gramsci e la questione religiosa.* Milan: Mazzotta, 1976.

Poulantzas, Nicos. "Political Parties and the Crisis of Marxism [Interview by Stuart Hall and Alan Hunt, April 5, 1979]" *Socialist Review,* no. 48 (November-December 1979), pp. 57–74.

———. "The State and the Transition to Socialism." Interviewed by Henri Weber. *Socialist Review,* no. 38 (March-April 1978), pp. 9–36.

———. "Towards a Democratic Socialism." *New Left Review,* no. 109 (May-June 1978), pp. 75–87.

Proctor, Joanne Barkan, and Proctor, Robert. "Capitalist Development, Class Struggle, and Crisis in Italy, 1945–1975." *Monthly Review* 27, no. 8 (January 1976): 21–36.

*Proposta di progetto a medio termine.* Rome: Editori Riuniti, 1977.

Pugliese, Enrico, and Mottura, Giovanni. *Agricoltura, Mezzogiorno e mercato del lavoro.* Bologna: Il Mulino, 1975.

Pugno, Emilio, and Garavini, Sergio. *Gli anni duri alla Fiat.* Turin: Einaudi, 1974.

Putnam, Robert D. "Interdependence and the Italian Communists" *International Organization* 32 (Spring 1978): 301–49.

Ragionieri, Ernesto. *Lenin e l'Italia.* Moscow: Edizioni "Progress," 1971.

———. *La Terza internazionale e il PCI.* Turin: Einaudi, 1978.

Ravaioli, Carla. *La questione femminile: Intervista col PCI.* Milan: Bompiani, 1976.

Ravera, Camilla. *Diario di trent'anni, 1913–1943.* Rome: Editori Riuniti, 1973.

Research Planning Group on Urban Social Services. "The Political Management of the Urban Fiscal Crisis: Italy." *European Studies Newsletter* 6, no. 5 (April-May 1977): 1–6.

Rizzo, Aldo. *La frontiera dell'eurocomunismo.* Bari: Laterza, 1977.

Rodano, Franco. *Questione democristiana e compromesso storico.* Rome: Editori Riuniti, 1977.

Ronchey, Alberto. "Guns and Gray Matter: Terrorism in Italy." *Foreign Affairs* 57 (Spring 1979): 921–40.

Rossanda, Rossana. "Twenty Years After." *Socialist Revolution,* no. 30 (October-December 1976), pp. 97–106.

Rossi, M. "The International Situation and the Stand of the Italian Communists." *World Marxist Review* 22 (March 1979): 47–51.

Rossi, Raffaele. *Il PCI in una regione rossa: Intervista sui comunisti umbri, a cura di Renzo Massarelli.* Perugia: Editrice Grafica Perugia, [1978].

Rubbi, Antonio. "The New Internationalism." *World Marxist Review* 20 (January 1977): 123–29.

Salvadori, Massimo L. *Gramsci e il problema storico della democrazia.* Bari: Laterza, 1973.

Salvati, Michele. *Il sistema economico italiano: Analisi di una crisi.* Bologna: Il Mulino, 1975.

Santini, Alceste. *Questione cattolica, questione comunista.* Rome: Editori Riuniti, 1976.

Sassoon, Donald. "Eurocommunism, the Labour Party and the EEC." *Political Quarterly* 50 (January-March 1979): 86–99.

———. "The Italian Communist Party's European Strategy." *Political Quarterly* 47 (July-September 1976).

Scalfari, Eugenio. *Interviste ai potenti.* Milan: Mondadori, 1979.

———. and Turani, Giuseppe. *Razza padrona.* Milan: Feltrinelli, 1974.

Schlesinger, Arthur, Jr. "Soviet Relations with Western Europe." *Marxist Perspectives,* no. 6 (Summer 1979), pp. 140–44.

Scroppo, Erica. *Donna, privato e politico: Storie personali di 21 donne del PCI.* Milan: Mazzotta, 1979.

Segre, Sergio. "The Communist 'Question' In Italy." *Foreign Affairs* 54 (July 1976): 691–707.

———. *Interview with Sergio Segre*. Privately printed: John Rossen: Chicago, 1977. For the reaction to this interview and other recent statements by Eurocommunist leaders, see Jim West, "For International Solidarity. . . ."

Serfaty, Simon. "The Italian Communist Party and Europe: Historically Compromised?" *Atlantic Community Quarterly* 15 (Fall 1977): 275–87.

Seroni, Adriana. *La questione femminile in Italia, 1970–1977*. Rome: Editori Riuniti, 1977.

*Sesso amaro: Trentamila donne rispondono su maternità, sessualità, aborto*. Rome: Editori Riuniti, 1977.

Sforza, M. Cesarini, and Nassi, Enrico. *L'eurocomunismo*. Introduction by Leo Valiani. Milan: Rizzoli, 1977.

Shaw, Eric. "Italian Historical Compromise: A New Pathway to Power?" *Political Quarterly* 49 (October-December 1978): 411–24.

Sheehan, Thomas. "Italy: Behind the Ski Mask." *New York Review of Books* 26 (August 16, 1979): 20–28.

———. "Terror in Italy: An Exchange." *New York Review of Books* 27 (April 17, 1980): 46–47.

Simmonds, J. D. "The French Communist Party in 1978: Conjugating the Future Imperfect." *Parliamentary Affairs* 32 (Winter 1979): 78–91.

Sklar, Martin. "Liberty and Equality, and Socialism." *Socialist Revolution*, no. 34 (July-August 1977), pp. 92–104.

Soboul, Albert. *The French Revolution, 1787–1799: From the Storming of the Bastille to Napoleon*. London: New Left Books, 1974.

———. *The Sans-Culottes: The Popular Movement and Revolutionary Government, 1793–1794*. Garden City, N.Y.: Doubleday, Anchor Books, 1972.

*Le Socialisme pour la France: 22e Congrès du Parti communiste français, 4 au 8 février, 1976*. Paris: Editions Sociales, 1976.

Spallone, Mario. *Vent'anni con Togliatti*. Milan: Teti Editori, 1976.

Spriano, Paolo. *Storia del Partito comunista italiano*. 5 vols. Turin: Einaudi, 1967–75. Vol. 3, *Storia del PCI: I fronti popolari, Stalin, la guerra*, 1970.

———. "A Turning Point in Human History." *World Marxist Review* 20 (September 1977): 41–43.

Stehle, Hansjakob. "The Italian Communists on the Parliamentary Path to Power." *The World Today* 34 (May 1978): 175–83.

———. "The Italian Experience and the Communists." *The World Today* 33 (January 1977): 7–16.

Sweezy, Paul, and Magdoff, Harry. "The New Reformism." *Monthly Review* 28, no. 2 (June 1976): 1–11.


Tarrow, Sidney. "Italian Communism: The New and the Old." *Dissent* 24 (Winter 1977): 54–60.

*Teoria e politica della via italiana al socialismo: I testi principali della elaborazione del PCI dalla Dichiarazione programmatica del 1956 al discorso sull'austerità*. Rome: Editori Riuniti, 1978.

Terracini, Umberto. *Come nacque la costituzione: Intervista di Pasquale Balsamo*. Rome: Editori Riuniti, 1978.

"Il testo integrale dell'ultimo scritto di Togliatti a Yalta." *Rinascita* 21, no. 35 (September 5, 1964): 1–4.

Thompson, E. P. *The Poverty of Theory*. London: Merlin Press, 1978.

Tiersky, Ronald. "French Communism in 1976." *Problems of Communism* 25, no. 1 (January-February 1976): 20–47.

———. *French Communism, 1920–1972*. New York: Columbia University Press, 1974.

Timmermann, Heinz. "Eurocommunism: Moscow's Reaction and the Implications for Eastern Europe." *The World Today* 33 (October 1977): 376–85.

Tiso, Aida. *I comunisti e la questione femminile*. Rome: Editori Riuniti, 1976.

Togliatti, Palmiro. *Comunisti, socialisti, cattolici*. Edited by Luciano Gruppi. Rome: Editori Riuniti, 1974.

———. *L'emancipazione femminile*, 3d ed. Rome: Editori Riuniti, 1973.

———. *La formazione del gruppo dirigente del PCI nel 1923–1924*. Rome: Editori Riuniti, 1962.

———. *Lectures on Fascism*. New York: International Publishers, 1976.

———. *L'opera di De Gasperi*. Florence: Parenti Editore, 1958.

———. *Opere scelte*. Edited by Gianpasquale Santomassino. Rome: Editori Riuniti, 1974. Togliatti's works are in the process of being published by the Editori Riuniti. As of 1979, four volumes in six tomes have appeared, covering the years from 1917 to 1944.

———. "Parliament and the Struggle for Socialism." *Marxism Today* 21, no. 9 (September 1977): 284–87. First published in 1956.

———. "Risposta a '9 Domande sullo stalinismo." *Nuovi argomenti* 20 (May-June 1956): 110–39.

Trentin, Bruno. *Da sfruttati a produttori*. Bari: De Donato, 1977.

Turone, Sergio. *Storia del sindacato in Italia, 1943–1969*. 2d ed. Bari: Laterza, 1975.

Urban, George. "A Conversation with Lucio Lombardo Radice (Communism with an Italian Face?)." *Encounter* 49, no. 5 (May 1977): 8–22.

———. " 'Have They Really Changed?' A Conversation with Altiero Spinelli." *Encounter* 50, no. 1 (January 1978): 7–27.

Vacca. Giuseppe. *Saggio su Togliatti*. Bari: De Donato, 1974.

Valenza, Pietro, ed. *Il compromesso storico*. Rome: Newton Compton, 1975.

Valli, Bernardo, ed. *Gli eurocomunisti*. Milan: Bompiani, 1976.

Vidal, Gore. "On the Assassin's Trail." *New York Review of Books* 26 (October 25, 1979): 17–23.

Vidali, Vittorio. *Diario del XX congresso*. Milan: Vangelista, 1974.

Webb, C. "Eurocommunism and the European Communities." *Journal of Common Market Studies* 17 (March 1979): 236–58.

Weber, Henri. "Eurocommunism, Socialism, and Democracy." *New Left Review*, no. 110 (July-August 1978), pp. 1–14.

West, Jim. "For International Solidarity Against Opportunism." *Political Affairs* 54, no. 4 (April 1977): 6–13. Attack on Carrillo, Segre, and Kanapa.

Wilson, Frank L. "The French CP's Dilemma." *Problems of Communism* 27, no. 4 (July-August 1978): 1–14.

Yergin, Angela S. "West German's Suedpolitik: Social Democrats and Eurocommunism." *Orbis* 23 (Spring 1979): 51–71. Excellent piece.

Zagladin, Vadim, ed. *Europe and the Communists*. Moscow: Progress Publishers, 1977.

Zangheri, Renato. *Il sindaco di Bologna: Enzo Biagi intervista Renato Zangheri*. Modena: Riccardo Franco Levi Editore, 1976.

———. *Zangheri Bologna '77: Intervista di Fabio Mussi*. Rome: Editori Riuniti, 1978.

Zorza, Victor. "Why Nationalization Matters to the Communists." *Manchester Guardian Weekly*, October 17, 1977.

# INDEX

# L

# M